12-

THE LAWYER IN THE PRISONER'S BOX

A True Story
by
OREST RUSNAK, B.A., LL.B.

THE TRUE STORY OF A LAWYER WHO
BECAME THE VICTIM OF ABUSE IN
THE CRIMINAL JUSTICE SYSTEM.

Author's Advocate Publishing Company Inc.
#2011 Esso Tower
Scotia Place
10060 - Jasper Avenue
Edmonton, Alberta
Canada T5J 3R8
Telephone: (403) 421-8557
Fax (for book orders): (403) 447-3982

Canadian Cataloguing in Publication Data:
Rusnak, Orest, 1950 - The Lawyer In The Prisoner's Box

Includes: Table of Contents
            Index
1. Criminal justice, Administration of – Canada.
2. Criminal procedure – Canada.
3. Rusnak, Orest, 1950 – I. Title
KE8813.R88 1992   345.71'05   Co2-091830-1

ISBN: 1-55056-262-2
OTHER TOPICS INCLUDED:

1. Justice System - Reform	17. Docket - Court
2. Legal System - Abuse, Manipulation	18. Arraignment -Court
3. Criminal Law - Case study	19. Judges -Provincial
4. Criminal Courts - How they work	20. Judges -Superior
5. Lawyers - Study of	21. Jury - trial by
6. Police - Actions and Abuse	22. Jury - selection of,
7. Police - Investigation by,	23. Jury - verdict of,
8. Police Department - operation of,	24. Charges -Criminal
9. Crown Prosecutors - Role of	25. Real Estate -Law
10. Criminal Lawyers - Analysis of	26. Agents -Realtors
11. News Media - in Court	27. Mortgages - Land
12. Courtroom - Procedure	28. Mortgage Brokers
13. Criminal Trial - An Analysis of	29. CMHC - described
14. Crown Witness - role of,	30. Application - Pre-Trial
15. Law Society - functions of,	31. Court Challenge
16. Certiorari - explained	32. Reform - aspects of

Portrait by Merle Prosofsky Photography
Editing by G.N.R. Editing and Composition Services
Book Layout by S & K Literary Consulting
Dust Jacket Design by P.D.Y. Designing Services

Printed and Bound in Canada
by D.W. Friesen & Sons Ltd.

DEDICATION

TO MY WIFE PAT;

*Because of her encouragement, support and understanding
I was able to persevere in my ordeal and ultimately
complete this literary project.*

TABLE OF CONTENTS

FORWARD

"WATCH OUT!
IT CAN HAPPEN TO ANYONE!
IT HAPPENED TO ME!
AND IT CAN HAPPEN TO YOU!"

These words have now become my words of advice to anyone asking about the police investigation that led to my prosecution for criminal fraud. The circumstances that gave rise to the criminal prosecution are so commonplace that almost everyone can relate similar experiences to what actually happened in my case. Yet the actual results of my case are so unbelievable that anyone would be prompted to believe that it was unusual and most certainly an isolated case.

However, as I conducted the research for this book, I discovered the shocking reality that my case of injustice was not an isolated example. Of the people that I have interviewed, many have described extreme cases of injustices. In too many cases, innocent people had been victimized by police investigations and wrongly convicted by the criminal justice system. Some of these cases are now being reported in the news media. As a result, abuses by the police, Crown Prosecutors, and Judges are becoming more recognized by the general public. Most notably, the cases of Donald Marshall and David Milgaard demonstrate how individuals who should not have been convicted were victimized by the abuses in the justice system. In those cases, each had spent a significant period of time in jail before errors and injustice were acknowledged by the Justice Department.

In this book, I have carefully recounted the story of how I was charged with criminal fraud and my experiences in dealing with police, lawyers and Judges. In writing this book, I have also described various aspects of the legal system. This was done to demonstrate how the justice system works and why it continually fails to protect the rights of all the citizens in our society. Few people are able to gain the perspective that I had simply because I was a lawyer. I understood what was happening and WHAT WAS WRONG. As my case was investigated by the police and later prosecuted before the courts, I experienced the horror and devastation that everyone involved in such a situation must suffer. Yet, as this epic of abuse and manipulation unfolded before me, I became determined to learn why it happened so that the lesson would not be wasted on me and could be used to benefit others.

Each story of abuse in the justice system is unique. Yet the theme is so familiar that it identifies the situation as commonplace. I have written my story from my personal perspective to allow the reader to understand and appreciate the full impact of such a situation upon the innocently accused victim. All of the events in this book have been described in a true and accurate manner but the events span over four years. Therefore, it has been necessary to edit and summarize certain aspects to maintain a readable account of the total event.

I have specifically avoided any attempt at writing a legal treatise of my case, but instead have provided brief and practical explanations of the law and the legal process where it was relevant. My main purpose was to focus on the abuses and manipulations that are so prevalent in the court system. I also used my experience and training as a lawyer to deliver a candid and objective assessment of the actions of all parties instrumental to my case and those involved in the legal system. Furthermore, I have attempted to explain the actual events in a way that would be instantly understood. In doing so, it is my hope that every reader will be able to empathize with all victims of similar devastating experiences.

In writing my story, I have specifically included examples of various cases and relevant anecdotes. It is my hope that the reading public might gain a better appreciation for the attitudes prevalent in the legal system and an awareness of the need for change in the way that our legal system works. Although this book will demonstrate the failures of the legal system, the specific types of changes that should be made are only dealt with in a general context for the better understanding of the reading public. The topic of necessary changes in the justice system is too extensive to cover in this book. I have instead chosen to simply dedicate this book to support the work of judicial reformers who have dedicated themselves to the task of building a better society for all of us to enjoy.

My greatest energies in creating this literary work were expended in my determination to deliver an honest and candid assessment of the failures of the legal system. This is an accomplishment that I would have found impossible as a practising lawyer. At that time, I found myself defending and denying the shortcomings of the legal system. I hope that my candid revelations will allow every reader to draw conclusions about the events and the people involved. I also hope that this book will provide the information and background foundation that will enable every reader to understand the desperate need that exists to eliminate the abuses in our legal system that I ultimately suffered.

Primarily, I would like this book to stand as a tribute to all those people in our society who have been wrongly victimized by the police and the justice system. I also hope that this book will serve as a mandate for the need to dramatically change our Justice system to cure such abuses. It is my hope that this book will inspire more people to speak out for change and support the movement for reform of our entire legal system.

In writing this book, I was fortunate to receive help and encouragement from many professionals and from family and friends who believed in this project. From them, I drew the inspiration to create this literary work that would demonstrate the blatant abuses that are so prevalent in our legal and judicial system. I would therefore like to take this opportunity to thank everyone who contributed to the process of helping this book to be published.

I also wish to express my heartfelt gratitude to all those people who provided to me and my family their unconditional moral support and encouragement. We were all overwhelmed by the gestures and assurances of those who believed in my innocence despite the damnation and humiliation that I suffered at the hands of our justice system as reported in the news media. Without their sincere encouragement, I would never have survived this ordeal or undertaken this literary project.

INTRODUCTION

"THE JUSTICE SYSTEM DOESN'T WORK ..."
"NOBODY KNOWS WHAT THE LAW IS ... "
"IN COURT, YOU GET SHAFTED ..."
"THE POLICE GET AWAY WITH EVERYTHING ..."

These comments are not unusual and are being made by a growing number of people from the general public and from within the legal system. We live at a time when governments have become more technically advanced and sophisticated in the manner in which they deliver services to their citizens. Yet except for marginal technical advancements in the Administrative operations and the filing of documents, the process for getting judicial decisions has in fact worsened. It is becoming evident to the general public that the legal system has deteriorated. Furthermore, the amount of abuse and manipulation in the justice system has steadily increased.

The basic feature of our justice system in Canada and the United States of America has always been the fairness of the court system. The forum in which justice is demonstrated and administrated is the Court House which traditionally occupied a prominent focal point of every community. Today, the Court room is a place that most people find interesting and intriguing when it is the setting in a television drama. Ironically, it is also a place that most people dread to enter for any reason. This is partly due to the stories of horror and disappointments that are commonplace from people who found themselves in a courtroom. No matter what type of circumstance initiated the need to be in court, most people leave with a negative reaction to the proceedings that they observed.

One significant attribute that makes a Courtroom an uncomfortable setting for the general public is the manner in which the justice system is administrated. To the general public, the court system is shrouded with mysterious procedures and operated by people wearing strange clothes and practising strange customs. To the general public, the legal language spoken in the Court room is difficult to understand and judges and lawyers seldom make the effort to explain any of it. To the general public, a definite feeling of alienation prevails as significant discussions and private jokes are shared between the judges and lawyers to the exclusion of the parties affected by the case.

The most curious reason why so many people avoid contact with the judicial system is the assessment of the general public that the decisions made in the Court room lack common sense. Instead, judges make decisions based on legal precedent which can be selectively chosen to justify any view that the judge wishes to incorporate into his decision. This is ironic since laws are usually validated on the basis of social need and common sense. It is also a reality that rather than common sense or law, the decision of a judge is often based on who the judge likes or favours.

The perception that one could get a better and more expeditious decision by flipping a coin is actually closer to reality than one would dare to believe. The Court room demeanour of some judges has deteriorated to such a degree that in one recently reported case, a judge actually offered a person accused of an offence the option of a coin toss to determine his verdict. The conviction in that case was entered on the basis that the accused lost the coin toss. A growing number of disenchanted people now wonder how often this happens without the knowledge of the accused person.

In a democratic society, the freedoms enjoyed by its citizens are the pillars of that society. The constitution which guarantees those individual freedoms are the society's foundation. The courts and the judicial system that protect those freedoms cover the society like a giant roof. They act as a shield to protect the citizens of that society from adverse elements that would impair those fundamental freedoms. By this analogy, the legal historian argues that the justice system is paramount in importance to any other interest of society. However, this dangerous presumption would have the effect of shifting control from a democratically elected legislature to an autocratic judiciary.

In Canada and the United States of America, we enjoy the security of knowing that our individual freedoms are guaranteed to us by the Constitution of our countries. These freedoms are protected by a system of justice that can even override the legislatures comprised of the elected representatives of the people. Obviously, this is a strange and unintended situation in any democratic society. However, it is justified as being necessary in order to protect the rights and freedoms of each citizen. As citizens of these countries, we put our blind faith and trust in our justice systems to make the"right" decisions and to protect us from all that is "evil". It is presumably unthinkable that these justice systems might be corrupted, abused, manipulated or improperly utilized by the very people entrusted by society to properly administrate them. Sadly, there is nothing to protect the citizen from these abuses of the justice system which continually occur.

So strong is our faith in the justice system that we dismiss any examples of miscarriage of justice as isolated situations. We routinely attribute such cases to human error or unusual circumstances which are not likely to re-occur or to affect us personally. So strong is our faith in the justice system that we dismiss and ignore stories as told in books and movies of abuse, manipulation and corruption in the administration of justice. Movies such as "AN INNOCENT MAN" as portrayed by Tom Selleck are dismissed as fantasy instead of being given serious consideration for the realistic portrayal of abuse that remains active in the criminal justice system. To believe otherwise would displace the comfort that we draw from our blind faith in the justice system. So strong is our faith in the justice system that we readily believe that anyone facing a criminal charge in the courts must be at least partially responsible for his problems. It is easier for us to believe that such a situation would not arise if a person lives by proper moral values. Yes, so strong is our faith in the justice system that we are blinded by it.

Although it is unusual for a lawyer to be arbitrarily investigated and charged with a criminal offence, my story of abuse in the legal system is not unique. It has become commonplace to read stories in newspapers and to view news documentaries on television about cases in Canada and the United States of America. We see people who have been "framed" by the police and other parties for crimes they did not commit. In many cases, people have been imprisoned on crimes for which they should not have been convicted. Three noteworthy cases are those of Donald Marshall, David Milgaard and Wilson Nepoose. These cases dramatically emphasize how the justice system can be abused and manipulated. The result in these cases was innocent people serving lengthy prison terms before the abuses could be proven and the convictions set aside.

Yet despite such increased publicity and awareness of abuse in the legal system, little or nothing has been done to correct the situation. Instead, the police and the justice departments have countered the criticism and silenced their critics with publicized justifications of their actions. One blatant example of this that received international recognition was the beating of Rodney King by members of the Los Angeles Police Department. It was horrifying to watch the videotape of the beating and torture that King received as he helplessly lay on the ground. It was even more intolerable to witness the police officers try to justify their actions and then be exonerated by the court. Yet, the justice system was manipulated to protect these police officers and to excuse their blatant discreditable conduct. It took a riot and a national protest to correct this injustice.

Unfortunately, atrocities in the justice system that attract sensational headlines are easily forgotten by the general public within days. It is impossible to investigate any wrongdoing in the operations of these venerable institutions because they are protected by a private investigative process that avoids public attention and scrutiny. Furthermore, the public relation efforts of both the police and the justice department have been effective in re-affirming the belief that there is really no need to change anything. The focus of these public relation campaigns is to reaffirm the comfortable notion in our society that nothing will ever happen to those that obey the laws. We are expected to believe that those people who the police investigate and the justice department prosecutes are the"bad" people who should be "rooted out" of our society. Regrettably, only those few members of the general public who are better informed can refute this superficial and simplistic presentation. As a result, there are very few people who can identify the real problems which are so blatantly being covered up.

The greatest misconception of the general public is that our laws clearly identify for ordinary citizens the conduct which is "right" and "wrong". We have faith in the premise that more modern sophistication and education will make the task simpler for such a determination. However, it is a reality that few people are truly familiar with the laws that affect them and this is also true of their lawyers. In response to this situation some lawyers have proceeded to develop expertise in a restricted area of law. The disadvantage is that the lawyer who specializes may not appreciate significant aspects of a case which do not fall within his legal expertise. This not only means that a citizen will not know the law but also that he will be poorly served by his specialized lawyer.

The situation in the Court room is even more appalling. A lawyer often finds himself presenting a case to a judge who has no knowledge or experience in the specific area of law. The lawyer is expected to present his case in a manner that would subtly educate the judge. In such situations, the judge makes a decision based on a superficial understanding of the whole case. One can hardly expect a judge under such circumstances to decide the case on any other basis than a coin toss.

The most disturbing aspects of the court system is the adjudications that take place in the criminal Court rooms. An accused person soon learns that any action can be interpreted by a witness or shaped by a police officer to fit the parameters of a criminal offence. Judges are allowed to draw inferences and rely on implied facts to support a conviction fora criminal offence. It is routine for Crown Prosecutors to build a case against an accused person based on theories, conjectures,and circumstantial evidence. The prospect of avoiding a prosecution on a criminal charge is therefore weighted heavily and unfairly against the accused person.

In this uncontrolled arena, innocent people are convicted of serious offenses which they neither understand nor can explain. Therefore this makes it impossible for them to question what has taken place. For that reason, the devastation suffered by the victims are seldom viewed by the public as being the result of abuses or improper conduct by police or Crown Prosecutors. Complaints to the police or justice department that do arise by some victims seldom result in retribution because the complainant cannot prove, or even understand, the abuses that have taken place. The complicated nature of the written law therefore contributes to the improper manipulation of the legal system.

Because the average citizen intentionally avoids contact with the justice system, such an experience is tainted with social stigma and viewed as unfortunate. An intrusion by the justice system in our lives is viewed in the same manner as the affliction of a terminal disease. Those people who find themselves before the courts are in many cases embroiled in a tragic circumstance that could not have been anticipated or predicted. A complaint and a police investigation can implicate anyone. The legal nightmare that follows would make that person an arbitrary victim to suffer the ordeal of the criminal justice system. Invariably, such victims are wrongly convicted and punished for the unprosecuted wrongs of society. The resultant suffering that accompanies such an experience invariably devastates and permanently impairs the victim and his family. In the larger context, the case creates shock and disillusionment regarding our justice system to all those with knowledge of the case.

For those few victims of the justice system that have enough strength to withstand the devastation of such an occurrence, hope will emanate from tragedy. The painful circumstances inevitably provide the victim with new insights into the lives of people who suffer as victims in the same situation. In a desire to help in the plight of others, some former victims will naturally speak out and work to change and improve the justice system. These efforts occasionally lead to small changes that benefit not only those who suffer but society as a whole. In some rare instances, the victim's suffering may become an example for others on the need for changing and improving a failing system. It is mainly through these efforts that the movement for change is mounted. Through such faith and dedication, we all have reason to hope for a reformed and effective justice system.

It is my hope that this book will assist in the movement for substantial changes and reform in the justice and legal systems. It is critical that governments take action to reduce and eliminate the growing abuse, corruption and manipulation. These debilitating viruses have desecrated this fundamental institution of our society. I also hope that this book will further the efforts of judicial reformers and populist activists who are demanding changes and improvements to our judicial systems. May they be inspired to continue their crusades for a better future for our society.

The obstacles to such reform include the reluctance and resistance of politicians, judges, lawyers and the administrators of the justice system. Because of their formidable influence, no changes will arise until the general public understands that there is a desperate need for change in every aspect of the legal system. Only then will the demands for such changes be heard and acted upon by our elected government representatives. Only then can we enjoy greater peace of mind over the protection of our basic rights and freedoms as guaranteed by our constitution. Only then can we hope to give to our children a legal and justice system that reflects the ideals that our constitution originally intended.

CHAPTER ONE

THE NEWS MEDIA IN COURT

As my conscious mind began to rationalize the sudden noise of music in my bedroom, I became aware of the reality that my radio alarm had activated. This meant that I would slowly have to motivate my exhausted body for yet another day of work. Like most people, I hated to get out of bed in the morning and so I allow myself the luxury of staying in bed for a few additional, luxurious minutes. This futile attempt to squeeze just a little more enjoyment out of every day had now become a ritual for me.

Typically, I stayed in bed until the news broadcast was completed. My self-serving justification was that everyone should listen to the daily news so as to be properly informed on the vital issues of the new day ahead. Naturally, I didn't listen to the news consciously as this would disturb the final moments of sleep that were quickly slipping away.

SUDDENLY, my conscious mind caught the words of a news item that froze me in terror. As I listened, I prayed that my worst fears wouldn't materialize into a nightmare of unbearable humiliation. My body began to tremble as the reality of the situation gripped my thoughts and I momentarily stopped breathing.

The words of the news announcer were terse and devastating as they shattered my private life:

"A ST. ALBERT LAWYER HAS BEEN CHARGED WITH FRAUD. OREST RUSNAK FACES ONE COUNT OF CRIMINAL FRAUD RELATING TO A COMPLICATED REAL ESTATE DEAL IN SHERWOOD PARK DATING BACK TO1984."

I quickly responded by hitting the off button on the radio alarm clock and sat in shock as I contemplated what would happen next. I knew that I would be suspended from the practice of law and I wondered how I would generate an income to support my family. I knew that this news would be broadcast by all the news media and I wondered how my wife and children would deal with the embarrassment that this news would create. I knew that our lives would never be the same again and I wondered if our family unit could survive the stress and adversity that this situation would inflict upon all of us.

I asked myself the same unanswered questions:
"HOW COULD THIS HAVE HAPPENED?"
"WHY WAS THIS HAPPENING TO ME?"

My rustling in bed woke my wife from her slumber and she immediately asked: "What's happening? What's wrong?" I couldn't even answer her as I sat there in momentary shock and disbelief.

Before I could respond, my throat became constricted and I began to feel sick with an uneasiness in my stomach. Instinctively, I jumped out of bed and rushed to the bathroom sink. For a moment I just stood there in agony, stooped over the sink and waited for my stomach to make the next move. After a few moments the nausea subsided and I began to splash cold water on my face for relief. I now felt more awake but badly shaken as I quickly returned to my wife to comfort her and to ease her fears.

My wife Pat was already sitting up in bed with a look of confusion over the unusual start to our morning. As I gazed at her I wondered how she would handle this latest development in a nightmare that was growing uncontrollably. Over the seventeen years that we had been married I had observed that Pat possessed the strange mixture of two conflicting attributes. She had a good sense of humour and a warm easing-going attitude to life. In contrast to that, she worried about anything that she could not accurately predict. She also had a strong extroverted personality and insisted on knowing the facts immediately so that she could deal with them in her own way.

I knew that I had to tell her exactly what had happened but still I dreaded having to tell her about the news report. It all seemed so unfair and I knew how much pain this would bring to her. I sat down on the bed next to Pat and began to tell her about the news story, bluntly and quickly. There was no time to calmly and tactfully explain the circumstances and I was in no condition to even think of such niceties. I simply blurted it out to Pat as I resigned myself to this hopeless situation:

"Pat, I just heard a news story on the radio about my criminal charge. I don't know if its just on this radio station but it will probably be on the other radio stations and in the newspapers."

"Oh, No!" was her shaken response. It was visibly evident that she was struggling to understand this bizarre situation. After a few moments, she asked:

"Why did the news media report THIS story?"

I tried to comfort her as I struggled to make sense out of the situation myself. Just yesterday, the concern about a news story in the media had occurred to me. I was satisfied that nothing like this would happen. Now we were living through another devastating development that neither of us had prepared for. With all my knowledge and prior experience, it still seemed that nothing was predictable. I now realized in horror that everything that was now happening made no sense.

As I looked at Pat it was obvious that she was in shock and physically disturbed about this latest set back in our lives. I was worried about her reaction to this traumatic event so I tried to discuss this with her in my most positive manner:

"I don't know, Pat! There are people being charged with fraud and even more serious crimes every day and the news media only reports the occasional ones. This charge must be sensational because it is a lawyer who is being charged with fraud. If I wasn't a lawyer, there would be nothing that was sensational about the charge to report. This charge had nothing to do with me being a lawyer but the new reporters made that the feature part of the story. I guess people love to see lawyers kicked around and knocked to the ground."

At that moment, my thoughts drifted to the news reporters that continually haunted the corridors of the Court House. During the fifteen years that I worked as a lawyer, I witnessed an endless stream of news reporters from radio, television, and the newspapers. Each news reporter scurried between courtrooms to find a story that would become his "scoop" for the day. Naturally, on most days there was nothing sensational in the subject matter of any of the cases. To satisfy their editors and reading public, the news reporters would resort to reporting an ordinary case but exaggerating an insignificant detail to make the story sensational. This was all in the business of news reporting but it brought unwanted publicity to people who already were suffering the grief of being in court.

Although the suffering of accused people is aggravated by the publicity of news reporters, their lawyers are most accommodating to such publicity. In fact, criminal lawyers revel over any publicity they receive from well publicized news stories because of its "recognition" value. In a profession where advertising was non-existent and is currently minimal, any publicity is welcomed by lawyers. Even publicity which is demeaning and embarrassing is welcomed by some lawyers who see such events as opportunities to communicate their reputations to the general public.

One well-remembered example of bad publicity being welcomed by a lawyer involved Peter Bruce Gunn who was jailed by Provincial Judge Ralph Chisolm for being in contempt of court. As one might imagine, this story garnered headlines in the newspapers and the other media. When interviewed by the news reporters, Gunn appeared to be amused by his experience in jail and commented that he was able to recruit new clients while in custody. He was also happy to admit that he was now "deloused", meaning that he no longer had lice. Gunn was referring to the shampoo he was required to use when he showered on his admission into custody which is supposed to rid the inmates of lice. Far from being embarrassed or humiliated by the experience, Gunn reacted with smugness over the news coverage.

The fact that the courts must function in an atmosphere of sensationalized stories created by hungry news reporters is always apparent in the Court room. The constant presence of news reporters motivate the Crown prosecutors to make grand speeches to the court on the need for harsher sentencing on every crime that comes before the court. These speeches are obviously intended for the benefit of the news reporters present who hastily jot down the exaggerated comments of the Crown Prosecutor and treat the details of the case as a footnote in their news story. The judges in turn must react to the situation knowing that their actions will either be applauded or criticized in the news story that is sure to follow. In this way, judges are pressured into imposing harsher sentencing on an accused person than they otherwise would if they decided the sentence on an objective basis. Regrettably, some judges actually begin to thrive on the publicity of the press and make grand speeches intended for the news media while victimizing the accused person with an unusually harsh sentence.

Although the court can ban news reporting of evidence at the early stages of a criminal proceeding, the final adjudications are always open to publication subject to an occasional ban on publishing names. Furthermore, in restricted situations, the news media is forever testing the limits of its freedom to publish news stories as they see fit. The typical argument of the press is that the general public has a right to know. However, the ulterior motive is that the early publication of a news story will sell more papers and draw a greater reading audience. Occasionally, the news media will be criticized for affecting the proceedings in court which may result in the disruption of a court case. However, none of this seems to dissuade the aggressive attitudes of the news media in pursuing any story.

A recent event in which a court case was disrupted by a news story put the newspaper staff on trial. The news story was published before the jury hearing started. The judge decided to adjourn that case and to bring contempt charges against the newspaper reporter, his editor and the publisher. In defending their position the newspaper argued that the jury members would not have been influenced by the news story. However, it was obvious to the judge who postponed the case that there was prejudice to the person on trial. Regrettably, this isolated case will do little to stem the continual deterioration of the court process by news reporters hungry for a story. The obvious reason for this is that the news media is not interested in the effective administration of justice but rather the sensational stories that will generate revenue. As the various news media reporters increase their presence in the Court room, we are destined to witness a stronger influence by them on the decisions of the judges.

The more sinister impact of sensational news reporting is the increase in violent crimes committed by disturbed people seeking attention and by serial killers. Because of the prominence achieved by news reporting in today's society, the general public is exposed to explicit accounts of atrocious crimes. Studies have now documented that some of the sensational crimes were committed because of ideas formed by the perpetrators from news reports. A recent example of this situation is Milwaukee's serial killer Jeffrey Dahmer whose crimes of murder and cannibalism were the direct influence of sensational news stories of similar crimes.

The victims who suffer because of sensational news reporting are not just the people whose cases are reported in the media. In a wider context, the victims are the general public for whose benefit the stories are presumably published. If the court process is hampered because of the presence of news reporters and the effect of those news stories, then justice is denied to those that appear before the court. In the current climate of the courts an accused person can no longer expect to receive a fair trial if the circumstances of the subject matter are sensational and attract the attention of the news media.

My thoughts of how I was being persecuted by the news media were suddenly interrupted by another question from Pat as she grasped for a better assessment of what was happening:

"I just don't understand this! Who would have leaked this story to the press?"

The answer to this question was obvious to me and I immediately responded:

"Pat, there are only two people who know about it and have any reason to leak this type of story. It would either be Don Christal, the police officer, or Eileen Nash, the Crown Prosecutor in charge. Consider the fact that Don Christal worked so intently on getting this charge laid even against the recommendations of the Crown Prosecutors office. Consider the fact that Don Christal is using this case as a stepping stone for a further promotion. It is a safe guess that he leaked the story using the media channels in the police network."

Pat was quite disturbed by this whole situation. She probed for something that would make sense and clear away all the nagging doubts of disbelief that she still felt:

"Why would he do such a malicious thing to you, or to anyone?"

Indeed, it was difficult for me to imagine anyone who was so callous or malicious that he would actively pursue an advancement in his career at the grief and suffering of others. My thoughts drifted to Don Christal and his cold, abrasive manner. I could still visualize him staring at me, dressed in his very expensive suit and shoes which were so uncharacteristic of police detectives. His off-colour red facial complexion admitted to high blood pressure which was accelerated by years of alcohol abuse. His demeanour fit the description portrayed to me of a narcotics investigator who kicked down doors and kicked around suspects during narcotic raids. In the drug climate, Christal could commit the most atrocious acts and then expect that his victims wouldn't complain since society has no sympathy for drug users. Such attitudes and abrasive actions are the natural result of such de-humanized work.

It was easy to understand how Christal would develop a callous attitude towards the legal rights of those that he investigated. He had spent years working in his hopeless battle against drug trafficking. As a result, he found himself in the familiar trap of turning to alcohol and drugs to find relief from work that was slowly consuming and destroying his total physical existence. After paying his dues on the frontlines of the war on crime, he was granted a promotion to the easier and more prestigious work of investigating commercial crimes. However, by that time, Christal's attitudes and investigative tactics had become a part of his very existence. His approach to investigating remained the same as he arbitrarily selected his victims and then harassed them while ignoring their legal rights. He knew all the tricks of the legal system and how to fabricate any form of evidence that would enable him to lay a criminal charge.

Through discussions, I had learnt that many fellow police officers dreaded and some even refused to work with Christal. Apparently they found his obnoxious attitude of harassing people he didn't like and his zeal for pursuing unwarranted investigations to be discomforting. However, none of this deterred him in his relentless pursuit to lay charges and gain greater recognition in the department. Over the years he also developed a hardened attitude that allowed him to justify his actions as proper. He excelled at disregarding the cries of sorrows that he inflicted on innocent families because of his abusive manner. Instead, he used his authority to investigate anyone in any manner he wished. His confidence came from the many faithful years of service that enabled him to learn all the techniques needed to justify anything he wished to do. He knew that he could always rely on the fact that everything he did was lawful because HE WAS THE LAW. As far as he was concerned, this was a police state and when he was on a case, he was always right and his word was final.

The answer to Pat's question seemed hard for me to fathom because we didn't know anyone in our daily lives that treated people in the manner that Christal did. In our lives, we adopted the attitude that there were too many nice people to spend time with and it didn't seem worthwhile to spend time with anyone that acted like Christal. Although I had learnt many things about Christal through informed sources, I didn't understand him. I knew that I would probably never have a conclusive answer to the question that Pat and I both wondered about:

"Why would he do something so malicious to me?"

For a moment, the images flashed through my mind of how a simple inquiry by a client had escalated into an investigation of my files and then resulted in a criminal charge against me. I knew that soon I would have to recount and document all of this for my lawyer in preparing my defence to this charge. However, there was no time to dwell on these details at this time.

As I looked at Pat I tried to soothe her fears and anxiety as I slowly responded:

"Pat, I really don't know why he is so malicious. Most police officers are not like him. I've met many police officers who work for the department and they're all nice people. Christal just happens to be one of the few rotten apples in the police department. I was told that he is very bigoted and enjoys slurring ethnic groups. He also has made it clear that he hates lawyers and apparently always wanted to nail a lawyer in a criminal prosecution. Maybe that explains why he is so malicious towards me. I was also told that he has openly stated that he was going to nail me in this case whether or not there was any evidence. I tend to believe the people who told me those things. It helps to explain why he'd push to have me charged in a case where there was no evidence."

Pat was now in tears, dreading what was happening to all of us and not knowing what lay ahead in this awful nightmare. In an attempt to find comfort in what seemed like our "darkest hour", Pat asked:

"Why did he have to pick on you? You weren't even involved in arranging the mortgage and yet he charged you with doing it. Why didn't he charge the people who were involved in that deal?"

The question defied all rational explanation. Even the criminal lawyers that I talked to could not answer this question. Usually if a police officer charges someone with fraud in arranging a mortgage, all the participants directly involved are also charged. Yet Don Christal singled me out and didn't charge anyone else, even though I was the least likely person in that transaction who could be accused of any wrongdoing.

As I sat next to Pat and agonized over the grief that we both harboured, I gave Pat the only answer that I could at the time:

"Pat, all I can tell you is what my lawyer, Patrick Murphy, said on this point. He says that Christal charged me because I am a lawyer. That gives his file a high profile in the police department. Murphy also believes that Christal made a deal with the other people in the mortgage transaction. He got them to agree to testify and implicate me in return for a promise that no charges would be laid against them. According to Murphy, this is a weak case. The Crown Prosecutor felt that they would never get a conviction against anyone. However Christal kept pushing the matter because he's content just to see me prosecuted. All we can do now is follow Murphy's advise and hope for a quick resolution of this matter."

Pat and I both resigned ourselves to this helpless situation. We both agonized over the frightening prospect that our destiny was in the hands of others and we simply had to hope for the best. We tried to maintain our faith in the justice system but we already saw how Christal had manipulated everyone to lay the criminal charge. We both feared that more abuse and manipulation would still be used in the prosecution of my case. I dreaded the feeling of launching our destiny like a ship into uncharted waters fraught with danger. However the winds of change were too strong to resist and our course was set. Maintaining a waterproof ship seemed to be our only hope of survival. I fell back on the bed momentarily, closed my eyes and prayed that God would help us through this difficult passage.

Pat got up from the bed and rushed out of the room in a frenzied panic only to return a few minutes later. She knew that this was an urgent situation and we had to immediately start assessing what had to be done to cope with this dreadful event. I sat up in bed and tried to piece together a sensible plan that would take us through this day. As we began to discuss the situation, we both felt sick and would have preferred to just climb back into bed and let the day pass. The children were the first priority and we agreed that we had to discuss this with them. We had to prepare them for any problems that they might experience with friends and playmates. Pat said that she would phone her parents and her aunt to make sure that they didn't worry. This was so ironic as we were both horrified with fear and didn't know ourselves what to expect next. Above all, we both instinctively understood that this was one of those times in our married life when we had to lean on each other. United we could face the storm that was threatening to shatter our lives. We had to pull together our strengths as a family to survive this hurricane of devastation that was upon us. There was no time for lamenting about our future at this moment. This was a full-scale emergency and firm action had to be taken immediately.

I always admired how Pat could handle these situations. She had the fighting spirit of a wilderness pioneer with irrepressible spirit to repel any form of danger. I had no doubt that Pat could rise to any occasion in confronting others who challenged her and this was certainly one of those occasions. I knew that she felt devastated, just as I did. However, she showed a formidable determination to persevere as she proceeded with her task of giving instructions to the children in a firm tone. Amid the usual morning commotion, she took time to telephone her parents and her aunt to assure them that we were working to resolve this situation and asked them not to worry. In those moments of despair, I was also comforted by her gestures in urging me not to give up. She encouraged me to fight back and to straighten this situation out. However, she must have sensed that I had doubts about my fate in the justice system. She proceeded to eradicate my fears by saying:

"Whatever happens and whatever we may lose, we should be happy that we are all together as a family and we still have our health!"

As one might expect, I laboured through my morning routine of shaving, taking a shower and getting dressed. My thoughts were riveted to what I would have to do to secure some income from the files in my control. I now knew that I could be called at any time to release them to a custodian appointed by the Law Society. I would have to clean up my files today and prepare myself for the events that I was sure would occur as a result of this highly publicized disaster in my life. I felt like a robot performing my usual functions without any feelings or expectations as I went downstairs to join my family. At breakfast I felt sick with grief but I maintained a positive appearance for the sake of our children. In their lives, this was simply just another day to experience. Perhaps only our oldest child felt any concern about the consequences of the news stories. We really couldn't know at the time how this affected them.

I realized at that moment how devastating this event would be on the lives of my wife and children. It occurred to me how unfairly this situation was in subjecting them to this humiliation. I wished that I could have endured all of the turmoil and discomfort in order that I might spare my wife and children of the grief and embarrassment that they had to endure. As I reflected on this situation, I pondered the strange custom of the Japanese of committing suicide to save honour. I realized now that it allowed their families to avoid embarrassment and was not such a strange custom after all. However, my religious beliefs and customs were different and I couldn't even imagine doing such a thing. Like most people in North America, my spiritual beliefs and customs directed me to fight against all adversity and to work to achieve a proper resolution of this devastating problem. With that resolve I proceeded to develop positive thoughts about what I would have to do to achieve the best resolution possible in these circumstances.

After breakfast I proceeded to my office located in the basement of our home to work on my legal files. There were important phone calls to make that would be necessary at this time to deal with the ramifications of the publicity that I received on my criminal charge. My first phone call was to Patrick Murphy who was not only my lawyer but my friend. I liked Murphy's good natured sense of humour and I treasured his warm and friendly disposition. I held the telephone receiver with nervous trepidation as I contemplated this current crisis that I needed to discuss with him.

Murphy maintained a law practice as a sole practitioner in the industrial area of South Edmonton but spent most of his time in court either in Edmonton or the surrounding suburbs. This made it difficult to speak to him directly but he was blessed with a good communication system through his office staff.

When I placed my telephone call to Murphy's office just after eight thirty in the morning, I was greeted by his receptionist who advised me that he went straight to court. I immediately explained to her that I was concerned that the morning news story would likely lead to my immediate suspension from the practice of law. I asked her to arrange for Murphy to call me so that we could decide how to communicate this situation to the Law Society. We could then determine what arrangements needed to be made on my law practice. Murphy's receptionist was quite sympathetic and tried to comfort me with encouraging words. She then explained that Murphy would be calling in for messages and she assured me that she would ask him to call me later in the morning. I thanked her and then said good-bye, knowing that my wait for Murphy's telephone call would be the most painful task of the day.

As I worked on my files I nervously anticipated receiving a telephone call from the Law Society with their directions relating to my suspension from the practice of law. As I sat at my desk in disbelief and contemplated what I would do to earn a livelihood if I could not work as a lawyer, I felt panic overpowering my thoughts. I had been an active practising lawyer for fifteen years, had established a satisfactory law practice, and enjoyed a comfortable life style. Now all of this was about to end. I realized that I wasn't trained to do anything else. All of this made me wonder:

"How could the governing body of the Law Society simply decree that a lawyer could no longer earn a livelihood as a lawyer? How could they take away a lawyer's employment without even conducting a hearing or giving the lawyer a chance to explain?"

I had no answers to these questions but I was satisfied that this would be my fate. Such arbitrary proceedings continually occurred to countless other lawyers at the whim of the Law Society. Although challenged, such proceedings had been approved and enforced by the courts. This was ironic since the same judges had been highly critical of any similar actions betaken by other professional associations.

I concluded that part of the answer to this conundrum related to the fact that it was not unusual for judges to have previously served as members of the governing body of the Law Society. The governing body of the Law Society also maintained an exclusive rapport with the Attorney General and with the government and openly influenced the types of laws to be passed in the legislature. As a result, over the years the governing body of the Law Society has succeeded in having laws passed that were expedient in their views and which have been oppressive to the general membership. This incestuous relationship between lawyers, benchers, judges and legislators resulted in an inherent problem of lawyers being the worst judges of the behaviour of other lawyers.

In contrast, the governing bodies of other professional groups never have the same access to the legislature or to the judiciary as has been the case with the legal profession. The result is that members of other professional groups are safeguarded from the unjust and tyrannical proceedings that the members of the legal profession face from their governing body. The prospect for change is quite remote since election to the governing body of the Law Society is almost totally controlled by large legal firms. For that reason the large firms can ensure that the rules will not be exercised against their members but will be used to exclude lawyers without influence from the profession.

It is little wonder that there is such a loud outcry for a different system that would ensure that lawyers are judged fairly. It remains to be seen if the new provisions of open hearings to the public for such matters will lead to any improvement. Most lawyers agree that this will not change the problems of influence which determine who gets subjected to such proceedings. Instead, some lawyers have indicated a preference of being judged by a board that does not consist of lawyers. However, with the resistance to such a change, this is unlikely to ever happen.

As I contemplated the unfairness of the situation, I was jolted to reality by the ringing of the telephone. I realized that I would have to face this moment and many like it for a long period to come before this ghoulish nightmare was over. I forced myself to face the situation with determination and all the inner strength that I could muster. After letting the telephone ring completely for a second time I grabbed the telephone receiver firmly in my right hand, brought it to my ear and answered it in my usual businesslike manner with a firm: "Hello!"

I listened in mortified silence for the agonizing words of the caller, dreading the termination of my law practice. Moments later the caller began to speak:

"Hi, Orest! It's David calling. Orest, what's all this on the news about a fraud charge that was laid against you?"

I stood speechless for a few moments not knowing exactly how to handle the conversation. David Boychuk was more than a client. He was also my friend and I wasn't about to brush him off with an idle comment. I didn't want to get into a conversation with him on the fraud charge either as I really felt awkward about the whole mess. Because I didn't respond immediately, David must have sensed that I was in a painful situation because he spoke up again to offer me his support:

"Orest, are you still there? Look, I understand if you don't want to talk about it. I just wanted to ask you about it. I know that you wouldn't have done anything illegal."

At that moment all my emotions began flowing out of me and I felt as if I might burst into tears. From my assessment, it seemed like everyone would probably believe that I was a thief or a con artist. Yet David Boychuk, who I only knew through my work, offered such sincere words of support and trust. I wasn't sure how to respond but I knew that I had to satisfy him that I was in control of this situation.

Finally, I took a deep breath and addressed David in a strong steady voice that disguised the turmoil that I felt within:

"David, it's very kind of you to offer such words of support. Listen, I really can't discuss the details of the charge. It's still a shock to me but I'll be dealing with it. I'm using Pat Murphy as my lawyer. I spoke with him yesterday and he feels that we should be able to clear this mess up at the Preliminary Hearing.

Let's have lunch in a couple of days and I'll be able to fill you in on it better at that time. In the meantime, I'll be working to complete your real estate deal and I should have all the paperwork ready shortly. If any problem arises that may affect the closing of the deal, I'll let you know."

David must have understood how I felt because he accepted what I said and we bid each other farewell. As I hung up the telephone I realized that this was just the beginning and that it would get much harder before it was over. I mentally braced myself for that dreaded telephone call that I knew would be less sympathetic and would terminate and ultimately bankrupt my legal business.

As I anxiously waited for my telephone call from Patrick Murphy, the telephone kept ringing. Each time the same dreaded fear would encompass my body and the same ordeal arose of answering the telephone. The telephone calls came from other clients and each one expressed genuine concern for what had happened. I began to realize that these people were not just clients but people who believed in me. In their eyes the criminal charge was not what determined my worth. Instead, my character was being judged by all that I had done for them prior to this event taking place. I had never thought of myself as having done anything impressive to anyone but I began to realize that I had served each of them in a way that they respected. Their inquiries about the charge were to ease my pain and not to convince themselves of anything. They already accepted the fact that I could not have defrauded anyone and they were prepared to accept that conclusion without any further proof or convincing.

I found it painful and almost impossible to concentrate on any work on my files and my mind kept asking the same questions:

"After having proved my honesty as a lawyer for so many years, why was I now being treated like a thief? Who did I wrong to deserve this type of treatment? Why was I suffering like this when the actual participants to the mortgage transaction were being excused from any blame? WHY ME?"

There didn't seem to be any conclusive answers. The explanations I had heard painted a bleak picture of a conspiracy and of corruption. At that moment, I knew that I would have to pull myself out of this state of mind and get on with resolving my situation. Otherwise, everything in my life would all surely fall apart and any hope of clearing this criminal charge would be lost.

As I set my mind back on my work the telephone rang again. Fortunately, I was already getting used to the shock that my system received each time I had to answer the telephone. Once again I answered the telephone in a strong business voice, hoping that it was only one more client calling. As I announced my usual "Hello", I nervously waited for the response:

"Hi, Orest! This is Pat Murphy calling. I just called in for messages and they said that you had called for me. We just talked yesterday. Don't tell me that you have already solved your case?"

I could visualize Murphy's facial expression with his perpetual smile as he tried to lighten the conversation on a topic that we both dreaded to touch on. His comments caused me to temporarily lose my mood of despair. My thoughts now turned to bitter-sweet melancholy as I responded:

"The only solution that I see right now is to have Christal struck by light-ning, and believe me I've got my prayers in."

The response to my jesting was immediate:

"I'm glad you told me that. Now if I see an unusual lightning storm, I'll know what's happening."

The tension in waiting for Murphy's call was now over and I could feel my body go limp. My whole system had already endured an over-abundance of adrenalin and it was time for a reprieve. I was relieved at the sound of his voice but I had so many pressing questions. I knew that I only had a few minutes to discuss them with him. I therefore quickly continued with my concerns as calm-ly as I could:

"Patrick, did you hear the news coverage of my fraud charge on the radio this morning?"

At this point, I was already drained of all emotions. I had already suffered the pain of the situation after hearing the news on the radio. I now felt partially revitalized by the encouragement of my clients. I was prepared for any comment that Murphy would make. However his reply came as a genuine surprise:

"Orest, I didn't hear anything about you on the morning news. Mind you, I listen to CBC radio because I don't care for the garbage that's reported on the other stations. But don't let that get you down. Those other stations are covering it because it's sensational but by afternoon they'll be onto something else. By this evening nobody will remember what your news story dealt with."

I appreciated Murphy's words of comfort but my mind was racing to deal with the pressing situation of my law practice. As soon as he finished speaking, I quickly interjected:

"Patrick, thank-you very much for saying that. I'm struggling right now to clean up my files as much as I can. I'm concerned that the Law Society will probably want to suspend me from the practice of law until this criminal charge is resolved."

I then hesitated momentarily as I struggled to work my next request for help from Murphy:

"I was wondering if you would be able to call the Law Society and explain the situation. Hopefully, you can find out what their position is with respect to when I have to stop practising law."

I knew that this was a new situation for Murphy but I was confident that he would do what he could to try and help me. Dealing with the Law Society was like dealing with someone who made up the rules as you proceeded into the game. You knew that they were going to finish first but you didn't know how much you were going to lose in the game. Similarly, with the Law Society you had to measure your success by the amount that you had lost. It was going to take a lot of Irish humour to make any headway in this situation.

Amid my apparent panic and apprehension, Murphy calmly reacted by say-ing:

"Take it easy, Orest! There is no reason to assume that you will be sus-pended right away. In all fairness they should wait until the trial is completed before they take any steps. The problem is that we know that they won't be that nice to you. If you weren't a sole practitioner but some lawyer who had friends on the Board of the Benchers, then it would be different. As you know, in the courts you have the benefit of being deemed to be innocent until proven guilty but that doesn't apply with the Law Society. They can basically treat you like you're guilty and leave it to you to prove your innocence. I think I'll give Ed Molstad a call. He's the Chairman of the Discipline Committee for the Law Society. I'll just explain the situation to him and see what he says. Why don't you come in and see me at the office tomorrow or the day after and we can discuss this situation better. Call my office, find out when I'm free and make an appointment."

As I listened to this new perspective of my situation I felt relieved of the burden that weighed so heavily on my mind. I quickly began to feel better and more confident of my situation. I then thanked Murphy for his concern and concluded our conversation. Murphy hadn't said much but what he did say offered some hope. I now had something to pray for as I worked to complete some of the files that could generate some badly needed income for my family. Before returning to my work, I telephoned Murphy's office and made an appointment to meet with him two days later. I then forced myself to put the nagging thoughts of despair out of my mind and to attend to the work at hand.

Because my work involved such total concentration, it was normal for me to lose my worries as I worked. However today, everything took twice as much energy and determination to do and the results were slow and minimal. Ordinarily this would have been disheartening but today it was therapeutic. I was happy to be making any form of progress on my work. I could only hope that this ordeal would get easier as I proceeded to take steps to resolve it.

As I struggled along with my work I finally got a reprieve with the sound of the garage door opening which signalled the return of my wife and our children. Pat had taken them for their annual medical check-up to our Doctor in St.Albert. Typically, such an excursion featured a treat for behaving: a visit to McDonalds Restaurant for hamburgers and french fries. Their return meant that the children would scurry off to find some games to play and I could enjoy a quiet tea break with my wife. I didn't anticipate the crest-fallen mood that I found her in when she returned. I instantly knew that this could only be more bad news. Instinctively, I quickly made some tea and brought it to her in our family room where we often sat to enjoy one of our true pleasures in life: hot tea and warm conversation.

As I gazed at Pat sitting on the couch, I could see that she was very disturbed by something and so I gently asked:

"What's the matter, Pat? Did you find out something at the Doctor's office?"

Pat responded in a sad voice, filled with anxiety and depression:

"The kids are fine, Orest! I had a little trouble getting them to sit still for the tests, but I expected that and I managed to get everything done. The problem is that the news report of your fraud charge was carried as the top news story on all the radio stations and in the newspapers. While I was at the medical clinic, the news report came on just as I was going in to see the doctor with the kids. All Dr. Grey said was "Don't worry about it, things will work out." He was being real nice about it, but it was still very embarrassing. Why do they have to make such a big story out of it just because you are a lawyer? They don't even say anything else in the story. All they say is that a lawyer was charged with fraud. They might as well convict you and hang you because you are a lawyer."

As I listened to Pat describe this latest development in our tragic saga, I wanted to ease her pain but I didn't know what to say to her. I felt just as devastated as she did and there appeared to be no immediate answer on a solution to our plight. This was a new experience for both of us and I didn't know how to deal with it, much less advise Pat on what to do. We were totally helpless and our destiny was like a ship that was sinking at sea. We didn't have any lifeboats and all we could hope for was that we could keep the water out until we could get back to land and dry-dock our ship for repairs. It didn't look promising and I was as worried as Pat. I tried to offer some comfort to Pat and to rationalize what was happening.

As I looked at Pat, my heartache intensified. I instinctively tried to soothe her pain and erase her fears as I softly spoke:

"Pat, you know that news reporters love to crucify lawyers. After all, everyone loves to hate lawyers. There's a lot of lawyers who deserve to be hated for the way they treat people in their practice of law. Because so many people get mistreated by lawyers, it seems that everyone has something spiteful to say about all lawyers in general. Unfortunately, I chose a profession that often creates misery and suffering for people. Most people seem to consider lawyers to be a necessary evil in society. It's too bad that I didn't know more about law as a profession before I chose it. I know now that I would have been much happier if I had entered the Education faculty and become a teacher."

My comments about lawyers and their perception by the public was old news and there was no need to comment on it further to Pat. As a lawyer I've heard all the uncomplimentary remarks that have been made over the years: some of it partially humorous but most of it critical and true. The unfortunate result of all this criticism is that some lawyers have begun to adopt the personas that were described by critics in jest. As a result we have lawyers who are flattered to have the image of a shark or a rat in their practice of law. All of these perverse developments create hardships for sensitive lawyers. Those who are sympathetic to the plights of their clients and are not prepared to stoop to such discreditable conduct, are still saddled with this public image. Ultimately many of these lawyers are forced to leave the legal profession and to start new careers unrelated to the practice of law. Ironically, some lawyers actually continue in the profession in order to generate an income but avoid mentioning their profession in their social life to avoid this very stigma.

I knew that I hadn't answered Pat's question pertaining to the news reporting media and so I now focused my attention on that specific concern:

"Why was the news media focusing so specifically on my case?"

This was the first time that I had ever had any kind of case that became the focus of the news media. I therefore found myself in strange waters. As I gazed at Pat, I tried to think of something comforting to tell her. After hesitating for a few moments, I found it safest to repeat some observations about the news media:

"Don't get upset about the news coverage. They obviously don't have any other news to report today and therefore are running this story because there is nothing else. One of my clients suggested today that even bad publicity is good publicity. However, I don't think that he would personally want this kind of publicity. All we can do is be patient and let this pass. I remember a reader's survey which concluded that anything reported in the news media today is usually misinterpreted by tomorrow and forgotten by the day after."

What I said was obviously not soothing to Pat so I continued with some advice for dealing with the situation at hand:

"Pat, we have to weather this storm out. Very few people in the general listening public even know me. Unless I run for political office, the news reports will never bother us. Since there's not much that we can do about it, there's not much sense in feeling worried about it all the time. Let's just try and put it out of our minds and deal with something else."

All of that is easier said than done! No matter what we started as a new topic, the conversation would always come back to a different aspect of our continuing ordeal. Instead of ducking the topic, we would try and deal with it and then move onto something more positive. The horror of the situation was darkening our skies and clouding out all signs of hope and recovery. We knew that we would have to ride out the storm and face whatever type of monsters that might rear their ugly heads in our future. I silently prayed that we could endure all the grief and anxiety that still lay ahead and that we could withstand the torment of such a colossal attack on the family. There was nowhere to hide and nowhere to run. I knew that I would have to enter the legal arena and hope that Murphy could advance a strong legal position. Perhaps he could still convince the Crown Prosecutors office to accept the fact that I was innocent of any wrong doing.

For the first time, the realization struck me that I only had a basic understanding of the criminal justice system. In reality, I had less of a knowledge of what happened in criminal court than the average repeat offender. A repeat offender has the benefit of picking up knowledge from other offenders who have seen recent similar cases argued before the courts. They get to know what lawyers to use, what defences work and how to manoeuvre through the system. Lawyers are not the best people to ask in these cases because they have an interest in dragging files as long as possible for the extra fees that can be earned. However, all I could do was put my trust in Murphy and hope that his assessment was correct as he proceeded with my case into the court system.

I was at once struck with the irony of the situation: I had never set out to commit a fraud or any other criminal act and was therefore ill prepared to deal with it. A repeat offender knows what to expect in these circumstances and immediately knows what steps must be taken and how to deal with it. Rather I was a typical law abiding citizen who never dreamed that this situation could ever arise. It was as if I was picked from out of a crowd of people for a magic trick, unaware that I would be standing under a guillotine. If the trick didn't work, I would lose my head.

There was no reason for Christal to single me out and only did so because I suited his purposes. I was in the wrong place at the wrong time, just as the person who was chosen for the magic trick that didn't work. The magician might apologize if the magic trick harmed an innocent spectator, but Christal didn't even have to do that. After all HE WAS THE LAW and if he singled you out, that was your problem.

It was the arbitrary actions of police officers that create the greatest resentment from the general public. The arbitrary use of force and investigative tactics continue to be excused and defended by the police administration, even in extreme cases. The arbitrary and unnecessary beating of Rodney King brought international attention to this problem. The most disturbing aspect of that case was that the police actions were actually condoned by members of the police community and excused by the courts. Only a massive outrage by the public was enough to cause the case to be re-evaluated so that proper sanctions would be imposed on the offending police officers.

In the same arbitrary manner, I was now to become a victim of our local police and there would be no apology for the abuse I suffered. Indeed, I was expected to be grateful if I was simply able to convince a judge that I should not be punished for being picked out of the crowd by a worthy member of our police force. Furthermore, I would get little sympathy from the courts since my plight would be no worse than the endless stream of victims that find their names on the dockets of the criminal courts. If I was ultimately vindicated, I would simply be considered fortunate that I escaped without dire consequences. The justice system didn't help people; it simply created victims.

I knew that I had to accept this situation as a new challenge. I was therefore determined to learn as much as possible about the law and the facts of my case to assist Murphy. All the complaining and self-pity that I could muster would only retard any effective progress that could be made in this case. A positive attitude had always been my strongest character trait and personal inner strength was what was needed at this moment. I became determined to organize my efforts, gather information, research law as needed and offer helpful suggestions to Murphy at the appropriate times. Still I had the nagging feeling that I didn't understand the critical factors in each of the steps in the criminal prosecution process. For that reason, I would logically miss opportunities to make decisions that could drastically affect my situation. I knew that I was unprepared for this situation but I was set in my resolve to become an asset in mounting my position on this criminal charge.

My course was set and the challenge lay before me. There was no way to change course or to roll the clock back. I felt like Christopher Columbus setting sail to prove that what he proclaimed was correct, while all around him everyone feared that he would simply fall off the edge of the earth. In my case there was a lot of optimism for proving my innocence. However I still had the nagging concern that the justice system might be compromised and manipulated and that a just decision might not be made in my case. There were simply too many instances that had occurred to my knowledge which demonstrated how such things happen in the justice system.

I knew that no amount of worry would help to solve my situation and that affirmative action was needed. I tried to put aside my doubts and to mentally prepare for my meeting with Murphy. I needed to find answers and he would help me do that.

CHAPTER 2

THE LEGAL PROFESSION

The location of the law office of Patrick Murphy was unusual but it fit the character of the man perfectly. It was hidden away in the industrial section and secluded from any well travelled city streets. Located on the second floor of a warehouse building, it was a small, functional and plainly appointed office space. This location was an inordinately long distance from the Court House, especially for a lawyer who spent most of his time in court. To new clients, the office space was hidden from easy access by an awkward configuration of streets. The only strong points for the location was that the rent was relatively cheap and there were no other lawyers located in close proximity to draw on prospective clients.

As with most delightful surprises, the charm of the office is located within and attributable largely to Murphy and his congenial staff. As with any professional practice, the size or location of an office is secondary if one can develop an office atmosphere that was comfortable for the clients. The other important factor for success is to satisfy the clients by providing the legal services desired by the clients. It is logical that Murphy's clients enjoy the friendly atmosphere of his office and the helpful concern of his staff. The main attraction, however, is the warm and friendly mannerisms of Murphy himself and the personal service which only sole practitioners give to their clients.

Although Murphy handled a significant number of criminal files, he also handled a large variety of non-criminal files in his office. For that reason, he was more correctly categorized as a "general practitioner", which referred to a lawyer who did not specialize in any particular area of law. In fact, he handled all types of files ranging from union arbitrations to wills and estates, and from real estate deals to prosecutions for the Department of Health. It seemed that if there was a fee involved, he could use his congenial charm to convince everyone that he was the best lawyer for the job. The result was a very successful law practice and a well-deserved income for his efforts.

In contrast to Murphy, most Criminal lawyers only handled criminal files and referred all other types of files to other lawyers. For that reason, most criminal lawyers are only knowledgeable in the field of criminal law and some actually specialize in defending specific types of cases. As a result, these lawyers have a very narrow perspective on the method for resolving cases and very little knowledge on the other areas of law. Therefore, a criminal lawyer who is unfamiliar with real estate law would not truly understand the actions of an accused person charged with a criminal offence arising from such a transaction. Instead, the criminal lawyer would ignore relevant factors to simplify the case to benefit himself, the Crown Prosecutor and the Judge. The result is that the true circumstances of the case are not properly argued, explained or even understood by the court.

By observing the appearance of criminal lawyers, one would conclude that it was mandatory for them to look untidy and to wear wrinkled and un-laundered suits. The reason for the lack of concern over appearance is that the clients don't object or even comment. In fact, the majority of clients of the criminal lawyer don't care about their own appearance or even have clean clothes to wear. As a consequence, some criminal lawyers actually foster the belief that they must dress and act like their clients to get the necessary respect and business from them. The result of their adapting to their environment is that these criminal lawyers become de-moralized by it.

Physical appearance is an easily observed attribute but the personality change that criminal lawyers adopt is seldom observed outside of the profession. Their personalities are shaped by the criminal justice system which treats the plights of accused people with cold and impersonal objectivity. Their mannerisms are rough and crude because of the exposure and work that they perform for hardened repeat offenders. As these criminal lawyers move from jail interviews to court appearances, their personalities become devoid of emotion. As a result, they begin to resemble the cold, heartless and cruel environment created to punish those who are suspected of breaching the criminal law.

Viewed in this way, it becomes easier to understand the need for many criminal lawyers to find solace in the company of other criminal lawyers. In order to relieve the stress and anguish, they naturally gravitate to having a social drink in the attitude of sharing in a professional obligation. For many, the alcohol becomes an anaesthetic for relief against the follies of a job that they cannot escape. Sadly, many criminal lawyers continue to function with severe problems of alcohol and drug abuse with the indulgence of other lawyers and the judges and to the detriment of their clients.

Murphy was fortunate in avoiding all of these trappings because of his obligations to his clients who were not criminal clients. After finishing in court, it was impossible for him to go for a drink because he was required back at the office to meet with clients. His general law practice required him to dress and act appropriately. His consumption of alcohol was therefore limited to rare occasions or social settings.

A recent example in which alcoholism in the legal profession was recognized was that of an Edmonton criminal lawyer, Clayton Rice. Because he was liked and respected by his colleagues, he was able to hide his alcohol problem for years. Ultimately, his problem became too apparent to his client during a trial that extended for five days. Rice was forced to admit to the Judge that he was intoxicated during most of the trial and had not conducted his client's case properly as a result. A mistrial was ordered in spite of the distress that it caused to the victims involved in the criminal trial. Ironically, many criminal lawyers deflected this obvious embarrassment to their profession by actually praising Rice for his courage in admitting to his alcoholic problem. The Law Society quickly reviewed Rice's conduct and concluded that Rice should be allowed to continue his practice of law on the condition that he took counselling for his problem. The reason for such leniency was that a harsh reprimand to Rice would have subjected many influential lawyers with the same problem to similar disciplinary action.

Drawing nearer to Murphy's office for my appointment, I reflected on the long acquaintance that I enjoyed with him. In our first year law classes, Murphy's personality was endearing to everyone he met. This was a refreshing change from the paranoia and the nervous anxiety that exuded from most of the other law students. He was a few years older than most of the first year law students because he had worked for a few years before enrolling at the University of Alberta. When asked about his relaxed attitude towards the prospects of successfully completing the first year courses, Murphy was quick to answer in his self-assured style:

"I don't see what there is to worry about. I know that I'm smarter that a few of the students here. If they have hopes of passing first year, what should I have to worry about."

It made more sense to me later as I reflected on these experiences. However, at the time, stress overshadowed common sense and most of us laboured with self-doubt. He was right about law school and I developed a deep respect for his wisdom. For that reason, I sought his opinions frequently after we embarked on our respective legal careers.

Murphy's greatest quality was his ability to be able to empathize with all of his clients. He understood personal hardship because he had a difficult start in life, having been born to a poor family in Ireland. He started work before completing school to support his family and immigrated to Canada in search of a better life. After working for a few years, he decided to complete his high school and then attended University to qualify for a degree in law. While in school, he continued to work part-time to support his family.

Because of Murphy's depth of understanding, his clients could relate easily to him and found it easier to share their feelings and secrets with him. Murphy never lost the common touch and understood the pain of the client who came to his door in search of help and re-assurance. His insights made it easier for his clients to accept his advise and to resolve their problems. His charismatic personality kept his clients coming back to his office in search of help for all of their legal needs.

As I opened the exterior office door to Murphy's office and began to climb the long staircase to his second-floor office space, I pondered on the difference between his life and mine. His daily concern was to generate enough money to meet his monthly expenses and to draw a monthly income. My daily concerns had now changed to planning a new career that was unrelated to the practice of law. I suddenly realized that I was only trained to be a lawyer and that I wasn't equipped to do anything other than perform the services of a lawyer. Who was going to hire a suspended lawyer who was now charged with criminal fraud? I concluded that the only solution was to continue to practice law as long as possible in order that I might generate some further income to support my family. My needs were the same as his but my career was about to end with the same sudden devastation as the crash to the ground of a jet plane torn apart by a bomb.

As I reached the top of the stairs and turned to find myself in Murphy's small reception area, I was immediately greeted by his friendly staff. It was comforting to hear their encouraging remarks about my deepening misfortune. As difficult as it was for me to comment on this turmoil in my life, I tried to present a positive attitude in spite of my feelings. Our light-hearted chatter was interrupted by Murphy's greeting to me as he entered the open office area from his inner sanctuary.

Murphy always appeared to be in the same cheerful temperament and treated everyone to the gracious warmth of his smile. He was of medium height and big-boned. Like the rest of us, he was struggling to keep his weight and his waist measurement within reasonable limits. Although he had to cope with the side-effects of enjoying a nice standard of living, he didn't suffer from the discomfort of a paunchy midsection because of his weekly forays into the racquetball courts. As he smiled, his eyes squinted and his cherub-like face would light up the room as he plied his Irish charm on his guests. Murphy's mannerisms made him ideally suited to be a politician who was liked even by his opponents. His charm was comparable to that of Pierre Trudeau of whom it was said that even if you had a reason to dislike him, you had to like him while you were with him.

As I looked around to acknowledge Murphy, he motioned for me to join him in a meeting room in the far corner of his office space. His secretaries returned to their work and I immediately turned and followed him. Murphy preferred to see people in this meeting room because he didn't like to move files off his desk. To do so would interrupt his personal filing system. As his secretary would often joke:

"There was no point in looking for a file in the filing cabinet because it was probably lost on Murphy's desk."

The meeting room was small and featured a small table and three chairs. It was the perfect amount of space for meetings involving one or two clients. As Murphy sat down, his smile lessened as he asked in a sympathetic voice:

"Orest, How are you doing? How's Pat? This must be a terrible ordeal for both of you!"

Murphy's comment told the whole story. As I sat there in momentary silence, I tried to visualize an appropriate response. We had undergone a terrible ordeal and it was just as hard for Murphy to imagine the torment and anguish that we felt as it was for me to describe it. Although I wanted to have a nice social visit with him, my mind was bombarded with questions that I needed to ask. Besides, there was no use in trying to dwell on sympathy. I decided to get the information that I needed and then start taking steps to clean up this awful mess. I felt sick inside but I took a deep breath, looked at Murphy and instinctively answered:

"I'm O.K. Patrick, and so is Pat! We're both still in shock over this whole thing but we're trying to stay busy. I'm just hoping that we can do something to get rid of this criminal charge as soon as possible."

Murphy's responded directly in a slow and serious tone of voice:

"Orest, we're going to have to make an appearance in Provincial Court to set a date for a Preliminary Hearing. At this point we don't know what they have for evidence. I've already been in touch with Eileen Nash at the Special Prosecutions Branch of the Attorney General's office. She will probably be prosecuting the case and she agreed to provide me with copies of any documents that she may have relating to this matter. When I get those documents, I'll let you know. Then we will be able to go through them to see what they really have for a case against you."

The words rang in my ears! For a moment, I could scarcely think because of the horrible implications of what Murphy was saying. The procedure he described was familiar to me from my first years as a practising lawyer. The horror was that these words were now relating to ME and not one of my clients. IT WAS I that was about to be put on trial on a criminal charge. IT WAS MY ACTIONS that were going to be scrutinized by a judge. Ultimately IT WAS MY INNOCENCE OR GUILT that would be the subject matter of adjudication. IT WAS MY FUTURE that would be changed in the process.

As I gazed at Murphy, I realized how easy it was for a lawyer to say these things and how difficult it was for a client to hear them and to accept what was happening. In a grasping attempt to elicit some words of hope from Murphy, I struggled to ask:

"You know, Patrick, I really would like to do anything possible to bring this whole thing to a head and clean it up as soon as possible. Is there any hope that during the production of documents, we can demonstrate that there is no evidence of any wrongdoing? If so, can we request that the Crown withdraw the charge without proceeding to a Preliminary Hearing?"

"Anything is possible!" Murphy responded. "Usually the Crown will proceed with a Preliminary Hearing just to see what the evidence is going to be before deciding to withdraw a charge. I wouldn't be surprised if they dropped it at that stage. Eileen Nash just told me the other day that she doesn't feel there is proper evidence for a prosecution. If it were up to her, she would not have laid the charge. However, the decision was made by her boss, Bill Pinckney. Eileen Nash really has got no choice but to proceed with it until she can satisfy Pinckney that this case should be dropped."

"Patrick!" I interrupted. "If Eileen Nash feels that there is no evidence for a proper prosecution, why is this matter proceeding? I just don't understand how something like this could happen. What's the point of proceeding with a criminal charge if the Crown Prosecutors themselves can see that there is no proper evidence to proceed with?"

Murphy answered me in his kind, patient manner, as he tried to calm me and soothe the pain that I was showing in every word that I spoke:

"Orest, as I explained to you, this charge was only laid because Christal was pushing it so hard. Finally, the Crown Prosecutors office gave in to the pressure he put on their department. Eileen Nash would be happy to see this charge dropped but Christal is still pushing it. The only thing we can do now is to prove your innocence. Let's see what we can dig up from the documents that Eileen Nash provides to me."

Murphy then paused for a moment as if to collect his thoughts and then continued:

"We're also going to have to put our defence file together. You should search your files to find any documents that might relate in any way to this whole transaction."

I was feeling exasperated but I knew that Murphy was only being candid about what had happened. I decided not to tire him with my continual laments. After another deep breath, I responded:

"Patrick, this was a real estate deal that happened almost five years ago. Any documents that I had would have been discarded long ago. I have very little recollection of the deal. The deal involved a purchase and a resale of property to people by the name of Garmaz. The Garmazs financed the property with a mortgage company and the mortgage company later foreclosed and lost money. I had nothing to do with that part of the deal. How they can charge me with fraud in a case like that is unbelievable. This has got to be just a bad dream. Nothing here makes any sense!"

Murphy could sense my frustration but his manner was still calm and unaffected. Trying to lighten the situation, Murphy responded with his infectious sense of humour:

"Orest, I've had lots of dreams myself. Some of them were so good that I don't tell anybody about them. This situation looks pretty real to me but if it is a dream, then relax and enjoy it. We seldom get to have dreams that are so vivid and unforgettable."

I smiled in response to Murphy's comforting gesture but I was still burning up inside. This situation was definitely out of hand. It seemed so ludicrous to me that I didn't want to just wait, without acting. It was hard for me to believe that a police officer could lay a charge and push a prosecution which was founded on little or no real evidence.

I always believed that cases were never prosecuted unless the Crown had a strong case. Yet here was a criminal charge that was proceeding against the better judgement of a Crown Prosecutor, was based on conjecture and lacked the necessary evidence. I couldn't believe that a case would be prosecuted only because a police officer was forcing the matter to proceed to court. I wasn't ready to accept the fact that our country was becoming a police state where the police controlled the justice system. However, all the facts of my case forced me to accept that conclusion.

Before I could speak, Murphy quickly interjected with a further request:

"Orest, it would be helpful to me if you would sit down and outline everything that happened during this investigation. You should carefully outline all the conversations that you had with Christal. Take your time in preparing it and be as accurate as you can. Christal will obviously be one of the Crown witnesses. To prepare for that, I would like to review your statements and notes on what happened."

I was happy about the change in topic and I immediately recognized Murphy's need for such an outline of the proceedings to date. I began to feel a little more relaxed. I saw this as an opportunity to help Murphy toward our goal in resolving this matter. I immediately responded to Murphy in a positive tone:

"I'll be happy to do that. I'll prepare a careful outline of everything that happened from the first time that I heard Christal's name. Whenever you need to review it, just let me know and I'll get it to you."

My next question for Murphy was a difficult one to ask, but I had been waiting anxiously for this moment. My heart began to beat uncontrollably and I could feel my throat swell. I dreaded the idea of getting any more bad news and yet I couldn't imagine any good news on this next topic. I braced myself mentally, took another deep breath and then asked solemnly:

"Patrick, did you speak to anyone with the Law Society about whether I will have to stop practising law because of this criminal charge?"

"Oh, yes!" Murphy responded. "I was meaning to give you a call but I didn't get around to it. I spoke to Ed Molstad. As you know, he's currently the Chairman of the Discipline Committee for the Law Society. He said that in his opinion there is no reason for you to be suspended at this time since you haven't been convicted of anything. He said that if anything further arises, he'll let me know. I don't think that there is anything to worry about at this time. Mind you, they could conduct their own investigation but we'll just have to wait and see on that. In the meantime, just go on with your work and we'll handle things as they come up."

I couldn't believe what I had heard. It was good news and it made sense. There was no reason for me to be suspended from the practice of law at this time but the Law Society was notorious for their tactics of suspending first and asking questions later. There was never any concern about the lawyer's loss of income or clients. Furthermore, fairness and common sense did not necessarily form the basis of their decisions. Miraculously, my situation was spared at least for the moment.

As I sat there in momentary disbelief, I was afraid to accept what I had heard as being true. Yet what Murphy described was a fair way of proceeding with my situation. I had to conclude that my knowledge of the way that the Law Society responded to problems facing lawyers had made me cynical. I just wasn't prepared to receive such good news and this was the best thing that had happened lately. I had to remind myself that this situation could change anytime but at least for now, I was content to proceed on the basis that no suspension was imminent.

I felt a positive wave of enthusiasm flowing over me as my thoughts drifted back to the problem at hand. There had to be something more that I could do to assist in the effort to resolve this matter. It was important for Murphy to know that I was anxious to help in any way possible. I tried to word my next suggestion carefully to avoid any indication that I was offering unnecessary help as I cautiously explained:

"If there is anything that I can do to assist in preparing this case for the Preliminary Hearing, you know I would be pleased to help. I could research any points of law that may be relevant and check on any information that needs a further explanation. But I would only do so if you requested me to do so."

Murphy seemed pleased with my suggestion. He immediately blurted out with his warm smile:

"That sounds like a good idea. Go ahead with the research but don't do any investigation work. I want you to stay away from any possible witnesses. I can get any of that information directly from Eileen Nash anyway. Let's leave this for now and we'll discuss this further at a later time."

I felt very positive as I stood to leave the meeting. Before leaving, I instinctively reached out to shake Murphy's hand and to thank him for his help. He casually waived it off as part of his job as my lawyer. He then quickly added as I was moving towards the door:

"Don't forget about our scheduled appearance in Docket Court. I need you there to enter a plea to the criminal charge and to set the date for the Preliminary Hearing. I'd like to see you there about ten minutes prior to the time that this is scheduled to be heard. We'll discuss any concerns about that appearance prior to going into Docket court. If anything comes up before then, give me a call at the office. If I need anything from you, I or my secretary will call you."

Murphy's comment brought to mind a procedural question which we had not discussed but which I partially understood from my early years of practice as a lawyer. Because this criminal charge was an indictable offence (which meant that it was a serious charge), I had the right of selecting from two alternative Courts for the trial. I could elect to be tried in Provincial Court or I could elect to be tried in Queen's Bench Court with or without a jury. In the event that I elected to be tried in Queen's Bench Court, a Preliminary Hearing had to be held before a Provincial Court Judge to determine if there was evidence on each of the various elements of the criminal charge that had to be proven by the Crown. Only if the Provincial Judge decided that there was evidence to necessitate a trial would I be required to stand trial in Queen's Bench Court on the criminal charge.

The benefit of electing a trial in Queen's Bench Court was that my defence lawyer would be entitled to hear all the evidence and question the witnesses of the Crown at the Preliminary Hearing. This step was viewed as a benefit to the defence lawyer in preparing for the trial in Queen's Bench Court. The disadvantage to the person charged was that such a procedure would triple or quadruple the time and the costs of resolving the criminal charge. Invariably, defence lawyers favoured the cautious route of electing a trial in Queen's Bench Court and using the benefit of a Preliminary Hearing. This certainly seemed to be Murphy's preference and I was inclined to favour a cautious approach in dealing with my criminal charge.

As Murphy was about to leave the meeting room, I called him back to clarify his feeling on the election that we would be entering during our appearance in Docket Court:

"Patrick, I know that you are inclined to hold a Preliminary Hearing in Provincial Court and to elect to have the trial in Queen's Bench Court. Is there any reason why we don't simply get this over with quickly by having the trial in Provincial Court?"

Murphy's mood became serious as he explained his assessment of my situation and his inclinations on how we should proceed:

"Orest, if you want to go directly to trial in Provincial Court, I'll be happy to comply with that decision. However this is an indictable offence and you are entitled to a Preliminary Hearing before you are required to make any answer or defence to the criminal charge. There is no harm in taking the extra time and your practice of law will not even be interrupted by it. The benefit is that you will be able to see exactly what the Crown Prosecutor has for evidence to use at the trial. If there is any evidence that requires an answer or a defence, then we will have plenty of time to prepare before the trial comes up in Queen's Bench Court. It's my opinion that we should proceed with a Preliminary Hearing first. If this case proceeds to trial, this is the safest and best way to choose. But like I said, it's strictly up to you."

Everything that Murphy was saying made sense and I didn't want to argue this point with him. However I was very anxious to resolve this whole mess without delay. Because I felt comfortable in confiding with Murphy, I responded in exasperation:

"I understand your point of view Patrick, but I just want to clear up this whole situation quickly. Your assessment of playing it safe is prudent and it makes sense to me. However, if there is no evidence to support the criminal charge, I'd like to see everything resolved at my first Court Hearing in Provincial Court. Do you think that we can resolve this criminal charge by having it dismissed at the Preliminary Hearing?"

Murphy was now more confident about this inquiry and boldly affirmed:

"Yes! I believe that this whole thing will be thrown out at the Preliminary Hearing. Eileen Nash appreciates that also. The Crown has to show that there is evidence on each element of fraud. From what I've heard, they can't show any evidence of fraud on anyone's part in that real estate deal. There is certainly no evidence that implicates you. I really feel that this is the best way to proceed and that we'll get it cleaned up at the Preliminary Hearing."

I then gave a sigh of resignation and nodded in agreement. At that moment, Murphy turned again and began to walk out of the meeting room. He then looked back at me and called out:

"Don't worry, Orest! I'll handle this for you. I'll see you on September 6 in Docket Court. Please meet me there about ten minutes before it starts."

While moving through the doorway into the main office area, I called back to Murphy:

"O.K. Patrick, I'll see you there."

As I walked through Murphy's outer office and said good-bye to his office staff, I felt a great sense of relief. My body felt relaxed and the great spurts of adrenalin which kept rushing through my body during those moments of anguish were now gone. I was relieved but the release of tension caused me to feel light-headed with blissful euphoria. After leaving the office, I began to realize that everything in my life would now settle down momentarily. I began to visualize that I and my family could enjoy a reprieve before the next onslaught of attacks came upon us. The situation was hardly one for celebration but I intended to go directly home and take the rest of the day off to relax. Everything else could wait until tomorrow. Tonight belonged to me, my wife, and my family.

As I drove home, my thoughts lingered on the last works that Murphy had said before I left. I would soon be making an appearance in DOCKET COURT. Although I didn't want to think about this and spoil my happy state of mind, the reality of that fateful day that was to come was stronger than my desire to forget about it. I was intent on bringing home a message of hope and a reason for happiness. The news that I could continue my law practice was good news at this moment. It had become my personal philosophy that at times like these, you had to enjoy your happy moments anytime that you could find them.

CHAPTER THREE

DOCKET COURT

The last days of summer vanished like dust into a vacuum. In the blink of an eye, the date of September 6, 1989, had arrived. My children were all back in school to start a new term. Naturally, we were struggling with the confusion that seems to dominate all families during the first two weeks of September every year. In a few more weeks the children would be settled into school work, sports programs, music lessons and art projects. Only then might parents everywhere be able to rest briefly before the next flurry of activities was upon them.

This day was not just another day for me. It was the date that I was required to make my first court appearance on my criminal charge in Docket Court. The experience was depressing and painful but I was determined not to allow my personal feelings to alarm any of my family. Instead of mentioning any of this to them, I focused my thoughts on the activities of my children and their latest "news" during our breakfast. The discussion around the table was loud and cheerful and I marvelled at how children were able to find so much excitement in each day of their lives. I hoped for their sake that they would also find excitement in each day as adults and enjoy life to the fullest.

My scheduled time for appearance was not until two o'clock in the afternoon. I intended to be at the Court House half an hour early and to wait until I could meet with Murphy. My morning was consumed by routine work on legal files and communicating with clients by telephone on the progress of their transactions. I tried to put the thoughts of the court appearance out of my mind but I was destined to suffer in silence as I waited out the clock. Finally I concluded my work and had a quick lunch. I decided to leave early and take a leisurely drive to relax before arriving at the Court House. I was determined to find solace in this depressing situation and the weather was perfect for a scenic afternoon drive.

Fall weather in Edmonton is limited to approximately six weeks before the snow falls but it can be the most beautiful weather of the whole year. Typically the evenings are cool with occasional frost but the days are warm and dry. I always love to drive through the beautiful river valley in the fall because of the spectacular array of colours that overpower the visual senses. Mother Nature offers a brief chance to view the splendour of her untouched landscapes before the leaves disappear and the snow covers the ground for another long winter. It is reminiscent of "the calm before the storm" and the only sadness that one feels is that the calm is beautiful and short and the storm is harsh and long.

I decided to drive down Keillor Road which wound its way along the river bank of the North Saskatchewan River in the direction of the downtown core. This road was a remnant of the past which survived because of its location and utility and because it offered a more direct route for its users. The road itself was a real driving challenge with no curbs or proper visibility and featuring sharp corners and steep inclines. The city planners were determined to close it from further use despite the outcry of large segments of the population. However, the road seemed to survive year to year and continued to be a well travelled artery for its many users.

As I drove onto Keillor Road I was struck by the beauty of the river valley as it began to take on its full spectrum of fall colours. I was as close to nature as I could be while driving in my car. The trees were almost touching the car as I passed beneath them and the view of the river relaxed my tension as it flowed along the side of the road. As the river flowed slowly and steadily towards the downtown core, I moved along at the slowest permissable speed. This allowed me the chance to take in the various scenes on display along the route. The last part of Keillor Road was a climb up the river bank which afforded a larger panoramic view of that portion of the river valley. As I enjoyed my final glimpse of this majestic landscape, my car emptied into a larger artery of traffic and I continued my destined trip to the Court House.

Moments later, I left behind the tranquillity of the country for the stress of the city as I drove along the busier streets leading downtown. My thoughts now focused on my professional work and I thought about how different it was for lawyers to appear in court as compared to their clients. Lawyers wander in and out of various courts expecting to be accommodated by the judges. They continually lament at their dissatisfaction at having to be bothered to show up for such attendances in order to comply with rules relating to the administration of the court system. On the other hand, their clients enter each courtroom with apprehension at the thought of some dire development that may result in further charges, fines or even immediate incarceration. For an accused person, these appearances were not simply inconveniences but rather stressful situations.

I was feeling impatient about meeting with Murphy. I was anxious to find out if he had spoken to the Crown Prosecutors Office prior to this Court appearance and if there were any further developments. My body trembled as questions flowed through my mind:

"Would the news media be there to report this matter?"

"Would there be any further charges laid against me?"

"Would I be held in custody pending the hearing of this matter?"

Nothing was happening the way it should and I was questioning everything that now occurred. As I approached the Court House and drove towards an outdoor parking lot, my thoughts focused on what Docket Court would be like. I had faint memories of Docket Court from my first few years in the practice of law. Docket Court is the place where all persons charged with a criminal offence make their first Court appearance to elect which court they wish to be tried in and to enter their pleas of Not Guilty or Guilty. The courtroom was typically packed with people whose names appeared on the Docket List outside the Court room. Each of them suffered a personal anxiety at being in court that day. Ironically, the only consolation was to witness some other person who was also appearing in court that day facing a more serious charge.

There were always a few spectators who came to enjoy the entertainment of watching the judge sentence people for a wide variety of crimes. In this group usually sat a few news reporters searching for a news story. Every few minutes a new case would be called and summarily dealt with. This routine expediency was followed to ensure that the rather lengthy Docket List could be concluded within two hours or less. For those unfortunate people who chose to plead guilty, the particulars of the offence would then be broadcast throughout the Court room for the entertainment of everyone present. The judge would then pass sentence to further add to the anxiety of the other accused people in the Court room. Without any doubt, these moments created the highlights of the entertainment sought by the spectators.

As I walked from the parking lot to the Court House, I anticipated the awkwardness of meeting lawyers who knew me and would naturally ask why I was there. I certainly was not a familiar face in the Court House as my legal practice did not require me to be there. Many lawyers would know exactly why I was there, having either heard it through the news reports or from the legal grapevine which effectively circulated this type of information. I tried to think of this situation as a humbling experience which arises in one form or another in everyone's life. Unfortunately, the reality was that this was more appropriately a humiliation and a degradation of my character.

After ascending the stairs to reach the correct floor, I proceeded to the large vestibule area which serviced a number of Court rooms, one of which was Court Room #265. The Court rooms were still locked and only a few people were seated intermittently throughout the vestibule area waiting for time to pass. I immediately proceeded to a less used alcove in the vestibule waiting area and took out some reading material to avoid contact with anyone passing through. The time dragged along and each few minutes I glanced up in the hope of catching a view of Murphy. Soon it was five minutes before two o'clock and he still hadn't arrived. By this time the waiting area was very active with people and the Court rooms were open for people to enter.

At last, feeling impatient and apprehensive, I stood up and walked into the main area in the hope that Murphy was somewhere in the crowd looking for me. Having glanced around frantically to no avail, I was about to return to my seat when I noticed the familiar face of Douglas Vigen who I had met through Murphy. Vigen practised criminal law and assisted Murphy with appearances whenever he had a conflict with another matter. Before I could ask Vigen about Murphy, he spoke up:

"Hi, Orest! Murphy can't make it today because he had to handle a trial out of town so he asked me to make this appearance with you. He said that he spoke to Eileen Nash and they're simply going to proceed with the one charge. Today we are simply going to elect Judge and Jury and set a date for the Preliminary Hearing. Eileen Nash will be here and after we set the date, we will be able to leave. Is that O.K. with you?"

At that moment I was simply relieved that I wouldn't have to appear before the judge with an apology that my lawyer had forgotten to appear. These situations happened quite often and created annoyances for judges. It was also an uncomfortable situation for the accused person who had to answer questions as to why the defence lawyer was not present. I was glad that there was no suggestion of any other criminal charges or any other surprises. I now wanted to simply get this appearance in Docket court finished. I quickly replied to Vigen:

"Doug, that sounds fine! If everything has been discussed by Murphy with Eileen Nash, then there should be no problems. We should be able to get through this quickly."

Vigen then gave me some instructions on how to proceed on this court appearance:

"Orest, we'll be going into the Court room now and you should have a seat at the back. When your name is called by the clerk, come up to the front and stand between me and the Prisoner's Box where the clerk and the judge can see you clearly. When the clerk reads the charge, I'll respond for you. Once I have the date set for the Preliminary Hearing, we'll be able to leave together. Any questions?"

It all sounded so easy but I felt so torn apart inside. I knew that these minutes of routine procedure would permanently destroy and alter my total self-image. I answered Vigen in a voice of resignation to the reality of the events as I began to move towards the Court room door:

"No questions! Let's get this over with."

As I entered Court Room #265, I noticed that there were a number of people inside. A few lawyers were speaking to the Crown Prosecutors in the front part of the Court Room. I immediately moved to a seat at the back of the Court room while Vigen made his way to the front. As I looked up from my seat, Vigen had already joined the other lawyers, who shuffled about as they waited for proceedings to begin. As I gazed at the various lawyers, I recognized a number of them who had spent their entire careers making Court appearances and trading their youth for the misery of their profession.

From the spectators benches at the back of the Court room, I began to appreciate the viewpoint of the multitude of strangers who sat there. These people reluctantly appeared in Court to make their dreaded appearances before the Judge. For the majority of them, this was a terrifying experience. Their facial expressions were unmistakable as they came ready to offer up pleas of mercy before their fates were decided.

In striking contrast were the other spectators who were familiar with the Court room setting and appeared calm and relaxed. Aside from news reporters, some of these were just spectators who came solely for the entertainment value in these proceedings. Rather than empathize with the unfortunate circumstances of those who must appear to be judged, these spectators actually enjoyed watching the sorrow that was paraded before the court. To them, it was a live-action soap opera that left them feeling happy to leave when it was all over.

Interspersed throughout the public seating areas were the repeat offenders who had come to court once again to answer to yet another charge. Because statistics prove that there was an eighty percent probability of an offender returning to court, the majority of the people appearing were in fact repeat offenders. These court veterans understood the system and were ready to offer the appropriate excuse that would prolong their case until they could conveniently dispose of it. To them, the prospect of going to jail was simply a temporary inconvenience which followed the inconvenience of appearing in court. Having been hardened by the judicial system which ultimately shaped their lives, they had become callous to the brutality of the system. These repeat offenders no longer viewed the appearance in court or the prospect of going to jail as a traumatic ordeal and humiliating experience. Instead, they had become as cynical as those who diligently work within the system.

Before the proceedings started, the only entertainment in Docket Court was to watch the lawyers as they paraded their important personas before the Clerk and the Crown Prosecutors present. Each lawyer was conscious of the pecking order of those lawyers present. The most senior lawyer expected to receive preferential recognition from the other lawyers present. For these lawyers, having a case called first or before another lawyer was an indication of that lawyer's importance before the court. This type of attitude was not just a result of individual arrogance but was also encouraged by the court. Provincial Judge Carl Rolf specifically delighted in calling lawyers in order of "seniority" so that their cases were dealt with before those of the junior lawyers present. Each lawyer snivelled in obedience to Rolf as he presided over his "Imperial" Court and all the lawyers present were expected to participate in this ego-enriching experience.

Other than in cases where judges like Rolf presided, the usual practice was for each lawyer to advise the Clerk and then the Crown Prosecutor of his case. The Crown Prosecutor then decides what order to call the cases for expediency. Invariably, the order of cases depended on the rapport of the lawyer with the Crown Prosecutor present. Each lawyer then patiently waited in the hope of completing his appearance first and leaving at the earliest opportunity.

As I reflected on the lawyers in the Court room, I could immediately identify lawyers who were at various stages of their careers. I marvelled at how the legal system shaped lawyers with characteristic traits which ultimately become the indicative results of their work. The first stage in the legal career was "the inexperienced lawyer" and consisted of the Students-at-Law and the young lawyers in the first years of practice. These lawyers appeared in court neatly dressed and displayed their presence like male peacocks hoping to impress their audience. At that stage in their careers, they were full of enthusiasm and displayed the energy, vitality and arrogance that was indicative of their youth to mask their naivety, inexperience and self-doubt.

After a few years, the legal system moulded the youthful lawyer into the second stage which is categorized as "the experienced lawyer". These lawyers develop a reputation for expertise in specific areas of practice and devoted all their energies to the task of distinguishing themselves in their careers. Working with excessive workloads, these lawyers toiled relentlessly even at the sacrifice of their social and family life. Their goals were to achieve a reputation before the courts and among their colleagues to guarantee a rewarding future in a competitive profession. Although the strain of over-working showed in their appearance, their presentations to the courts were professional and envied by the other lawyers.

After ten years of practice, many lawyers began to enter the third stage of their legal careers of "the disillusioned lawyer". After years of dedication to his professional career, a new perspective was formed by the misery and hardship that he had witnessed over the years. By this time, the lawyer realized that he had to persevere with the practice of law. In most cases, financial obligations made it impossible to quit and re-train for another vocation. These lawyers had now lost their enthusiasm and become cynical about the legal system. However, they could not change it or speak out against it so they sought diversions and generally appeared dissatisfied with their work. These lawyers appeared in court with less enthusiasm and spoke with resentment and intolerance in private conversations about the general state of the legal system. Many of these lawyers found solace by sharing gossip with other lawyers over the misfortunes of their colleagues.

Some lawyers who become disillusioned try to leave the practice of law to work as legal advisors to corporations or in government. Some even manage to leave the practice of law totally. Of the disillusioned lawyers that continue, some inevitably enter the fourth stage of their legal career of "the burnt-out lawyer". This category of lawyers include the victims who are examples of the stress created by the legal system. After having witnessed too much misery and misfortune resulting to their clients, many in this category found relief from stress and disappointment in their consumption of alcohol or drugs. Such addiction was always commonplace in the legal profession and most noticeable with the criminal lawyers.

The burnt-out lawyers continue to work in their legal practice and generate new clients solely because of the reputations that they made in their earlier years. They are sustained by naive clients who believe that their lawyer will sober up long enough to help them resolve their problem. These lawyers are clearly noticeable by their appearance and the difficulty that they display in functioning in Court. However they are tolerated because of their long acquaintance with the Judges, Prosecutors and lawyers present. As they stumble in and out of court with their unsuspecting clients, the other lawyers joke about the dilemma of the client who would be better off without a lawyer. Clayton Rice had ultimately found himself in this situation.

None of this was new to me but it was interesting to sit back and observe this menagerie of lawyers as they displayed their quirks for their watching public. As I watched an array of their habitual gestures, I began to appreciate the critical comment made about lawyers as being obnoxious and ill-mannered. Aside from the physical appearance of many of the lawyers, there was a display of mannerisms that would be laughed at in any other setting. Along with the other spectators, I watched these lawyers as they picked their noses, scratched their bums, tugged at their pants or played penis pocket pool. I wondered if any of them realized that they were in a public place and not a locker room. The fact that there were women present who were observing these antics didn't seem to concern them.

As I watched Vigen approach one of the Prosecutors to identify his case on the Docket List, I glanced around the Courtroom and noticed that the seating area was only partially occupied. The afternoon docket was usually shorter than the morning docket and this meant there wouldn't be a long wait before my case was called. As I focused on various people seated in the Court room, I began to feel the despair that hung in the air. Each of us contemplated that moment when our name would be called and we would have to answer to the Court. As I looked around the Court room my thoughts were shattered as the Clerk called out "ORDER IN COURT". Immediately, everyone stood up as the Judge walked in to take his place on his elevated perch.

The Judge presiding today was Dean Saks, a veteran of the Provincial Court and a familiar face in Docket Court. I remembered him from the time when I was still in Law School and making appearances for clients through Student Legal Services. Saks still wore the same dark rimmed glasses and proffered the same smile as he happily surveyed his domain from his lofty position. The smile was an unsettling attribute of a man who appeared mild-mannered in demeanour when you approached. However his mood could instantly change to anger as he would admonish anyone in court or prescribe an arduous sentence because of his undetected displeasure. Although he did not make the "List of Worst Provincial Judges" published by the Canadian Lawyer magazine, many lawyers felt that he should have received an Honourable Mention for this uncomplimentary distinction.

Provincial judges in general are cited as the main reason for such widespread dissatisfaction by the public with the justice system. It is the Provincial judges that deal with the greatest number of cases and most members of the general public will usually experience the justice system through the Provincial courts. Many of the appointments of Provincial Judges are clearly political rewards that staff this judiciary with many incompetent and inappropriate candidates. Many Provincial judges display callous and arrogant attitudes with frequent sessions of ranting and bullying. Because of the criticism that has been made to improve the quality of the Provincial Court, there is some movement to better selection of candidates. However, there is no way of removing a Provincial judge who is abusive and incompetent so everyone is forced to wait for their voluntary retirement.

As the clerk began to call the cases on the Docket for the afternoon, Saks began his repetitive work of dispensing with the cases by assigning trial dates and considering adjournment applications. Each time a name was called, panic momentarily filled my body. I then slowly relaxed as one of the other victims present responded and moved to the front of the Court room to deal with the specific charges.

In order to distract my thoughts, I began to focus on the faces of the different people approaching the judge. My immediate observation was the increase of the number of people who were processed through the criminal justice system. Naturally, I could only make a subjective assessment based on my recollections from my early years of practice. However it was obvious that the proportionate number of people coming before this court was dramatically greater than the increase in our general population. This is consistent with other studies that document the increasing amount and rate of crime in our city and in our country. Consequently, this leads to a disturbing feeling of failure to solve or curtail a serious problem in society.

One reason for the dramatic increase in the number of offenders was evident from observing the people who appeared in Docket Court. Instinctively, I made a quick assessment of their physical appearances. From hearing the charges against them, I was immediately reminded of recent studies conducted which concluded that most of these people had a problem functioning in society. The research of the organizations which try to help repeat offenders confirmed that in over ninety per cent of the cases, the problem was either alcohol or drug abuse. Yet these are problems that our society was doing very little to understand or cure. To an observer, it became painfully obvious that most of these people were not criminals, but outcasts. A more compassionate and realistic assessment was that these people were simply victims of a society that could not accommodate their problems.

Suddenly, through the continual noise of people talking and shuffling, I heard the Clerk's voice say "Orest Rusnak". My heart began to beat uncontrollably again, I felt flushed and my body felt momentarily paralysed. Instinctively, I struggled to compose myself and then to rise to my feet so that I might be recognized by the Clerk. I noticed the Clerk visually scanning the Court room for my presence and nodding when she spotted me. As soon as I was on my feet I began to move slowly to the aisle, and then forward to the front of the Court room. Each step that I took required laborious determination and I felt so weak that I was afraid that I might collapse. One would have thought that I was approaching a guillotine and that I was about to be executed by a hooded, axe-wielding goliath who was outraged with his severance pay. In a sense, an execution was taking place of my personal self-image. After this date, I would never again be the same person that entered this Court room.

As I walked to the front of the Court room, I could see Saks staring down at me with a look of contempt in his eyes. In his view, I was simply one more lawyer who had committed a criminal act. I sensed from his expression that he certainly would have had no difficulty in disposing of my case in an expeditious manner if he could have done that. I concluded that it was only natural for Saks to feel that way, having regard to the perspective that he had developed over the long span of his career as a judge. The repetitious work of sentencing people over that period of time had made him cynical and unsympathetic. One could hardly blame him for failing to feel any empathy for anyone unfortunate enough to appear before him.

The formality of the proceedings commenced while I was making my way to the front of the Court room. Vigen spoke up to say that he would be acting as Murphy's agent on this appearance. Eileen Nash stated for the record that she was representing the Crown in this case and that it was my first appearance in court. All of this appeared to be happening for the benefit of the Court Record and was being recited so that the Clerk could note it on her files. Strangely, no sound emanated from Saks; not even an acknowledgement that he had heard what had been spoken.

Having reached the front of the public section in the Court room, Vigen walked over to me and directed me to stand in an open space near the Prisoner's Box. As I moved near the Prisoner's Box, I was horrified at the thought that I might one day have to appear in it. Its structure was a wooden enclosure that featured a four foot wall which was built against the side wall of the Court room. The structure was complimented by the unnecessary addition of wooden beams that extended from the wall toward the ceiling. All of this made the structure obtrusive and generally a visual blemish. The purpose of the Prisoner's Box in Docket Court was to confine those people who were in custody during their appearance in Court. In other Courts, the use of the Prisoner's Box was to put the accused person on display while his case was dealt with by the Judge. Within the Prisoner's Box was a locked door in the wall that led to the cell area which was connected by tunnels to the Remand Centre. Everything was designed for the smooth movement of prisoners with no regard for the dignity of those who were forced to appear in these "cages". The appearance of the Prisoner's Box was a grotesque reminder of the fragility of one's freedom and how easily such freedom could be curtailed.

As I turned to face the Judge and the Clerk, Vigen walked over and stood next to me. Our attention was then focused on the Clerk as she stood by her desk located next to the Judge's elevated loft. With a gesture from the Crown Prosecutor to proceed, the Clerk spoke as she read from the papers before her:

"Orest Rusnak, you stand charged that between the 1st day of July, 1984, and the 1st day of April, 1985, both dates inclusive, at or near Edmonton, Alberta, did by deceit, falsehood or other fraudulent means, unlawfully defraud Heritage Savings & Trust of property, money or valuable security, to wit: money, of a value exceeding $1, 000.00, contrary to Section 338(1)(A) of the Criminal Code of Canada. On this charge you have the option to elect to be tried by a Provincial Judge without a Jury, or a Judge without a Jury or a Judge with a Jury. How do you elect to be tried?"

Vigen spoke up in reply by stating: "Judge and Jury". He then walked back to the table next to the Crown Prosecutor and waited for a Court date to be suggested. While he glanced through a Day Timer Appointment Calendar that he was holding, Saks inquired:

"How long do you expect that Preliminary Hearing will take, Miss Nash?"

In reply the Crown Prosecutor, Eileen Nash stood up and responded without hesitation:

"I have discussed the amount of time needed with Mr. Murphy and we have agreed to set it for five days, Your Honour."

The Clerk then suggested: "January 15 to the19". Both Vigen and Nash confirmed that these dates were satisfactory with their calendars. At that point Vigen and Nash busily made notes to record the dates in their calendars while I waited in muted silence for this painful moment to end.

Saks then looked at me and stated in a monotone and deliberate voice:

"Orest Rusnak, you are hereby remanded to January 15, 1990 and for each day thereafter for a Preliminary Hearing on this Charge to be held in Court Room #67."

Both Vigen and Nash then advised Judge Saks that this concluded their matters in Court. As they began to walk away from their positions, I turned and began to leave the Court room. Vigen followed me to the door without either of us speaking. Before leaving, Vigen stopped to bow as a sign of respect to the Judge. This custom continued to be practised by lawyers in Canadian Court rooms as one of the traditions inherited from the Courts in England. This gesture was a sign of respect and obedience that lawyers were expected to show to judges as a matter of Court etiquette. Failure to do so was looked upon as an indication of disrespect and would certainly be remembered by the judge on a future appearance in his court. Unfortunately, this was one more factor that added to the image of the general public that the Courts are not approachable by the average citizen. Indeed, Courts were the stage on which only lawyers and Judges were allowed to perform and the accused person was simply a convenient "extra".

As I watched Vigen complete his bow, I hesitated temporarily about leaving the Court room without doing so myself. I felt odd about doing so because I was now appearing in Court as an accused person and NOT as a lawyer. Yet this always was my custom before this incident had happened and I was still working as a lawyer. I realized that old habits die slowly but I decided to leave it alone and simply left the Court room.

A strange feeling of emptiness now filled me as I tried to mentally accept this latest development in my life. My status as a lawyer was slowly being stripped away from me and I didn't feel in control of any part of the situation. A decision could arbitrarily be made by a Judge like Saks that could end my legal practice and even put me in jail. Strangely, it now seemed that there might be nothing that could be done to prevent such an occurrence. As that thought gripped my mind, a cold shiver flowed through my body. Such an occurrence at one time seemed impossible but now I wasn't so sure.

I have often contemplated how helpless everyone charged with a criminal offence becomes while grappling with the criminal justice system. Being right and being innocent didn't count for much if the judge didn't like you or was inclined to convict you even before he hears any of the evidence. It was frightening to discover something that I had never questioned before. I had always wanted to believe that judges were impartial regardless of the case before them. In spite of the fact that I knew that to be untrue, I clung to this belief because it was more comforting to live with that illusion. Now I had to confront the ugly reality. This new perspective was one that I wish I never had to accept. However, after this court appearance, I had officially joined those lawyers in the category of the "disillusioned lawyer".

Once outside the door and beyond hearing distance of the Court room, Vigen turned to me looking for my questions or comments on what had transpired. I immediately blurted out:

"I got the feeling that Saks was not very pleased with me in there. You would think from the look on his face that I had either taken some money out of his pocket or perhaps scratched his brand new Mercedes."

Vigen was usually quiet, but the occasion called for an observation and he certainly had one:

"I noticed that! It's a good thing that you weren't appearing in front of him to argue your case. If you had, he certainly would have hung you out to dry in your shorts."

This may have been an old joke with lawyers, but in this case it was true and I couldn't help agreeing with him:

"He looked mad enough that he probably would have hung me out to dry without my shorts. Everyone would have had a good laugh and he would have taken my shorts home as a souvenir."

Our jesting was enough to lighten the mood from the anxiety and tension of the Court room. Since there was nothing more to discuss, Vigen proceeded to walk toward the doorway leading to the Exit. As we were about to part company, Vigen suggested:

"I'll report to Murphy about the date for the Preliminary Hearing. Why don't you call him if you have any questions about your case."

I immediately called back to Vigen:

"I'll do that. Please tell Murphy that I will be working on that written summary that he wants of all my contacts with Don Christal leading up to the laying of the criminal charge. I should have that ready for him shortly. I'll be happy to sit down with him to review this anytime that he wishes."

Vigen acknowledged that he would communicate this to Murphy. With a waive of his hand he was off into the adjacent Court House and I went out the door back onto the street and then to my car. I had endured a very difficult, emotional ordeal and I was just happy to be on my way again. Tomorrow was another day and I had work to do for Murphy. It was now time to recount everything that had happened in careful detail. My next task was to prepare a detailed account of all the events leading up to the laying of my criminal charge.

CHAPTER FOUR

THE POLICE
INVESTIGATION

The task of preparing a written report on my dealings with Don Christal sounded easy when I first discussed it with Murphy. However, when I began to summarize the numerous visits and events, I soon realized that it would be more difficult than I first envisioned. The important events and conversations were very clear in my mind, but so was the pain and the horror that I lived through on each of those visits. It was important for me to prepare an objective summary of "Just the Facts". I was determined to do so in a professional manner so that my contributions would be useful without hindering or complicating the process of preparing my case for the Preliminary Hearing. Yet, it seemed impossible to prepare a written summary of Christal's actions without commenting on his devious, malicious, and callous actions. Ultimately, I decided to document and report all of the facts and allow Murphy to isolate those items that he deemed to be of primary importance in this case.

Intentionally, I began to set aside time during my working day when I could sit at my desk and make notes of my various meetings with Christal. I decided to start with my first contacts and simply report the facts as I became aware of them. Obviously, this would be a longer process but would also be a better documentation of everything that transpired. I was careful to arrange my notes in a format that would be useful to Murphy as a sequential itemized reference.

Often, I had to struggle with my conscious thought process to pinpoint those precise moments of primary importance to the report. As I wrote, I had to subdue the anguish that was instantly recalled and to cope with the jolts of pain and heartache that re-ignited the turmoil that I suffered. At times, I wanted to quit and to ask Murphy to work without this report but I knew how important this was for him. I was determined to rise to the challenge, no matter how painful and distasteful it might become. It was my responsibility to provide any assistance that would be helpful in preparing the defence case. My report began with the first encounters that I had with Detective Don Christal of the Edmonton City Police, Commercial Crime Division.

The first mention of the name Don Christal came from Kenneth Klushin, in November of 1988. I first met Klushin about ten years earlier at my legal office. As I continued to do legal work for him, we became good friends. Through the years, we had enjoyed many family visits and social occasions together. Klushin's primary business was construction of pipelines, waterlines and sewer lines. However, he also undertook other projects and developments including an acreage development of his land. Typically, such projects gave rise to unresolved claims and contested applications for permits which occasionally erupted into bitter disputes and heated arguments. It was necessary to meet with Klushin regularly to review these matters, to provide advise and to receive specific instructions on resolving these ongoing concerns.

Klushin always fostered a positive outlook and a cheerful attitude but his best characteristic was his choice of hairstyle. When faced with the hereditary problem of baldness in early adulthood, he elected to shave his head. By doing so he created an image that was unmistakable everywhere that he went. His shaved head became the object of one of the most amusing incidents that I witnessed during my legal career. On that occasion, we were having coffee at the Court House cafeteria during an adjournment on one of his cases. Our intense conversation on the resolution of his case was interrupted when Klushin became aware of the sensation of someone rubbing a hand on the top of his head.

Klushin slowly turned around with a startled expression and gazed into the smiling face of a nicely-dressed middle-aged woman. Klushin's expression called for a response and the woman quickly explained: "I just had to do that. I had to know what it would feel like." Klushin's sense of humour immediately shone as he smiled and asked: "Did you like it?" The woman responded with a smile: "Yes, I did." The woman then walked away to join her friends at another table. As we listened to the laughter from their table, we both broke out in laughter. I then advised Klushin: "I wish your bald head would attract a solution for some of your legal problems." I always enjoyed a good sense of humour and Klushin's was a delight to everyone.

On this occasion Klushin was telephoning me to request my assistance with a new situation that had just arisen. He was obviously upset and I listened intently on the telephone as he explained:

"Orest, I got a telephone call from the Edmonton Police. They said they wanted some information on an acreage that I am involved with. I guess someone must have complained about my acreage development. Could you get a hold of the police officer and find out what exactly is the problem and see what we can do to clear it up. His name is Don Christal and he's at the police station downtown."

As I listened to Klushin, I immediately adopted his conclusion that the police must have received some type of complaint about him. I couldn't imagine any serious problem and so I replied in a positive manner:

"Ken, it's obvious that they're probably just following up on some complaint. However that doesn't mean they are going to proceed any further. I'll be happy to give this Christal a call. I'll probably have to meet with him since they usually don't give any information over the phone. Once I find out more about the complaint, I'll let you know. Perhaps we can arrange a meeting with him to clear the whole thing up. Don't worry about it! I'll check it out."

We concluded our conversation and I immediately telephoned the Edmonton City Police and asked for Don Christal. The receptionist advised me that he was out so I left a message for him to call me back on his return. Later that afternoon I received a telephone call from Christal. After he identified himself, I proceeded to explain the purpose of my earlier telephone call:

"I am the lawyer for Ken Klushin who got a telephone call from you. He said that you wanted some information on his acreage deal. He wanted me to talk to you and to provide you with any information that you may require. I have a file on his acreage deal and perhaps I might have the information that you are interested in. Can you tell me specifically what your inquiry concerns? Do you have a specific complaint that you are investigating?"

Christal immediately responded to my questions by avoiding my inquiries and saying nothing further except:

"I would prefer if we discussed this matter at a meeting rather than over the telephone. Would you be prepared to meet with me at my office here at the downtown police station?"

His response seemed typical, as police officers seldom agree to telephone interviews. I immediately responded in a cooperative manner:

"Sure, that would be fine. When would it be convenient for you to have this meeting?"

Christal responded in a serious tone: "Would December 6 at one o'clock in the afternoon be O.K.?"

I agreed and we concluded our conversation. I then telephoned Klushin to tell him that I would be meeting with Christal. I confirmed that I wouldn't be able to advise him on anything further until I got more information from him. Klushin was noticeably worried and I was concerned for him. However, I assured him that it was probably something that could be easily resolved and not to worry. After all, until I had a chance to find out what was going on, we couldn't be sure that there was a problem.

I heard nothing further from Christal or Klushin after that. Because I was busy in my law practice, the date of December 6 arrived without any further dis-cussions or preparations being made for the pending meeting. That morning, my work required that I schedule other meetings outside of my home office to com-pliment my outing to meet with Christal at his office downtown. I therefore left my home office right after breakfast and I knew that my wife would be going out later in the morning as well. We agreed that I would call home when I had a chance to check for messages from my clients.

My first meeting was with a client to discuss a new business venture that required some legal work. We met at a restaurant over coffee to discuss his con-cerns and our meeting concluded at eleven o'clock. I agreed to prepare some documents that he could review at a further meeting to be held a few days later. My meeting had extended longer than anticipated and I was already pressed to go downtown for a meeting with a real estate agent set at 11:30. I decided to telephone my home office in the hope that my wife was there and could give me any messages from the morning. I dialed the number on our private telephone line and a deep male voice answered "Hello".

I became totally bewildered at the sound of this strange voice on our private telephone. I couldn't recall my wife saying that anyone was coming to the house that morning and I was sure that she had plans to be out for part of the day. It never occurred to me that I might have dialed a wrong number and I proceeded to ask questions of this strange man who had answered MY PERSONAL telephone. With an authoritative voice, I demanded:

"WHO IS THIS?"

I was mentally unprepared for what had just happened and I certainly could never have anticipated the next response from the strange voice:

"This is Detective Don Christal. Who is this calling?"

At that moment, I felt totally confused and momentarily disorientated. I was sure in my mind that my meeting with Christal was scheduled for one o'clock at HIS DOWNTOWN OFFICE. Was it possible that I made a mistake on the time and place of our meeting? I also couldn't understand why Christal was at my home office as I never had meetings of any nature at my home office. It was designed and used specifically for preparing documents, making and receiving telephone calls and personal administrative work relating to my legal practice. I instinctively proceeded to clarify why he was at my home office by responding in a direct manner:

"This is Orest Rusnak calling. What are you doing at my home? I thought our meeting was scheduled for one o'clock at your office downtown."

Christal then responded in a loud demanding voice:

"Mr. Rusnak, I have a search warrant to search your home. I want to see you here immediately so that I can ask you some questions. How long will it take you to get here?"

My confusion now heightened to a state of shock at what Christal had said. As a lawyer, I was aware of how search warrants were executed. However, they were seldom used to search the records of a lawyer because such documents were protected by law for the benefit of the lawyer's clients. Yet, my office was now being searched for documents pertaining to my client, Ken Klushin, pursuant to a search warrant that must have been approved by a Judge.

As my shock subsided and rational thought settled in, it become obvious that this had now become an emergency that required my immediate attention. I immediately responded to Christal by advising him:

"I'll be returning home immediately. I should be there in about 10 minutes. Can you let me speak to my wife for a minute?"

I could hear the telephone receiver being handed to my wife as Christal told her that I wished to speak to her. As she said "Hello, Orest" I could tell that she was upset so I tried to re-assure her:

"Hi, Pat! I'm on my way home right now. I should be home in about ten minutes. Don't worry about anything! I'll straighten everything out when I get home."

"Why is this happening?" Pat asked, in a quivering voice. "What do they want from you?"

I didn't know how to answer this. I tried to assure Pat that everything would be resolved by saying:

"I don't really know, Pat! But I'll find out as soon as I get there. Don't worry! I'll see you shortly."

As I said "Good-bye", her questions stuck in my mind and I asked myself:

"Why would they be searching my records for anything?"

I had to get moving quickly to respond to this sudden emergency. I immediately placed a telephone call to cancel my other scheduled meeting. Seconds later, I was running to my car and rushing home. As I drove, I felt very confused and apprehensive over what was happening at my home. I was so distracted that I could hardly concentrate on avoiding traffic on the freeway.

I had never had a police officer treat me like Christal was behaving. That is not to say that I had never experienced obnoxious and rude behaviour from police officers. However, I had never had a police officer lie to me by agreeing to meet me at the police station and then surprise me by showing up at my home. What didn't make sense was Christal's actions to obtain a search warrant. Why would he want to seize the very documents from me that I would have provided him willingly at a meeting at his office.

Obtaining a Search Warrant was not a simple task of asking the police department to requisition one. The legal process required a police officer to justify a Search Warrant by providing a sworn affidavit describing the reason for it. A judge must then review the information in the sworn affidavit and satisfy himself that there was a justifiable reason for granting a Search Warrant. Because the intended target of the search is not aware of the application for the Search Warrant, this process is critical to protect the civil rights of every citizen. In good faith, the general public relies on the police to follow this procedure explicitly.

Unfortunately, this important safeguard to prevent unwarranted breaches of privacy has deteriorated and in most cases is treated like a technical formality. The common practice is for search warrants to be approved routinely based on affidavits that follow a standard form touching on the specific requirements. Only those judges that show a lenient attitude for broader investigative powers by the police are approached so that the affidavits will not be scrutinized for information. Frequently, these search warrants are authorized in mass numbers and the selected judge relies on the assurances of the police officer that the necessary information is set out in the supporting affidavits. In reality, the process is actually one of obtaining a series of autographs from a complacent judge.

These blatant non-conforming practices have resulted in police officers simply processing the paper work for a search warrant, whether or not there are proper grounds for obtaining one. The police have become complacent about the specific procedures required or the rights of those involved because of the ease in which search warrants are made available. Because search warrants are seldom challenged in later court proceedings, these abusive practices remain undetected.

Occasionally, a search warrant is challenged in court to disallow evidence obtained under an improper search warrant to be used at a trial. In such cases, the abuses become painfully evident and publicly noted. If a judge chooses not to overlook the abuse, then evidence will be disallowed and charges dismissed. In recent court cases, police officers have been criticized for improper procedures in securing search warrants and in a few cases for swearing false affidavits. Sadly, such breaches of conduct seldom result in any form of reprimand to the offending police officer.

These improper practices in obtaining search warrants in unwarranted situations is a growing concern. As we witness an increase of complaints relating to these improper investigative conduct of police officers, their supervisory officials have promised to review these cases. Politicians have responded by promising to increase the role of Disciplinary Boards that investigate such complaints. However despite hopeful promises, no significant changes are proposed and we can only expect the current situation to deteriorate further.

The thought of a search warrant being used to search my home was now extremely disturbing and confusing. I couldn't understand what might be so important about the documents that I had for Klushin that would merit a search warrant to be executed on my files. Surely, Christal could have searched for the same documents at Klushin's home. If he had, Klushin would certainly have called me and advised me of this. I resolved in my mind that I would try to resolve this matter as much as possible for Klushin pursuant to my instructions from him.

After arriving and entering my house, I became upset at the thought that Christal would violate my home by forcing his way in with the use of a search warrant. My wife and I had always valued our privacy and our home was our personal refuge from the rest of the world. I never saw clients at my home office because that would disrupt the comfort of my family which always was the paramount consideration in our lives. Yet, here was a police officer walking through our home and trampling on our privacy without invitation and without any regard for any personal feelings.

As I entered, I saw my wife and noticed that she had been crying. Without asking, I knew how traumatic this was for her. I felt angry that anyone would act in such disregard for her feelings. It was painfully obvious that there was no need for this. Surely, this could have been arranged so that I could accommodate Christal without victimizing my wife. I tried to comfort my wife as much as possible by explaining:

"Pat, I'm really sorry about this! I didn't know anything about this or I would have been here. I'll get this straightened out and then we can sit down and talk about it. Why don't you go and relax and let me handle this."

Pat responded in a voice that confirmed that she was shaken by this shocking event:

"It's O.K., Orest! They wanted to see some banking records and I showed them what they wanted to see. I'll come down and help you find any other documents that are needed."

What Pat said made a lot of sense to me at that moment. I couldn't understand what sort of information they could possibly be after. However, I didn't want to argue with her or upset her any further. Also, Pat knew where all the records and accounts were kept as she helped me to prepare and file these. I would have been lost trying to locate these on my own. In an attempt to calm her, I responded:

"That's sounds good, Pat! Please don't let this upset you any more than it already has."

I could see that my words were not having any effect on her and she appeared to be in a state of shock. This unusual occurrence was also causing me to feel drained. I was still adjusting to my father's death which happened two weeks earlier. Now, I had to contend with this disturbance at our home because an over-zealous cop couldn't wait to obtain documents during our scheduled meeting. I could only hope that whatever he wanted, we could satisfy quickly so that we could end this ordeal quickly.

I immediately proceeded downstairs and Pat followed me into my office. As I entered the room, I noticed two men in business suits. One was at my filing cabinet flipping through my legal files while the other man was at my desk looking at my trust account records. I was upset that they were violating the sacred rights of my clients by looking at their confidential files but I resolved not to argue with them. I had decided that a rational and calm approach would help to resolve this matter in the most expedient manner.

As soon as he noticed me, the man searching through my filing cabinet immediately turned to me and spoke in a forceful, interrogative manner:

"Mr. Rusnak, my name is Detective Christal and this is Detective Hnatiuk with me. We're here to execute a Search Warrant on your home. Your wife told us that you keep all your documents in this room and we have been conducting a search of all the documents you have here."

As he spoke, Christal handed me a document entitled Warrant to Search and then continued with his task of searching through the files in my filing cabinet. It was obvious that the files that he was looking at pertained to various clients on their legal matters. None of this concerned Christal as he fingered and browsed through them. I felt stunned to see how the rights of so many clients could be simply disregarded by a police officer. Although he was relying on the authority of a Search Warrant, his investigation had no bearing on those clients.

As I focused my attention on Christal, it suddenly occurred to me that he was dressed so strikingly different from his partner. Both of them worked for the police department as detectives and presumably earned a similar salary. Furthermore, I was accustomed to seeing police detectives dressed much like Hnatiuk. Typically when police detective dress up in business suits for court appearances or office work, they dress modestly and usually wear inexpensive sports jackets with coordinated slacks. Yet Christal was decked out in an expensive tailor-made suit, professionally matched by a designer shirt and silk tie and complemented by expensive Italian-made shoes. Christal was certainly out of place and presented an appearance of money that was inconsistent with the type of salary that his job paid.

His striking appearance suddenly triggered a recollection of stories I had heard from lawyers and police officers in candid conversation. Over the years that I worked as a lawyer, I heard so many stories of various members of the police force that made a generous second income from their off-duty activities with drugs, theft rings and prostitution. Naturally these types of off-duty activities are kept undetected, usually with the help of instrumental people in the police department. A fascinating and noteworthy anomaly is that such police officers are easily recognizable because they have difficulty refraining from spending such funds on themselves.

An interesting aspect of this anomaly is that flashy sports cars and expensive clothes are positive indicators that a police officer has secured a more-lucrative second income. One police officer suggested that this was actually done to flaunt the fact to other police officers. These actions spoke louder than words which could be overheard by the wrong people in the police department. The incredible irony is that the police department is known to prefer not to uncover or expose such activities which would eliminate these illegal activities by police officers. The head Administrators prefer instead to avoid scandal to the police department and to denounce such activity only when such an incident becomes public knowledge. This unwritten policy creates an understanding between police officers to suppress their knowledge of these activities unless they are confronted to reveal it. The result of this situation is to give the participants a certain amount of protection and immunity in such activities.

My legal training forced me to be careful not to draw assumptions from unconfirmed stories since there was no way to prove these facts or substantiate the suppositions. However, I never doubted the truthfulness of the stories and there was no doubt that such off-duty activities by police officers did occur even in our quiet northern metropolitan city. Because I didn't personally know anyone who was involved in such activities, I never thought about the situations described. Now I was looking at an obvious example that fit the stories and I felt surprised and uncomfortable with the discovery that I had made. I tried not to show any reaction as I quickly I focused my attention on the Search Warrant I received from Christal.

The Warrant to Search was a one-page typed document set up in a format that was difficult to read. To a lawyer or a police officer who was familiar with such documents, it would have been instantly assessed for pertinent information. Conversely, I had no personal experience with such documents since I had never encountered them in handling files for my clients. In law school I studied search warrants in a general way but I had never gained any further knowledge through research or working experience. I therefore found myself wrestling with a new situation and struggling to understand what specifically the document was referring to.

As I glanced through the search warrant to see the reference to Klushin, I immediately noticed the location to be searched described at the bottom of the Warrant to Search. The description set out was my home address in Edmonton, Alberta with the further description: "the law offices of Orest Rusnak, Barrister and Solicitor". Beneath that, the time for the warrant to be executed was described as "between the hours of 8:00 and 5:00 on the 6th day of December, 1988." All of this appeared to make sense and I then began to read the small print in the balance of the document.

The rest of the document made no sense and I soon began to think that perhaps there was some type of mistake. Was it possible that perhaps they had instituted a search at my residence in error? I was about to ask Christal about this when I noticed a passage in the middle of the document. It stated that the purpose of the search warrant was to find evidence to be used to prove the following charge:

"THAT Orest Rusnak at or near Edmonton, Alberta, between the 17th of July A.D. 1984 and the 22nd of April A.D., 1986, did by deceit, falsehood or other fraudulent means, to wit by arranging for Stephen and Gayle Garmaz to make fraudulent misrepresentations which caused Heritage Savings and Trust to advance mortgage funds of $151, 500.00 on property at Lot 15, Block 2, Plan 3896 R.S., municipally known as 541-22560 Wye Road, County of Strathcona, Alberta, did defraud Heritage Savings and Trust of monies of a value exceeding $1, 000.00 contrary to Section 338(1) of the Criminal Code."

As I read those words, my body froze. I couldn't make any sense out of what was happening. This was not an investigation regarding Klushin. Everything that Christal had said about Klushin must have been just a trick to disguise the fact that he was charging me with fraud. For endless moments, my mind was blank as I struggled to understand what was happening.

While gazing at the document, I could hear Christal and Hnatiuk talking to my wife and asking her where certain entries were in my trust records. As they busily shuffled through my client records, I tried to reach some type of a conclusion of what had happened. I surmised that people by the name of Garmaz had laid a complaint against me with the police which resulted in a charge of criminal fraud. The police were probably searching for information that I had on that file.

At that moment, I became mortified at the thought that I would be charged with a criminal offence. All of my life, I had always governed my life in strict compliance with the law. For fifteen years, I had instructed and counselled countless clients on how to conduct themselves in accordance with the law. It was inconceivable to me that anyone would ever suggest that I had done anything unlawful. Yet, here I was charged with a criminal offence. Furthermore, fraud was a very serious criminal offence with extreme and dire consequences.

As my thought patterns began to develop, my mind still remained in shock. I slowly began to rationalize what should be done under the circumstances. As I looked up at Christal, he asked in a cold and indifferent tone:

"Your wife said that you don't have any files that go back to 1984, 1985 or 1986. Is that true?"

"Yes, I'm afraid so, " was all that I had the strength to utter to him in response to this question.

Christal immediately retorted in a demanding voice:

"Do you have any files relating to a transaction involving people by the name of Garmaz that date back to that time period?"

Without further thought, I immediately responded:

"I'm sure that I don't! I usually discard files after a few years and anything that old would be discarded."

All at once, something familiar began to settle into my mind: the name "Garmaz". He was not a client of mine but rather someone who had purchased a real estate property from me. The transaction happened a long time ago and that explained why I had difficulty recalling it. As I looked down on the document, it started to become clear to me that the police were investigating that transaction. But why were they searching my law office? I had never acted as Garmaz's lawyer in that transaction. And why were they charging me with criminal fraud? If Garmaz had done something illegal, why was I implicated? How many other people were being charged with fraud? What could anyone have possibly said to implicate me in an act of criminal fraud? None of this made any sense! I would have been relieved to wake up at that moment and to find out that this was simply a terrible nightmare that would vanish with the night. Perhaps I could wake up and find that time had been rolled back just as they did in the "Dallas" television series when they brought Bobby Ewing back to life. I was to find out later that this terrible nightmare would never vanish and that it would only get much worse.

Suddenly Christal's attention was called to an entry in my trust records that his associate, Hnatiuk, found relating to funds received on the transaction. This prompted Christal to telephone Eileen Nash at the Crown Prosecutors Office to confirm the procedure he should follow. After all, these were trust records and were considered different in terms of evidence that could be seized in such an investigation. In a moment he had concluded his telephone call and was using my photocopy machine to make copies of the trust entries and the trust cheques. Within a few minutes this task was completed.

At this point, Christal appeared to be satisfied that there were no other documents that could be seized. He then instructed Hnatiuk to continue reviewing the trust records for any other possible entries. This seemed like a useless task but Christal was giving the orders and Hnatiuk indicated his willingness to comply. He then reluctantly proceeded to read through the endless columns in the trust ledger for anything that might refer to the transaction under investigation. Christal then turned and stared at me with a glaring look of contempt in his eyes and spoke in a loud, demanding voice:

"Mr. Rusnak, I want you to come with me upstairs. I want to speak to you alone. Mrs. Rusnak, I want you to remain downstairs with Detective Hnatiuk."

At that moment, I knew that I would be arrested and then taken to the police station to be charged with criminal fraud. My body went into a terrifying shock. I couldn't believe that I was being charged with a criminal offence because of a real estate deal that happened so long ago. As I glanced at my wife, I could see the look of despair in her eyes. I wanted to reach for her and hold her to comfort her. However, the demanding voice of Christal would not allow for such moments of solace as he trampled on our personal feelings.

As I tried to move, I realized that my body was too weak from the shock of this traumatic encounter to make it up the stairs. However, I was afraid that Christal might use force on me for failing to comply so I forced myself to move.

For a moment, I could visualize the many horror stories that were prevalent of police brutality that arose in situations like mine. I knew that Christal only needed an excuse to use his position to brutally assault me. His angry and demanding demeanour left no room for questions or requests so I decided to cooperate and do what he said to appease him.

I slowly followed Christal out of the room and up the stairs. As I was leaving the room, I could hear my wife tell Hnatiuk that she had to go upstairs for a minute. Hnatiuk's response was:

"NO! You have to stay here."

On hearing this, I immediately became concerned for my wife's safety. I couldn't believe how we were being treated in our own house. We were now treated like prisoners under house arrest and every whim that they might have demanded would have been carried out with the full force of the law. This situation now took on a sinister edge as I recalled recent stories of police officers who had beaten suspects and sexually assaulted women in similar circumstances. I knew that some members of this police department had even shot and killed people on the pretext that the suspect made a gesture of resistance. Although the inquiries that followed concluded that such extreme actions were improper, this offered no consolation to the victims' families.

As I contemplated our plight, I began to panic as I realized that we were totally helpless in this situation. If anything like that started to happen, how would I be able to stop it? This was truly a hopeless and desperate situation. The horror of what was happening began to magnify itself as I watched the cold and calculated moves of Christal. I began to empathize with the true accounts that I had read over the last fifteen years in which innocent people endured the brutal abuse of police investigations. In those situations, the police would break into any home and terrorize the family. In the process, they would trample on everything that the family had, victimize the family in any way that they wished and use immeasurable force to carry out their goals. It was obvious from the way that we were now being treated that there were no civil rights and liberties to protect us when dealing with the police. In such a situation, the victims are totally helpless and defenceless and must endure the ordeal. I now realized that there was no protection from those legal rights that everyone assumes must exist to prevent these atrocities.

On reaching the top of the stairs, I began to feel weak from nervous exhaustion. In desperation, I called to Christal:

"Please, I'm not feeling well. I need to get some water, or I'll pass out."

Christal responded in a cold and callous voice: "O.K., get some water and then come into the living room immediately. I don't want to waste any time."

My whole body began to tremble as I struggled to walk to the kitchen without collapsing. My knees felt weak and I needed to lay down and rest. However, that was out of the question. As I made my way to the kitchen sink, I wrestled with the horror of what might happen next. It seemed that Christal was capable of doing anything. There seemed to be no limitations of what he might do in this situation. He was a police officer out of control and that was becoming a real concern to me. I knew that I had to be as cooperative as possible and perhaps my worst fears would pass without further incident.

As I approached the kitchen sink, I reached into the cupboard for a tall glass. Then with trembling hands, I poured some water from the water faucet. The water was luke warm but it seemed to replenish my body temporarily with the strength that had drained away during my short encounter with Christal. Having finished my first glass of water, I now let the water run until it was colder and quickly poured for myself a second glass. Having quickly gulped down my second glass of water, I now felt reconstituted and ready to return to my meeting with Christal. I worried that if I didn't appear quickly in the living room, Christal would come for me. I didn't want to initiate an incident that would prompt him to use force. Before leaving the kitchen, I filled the glass with cold water to revitalize my body during the upcoming ordeal.

As I walked back to the living room, I accepted the reality that I was about to be charged with criminal fraud. I now assumed that he wanted to speak to me in the living room to serve me with formal documents relating to the criminal charge. I only hoped that he would not arrest me and take me into police custody and detain me until bail could be arranged. Although this was totally unnecessary, I knew of many cases where police had done just that simply to add to the torment of the accused person.

In desperation, I decided that I would be pleasant and co-operative by discussing my involvement in the transaction openly with Christal. Because of my cooperative attitude, I hoped that he might simply issue a standard Appearance Notice. This would allow me to appear voluntarily in court and would not necessitate his actions of placing me in custody. The thought of being placed in a jail cell and then waiting for a Bail Hearing before a Justice of the Peace or a Judge was more than I could endure at that moment. I therefore resolved to answer his questions as much as I could and then hope that this situation would not digress into a more disastrous mess.

On my entry into the living room, I focused my attention on Christal who was now seated on my living room couch. My eyes were drawn to a file and a portable tape recorder set up on the coffee table before him. As I sat down on the couch across from Christal, I placed my glass of water on the coffee table. Moments later, I began to silently take deep breaths so that I would feel more relaxed. I could feel my heart pounding inside my chest as I waited for the inevitable words that would send yet another jolt of shock through my body. I prayed that my heart could withstand the stress that was being inflicted upon my body as I patiently waited for Christal to speak.

During that momentary silence, I looked into Christal's face which hung like a mask that was devoid of emotion or compassion. His face told a familiar story of misery and disappointment that shaped his career. While lamenting his wasted youth and wasted opportunities, he became bitter and vindictive against those people in society who prospered while he toiled for what he viewed as a meagre salary. Now, with his new position of power and authority, he could derive satisfaction in causing an even greater misery and hardship on those that he might choose to victimize at whim. Having learned how to manipulate the legal system without detection, he could expect to execute these malicious actions with the total blessings and sanctions of the police department. I knew of a few examples of such police officers in the department but there was no doubt in my mind that Christal was the most blatant example of such abuse.

Having turned his portable tape recorder on, Christal now began to speak to me:

"Mr. Rusnak, before we go any further, I'd like to let you know that you haven't been charged with any criminal offence. However you may be charged with fraud and I want to read the standard caution to you. Do you wish to say anything?"

I blurted out my answer instinctively, knowing that I was in no condition to discuss this matter. Furthermore, I wanted to find out what was happening before any statement was made to the police. My answer was clear and emphatic:

"NO! Not at this time."

Christal must have recognized that I was upset and disorientated. Having sensed that I was unable to resist his interrogation, he began to question me in spite of my answer. He was intent on getting a statement and was not to be deterred by my decision to wait until a later time. I sat there facing Christal, frozen with fear and hoping to appease him by showing a co-operative attitude. As he asked his questions, I realized that nothing he said made any sense. It was obvious that I had forgotten almost everything about this transaction which had happened four years earlier. He mentioned names such as Doug Hawryluk, Nadia Foster, Doug Thompson, Peter Pilip and of course, Stephen and Gayle Garmaz. All of these names were familiar in some vague indeterminable way. Unfortunately, none of these names bore any familiarity to a real estate transaction that happened four years ago and which was now the basis of his criminal investigation.

After it became obvious that I couldn't recall anything or make any statement from personal knowledge, Christal began showing me documents to try and refresh my memory. My mind was still blank and I couldn't think of anything that was familiar to me from that time. I began to feel sick and quickly drank the water before me. Then came an interruption as Hnatiuk called Christal to take a telephone call. I quickly rose to my feet to run for more water. My hands shook uncontrollably but I managed to drink another glass of water. As I was finishing it, I could hear my name being called by Christal. For a second, a flash of fear paralysed my body as I contemplated the ordeal that would soon follow. I struggled to fill my glass again with cold water and then reluctantly returned to the living room to continue our meeting. Once I was seated he continued to show me various documents. I struggled to make sense out of each document but my mind was blank. As I tried to respond it became obvious that my answers were the result of feeble and desperate conjecturing on what might have happened.

Finally, the questions stopped and I waited for the next bombshell to fall. Christal could do anything that he pleased and I was now sure that I would be charged. I now feared that I would be arrested and taken to the downtown police station to be charged and held in custody until bail could be arranged. Christal abruptly stood up and walked downstairs to confer with Hnatiuk on his search on my trust ledger. Having located nothing further, both of them returned upstairs. Christal then informed me that the search was completed and that they would be leaving.

For a moment, I stood there in disbelief as I realized that nothing further would happen. Christal advised me that he would be reviewing the results of the search warrants before taking any steps to lay charges. He then indicated that he would be reviewing his findings on this matter with Eileen Nash at the Crown Prosecutors Office and that my lawyer could obtain any information that we desired from her. At that juncture, I advised Christal that I would be consulting with Patrick Murphy on this matter and that he would be in touch with Eileen Nash to discuss this further. With that parting comment, both Christal and Hnatiuk left through the front door. Their departure left me and my wife in emotional shambles as we collapsed on the couch to comfort each other.

Moments later, I rushed to the kitchen to make some tea so that we could relax from the stress of the whole ordeal. We were both drained of all our emotions and didn't have the energy to be angry or even cry. In shock, we sat there in terror contemplating what was sure to develop from this devastating situation. Instinctively we both knew that we would have to prepare ourselves for the worst conceivable outcome. The problem was that this was a situation foreign to us and we could never have anticipated that anything like this could ever happen. We lived a quiet and sheltered life and had never witnessed this form of a crisis in our families or even with friends. Now we were about to be devastated by this unpredictable disaster and we had to prepare ourselves emotionally and physically.

As we began to relax, our emotions started to pour out. I gently spoke to my wife to offer her comfort after this terrible encounter:

"Pat, I'm really sorry that you had to go through this. I was supposed to meet Christal downtown today at one o'clock. If I had known that he was coming here, I would have been here. I wish you could have been out of the house during this ordeal. You shouldn't have endured this. I feel badly about what happened to you."

As my wife started to speak, it was evident that her body was wrenched with stress. I knew that she was having difficulty comprehending what was happening:

"I thought that they were going to arrest you and put you in jail. I didn't know what to do. I was so scared. I'm sorry that I was crying. I must look awful. My eye mascara has been running. I just feel awful."

I tried to comfort Pat on her appearance and told her that she had done everything properly. I didn't know how to explain this situation myself and I had no idea what was really happening. I wanted to know what Christal had done before I got home and so I asked her to tell me what she remembered of this whole situation.

Pat responded in a strained voice. She struggled to contain her emotions as tears filled her eyes:

"I was just leaving the garage to go meet a friend when they pulled up and stopped me. Christal handed me that document and said that they wanted to search the house. I couldn't understand anything on it and I just asked: "What is this all about?" Christal then said: "It's a Search Warrant to search your house." I asked them to wait until you got home but he said: "If you don't open the door right now, I'll break it down." He started walking toward the door and I knew that he was going to kick it down. I began to run to the front door with my keys and I slipped on some ice in front of the steps. I fell down and bruised my knees and my elbow on the cement. I hurt my leg badly and it was bleeding but he did-n't even care. I started to cry because my leg hurt but all he said was "Open this door". When I opened the door, he walked in and started demanding: "Where does your husband keep all his records?" I told him: "Downstairs, in his office." He was shouting and I knew he was going to do something terrible. They both went downstairs to your office and began to look through your files. I asked them to wait until I could call you but Christal said he was getting a truck to haul everything in your office away."

Pat was now sobbing and I softly held her hand to comfort her as she con-tinued to describe her terrible ordeal:

"I asked him: "Why are you doing this?" and he said: "Your husband has committed fraud which is a criminal offence." He gave me the document again but I couldn't even read it. I told him that I knew that you wouldn't have done anything like that and then he said: "You don't know the kind of things that your husband has been doing without telling you. Your husband has been doing all kinds of illegal things and has been hiding these things from you."

At this point, my wife was crying. I could sense her deep emotional pain as I interjected to comfort her:

"It's all over now, Pat! They came and searched the house. Now they know that there isn't anything here that they were looking for. I'm sure that they only took the banking records so that they wouldn't leave empty-handed. Just relax and don't worry anymore."

I could hear myself saying these words but my feelings were totally con-trary to this assessment. I really didn't know if the police were satisfied with their search. I felt sick thinking of the prospect that they might appear again at any time. I worried that nothing would prevent them from coming again to ter-rorize me and my family. Silently I prayed that this was the end of the ordeal and that we could soon forget this awful incident.

My wife was groping for answers to explain the horror that she witnessed. Similarly, I was groping to understand what had happened four years ago in the real estate deal that they had construed to be a fraud. If it was so obvious that I had committed a criminal act, then why was I having such difficulty determining what was illegal in that transaction. This whole situation was ridiculous and I wondered how anyone could accuse me of committing a fraud under such circumstances. Nothing made sense to me. I began to feel sick over the prospect that I could be charged with a criminal offence without knowing what had happened. I dreaded to think of how our lives and my legal career would be devastated if this police officer decided to lay a criminal charge. Whether or not there was any proper basis for laying such a charge would be irrelevant, as the consequences would devastate everything.

Pat interrupted my thoughts with a question that seemed disturbing to her:

"Orest, why are they saying that you committed a fraud? They kept saying that you committed fraud and hid it from me. I know that you wouldn't have done anything like that. Why are they doing this to you?"

The question was one that I was having difficulty understanding but I realized that I had to comfort Pat after such an agonizing ordeal:

"Pat, I know that I didn't commit any fraud. I don't understand why they are investigating me. Christal said he hasn't charged me yet and that he will be reviewing this with the Crown Prosecutors office. I am going to get some information on this. I'll need to get Patrick Murphy to contact the Crown Prosecutors office to find out what is going on. Let's not worry about this! We'll be able to understand this better when I get more information. I'll call immediately to arrange a meeting with Murphy."

Pat was not comforted by these comments and neither was I. Christal's actions left no doubt that he was going to charge me with fraud. This search for documents may have been nothing more than a formality to justify his actions in laying the charge. Maybe he was hoping to find something that might be construed as useful evidence. However, his failure to find anything was secondary to his attitude that he intended to charge me with fraud. I began to wonder why there was such personal animosity by Christal towards me. I wondered why he would act with such unnecessary force and use such overbearing tactics. After all, this was a situation where nobody was offering any difficulty or resistance to him. I concluded that there must have been something personal in his motives which explained why he treated me and my wife in the manner that he had. I was sure that I never had any cases that involved him and I had no idea what might have happened to cause him to feel that way.

My whole body felt uncomfortable and restless and I knew that I couldn't just sit and relax after what had just happened. In every situation that I had faced in the past, there was always something that could be done to resolve a problem or complaint. Now I was facing a devastating situation and there seemed to be nothing that I could do about it. It was ironic that as an experienced lawyer, I was still helpless in resolving my personal legal problem.

I wondered why it was that the criminal justice system did not provide an avenue for complainants to resolve complaints before taking steps to lay criminal charges. In civil matters such as this one, the dispute is usually over money that was lost. Usually, these types of situations are best resolved through negotiations and settlements. At the very least, such a procedure would provide for an exchange of information that would be helpful to all parties if criminal proceedings were instituted. I was aware of various reform proposals advocating such a system to lessen the backlog of cases before the courts. Unfortunately, most of these were ignored by the government for fear that it might disturb the established court process. Any reform that would affect the judicial mandarins was difficult to implement without offending their egos.

The need for this type of reform is obvious to those that continually work with criminal cases. Often, such cases are referred by the Crown Prosecutors office to civil court since that is the more appropriate forum. When such cases are brought before the criminal courts, occasionally judges will refuse to proceed on criminal charges on the basis that the complainant is abusing the criminal justice system to simply collect a debt. Unfortunately, the criminal courts continually receive such cases because no specific policy has ever been established to systematically curb this abuse. As a result, when such a case is pursued by a zealous police officer or Crown Prosecutor, another victim is created by an unnecessary prosecution.

The solution to eradicate this problem is simple and has become a topical issue with justice reform advocates. Many concerned action groups have advocated the creation of a special arbitration tribunal that could hear and resolve such cases in a non-criminal setting. This change would drastically reduce the number of cases before the criminal courts and provide a better solution for such disputes. Instead of penal sanctions, the complainant would receive retribution and the accused person would avoid the protracted and demoralizing process of the criminal courts. This alternate means of dealing with these cases would benefit everyone and reduce the number of people in our prisons. Alas, very little movement by the government has been made that would signal any reform that faintly resembles the virtues of such a reform program.

As the tension within me began to build, I jumped up. The sudden movement startled my wife and she immediately inquired:

"What's the matter? What are you doing?"

My frustration and agitated manner were evident from my movements and were causing her to have concerns about my reactions. I tried to calm her again by explaining:

"Pat, I just can't sit and relax! I'm going to call Murphy's office. I want to make an appointment to meet with him on this whole thing. The sooner we start making inquiries, the sooner we'll have some answers on what is going on. Why don't you lay back and rest."

As Pat slouched on the couch and closed her eyes, I walked to my office in a determined manner. On reaching my desk, I located Murphy's number and dialed it. His secretary answered and advised me that Murphy was in court. I then advised her that I had to see Murphy on a serious matter so we agreed on an appointment the following day. As I hung up the telephone, I began to feel better about the steps I was taking to deal with this traumatic situation. For a moment, I tried to adopt a positive attitude that there must be a way of demonstrating that this whole investigation was improper and should be discontinued. It was wishful thinking but it provided some desperately needed comfort at that moment.

And now the challenge was to try to relax. All I could do was wait to see what tomorrow would bring. As the realization of what had just happened in my life began to settle in, I knew that I had to get some immediate answers. Unfortunately, I was inexperienced to handle this case. This was a criminal matter and I need the help of a criminal lawyer. I was sure that Patrick Murphy would help me to get those answers.

CHAPTER FIVE

THE CRIMINAL LAWYER

Although it is common and fashionable for lawyers to specialize and restrict their law practices to specific types of cases, the designation of criminal lawyer also has historic roots. From the earliest inception of the legal profession in England, there was a recognized need to distinguish between lawyers who appeared in Court and those that did not. As a result, lawyers who appeared in Court were described as "Barristers" while lawyers who limited their legal practice to other work were referred to as "Solicitors". In practice, a lawyer could become a solicitor easily after successfully completing his legal studies. However, a lawyer could only become a Barrister by "articling" or training with a Barrister and then ultimately joining an "Inn" that regulated his conduct. The most common cases of Barristers was that of a Criminal Lawyer. As a result, some criminal lawyers still foster an attitude of aloofness which they flaunt over the general public and those lawyers doing less prestigious work.

The distinction between a Barrister and a Solicitor still exists in England although it is now slowly disappearing. In Canada, every lawyer can identify himself as both a Barrister and a Solicitor. Today, this distinction has become almost non-existent since almost every area of practice may require at least an occasional appearance in Court. However, the Criminal Lawyers still consider themselves the true Court room Lawyers and some even prefer to identify themselves as Barristers. Lately, this image has diminished in the eyes of the general public. Ironically, criminal lawyers have received much criticism for frustrating the criminal justice system with their legal tactics in Court. In order to defend themselves and to develop a better image, they have formed a Criminal Trial Lawyers Association. Whether this will improve their negative perception by the public is difficult to predict but they have succeeded in generating news media attention for themselves.

A Criminal Lawyer is regarded by the judiciary as an "Officer Of The Court". With this historic privilege comes an expectation of unquestioned integrity. Unfortunately, this highly regarded status of Criminal Lawyers has diminished because of blatant abuses and inappropriate conduct. Of these indiscretions, the most inexcusable are instances where Criminal Lawyers have lied to the Court, sworn false documents and conducted trials while intoxicated. Because of the recent proliferation of such cases, investigations have been conducted by the judiciary, the legal professions and the governments in Canada, the United States and Britain. These investigative boards have issued reports that criticize Criminal Lawyers for intentionally disrupting Court procedures by preventing the administration of justice and casting the legal profession in disrepute.

Most recently, the Law Societies and the Legal Profession in general have acknowledged the diminishing public perception of lawyers. They have acknowledged that the public now perceive lawyers generally as being greedy, dishonest to clients, self-serving and uncaring in attitude. This public perception has become so bad that many lawyers are embarrassed to discuss their profession and even lie about their involvement in the legal profession. This general image problem has sparked debate in the profession on how to rectify this deteriorating situation. Although there have been small efforts to convince the general public of a movement to improve, most of these changes are simply cosmetic and do little to hide the blatant problems that exist. As a result of that general attitude in the legal profession, the bad image problem may always stigmatize lawyers.

Criminal Lawyers not only share in the bad image problem but are perhaps the worst culprits in creating it. Furthermore, Criminal Lawyers are unpopular to the public because of the type of cases that they handle. In the eyes of the general public, the Criminal Lawyer is the "snake" who represents guilty people and uses trickery to inhibit their punishment by the justice system. Unfortunately, in many instances that is a reasonably accurate assessment.

It is also this perception by the general public that creates a stigma for anyone who seeks the advice or assistance of a Criminal Lawyer. No matter how irrational this may seem, a person naturally feels that he must be guilty of a criminal offence to enlist the help of a Criminal Lawyer. After all, it is a widespread belief that only those who wish to avoid rightful punishment from the Courts would ultimately need to turn to a Criminal Lawyer. Even the innocent people feel the burden of this public perception as they endure the torment of the humiliating procedures of the criminal justice system. I also began to understand and appreciate these feelings as I enlisted the services of a Criminal Lawyer.

As I drove to Murphy's office, my thoughts were riveted to the traumatic experience that I and my wife had just endured. Although I didn't have a restful evening, I now felt slightly more relaxed than I was yesterday. My thoughts drifted to the various possibilities that could arise as a direct result of Christal's investigation. I reasoned that the most likely possibility was that I would be charged with criminal fraud, if such a charge was not already processed. A deep depression swept over my body as I contemplated the devastating effects of such a situation on my family and on my career. The stigma that would result and the conclusions that everyone would draw from such an occurrence would create inexplicable horror to all of us. Our quiet, tranquil lives would inevitably crumple into a turmoil that would leave its marks on our lives forever. The most devastating consequence of such an occurrence was that my legal career would be over. If my license was suspended, I would lose the only means that I ever had of supporting my family.

As I contemplated the ramifications of this situation, I began to feel upset about the effect that this entire matter was having on my family. How would we cope with the endless questions that would come from relatives, friends and acquaintances? How could we explain this to curb their curiosity relating to the circumstances of what happened? How would we manage to support and maintain our lifestyle if I could no longer generate an income from practising law? How would we survive the stress that would accompany this situation? How could I prevent my family from dissolving as so many family units do in similar circumstances? If we were ostracized by our neighbours and our children were ostracized in school, where would we move to? Would we survive this situation without a tragedy such as a suicide, a fatal heart attack or a mental breakdown?

My mind drifted to stories that were all too prevalent about people who had committed suicide because of a perceived hopeless situation. Often, the stress that caused a person to commit suicide was not even obvious to those closest to the victim. Yet, a suicide would occur and would devastate everyone who knew the victim. The legal grapevine would always feature stories of lawyers who chose suicide to avoid the consequences of some major indiscretion. None of the cases made any sense and this made the circumstances all the more tragic. A fatal shot from a handgun seemed to be a favourite choice but one local lawyer elected the mundane method of jumping from a high bridge into a polluted river. Some lawyers demonstrated their macabre attitudes by debating if it was the jump or the polluted water that actually killed him. The consensus favoured the polluted water.

These shocking and tragic situations bothered us and I and Pat realized that anyone is susceptible to such a situation. We therefore raised the topic with our children to offer them accurate information and tangible evidence of our moral support. Our concern was that studies had demonstrated that suicides can happen at any age and to any family. My thoughts now wrestled with the foreboding concern of how my wife and children would handle this devastating situation if it began to look hopeless?

As I shook myself to clear my thoughts of these depressing prospects, I fixed my thoughts on what I could do to prevent such a devastation to my family. As a lawyer, I should have been able to immediately determine the various legal recourses that could be used to resolve any situation. However, this was a situation in which I had no real experience. Although I learned some case law while at law school to develop a general overview of criminal law, none of this was helpful or easy to recall sixteen years later. I had some slight experience with a few criminal cases during my articling year and my first few years of practice. Unfortunately, none of these cases involved serious charges or these types of investigations. It was frustrating to realize that so little of what I knew was relevant to this situation. For the past twelve years, I had only handled commercial files and collection files with no involvement in any criminal files. I now had only a vague familiarity with the criminal justice system and I knew that I would have to rely entirely on the advise of my lawyer in resolving this matter.

As I arrived at the law offices of Patrick Murphy, I parked my car and realized that I was a few minutes early. I decided to stay in the car for a few minutes to develop a positive framework in my mind that would assist me in conducting my meeting with Murphy on a productive level. I began to speak out loud to quickly adopt a positive outlook on this growing crisis. I told myself that nothing had happened yet and that Murphy's involvement might enable us to sort this out before anything further happened. After all, I knew that I had done nothing illegal. Therefore, even if Christal wanted to charge me, the Crown Prosecutor would have to conclude that there was no evidence on which to proceed. Recalling some personal aspects of my case, I convinced myself that there was nothing to fear. Obviously, the truth would prevail and ultimately clear me of any accusations of wrongdoing. With these thoughts now firmly implanted in my mind, I said a silent prayer that all of this turmoil would end quickly for me and my family.

With a deep breath, I turned off the car engine. Grabbing my briefcase, I stepped out of the car into the snow and the cold wind of an Alberta winter. My mind quickly focused on making a strong effort to get into the warm building before I experienced any chills or frostbite. Steadfastly, I moved in a determined gait through the parking area towards Murphy's office. I realized at that moment that one advantage of a cold winter day is that while outside, everyone's thoughts are focused on survival rather than everyday worries. No matter how oppressive the other concerns might be, the blast of a cold wind is sufficient to capture anyone's attention. All is forgotten in the instinctive reaction to preserve oneself.

On reaching the front door of Murphy's office, I quickly stepped inside. I had to force the door shut to keep out the wind and snow that tried relentlessly to invade and dissipate the inner warmth of his office. As I walked up a long staircase, I brushed snow away from my winter coat and pulled my gloves off. On reaching the top landing, I turned to be greeted by Murphy's office staff. They were obviously busy as they continued their work on files that were arranged all over their desks. I was told that Murphy was in but that he was still with a client. In response, I acknowledged that I would be happy to wait.

I proceeded to remove my coat and hang it in the coat closet before reaching for a magazine and sitting down in the waiting area. As with most offices at this time of year, there were Christmas decorations displayed everywhere. Attention was now focused primarily on trying to complete work that was critical before leaving for the Christmas break. In legal offices, December was a difficult month since many emergency files would arise that required completion before the end of the month. Yet it was difficult to complete work with everyone partying and taking long lunch breaks. For the same reason, registration in government offices usually took twice as long as it did normally. It was difficult getting anyone by telephone and even more difficult arranging a meeting to discuss anything. All of this created frustration and exhaustion which was rampant at this time of year.

As I glanced through a magazine in Murphy's reception area, I found that I couldn't concentrate enough to read anything. Instead, I found it somewhat relaxing to simply glance at pictures and focus on various articles without trying to seriously engulf myself in them. As I worked my way through the magazine, I suddenly became aware of Murphy's voice getting louder. I looked up to see him emerging from his meeting room with two clients. Murphy noticed me but continued his final remarks with his clients. He then directed them to make another appointment with his receptionist to come in and sign documents. Looking toward me he said "Hi" but before we could say anything further, his receptionist gave him an urgent telephone message. He advised her that he would make the call and then called out to let me know that he would be with me in a few minutes. With a wave of his arm he gestured for me to wait in his meeting room and I immediately responded in compliance.

As I entered his meeting room, I expected it to be cold as I had experienced before. This time I noticed that Murphy was employing a portable electric heater to bring more comfort to the room. I sat down in the warm environment and looked out the window at the snowflakes dancing in the torrents of wind currents. This was yet another example of Nature's magical choreography set to the music of the dull whine of the raging Northern wind. The scene at once became a vision of wonderment and I began to experience the sheer delight of the living world around us. It seems that such a scene is only truly enjoyed by children and is lost in the serious and busy world of adults.

Soon I began to feel more relaxed as I marvelled at the Snowflake animation. Suddenly, I heard Murphy's voice in the background as he drew nearer. I turned around and Murphy called to me as he came through the door:

"Orest, it's nice to see you again. How's Pat and the family?"

It was so comforting to see Murphy's smiling, friendly face. I adopted a similar smile as I responded to his opening question:

"We're all fine, Patrick! Thank goodness, we're all healthy! The kids are growing fast and doing reasonably well in school. How has everything been with you and your family?"

This was a typical opportunity for Murphy to bring out his humour, which I always enjoyed:

"We're fine, Orest! There's no point in me complaining because nobody around here takes me seriously anyway."

With that remark, I could hear sounds of agreement from the outer office. Murphy smiled at his secretaries and then closed the door. With a cheerfulness that was perfect for the season, he sat down at the table and reclined in his chair. As he looked across at me, his expression became more serious as he asked:

"Orest, you said on the telephone that you had something important that you needed to talk to me about?"

I looked at Murphy and calmly responded: "Yes, I do. I had a terrible experience yesterday and I'm going to need your help to get this situation cleaned up. Let me show you a document that I got and this should explain what happened."

With that remark, I reached into my briefcase for the Search Warrant that I received from Christal. As I placed it on the table before Murphy, he reached for his reading glasses and surveyed the contents of the document. The atmosphere in the room became tense as I began to explain to him what must have been obvious at that moment:

"They're charging me with fraud, Patrick! I don't know what the hell is going on. I wish I could tell you why but I really don't know. I'd like to get this cleared up without any further problems. Is there anything that you can do to help me?"

As I finished talking, Murphy's facial expression changed to a frown on his forehead and a squinting in his eyes. Finally, with a sigh of exasperation, he put the document down, took off his reading glasses and responded to my question:

"Orest, I'll do whatever I can to clear this up for you. Have you received an appearance notice along with this Search Warrant?"

I quickly responded as I intently watched for his reaction:

"No, Patrick! The police officer who conducted the search took a statement from me. Before he left he said that he was not laying any charge against me at that time but that he might do so later. He also said he would be reviewing this with the Crown Prosecutor before deciding what to do but he acted as if the charge was going to be laid shortly. Can anything be done to resolve this before a charge is laid against me?"

Having blurted out those agonizing words with my pleas for help, I felt drained of energy and slouched into my chair. I sat there pensively and stared at him. As the seconds passed, my heart began pounding in my chest. I anxiously waited in total alert to hear any words of hope that Murphy might offer to me. I could feel the seconds slowly passing as I focused my total attention on Murphy.

Murphy looked at me sympathetically, reclined on his chair again and spoke to me in a philosophical manner:

"There is nothing that can be done to stop a police officer from laying a charge. Nobody seems to intervene with what they do. It doesn't become a concern of the Crown Prosecutors Office until after there is a charge before the Courts. Generally all Criminal Lawyers simply wait to see if a charge is laid. If that happens, we then start our work of preparing a case to defend the accused person on the charge. I'm sorry to disappoint you but that's just the way the system works."

This explanation by Murphy was not what I wanted to hear. I just couldn't accept the fact that any police officer could simply and arbitrarily lay a charge against anyone. I couldn't believe that there was no control in the legal system to insure that he was acting properly. The implications of a decision to lay a charge would be devastating to anyone. Yet, Murphy accepted such a result as the norm, based on his extensive experience. With exasperation, I exclaimed:

"Surely, Patrick, this can't be the case! In the United States, they have a hearing before a Grand Jury before a charge like this is laid. There must be some kind of procedure here in Canada to review whether there is proper evidence to warrant a charge being laid. There must be something that a lawyer can do before it proceeds to the stage of a person being charged. Isn't there any kind of procedure that can be utilized here?"

The truth was painfully obvious from Murphy's reaction to my expressive ranting on the injustice of this situation. Patiently, Murphy responded in a tactful manner:

"Well, there is no system for reviewing evidence before a police officer lays a charge. I suppose that I could contact the police officer to discuss what he is doing, if he'll talk to me. If he hasn't decided to lay the charge, maybe we can demonstrate to him that there is no evidence to support a fraud charge. There's a chance that he might accept our explanation and then simply close the file. That's about all that I can suggest in this case. What is the name of the police officer who spoke to you yesterday during the search at your home?"

A glimmer of hope had shone through Murphy's dismal assessment of my crisis. Anxiously, I focused on that prospect and immediately responded:

"The main investigating officer is Detective Don Christal from the Edmonton City Police at the Downtown station. His assistant's name is Hnatiuk. Do you know either one of them?"

Murphy looked at me thoughtfully and then responded in a cautious voice:

"I think I've seen Christal in court before. The name Hnatiuk also seems familiar. Let's hope that they remember me. Maybe I can get some information from them on what is going on."

I then interjected with another suggestion that I thought might interest Murphy:

"Christal said that he would be speaking with Eileen Nash. He suggested that I tell my lawyer to contact her to get information on this. Have you had any previous dealings with her?"

Murphy responded to this inquiry with the typical gestures of an experienced Criminal Lawyer:

"Oh, Yes! Eileen Nash is with the Special Prosecutions Branch of the Attorney General's department. Christal must be talking to her to get advice on whether there is enough evidence to lay a charge. If a charge is laid, it would be prosecuted by that department. She would be one of several lawyers who might handle the prosecution. It would probably be better for me to call her as she would probably be willing to give me more information on this than Christal."

Murphy then reached for a pad of lined paper and a pen from the table and began to ask:

"Orest, I'd like to make some notes of what has happened here. This will give me a better understanding of your situation when I speak to Eileen Nash. Can you tell me what you recall of the transaction that they are referring to in the Search Warrant?"

"Patrick!" I muttered with disappointment in my voice. "I hardly remember anything about the transaction. This happened over four years ago. It was an ordinary real estate deal. The only thing I can remember is that I purchased this acreage property through one of my companies. It was then sold to people by the name of Garmaz. They arranged a mortgage on it and the deal was completed. The Garmazs had their own lawyer on the deal. I don't understand how I could be accused of defrauding them if their interests were being protected by an independent lawyer. That's basically all that I recall about the real estate deal. My files were discarded a long time ago. I don't have anything to refresh my memory on what actually happened. In any event, I'm sure that I didn't do anything fraudulent, Patrick. I never did anything illegal in my whole life. I'm convinced that I didn't do anything dishonest or illegal in this real estate deal."

Murphy then interjected with his reassurance and his assessment of this whole matter:

"Look, Orest! I've known you for a long time and I know that you are one of the most decent and honest guys around. I'm sure that the only reason that Christal is trying to find something to charge you with is because you're a lawyer. Hopefully, we can satisfy him that you did nothing wrong and then this whole thing can be forgotten. Now tell me what they seized at your home under this search warrant."

Murphy's words gave me a sense of momentary comfort. I struggled to compose myself as I responded:

"Nothing much. He took a photocopy of a page from my trust journal and a card from my trust ledger which related to the real estate deal. He also took a couple of cheques showing the money that was disbursed from my trust account in the real estate deal. The funds went into my trust account because I represented my company in the real estate deal. There were no other documents that he could seize."

At the sound of this information, Murphy responded with indignation:

"He had no right to look into your trust records. These documents are protected by solicitor-client privilege! Why did you allow him to go through your trust books?"

What Murphy was saying was absolutely true. Christal had no right to be looking into my legal files or into my trust records. This was just another example of the way that police officers can override the rights and liberties of anyone. Christal had intentionally disregarded sacred principles protected by the courts. Ironically, he did this in the name of the law which he was supposed to uphold. This was one more case where the very people who are given the trust and responsibility of upholding the law are most guilty of abusing that privilege and breaking the law.

I looked at Murphy apologetically as I tried to explain how this all occurred:

"I was not at home when they first arrived with the Search Warrant. Christal ordered my wife to open the door and even threatened that he would break it down. When they got in, they went downstairs and Christal immediately decided that he would be seizing and removing everything from my office. They began looking through everything before I got home. Christal kept ordering my wife to show him whatever he wanted to see. By the time I found out about this and got home, they already had the trust records and were taking it with them. I had nothing to say in this whole process and anything I would have said would not have made any difference."

Murphy was noticeably upset about what I had described. He then tried to reassure me about his position relating to Christal's conduct during the search for documents:

"I'm going to speak to Eileen Nash about this and tell her that it is my position that this search was done totally improperly. It's wrong for them to be going through your legal documents without you being present. She knows that Christal has to give you a chance to object to their search of legal files on the basis of your clients' rights to privacy. If this ever goes to court, I'm going to object to the introduction of any evidence that was obtained in that manner."

Murphy then made a note on his paper while I glanced at the scrawl marks that he was making. Murphy's writing was illegible to anyone else and it was a wonder that he could read it himself. The familiar joke relating to all professionals is that they spend so much time going to school and yet nobody ever teaches them how to write. His writing might have prompted a remark from me if I hadn't been criticized by others for my own handwriting. It was as if poor and illegible handwriting was a distinguishing feature of lawyers and other professionals. The only justification ever given for this was that sloppy handwriting disguises what was written to insure that the information could not be read by anyone except the author. Although this may have been said in jest, I suspect that it is closer to the truth than anything else that has ever been suggested.

As he continued to scrawl in his notepad, Murphy asked:

"Did you make any kind of a statement to the police officers during or after their search?"

I hesitated momentarily as I anticipated Murphy's reaction to what transpired. Instead of answering directly, I proceeded to explain in detail what had happened:

"Yes, I did. Shortly after I got home, Detective Christal said that he wanted to talk to me alone. He acted as if he was going to arrest me. Because of his actions, I was worried that he would use force. I was concerned that things would get worse if I resisted his investigation in any way. Christal was acting like a cop out of control and I was really concerned about his disposition. I decided to co-operate and do as he ordered. He took me upstairs away from everyone and began asking questions about the real estate deal. I told him that I did not want to make a statement but he kept pushing me for answers. I basically told him that I just couldn't remember anything specific about the real estate deal at this time."

Murphy completed his notes and then began to admonish me for my actions:

"You should have just clammed up and said nothing! The police shouldn't badger people when they say that they don't want to make a statement. The police use that tactic to force people to say anything. The police can then take whatever a suspect says and stretch it to make it look like he is admitting to something or trying to hide something. You should know that when the police question you, nothing you say is ever used to your benefit. Instead, it is typically twisted around to contradict you or make you look bad in court."

Murphy then reclined in his chair and began to advise me on his position regarding the giving of statements in these types of investigations:

"I always tell my clients not to bother answering any questions because the answers will usually be used by the police in a different context than it was given. In my experience, most statements to police officers are put into evidence before the court in a different way than it was intended. Most people think that giving a statement to police will clear them of any suspicion. However, in most cases, the opposite happens. The Crown Prosecutor will always try to show that the person was hiding something or trying to distract or confuse the police officer. The usual result is that the statement to the police officer will ultimately be used to make the accused person look bad in court."

I tried to interject so that I could clarify my actions, but Murphy continued with his explanation:

"All Criminal Lawyers seem to give the same standard advice to their clients on this topic of making statements to police officers. The advice is that if you are being investigated by the police and you are asked any questions by the police officer, you should SHUT UP, STAND UP AND CALL A CRIMINAL LAWYER. All police officers will try and get you to say something and they will record and repeat in Court even the most inconsequential reactions to their questions. The best thing to do is to simply tell them politely that you won't say anything to them unless your lawyer is present. When you do that, they shouldn't pressure you further and they have to let you call your lawyer. In that situation, I can be there when you are being questioned. Then I can make sure that the questions are proper and the answers are properly stated so that the police can't misconstrue them. If the Crown Prosecutor tries to introduce such a statement in an improper context, I am able to object more easily since I can state what actually happened when the statement was given."

Instead of protracting the conversation on this point, I simply decided to accept Murphy's advice as a reflection of his concern for me. I therefore responded by nodding to acknowledge his directions. He then looked down at his notes and scrawled something further on his note pad before asking:

"Is there anything else that happened that I should know about?"

For a few moments my mind raced through the events of the previous day to target any events that were relevant. There was so much to say but Murphy was inquiring about facts or events that were relevant to the transaction being investigated. I was unable to recall anything else at that moment that would have assisted him. No doubt, Christal's conduct and manner during his investigation was relevant. However, at this moment, Murphy was more interested in the facts of the case and not the incidental occurrences that might be mentioned at the Preliminary Hearing or the trial. After hesitating for a moment, I concluded that I had related everything that I could recall. In a confident tone of voice, I responded to Murphy's inquiry:

"That's all I can think of right now!"

Murphy looked over his notes, made some corrections and then took off his glasses. As he reclined in his chair again, he commented:

"O.K. Orest, I'll look into this. I'll give Eileen Nash a call. I get along with her quite well. I'll ask her to give me a breakdown of the information that they have on this case. It may take her some time to review this file. That will depend on the amount of stuff that they have collected during the investigation. In any case, I'll find out if you are going to be charged. If so, I'll be able to get particulars of their case. I'll call you as soon as I've had a chance to talk to her."

What Murphy said reflected my worst fears but I knew that it was an accurate assessment of my situation. I felt encouraged by Murphy's comments that he knew Eileen Nash at the Crown Prosecutor's office. I hoped that this might open the door to an exchange of information between them. Maybe it was still possible to resolve this mess before it got out of hand. It was dreadful to think that Christal could lay a charge even if he didn't have proper evidence to support it. If that happened, nothing could be done to avoid the devastating consequences that would surely follow. It was more comforting to think that perhaps the Crown Prosecutors Office could intervene to avoid this type of uncontrolled conduct. I prayed that the Crown Prosecutor would review the whole file before any decision was made on whether a charge would be laid against me.

As we both stood up to conclude our meeting, I smiled at Murphy and said:

"Thanks, Patrick! I really appreciate your help in this matter. I'm going to be praying that we can clean this mess up before it falls on me like a ton of bricks."

Murphy smiled and then remarked in his typical, humorous style:

"Just make sure you don't get squashed in this office. We have enough trouble cleaning up the mess around this place as it is."

As Murphy finished speaking, he stood up and gathered up his notes and the Search Warrant. As he walked into the outer office, I grabbed my briefcase and followed him out. Murphy then called back to me before he disappeared into his private office:

"Take care of yourself, Orest! I'll call you when I hear something."

As I walked out towards the waiting room, I called back to him:

"Thanks Patrick! I'll wait to hear from you."

I then retrieved my heavy winter coat and struggled to put it on. As I looked into the general office area, Murphy's staff was busily working amid all the commotion of people coming and going. Having buttoned up my coat, I grabbed my briefcase and headed to the stairs as I echoed the familiar parting greeting of: "Merry Christmas." As they continued with their work, they responded with:

"See you, Orest! Merry Christmas to you too."

Moments later, I was going out the door and confronting the cold weather outside. Instinctively, I made a quick dash to the car and started the motor. While I shivered in the car and waited for the motor to warm up, I began to reflect on my conversation with Murphy. In an attempt to relax, I tried to mentally highlight the positive aspects of what he said. I was happy to hear that there was a Special Prosecutions branch that was assigned to these types of prosecutions. Typically, a Crown Prosecutor is handed a file only days before the date set for the matter to proceed in Court. It is therefore difficult to find out anything in advance from the Crown Prosecutors office on most files. Furthermore it is even more difficult to get any type of feedback since there is nobody who is that familiar with the file.

I was also more enthused when Murphy indicated that Eileen Nash would probably be familiar with the file. It was possible in that situation for Murphy to find out what was going on, perhaps even before any charge was laid. If a charge was laid, we could at least expect to get more cooperation from the Crown Prosecutor if they had the file in advance and were familiar with it. If Murphy in fact had a good working relationship with Eileen Nash, she might be more candid in telling him about the type of evidence that she would be relying on. We could then better assess how to prepare our defence on the charge.

As my thoughts became clearer, I began to adopt a positive attitude that the charge might not have been laid yet. I therefore believed that Murphy might be able to convince Eileen Nash and Christal that there was no evidence, or at least insufficient evidence, to lay a criminal charge against me. It was obvious that someone had made a statement which implicated me in something that was illegal. However, I couldn't accept the fact that the charge would be laid simply on the basis of a statement from one person. In this type of criminal prosecution, there had to be ample evidence to show that I had done something illegal in the transaction and that just was NOT the case.

As I started to drive my car out of the parking lot, I was satisfied that I had at least gotten a positive indication that Murphy would take steps to check into this problem. I knew that he would work on my behalf to resolve this misunderstanding before a charge was laid. This was good news to take home to my wife and it was at least something that would brighten our hopes at Christmas and for the New Year.

I could hardly wait to hear more news from Murphy. I silently prayed that he would be able to shed some light on this mysterious conundrum: What had I done wrong? Now that he was representing me as my Criminal Lawyer, I was also satisfied that I wouldn't have any further problems with Christal. Anything that Christal would request could now be arranged between Murphy and Eileen Nash. The abuse and harassment that we suffered from Christal would not occur again and we could now relax and forget that ugly experience.

CHAPTER SIX

POLICE HARASSMENT

In recent years, a growing feeling of alarm has become more identifiable for the citizens of Canada and the United States of America due to a loss of confidence in the justice system. Aside from continual examples of miscarriage of justice, we have witnessed some extreme examples of police misconduct. Many of these cases involved inappropriate conduct by police officers in the harassment and abuse of people subjected to an investigation. Because the frequency of such conduct has increased, the general public has now demanded that such abuses of power be investigated and alleviated.

Although cases involving assaults and beatings by police officers have increased, we now witness an increase in reported cases involving sexual assaults and falsifying evidence. One inherent reason for this increase of abuse of power by police is the climate fostered within the police department. Too often, police officers can abuse the privilege of their position of power and expect to enjoy immunity. The abusive police officers know that most of their victims are afraid to complain and that any complaint that is made would inevitably be muted in the investigation that follows.

The most common form of abuse of power by police officers is that of harassment, simply because such abuses are difficult to prove in the face of denials. Police officers can use their position to torment, humiliate and violate the rights of anyone they choose and then disguise it as part of their routine work. Since it is difficult to prove such harassment, it is easy for the police department to excuse and even justify such behaviour.

Although police harassment is a serious violation of a person's constitutional rights, the average citizen fails to recognize such abuses or complain when these abuses of power occur. One reason for this situation is the portrayal of such tactics in television shows and popular movies as an effective means of entrapping the most fearsome criminals. The unfortunate result of this latitude by the general public is that police officers with a bankrupt social conscience actually believe that harassment is part of their expected work. Fortunately, the large majority of police officers seldom resort to these despicable tactics. However, the dramatic increase in complaints and reported cases of improper abuses by police officers signals an ominous trend that must be curtailed.

My brief encounter with Christal was sufficient for me to understand that he had become skilled in abusing his powers. From Murphy's insights and information from others, it was becoming increasingly clear that Christal's character was flawed by his tendency to abuse his position. His moral and ethical conduct in this investigation removed all doubt that he was indeed a "COP OUT OF CONTROL". As I evaluated his abusive and callous attitude during his visit to my home, I had no doubt about his motives. He openly used harassment as his main tactic to force his targeted victims to submit to his investigations. The worrisome factor of such police officers is that they were totally unpredictable and irrational in their actions. I laboured with the unsettling feeling that nothing could be done to secure the cooperation of the Crown Prosecutors office to monitor and evaluate this investigation. All I could really do was to pray that there would be no further problems or encounters with Christal.

A few days after my meeting with Murphy, I found myself submerged in my work as I tried to complete a few legal files before the Christmas break. I was working fervently with deadlines when in the midst of this mayhem, the telephone rang. As I answered it, I recognized the jovial voice of Murphy with his yuletide greetings followed by his jesting remarks:

"I just bet the girls in the office here that you had already closed your office for Christmas. I'm just phoning to see if I won the bet?"

With that remark I could hear Murphy chuckling on the telephone and background sounds of a party in his office. I immediately dropped everything and allowed myself to jump into the merriment that Murphy was projecting:

"Not a chance, Patrick! With my luck, I'm going to have to work until Santa Claus comes down our chimney and relieves me so I can go to bed. It sounds like your office is in the middle of a party. Boy, I sure wish I worked in your office!"

It was nice to take a momentary break from the stress of the legal work that I was doing. Murphy was in the right mood to help me do that. I always enjoyed conversations with people who maintained a positive and happy outlook in their everyday lives. It was always a pleasure to talk to Murphy because he always tried to bring sunshine and laughter into the lives of others. By doing so, he found that his life was filled with sunshine also. Because this attitude defined his character, it didn't take much to provoke a jesting response:

"Actually, we're just wrapping things up for the day. But there is enough partying going on around here just the same. Maybe in the New Year, I'll ask the girls to schedule some work time in between all the other activities that go on around here. Anyway, the reason for my call is that I finally got a chance to talk to Eileen Nash about your problem. It looks like you've got nothing to worry about. She has now reviewed the evidence that Christal brought her. She told me that there was no evidence of any fraud by you in that transaction and certainly nothing that would justify the laying of a criminal charge against anyone. It appears that Christal doesn't know what he's doing in this investigation and he doesn't understand the law on criminal fraud."

For a moment, I couldn't believe what I was hearing. This almost seemed like a dream that was too wonderful to be true. I knew that there couldn't be any evidence of me doing something illegal. Yet, Christal's conduct left no doubt that he was going to charge me with fraud. Now it was obvious that the Crown Prosecutor had determined that no charge should be laid in this case. I felt vindicated at last and was pleased that this investigation was now at an end.

The joy from inside me erupted like a suppressed volcano and I had to calm myself in order to respond to Murphy:

"Patrick, that's wonderful! I'm so glad to hear you say that. Am I correct in assuming that no criminal charge was laid against me by the police?"

In deep suspense, I held my breath as I waited for Murphy's response:

"That's right, Orest! No charge has been laid. It was only an investigation. Apparently, the mortgage company that was involved lost money when they foreclosed on their mortgage. When they couldn't collect it, someone decided to have the police investigate. That's all that has happened to date. According to Nash, the mortgage was arranged by a mortgage broker and not by you. If anyone did anything wrong, it was the mortgage broker. Also those people, the Garmazs, who bought the property and applied for the mortgage look suspicious. However, there is no evidence that you were involved in any of that. You can stop worrying and enjoy your Christmas!"

The news seemed so glorious and so wonderful that it truly was a blessing of this festive season. Now I could look forward to enjoying all the joys of the season. The distressing thoughts of a criminal charge that would devastate my life and my legal career were now meaningless. This was such wonderful news and I felt such a relief at that moment. I knew then that nothing could make my Christmas any happier.

I wanted to conclude this matter with Murphy properly with an invitation:

"Thanks for everything, Patrick! I'll make a point of coming in to see you at your office in the New Year to look after your account for the work that you've done. I'll be delighted to see you close this file."

Murphy responded kindly in his gracious and modest style:

"Don't worry about it, Orest! I didn't do much. Let's get together for lunch in the New Year and we'll work something out. Now forget about this stuff! I want you and your family to enjoy a happy and beautiful Christmas season."

I immediately wished Murphy and his family a joyous Christmas season and hung up the telephone. As I sat there silently at my desk, I basked in the euphoria of the news. Now I knew that all those horrible anticipations and fears that had filled my mind for the past week would never concern me again. My life could now go on in its normal and tranquil manner.

I soon began to reflect on how fear can dominate our thoughts and actions. It can ruin the happiness of each precious day if you allow it do so. I recalled an intense conversation that I had with Kenneth Klushin about research that had been conducted on the topic of the fears that are most prevalent in our society. There are a countless number of phobias and fears that have been identified by the medical profession and it is not unusual for a person to suffer from one or more of them. The research disclosed that a large majority of people surveyed identified specific fears such as the fear of heights or flying or enclosed spaces. However the fears that seemed to be most commonplace among people were the more generalized fears of public speaking and dying. What surprised the researchers was that the fear of poverty was the one most chosen by the greatest number of people as their worst fear. This conclusion was the same in all the income groups. Furthermore, the wealthier the individual, the more often such a fear would arise in his daily life.

It occurred to me that all my fears and apprehensions which resulted in the horror that almost immobilized my body were nothing more than the irrational fear of poverty. My fear related to my possible loss of my right to be a lawyer and the loss of esteem that I and my family would suffer. This was not a situation of imminent danger that could result in injury or death. There was no reason to believe that any resulting consequence could not be dealt with in a favourable manner. As my thoughts became more philosophical, I realized that my strong faith in God would guide me though these moments. I had to stop doubting my own integrity just because someone maliciously stated false things about my actions. For the future, I resolved to remain undaunted in my belief of myself. It was important to accept life as it unfolds, no matter what the consequences might be or what might develop.

I found myself in such an elated mood that it was difficult to concentrate on my legal files. However, I felt obligated to complete some work before the children arrived from school and my wife returned home. I continued to work and tried to contain my irrepressible desire to dash all the files on the floor and to run out and celebrate. My subconscious infused guilt about these irrational thoughts to coax me to act responsibly and complete my work. Time was quickly evaporating and the days before Christmas were quickly disappearing. I became determined to delay my celebrating until that evening when I could share this wonderful news with my wife.

I could never resist the magic spell that descended on the world at this time of year. It was in this atmosphere of excitement that our household celebrated the latest news from Murphy regarding the Crown Prosecutor's decision. As I relaxed in the glow of the season, I once again began to appreciate how much our family had been truly blessed. We enjoyed the joy of a close family relationship, close friends, good health and a comfortable standard of living. I was pleased that we could once again enjoy the peace and harmony that one feels when everything proceeds from day to day in a predictable manner. The stress that had dominated our thoughts and actions only a week ago were now gone and forgotten. We were now confident that nothing would ever disturb our household again.

This feeling of euphoria was shattered again on the afternoon of December 16, 1988. As I arrived home from meetings with clients I noticed a compact sedan parked in our driveway. This inconvenience forced me to park on the street and walk to the house. I deduced that this was a delivery company or perhaps someone visiting with my wife. I casually walked to the front door and used my keys to unlock the door. On entering, my children immediately came to greet me and to tell me "that there was a man talking to Mommy in my office." This seemed odd to me so I quickly removed my winter shoes and coat and went downstairs.

As I entered my office, I instantly felt the forgotten pangs of panic and distress. The sight of Christal and the look on my wife's face told me more than I wanted to know at that moment. His cold, piercing eyes and his demeaning facial expression made it obvious that he felt contempt for us. On seeing me, he immediately reached for a document on my desk and presented it to me while saying:

"I have another Search Warrant. I've come to seize a cheque that I located during my first search. Your wife showed me your returned cheques. The one that I want is not there. I guess that I must have seized it on my first search."

I had a hard time understanding what Christal was doing and I couldn't make any sense of this situation. Was Christal really that incompetent that he didn't know what he seized on his first search of my office? Was this perhaps a ploy to show that he was still continuing his investigation? Was he really here to search for anything? Was it more likely that he had come here to harass and upset me and my family? From his demeanour, I detected a sinister motive. It was obvious that this visit with a Search Warrant was not made for the purpose of securing any new evidence. Christal's actions were now transparent. There was no doubt that this was nothing more than police harassment.

As I looked at Christal, I momentarily reflected on how he was conducting himself at this time of year - totally devoid of the Spirit of Christmas. Christal was not just emotionally bankrupt in his actions at Christmas like the Charles Dickens character "Scrooge", but was also malicious and vindictive. The closest comparison that I could make to Christal was the Dr. Seuss character "The Grinch" who hated everyone that enjoyed the Christmas season. As I gazed at Christal, his similarity to "The Grinch" was manifest and obvious. There was the scrawny body and the wrinkled face that scowled and frowned, the cold and demeaning voice and the wicked expression in his eyes. Christal could personify "The Grinch" better than anyone that I could imagine. There was a significant difference however: the problem with "The Grinch" was that he had a heart that was two sizes too small; the problem with Christal was that he had no heart at all.

My body was quickly becoming accustomed to the new situation that I now faced. As I relaxed, I began to feel sick as I realized that the whole ordeal was not over yet. While collecting my thoughts, the obvious questions kept plaguing me: What was really going on? Why was he really here? What did he really want from me?

I was determined to try and obtain some answers to these nagging questions. Without being insulting, I proceeded to ask him:

"Why are you still searching for documents? I understood from Pat Murphy that the Crown Prosecutor had decided not to proceed with any criminal charges in this case."

Christal appeared to be oblivious to the effect of his actions. He responded coldly and totally devoid of any feeling or concern for the hurt that his actions were causing:

"My investigation isn't over yet. I still have a few documents to present to the Crown Prosecutors Office. THEN I'LL DETERMINE IF A CHARGE IS GOING TO BE LAID."

At that moment I felt angry about the manner in which he was conducting this investigation. It was now obvious that he intended to charge me with fraud, whether or not there was any proof to support it. I quickly resolved that I would not show any expression of anger as this would only worsen my situation so I simply stated:

"That's fine, then! I'll be speaking to Pat Murphy about this. I'm sure he'll be in touch with you through the Crown Prosecutors office."

On hearing that remark, Christal walked past me and up the stairs without saying anything further. My wife followed him upstairs to see him to the door. I remained in my office to contemplate this new development. It just didn't seem proper that Christal could conduct an investigation that the Crown Prosecutor had concluded was not supported by any evidence. Yet, that was what Christal was intent on doing. It was sickening to think that the police were not accountable to anyone and could freely harass anyone with impunity.

Sadly, I now realized that nothing could be done to prevent such an abuse by a police officer. It was frightening to think that the police investigative system had degenerated to that degree. Unfortunately such conduct was now very commonplace among police officers. It was therefore difficult for the police department to control it. As a result, the unwritten policy was to ignore it and only deal with those cases that arose because of complaints that couldn't be resolved through public relations.

After a few moments of reflection, I decided to telephone Murphy's office to leave a message for him to call me. I then rushed upstairs to comfort my wife and to dispel her worst fears. This incident had tarnished our hopes for a happy and carefree festive season. Reluctantly, we accepted the fact that this matter was not resolved and that we would still have to wrestle with this whole ordeal for some time to come. It was a sickening thought and the vision of Christal in our house was once again emblazed in our consciousness. Our future was again clouded by Christal's actions which were conducted with no compassion or respect for our rights. We now feared that he would come again to ruthlessly disturb the privacy of our home. We now knew that more police harassment would follow as he continued his crusade to fabricate evidence that might justify a criminal charge against me.

Murphy called back a little later and I informed him of this latest development involving Christal's visit. Murphy reacted with noticeable confusion on hearing the news, especially in light of the fact that there was no purpose for the visit. He then surmised that Christal was just checking for more evidence and assured me that there was nothing to worry about. We both acknowledged that nothing would be learned on this matter until after the Christmas break. However, he promised to look into this new twist in the case and to find out what Christal was up to. I felt comforted to hear Murphy speculate that Christal was just "fishing" in the hope of finding something to build a case on. He then reassured me that there wasn't any evidence that showed that I was involved in any unlawful activity. As he spoke, I detected a suspicious attitude relating to Christal's true motives and I hoped that Murphy would find out what was really happening behind the scenes. I appreciated his words of encouragement and I promised to share them with Pat.

Thankfully, the Christmas festivities overtook us. Our business lives were put on hold as we shared the joy of the season with our family and friends. In the New Year, there would be new hope and new challenges. Unlike other business-es, lawyers often find themselves working on files during the odd business days which fall between Christmas and New Years. Typically, lawyers only do so because of necessity to complete some work that has imperative deadlines. It is difficult to work on larger files because of the inability to concentrate. Furthermore, it is difficult to communicate with anyone else during the festive season. For this reason it is nice to get back to work in an atmosphere where everyone is again back at their desks even if the general mood is that of apathy and depression.

My work resumed as well after the Christmas break. As I laboured on my legal files and attended meetings with clients, one thought festered silently in the channels of my conscious mind: When is Murphy going to call with more news? I was tempted to telephone his office just to check on him but I resolved that I wasn't going to bother him unnecessarily. This was not the only file on his desk and I was satisfied that he would look into it as soon as he could. I had to be patient and to focus my thought on work before these deadlines became a prob-lem. I realized that it was best to suppress my thoughts of this ugly incident and to proceed into the New Year with a positive attitude.

As I became immersed in my legal work, it came as a pleasant surprise to answer the telephone and hear Murphy's voice:

"Hi, Orest! It's Pat Murphy! Have you finished with your Christmas cele-brating or are you still hung over?"

As he chuckled, my spirits lifted as a happy mood swept into my office. Instinctively, I found myself responding in warm laughter:

"Well, Patrick! With all the celebrating I've done, I'll probably be hung over into next month. But, as you know, lawyers don't have to be sober to be at work. So here I am! And how was your Christmas vacation?"

Without delay, Murphy quickly responded: "Oh, just great! We had a nice, quiet Christmas with the family. We don't get too carried away with celebrating. It's too hard at our age. Besides, I don't want to die young so I have to take it easy."

We both laughed and then Murphy continued: "Anyway, I had a chance to talk to Eileen Nash again about this investigation that Christal is doing. She was a little surprised that he's still investigating this thing. She says that there is no evidence of any fraud in this case. Everything that Christal has is speculative and circumstantial at best. It's pretty clear that she would never lay a fraud charge in this case."

What Murphy described was again reassuring but I didn't feel as comforted by it this time. I had spent a lot of time thinking about this whole calamity and studying the Search Warrants. Yet, something just didn't make sense. I couldn't visualize any fraud in the transaction or the mortgage that was placed on the property. Even Murphy and Nash agreed that if there was a problem with the mortgage, I was the least likely person who should have been investigated. There was suspicion about the Garmazs who applied and obtained the mortgage. The mortgage brokers who arranged the mortgage with Heritage Trust were also suspect. Surely, nobody could seriously believe that I had anything to do with arranging that mortgage. It was pretty clear that all I did in the transaction was purchase the property and then resell it to the Garmazs. It was also clear that when the transaction was completed, Heritage Trust had a lawyer representing it and Garmazs had a lawyer representing them. The obvious questions remained: How could anyone say that I had anything to do with influencing anyone in this transaction? How could anyone suggest that I had any opportunity to misrepresent anything to anyone? Most of all, how could anyone suggest that I had done anything illegal?

I was now desperate to get some answers to these nagging questions:

"Patrick, if you've got a minute, I'd like to ask you more about the case that Christal is trying to build against me. From my reading of the Search Warrant, it appears that Christal is taking the position that I had something to do with the Garmazs making a fraudulent misrepresentation to Heritage Trust. What was this fraudulent misrepresentation? Why do they say that I did it? After all, there was a mortgage broker who arranged the mortgage. Isn't it obvious that those people are the ones to be investigated?"

Murphy then began to explain some of the details that he had obtained from Eileen Nash which I was now hearing for the first time:

"It appears that Heritage Trust is saying that they were told by the mortgage broker that Garmazs had a clear title home. They insist that this was the proof of down payment by the Garmazs on the deal to purchase the acreage property. Heritage Trust didn't bother to check the title at the time they approved the mortgage loan to the Garmazs on the acreage property. When they checked the title to their home later, they found that the broker and possibly the Garmazs had lied because there was a mortgage on Garmazs' home. The Garmazs never had a clear title to their home. Heritage Trust lost money when they foreclosed on the mortgage they placed on the acreage property. Now the people who used to work for Heritage Trust are trying to find someone to blame for that loss."

As I listened carefully to every word that he uttered, two questions kept nagging at me: What did this have to do with me? Why would I be charged with fraud? When Murphy finished, I quickly interjected:

"If Garmazs made a false statement on their mortgage application, how does this relate to me doing something fraudulent?"

Instantly, Murphy responded: "Apparently, Christal got a statement from Garmaz blaming you for what happened. Nash told me that Garmaz claims that they only said that they had a clear title house because you told them to say that. On that basis, Christal is pressuring Eileen Nash with the position that you should be charged with fraud, and not the Garmazs."

When I heard this, I felt outraged that the Garmazs had lied about this to Christal. I interrupted Murphy again to correct his information:

"This is nonsense, Patrick! First of all, I did not have anything to do with the Garmazs' mortgage application. Whatever he may have told the mortgage broker had nothing to do with me. I didn't even know if he had a clear title home when we did the deal. I certainly didn't tell him what to say to the mortgage broker. Secondly, it's obvious that the Garmazs made the false statement and committed fraud. It's nonsense to believe that they can escape prosecution simply by blaming it on me. Surely Christal is not that dumb to buy an explanation like that."

After my rambling, Murphy again tried to reassure me about his general attitude towards the investigation conducted by Christal:

"That's why this is such a weak case. There is only questionable evidence that there was any false representation made. On the evidence they now have, there is simply no way that the Crown Prosecutor would proceed to prosecute anyone in this case. What Garmaz said about you is so suspect that Nash doesn't even want to consider it. Aside from that, there is no evidence that you did anything illegal in this case. From everything I've seen, this case is finished. It's possible that Christal may fish around a little longer to try and find something. Then he'll simply close the file and we won't hear anything further on it."

I tried to understand Murphy's point of view on my case. I respected and trusted his assessment of it but I still felt uneasy. There was something wrong with the way this whole situation was being investigated by Christal. I desperately wanted to know what the real story was behind the investigation. I decided to push Murphy further for more answers and to get his personal and candid comments of this case:

"Patrick, this whole thing doesn't make sense! Why is Christal so intent on trying to charge me with fraud? There couldn't be any pressure from a complainant. After all, Heritage Trust is not in business any longer. The Alberta government paid up any losses of Heritage Trust and put all its assets into the NorthWest Trust Company. There doesn't seem to be any reason for Christal to push this investigation. Surely there are more pressing files needing investigation than this one! Why is he so obsessed to dig into something that happened so long ago? I can't understand why Christal is still proceeding with this investigation. What reason could he possibly have for wanting to charge me with fraud?"

Murphy's voice became softer and quieter. The tone of his voice immediately alerted me to the fact that he was now speaking "off the record" and as a friend:

"The very same thing occurred to me so I asked Eileen Nash about that. It's pretty obvious to us that the only reason Christal is pursuing this investigation is that you are a lawyer and he wants to nail a lawyer. Charging you with fraud would really look good on his record as a police detective, even if it's thrown out in court. The other thing I found out is that Christal really hates lawyers. That's a typical attitude with some cops but Christal really has it in for lawyers. That's why he's doing everything he can to keep this investigation alive. He'd do anything to try and make a case so that he could lay a fraud charge against you. His problem is that he doesn't have any evidence that will stand up in Court and everybody knows it."

I listened to the words that Murphy spoke in horror. I now had a clearer vision of Christal and the manner in which he was investigating this case. I had no doubt that everything that Murphy said was true. I knew that what he said was probably common knowledge in the gossip corridors of the police station and the Attorney General's department. Murphy spent time socializing with the Crown Prosecutors and with different police officers either over coffee or sometimes at racquetball games. For that reason, everything that Murphy said was not just speculation but was instead based on information from reliable sources. As always, this type of information was "Off The Record" and difficult to prove. This meant that he was prepared to tell me about it on the understanding that he wouldn't have to disclose his sources. However, whether it could be proven or not, the shocking reality was that it was unequivocally true.

Everything that Murphy described about Christal's motive and conduct was obviously improper. However, I was aware that such situations existed and were allowed to continue unchecked by the Police Department. As I reacted to Murphy's statements, I tried to rationalize this discovery:

"Patrick, what I don't understand is why Christal is allowed to continue the investigation in this case. It must be obvious to everyone that he has no evidence to proceed on and that he's only doing it for his own personal reasons. You said that Nash has already made her objective assessment of this case and concluded that there is no evidence for prosecuting this case. Why doesn't she simply tell Christal to close the file?"

In response to this inquiry, Murphy explained the relationship between the Crown Prosecutors office and the police relating to charges laid and prosecuted before the Courts:

"Well, first of all, the Crown Prosecutors don't have any control over the investigation of these charges. They may be consulted by the police to determine the proper wording for a charge or whether there is enough evidence for a conviction. However, the decision to lay that charge is with the police officer. Christal could have laid this fraud charge already. He can still do so and nobody can stop him from doing it. However, he knows that he doesn't have any evidence to sustain a prosecution against you for fraud. If he were to do so, the charge would be thrown out in the first hearing before the Court. So unless Christal can come up with some convincing evidence, I doubt that he will lay any criminal charge in this case. It's not so much that he can't but rather that it's just not good practice for him to do so."

After a short interruption, Murphy continued:

"The second thing to realize is that if a charge is laid by the police, the Crown Prosecutors have to prosecute it. Although they are not forced to prosecute a criminal charge, they do so to maintain a good relationship with the police. The Crown Prosecutors prefer to see a judge throw out a criminal charge rather than decide on their own to drop or withdraw the charge. Otherwise, the police officer complains to the Chief of Police and he complains to the head of the Attorney General's Department. This all creates bad public relations. Therefore the Crown Prosecutors will go ahead with cases that shouldn't be prosecuted just to avoid the complaints that are made if they don't prosecute the charges. That's why Prosecutors seldom make decisions about dropping charges. One good example of this is what happened in the case of George De Rappard and George Brosseau. The Crown Prosecutors Office would never have withdrawn those charges. That's why the Attorney General appointed Ron Berger as a Special Prosecutor to do that."

The case that Murphy was referring to was a very good example that demonstrated that if one had good political connections, one could arrange for any criminal prosecution to be dropped. Two prominent Albertans who had close friendships with our then premier were charged with fraudulent activity as a result of the demise of a mortgage company that they directed. George de Rappard was a good friend of Alberta's Tory Premier, Peter Lougheed. He held a high profile position in the Premier's office during the Lougheed years of undisputed political power in Alberta. George Brosseau was an Edmonton lawyer with a legal practice chiefly handling real estate transactions. Being a good Tory, Brosseau had no difficulty securing a prestigious Q.C. designation although he seldom if ever appeared in court.

The Q.C. designation stands for "Queen's Counsel" and is supposed to be awarded to lawyers who distinguish themselves before the courts as experienced counsel. In reality, the designation is only given as a political favour to those exceptional supporters of the political party in power. This ceremonial designation is attached to their names so that they may flaunt it to attract more credibility and respect from an uninformed and unsuspecting public. Because of this and other abuses, the Ontario government legislated the abolishment of the use of the Q.C. designation in that province. However, other provincial governments have been slow in curbing this situation because of its political benefits.

This case drew media attention when these two politically prominent men were charged with fraudulent activity relating to false statements in a Prospectus document filed with the Alberta Securities Commission. After the charge was laid, the attention focused on the Attorney General's department to see if they would in fact prosecute this case involving two men so dear to the heart of the Premier. Obviously, the Crown Prosecutors Office couldn't just withdraw the charge, even if the evidence was weak, for fear of negative publicity from the news media. A unique solution had to be found and hastily a new innovation was developed to quiet the news media and achieve the desired result.

Shortly after the criminal charges were laid, an announcement came from the Attorney General's department that a "Special Prosecutor" would be hired separate from the Crown Prosecutors Office. The role of this Special Prosecutor was to advise the Attorney General directly if there was sufficient evidence to proceed with this prosecution. No doubt, this could have been done by any of the Crown Prosecutors employed by the Attorney General's Department. However, there was a need to distance the government from any embarrassing questions that would be asked if the decision was made within the department.

Because the Special Prosecutor would automatically refuse to comment on the case, all the news media publicity would end abruptly without scandal. This innovative procedure was simply another miracle of Government to create a board to solve a problem. Unfortunately, such miracles are seldom utilized to create anything useful for the general public.

The lawyer hired to be the Special Prosecutor and to provide the necessary decision was Ron Berger. Berger was an Edmonton lawyer in a small private practice who arrogantly flaunted a snobbish English accent. No one doubted his knowledge of the law but it was painful to endure his nasalized voice and his demeaning attitude as he expounded on some insignificant legal point. To his credit, he was politically astute and capably promoted himself with senior lawyers and judges. Because he could be trusted to make the right decision to advance his own career, he became an obvious choice for this unusual assignment. To no surprise from anyone, Berger wasted no time in looking into the case and preparing a report. Nobody with political astuteness was surprised to hear that it conclusively recommended that the criminal charges be withdrawn because of a lack of evidence. This decision abruptly terminated a media event that would have been followed closely in the province. After all, these criminal charges were the result of a lengthy investigation by the Alberta Securities Commission into the sudden collapse of a large mortgage company, Dial Mortgage Corporation. Their investigation concluded that blatant misrepresentations in various documents which were signed and approved by these directors resulted in losses of millions of dollars to Alberta investors. Because of the strict responsibility of directors to file accurate and truthful statements, there was no excuse for these misrepresentations. For that reason, the Alberta Securities Commission, as an independent government body, was compelled to direct that charges be laid against these notable public figures.

Prior to the collapse of Dial Mortgage Corporation, George De Rappard and George Brosseau were its primary directors and Brosseau did the majority of the resulting mortgage and legal work. The investigation and resulting criminal charges created a temporary inconvenience for both men. However, after being vindicated, everything ended happily for them. George De Rappard returned to his position at the Premier's office and George Brosseau continued in his legal practice without any interruption. Berger collected a large fee and shortly thereafter received an appointment as a Justice with the Court of Queen's Bench of Alberta. The only unhappy people to be forgotten in the process were the financially devastated investors of Dial Mortgage Corporation. These people were not destined to receive any satisfaction from the Alberta Securities Commission, the Government or from the Courts. After enduring the protracted investigations of the Alberta Securities Commission and witnessing the swift and secret disposal of the criminal charges that resulted, nothing else could be done. Since the sympathy for these investors had since dissipated through the erosion of time, the news media, the Government and the general public were now ready to forget about their plight.

Murphy's words of wisdom left me speechless. Slowly, the images of horror that I had witnessed as a lawyer in the legal system began to flash in my mind. At that time, I rationalized the complaints of harassment and abuses of power by police officers as isolated examples. Now I was starting to accept the fact that such abuses of power were a constant reality of the legal system. Although one can generally accept that flaws arise in any system, this situation was an example of extreme abuse. A growing sentiment was also starting to be heard throughout the news media to stop the manipulation and abuse of power by all those involved in the administration of justice. Sadly, very little was being proposed to curb this.

I was now experiencing a situation of harassment and abuse of power by a police officer. Rather than lamenting about it, I decided to use a different tact. After a brief pause, I responded:

"Patrick, I know that I shouldn't worry about this but I have a hard time keeping it out of my mind. Is there anything that we can do to bring this to a head? Isn't there any way that we can clean this up right now?"

Murphy responded in the typical style of an experienced Criminal Lawyer:

"Orest, there's nothing to do right now. There is no charge and I'm sure that there isn't going to be one. You just have to forget about this whole thing and it'll wind up on its own. I'll stay in touch with Eileen Nash. If anything further arises, I'll call you."

At that point, I had nothing further to add and so I thanked Murphy for his efforts. As I hung up the telephone, I felt that I understood everything better. I rationalized that in spite of the fact that this situation was still ongoing, there was no cause for worry. I resolved to take Murphy's advice to forget about it and allow it to run its course. After all, there was nothing more that could be done about it. It was foolish to preoccupy oneself with needless worry.

As I returned to the task of the legal work on my desk, I reflected on the disillusionment with the legal system that was frequently commented on by so many clients and acquaintances. There were too many significant cases that affected a large amount of people where the law and the justice system failed to protect their interests. Many people had become bewildered by a legal system that was out of step with the times. Too often, it failed to produce the results that society expected from it. Too often, it was misused by those entrusted to enforce and defend those ideal principles for which the justice system was created. It was becoming an obvious reality that our society was plagued with too many laws and not enough justice.

The complaints about the legal system were not confined any longer to those who were charged and prosecuted for criminal offenses. Those people that became involved in the legal system as complainants or witnesses felt more like victims than participants. The only beneficiaries appeared to be the lawyers, clerks, judges and police officers whose employment was needed to maintain the growing legal system. It was no mystery that these people defended the virtues of the legal system even though they knew how often it failed to deliver justice.

The virtues that were intended to be preserved in the legal system have now become obscured by the many examples of injustice that the system produced. However, the very worst part of the legal and justice system was that there was no control over the actions of anyone in authority. These people - the police, the Crown Prosecutors and the judges - did not answer to anyone and could act without reprisal according to their personal whims. The legal system usually defended and covered up their conduct rather than reprimanding and removing them. It was easy to conclude that what we had was a legal system that was out of control and totally unsatisfactory. Yet, the prospect of change was remote because few people understood it enough to speak up for change. Indeed, the legal system had become a poignant example of decay in the foundations of our society.

The passage of time introduced the changing of the seasons from winter to spring. Sadly, it was also at this time that my mother passed away suddenly. Within two months, I had lost both of my parents and was now saddled with the hassles and disputes arising from their estates. The needless bickering that resulted would continue to draw on my energies for the next four years before it was finally resolved. For me, this season was always the time to personally experience the miracle of new growth and cherish the joy of life. The changes in the season also brought hope for a new beginning so that the worries of the past could be forgotten.

This time of renewed expectations in the Spring of 1989 was suddenly disrupted again by a visit from Christal. In his normal pattern he appeared again at my house with a Search Warrant in hand and again demanded to see our cancelled cheques. Again, instead of searching our records, he simply wanted to seize a specific cancelled cheque: the one that he obtained on his first visit. Christal again came without notice and again I was not at home when he arrived. Only my wife was there to receive him.

As if by coincidence, I did return home to find Christal in my office and speaking to my wife. These visits should have been easier to tolerate since this was now his third visit. Furthermore, Christal's manner and the other circumstances surrounding his visit were now becoming more routine. However, this visit seemed more tortuous because it dashed all the hopes and plans that we had carefully built. We were relying on the premise that nothing further was developing and that this whole nightmare had surely ended. Now I worried that this nightmare would never end. It seemed that nothing would stop Christal from prolonging this investigation needlessly to achieve his objective of laying a fraud charge against me.

By now, it was becoming evident that Christal was not really interested in any documents. Instead, he had come to demonstrate that his investigation was still proceeding. According to Murphy, there was no evidence to support Christal's position for laying a fraud charge so it was evident that Christal would either have to close his file or continue to take further steps, even needless ones. His actions had now become a blatant example of a police officer abusing his powers and position. His investigative tactics were directed at disturbing and

harassing our lives by the continual use of search warrants for unnecessary purposes. Yet, there seemed to be nothing that could be done to challenge his right
to do so or to stop him from harassing us in the manner that he conducted his
investigation. As I reflected on this situation, I marvelled at how easy it was for
a police officer like Christal to secure a search warrant to needlessly harass people who were the targets of their investigation. The actual procedure that
Christal had to follow was to prepare an affidavit to show a good reason for a
search warrant and then present it to a judge for his review and decision.
However, in actual fact, the judge simply signed the search warrants without any
consideration or evaluation since there was never any opposition to such a
request. These applications were always made without the knowledge of the victims to be targeted. Because Provincial Judges are overworked and must consider these requests for search warrants in addition to their other work, many of
them simply sign these search warrants on request. This relaxed practice quickly
becomes common knowledge to the police officers, resulting in a cooperative
rapport between favourable judges and devious police officers. As a result, a
police officer who knows the system can obtain these search warrants as often as
he likes and nobody can prevent this abuse.

As I gazed at Christal, decked out in a different designer suit and expensive
shoes, I could feel how deeply he disliked me. This troubled me because I could-
n't understand why he had any reason to be so vindictive towards me. It was evident from his manner that Christal found personal satisfaction in tormenting us
as he prolonged this investigation to manufacture a case against me. It was now
clear from Christal's actions that he would continue to harass witnesses and
manipulate evidence until he could convince the Crown Prosecutors office of his
case. Then, with the support of the Crown Prosecutor, he could proceed to lay
the fraud charge.

As I approached Christal in my office, he reached for a document laying on
my desk and handed it to me, saying:

"I've come again with another Search Warrant to seize a different cheque.
Your wife helped me find the cancelled cheques but it seems that I took the
cheque with me on my first search. I must have forgot that I already had it."

I was filled with anger at the thought that he would continue to harass me
and my family in this way but I responded in a civil tone:

"Why didn't you simply request it through my lawyer? Why is it necessary
to keep bothering us like this?"

Christal's response was cold and without compassion:

"I don't have to give you any reasons for being here. I have a Search
Warrant and I'm entitled to come anytime I want without notice. If you refuse to
cooperate, I will use force. The cancelled cheque was the only document that I
was interested in seizing today. If I need anything further, I will return with a
new Search Warrant."

As he finished speaking, Christal walked past me out of the room. My wife
followed him upstairs to see him to the door. When my wife returned downstairs, we both looked at each other. At that moment, neither of us spoke as it

was unnecessary to say anything. Both of us had been stripped of all feeling by this callous, insensitive Robo-cop who was programmed to destroy our lives. There seemed to be nothing that could be done to reason with him or to explain the reality of this situation to him.

Christal now behaved like a badly programmed computer with mechanical actions lacking compassion. With his Terminator mentality we were destined to fall victim to his rampages. There was no escape from this fated plan of destruction as society had adopted the attitude to safeguard his existence at the expense of those that might be destroyed. All of this was justified for the sake of expedience and progress which took precedence over human rights. I suddenly had a scary thought that this explanation of Christal's actions was just as plausible as any other. Ironically, it now seemed that the final result in my case might actually be the same as it would be in the science fiction analogy.

The conversation that followed with my wife was a familiar repetition of so many earlier ones. The same questions were raised with no satisfactory answers being available to respond to them. What does Christal want from us? Why is he still investigating this matter? Will he be charging me with fraud? The questions couldn't be answered because nobody but Christal knew the answers. Although neither one of us said anything, both of us suspected what those answers were. Neither I nor my wife could talk about it because we did not want to imagine the horror of such a situation taking place and changing our lives.

The only comfort that I could give my wife was to telephone Pat Murphy to report this latest encounter with Christal. I assured her that I would ask Murphy to check with Eileen Nash to determine why this investigation had not be discontinued. On calling Murphy's office, I spoke to his receptionist and left a message for Murphy to call me as soon as possible.

On hanging up the telephone, I found myself seated at my desk and feeling shattered by this incident. I wondered what the point was in continuing with my legal work. It seemed inevitable that this roller-coaster ride was not going to arrive safely at the starting platform. Instead this ride was going to be interrupted suddenly and we would helplessly fall and crash on the concrete floor below. I was drained emotionally and felt like I was staring death in the face.

The following morning, I received a telephone call from Murphy. I was now in a better state of mind to discuss this new turn of events with him. Murphy could only offer to speak to Eileen Nash at the Crown Prosecutors office and call me with any news that she had to report. I then resolved to adopt a positive attitude, ignore my worst fears and return to my work. However, my heart was sick with grief and worry and my efforts were only dismally effective in completing any work that I had planned to complete. I now knew that I would be unable to work effectively until this whole nightmare was settled. I could only hope that Murphy would telephone soon with encouraging news.

The days seemed to pass slowly after that latest intrusion by Christal into our lives. My wife and I found ourselves preoccupied with the wide variety of urgent responses that are necessary in coping with a family of four children. For them, it was true that they always looked like angels when they were asleep. It was also equally true of our children that it would be out of character for them to act like angels during their waking hours. The mischief that our children stirred up always kept the conversations very interesting at our breakfast and supper table. This presented an effective distraction because during these dreadful moments of uneasiness and distress, the best antidote for us was our children. They always commanded our full attention and energy to sort out their urgent problems that continually arose on a daily basis.

It was almost two weeks later that Murphy finally telephoned me. His call came on a late afternoon after my children had arrived home from school. I had to ask Murphy to wait while I directed the children out of the room so that I could discuss the situation candidly with him. As I picked up the telephone receiver again, my heart was already pounding wildly and adrenalin flowed throughout my body in preparation for what was about to happen. The moment that I had waited for so patiently had arrived and I trembled as I held the telephone receiver.

Murphy began in a serious manner which was in direct contrast to all of our earlier telephone calls. He was not relaxed this time and he was making no effort to joke with me. I held my breath as I braced myself for the news that Murphy was about to deliver:

"This whole investigation by Christal has really gotten out of hand. I just talked to Eileen Nash and she said that she has met with Christal a few more times since we last talked. He keeps bringing her more paper but basically its the same stuff that she already has. None of it shows that you had anything to do with arranging the mortgage with Heritage Trust. Eileen Nash still insists that there really is no evidence for a fraud charge against you. She also told me that no fraud charge is going to be laid. It looks like this whole thing is dead. I think that Christal was just trying to keep this case alive by coming to your place with a new Search Warrant."

I couldn't believe what Murphy was saying. It was obvious now that this had to be the end of Christal's investigation. After all, this was a case where the Crown Prosecutor was now satisfied that there was no evidence to prosecute a fraud charge. Even if Christal wanted to lay the criminal charge, the Crown Prosecutor would know right from the start that this whole case would be thrown out at the Preliminary Hearing. Now it was certain that the Crown Prosecutor would convince Christal that there was no point in laying the criminal charge against me and that would end his investigation.

My body suddenly went limp with relief as I slouched into my chair behind my desk. I began to take deep breathes to relax and rejuvenate myself. The joy of the moment immediately displaced my growing fears and I chanted in response:

"That is good news, Patrick! I was really concerned about this last visit to my house by Christal. He was not only obnoxious; he was also talking mean. I'm sure that if I had said anything that he felt was insulting, he would have cuffed me and taken me downtown."

My comments about Christal prompted Murphy to ask in a curious manner:

"You know Orest, that's an interesting point! Eileen Nash made a comment to that same effect. We're both wondering if you ever had a problem with Christal or anyone that he knew. The way he's carrying on, its obvious that he's really out to get you. Certainly, neither of us can see anything in this deal that would make a police officer want to nail you. After all, there was no fraud here and it's obvious that you didn't do anything illegal. Nobody lost any money and there's no victim. We both agreed that it was ridiculous for Christal to spend so much time on a case like this. We just can't figure out what he's got against you. Are you sure you never had any dealings with him in court or in your legal practice?"

Hearing Murphy ask it in that way startled me. I now knew that it was not just a question of my paranoid reaction to Christal but rather something that was obvious to objective onlookers. There was no doubt that Christal resented and despised me but I just couldn't recall any connection or dealings with him. After a momentary pause, I responded:

"Patrick, the same thing has been going through my mind from the time I first met Christal. I've dealt with different police officers but Christal is a breed all unto himself. This man is callous, insensitive and actually malicious towards me. It's so obvious from the way he's investigating this case that he is desperate to charge me with fraud. Unfortunately, I really can't recall any past dealings with Christal. If I ever had a problem with him, I'm sure that I would have remembered him. He's not the kind of cop that is easy to forget."

Murphy then tried to comfort me with his usual charm and wit:

"Orest, it's obvious to me that he's only trying to get a criminal charge laid against you because it would be good for his career. He'd probably be in line for a promotion if he could turn this case into a high profile prosecution. If he could lay a charge of fraud, you can bet that he'll be trying to get a promotion in the department out of it. You know, he hasn't been a detective that long. Before that he spent a long stint in drug enforcement. You can basically guess that from the way he treats people. He would rather punch you in the face than talk to you. Most detectives are reasonable and easy to talk to but Christal is different. He has made up his mind and you can't reason with him."

My mind was riveted to every word that Murphy spoke. His explanation helped to answer some of the questions that puzzled me about Christal. As I reflected on the way that Christal acted during his three visits to my home, I could now clearly visualize how Christal evolved into the monster that he had become. In Drug Enforcement cases, police officers conducted themselves as if they were at war. Conducting raids without notice, kicking down doors and harassing suspects was all part of the job. Aside from the deadly and depressing consequences of drug use, the underworld activities made the work very dangerous. As a result, police officers involved in this type of work become hardened and cynical to everything around them. Christal clearly showed the attributes of being hardened by this type of work.

The more tragic consequence of such work is the permanent change of attitude and loss of compassion that most police officers suffer. The scenario occurred too often and the stories of such transformations were too many to consider individually. After years of drug enforcement which primarily involves investigating people trafficking in narcotics, a police officer soon develops a cynical attitude towards everyone and view any target with suspicion. Too often, such investigations are frustrated by a lack of evidence but that only deepens his cynical attitude and his desire to charge everyone. In his eyes, everyone that he investigates is guilty. This often leads to illegal activity to compensate for such frustration. To simplify his work, if he doesn't find drugs on a suspect, he can plant it on him or simply stretch the facts to implicate the suspect.

When such a police officer moves to another department, it is illogical to believe that he can adopt a new attitude. After being transferred to commercial crime investigation, Christal carried on with the same attitude and tactics as he used before. However, such conduct in his new position was now unusual and very inappropriate. In combatting the war on drugs, he could count on the sympathy of the public to excuse his abuses of power. However, in his new position, his blatant abuse of power was clearly evident and objectionable. In these cases, the Crown Prosecutors and Judges find it more difficult to excuse or ignore these indiscriminate abuses.

As I visualized Christal continuing to pursue his misguided crusade, I knew that the turmoil in my life would continue. Suddenly, I blurted out:

"I know that I've asked this already but I must ask again. Isn't there something that we can do to stop all this nonsense?"

When I completed my latest plea for help, I waited a moment and then Murphy began his slow response:

"Orest, as I've said before, there is no evidence of fraud here. Now, Everybody knows that. Eileen Nash says that there is no basis for a fraud charge against you. As far as I can see, this thing is at an end. Christal may continue to do some fishing but I don't think you'll ever hear from him again. Just put this whole thing behind you, now. It's best that you direct your attention to your law practice and to raising your family."

There was no doubt that Murphy was right. I accepted the fact that nothing more could be done. It was simply best to put this whole ordeal out of my mind and get on with my life. There was simply no point in re-hashing the details of this situation further or engaging in paranoia. I decided to embrace the positive news that Murphy had delivered.

CHAPTER SEVEN

THE CRIMINAL CHARGE

When I operated a general legal practice, I had many instances where clients consulted me on various criminal matters. Typically the "criminal charge" involved a Highway Traffic offence or an infraction of a provincial statute or by-law. All of these charges took the form of a Notice that directed the person to appear in Court to enter a plea of "Guilty" or "Not Guilty". In such cases, there was no formal charge and the Judge simply adjudicated on the basis of the original copy of the Notice issued by the police officer.

In contrast, a criminal charge under the Criminal Code of Canada required a formal charge to be sworn in the format prescribed in the Criminal Code. A failure to meet the exacting requirements in the wording of the charge was sufficient cause for the Court to dismiss the criminal charge. In such instances, the general public perception was that the charge was dismissed on a "technicality". However, the advantage of this system was that the lawyers and judges could clearly assess the specific charge to be proven. The Defence lawyer was only concerned with disproving the specific allegations in the criminal charge. Sadly, this organized process for assessing criminal charges was seldom followed in actual court proceedings. Judges often ignored complaints raised by Defence lawyers on technical flaws that existed in a charge. Furthermore, Crown Prosecutors were allowed to amend the wording of a criminal charge at virtually any stage of the proceedings to defeat such objections.

The irony of this precise requirement of the criminal process was that the sworn formal charge was never provided to the accused person by the police. Instead, this formal charge simply became a part of the Court document on which the Judge endorsed his disposition of the case. The document that was provided to the accused person was called an "Appearance Notice" which contained minimal information. Its main purpose was to advise the accused person of the time and place of the Court Appearance to respond to the charge. In order to prepare for the Court Appearance, the Defence lawyer was forced to order a copy of the formal charge from the Clerk's office. Unfortunately, most criminal lawyers failed to do this and simply relied on their dulled memories to absorb the details of the criminal charge as it was read to the accused person during his first court appearance.

These technical aspects of criminal proceedings essentially remained unchanged from the time that I first began to work as a lawyer. However, the Court administrators and judges were always introducing new procedures and the law continued to evolve. Knowing the technical aspects of the system still left me quite unprepared for the realities of the criminal court system. With each new development in my case, I was forced to accept the practical realities of a legal system that had become unpredictable because of the unwritten exceptions to the prescribed rules and procedures.

Nothing works as well as the passage of time to create new priorities that can eclipse yesterday's problems. As summer arrives, so does the busy season in a real estate law practice. Traditionally, it is difficult for lawyers with this type of legal practice to take any time off at this time of year. It is much different for lawyers involved in a criminal law practice or a civil litigation practice since the superior courts do not hold trial sittings in July and August. Presumably, superior court judges need more vacation time to rest from their burdensome work than do Provincial Judges who continually preside at trials throughout the year and get much less time off.

During the summer months, I found that it was best to only take short breaks of less than one week. This was necessary to meet my critical deadlines and did not unduly upset real estate clients. For this reason, our summer vacation trips were nothing more than extended week-ends. We had become accustomed to visiting local attractions and events. Such was to be the case again this year and I happily anticipated the prospect of adventuring from home to the numerous summer festivals and activities within our city. We typically found enough activities for our children to enjoy and the months of July and August always disappeared too quickly.

In the summer of 1990, we began to follow the familiar routine of previous years. We were again pre-occupied with the cares and concerns of our children as they experienced the joys and endured the frustrations of their adolescent lives. Additionally, we found ourselves toiling during the long days of summer to complete the multitude of outdoor work projects at home that lay dormant during the other seasons. All of this activity and commotion consumed our total energies and thoughts and replaced anxiety with physical exhaustion. Our diminishing youth was tested continually as we laboured to cope with all the demands that were made for our attention.

As the first days of August arrived, I found myself submersed in my legal work, struggling to complete files that always had urgent deadlines. The delays in completing work were now attributable to vacation time for lawyers, their secretaries and for government employees. In the midst of this beehive of activity, my happiness was disrupted with our doorbell ringing one morning. I went to answer the door assuming that I would be receiving the delivery of documents on one of my legal files. Instead, I found Christal with another police officer. The sight of Christal immediately brought a sickening feeling to my stomach. There he stood smugly in a new tailored suit. From his expression, it was evident that he had come once again to disrupt and torment my life. It was now obvious that his quest to charge this lawyer with criminal fraud was not over.

Christal's attitude and demeanour did not allow for any pleasant greetings. When I asked him what he wanted, he handed me a document, saying:

"I have another search warrant and I'm here to search your office again."

Having said that, Christal and his partner walked past me into my home. I stared at the document that he handed to me. As I turned around, I saw him walking downstairs to my office. I then looked around to see my wife coming in from the kitchen. The expression on her face was a reflection of my feelings of horror and despair. As I wrestled to compose myself, I could hear Pat ask:

"What does he want now?"

At that moment, I felt totally unprepared as I mentally tried to cope with this drastic change of events. I wondered why this was happening and began to sink into despair over the futility of my situation. As these thoughts flashed through my mind, I soon realized that it was necessary for me to act. I then firmly responded:

"I'll take care of this and find out what he wants. Please stay upstairs with the kids. I'll call you if I need any help."

I then quickly followed Christal and his partner down the stairs. As I entered my office, Christal turned to me and asked in a demanding voice:

"We're here to conduct another search of your financial records. We're looking for bank records relating to your company Eleventh City Developments Ltd."

At this point, I felt upset with Christal. It was now obvious that he was just doing this to demonstrate that he was still conducting an investigation. I immediately responded:

"You asked for those records the first time you were here, back in December. My wife and I told you then that any financial records relating to that company had been discarded. That company has been dormant for a number of years. There was no need to keep any of those records. The only records I have here are those of my law practice."

As I finished speaking, I reflected once more on how easy it was for Christal to manipulate the legal system. There was no proper reason for him to secure a fourth Search Warrant from a judge for the same documents that he asked about on the very first occasion. Yet, he could obtain a search warrant at his personal whim since the judge would never even question his reasons for the request. The approval process was in fact a "rubber stamp" affair since no determination was ever made by the Judge about whether it was proper to authorize it. Christal knew that he could abuse the legal system and use search warrants to harass anyone since nothing could be done to stop that.

Christal looked at me tenaciously. His cold, piercing eyes vividly described the hatred that he felt towards me. After a momentary pause, he responded in an arrogant manner:

"I see! I must not have made a note of that. In that case, there is nothing for us to seize here today. I'll be making my report to Bill Pinckney at the Special Prosecutors office. You'd better get your lawyer to call him."

What Christal said about Pinckney was confusing so I immediately inquired:

"Isn't Eileen Nash handling this file at the Crown Prosecutors Office?"

His chilling response left me feeling uneasy:

"Eileen Nash is on vacation right now. I'm dealing with Bill Pinckney who is the head of that department. Your lawyer should call him now."

Having said that, Christal turned and walked out of my office. His partner trailed behind him like a puppy showing obedience to his master. I followed them up the stairs and then watched as they disappeared out the front door, only minutes after they had arrived. Pat soon joined me but didn't say anything as we watched them leave. Their arrival and departure was so sudden that it left both of us in shock and disbelief. For a moment, we both wondered if this had really happened. My wife then asked what they wanted and I briefly explained to her what had happened. I then reassured her that I would call Murphy and have him make a further inquiry. I tried to comfort her and myself by recalling Murphy's last words on this investigation and his advise that we should not worry. However, both of us felt distraught as we struggled to contain our emotions. Suddenly, my life again went into a downward slide like a roller coaster making its longest and most frightening descent.

As I turned to go downstairs, Pat returned to the children. We both endeavoured to proceed with our planned activities for that day and to set aside all thoughts of this latest intrusion into our lives. On reaching my desk, I immediately reached for the telephone, dialed Murphy's office and found to my surprise that he was in. After waiting for a few minutes, Murphy's voice came on the line in his usual jovial manner:

"Hi, Orest! Are you getting enough sun these day?"

I tried my best to respond in a warm, uplifting manner. Unfortunately, my body was still in shock and my efforts at being cheerful were dismal but I responded in the best mood that I could muster:

"Patrick, I never get enough sun and warm weather but I'll settle for what I do get."

Before Murphy could say anything further, I continued:

"I'm sorry to call like this but I just had another visit from Christal. If you can imagine, he came again to ask for documents which he knew we didn't have. This is his fourth Search Warrant on my home and its blatant police harassment. He was asking about financial records for my company, Eleventh City Developments Ltd. He knew that I didn't have these any more. He asked Pat and me for these on the first day that he searched my home. We told him then that we didn't have these records anymore. He didn't even make any attempt to search for anything this time. It was obvious that he was here just to show that he was still investigating this matter."

Murphy tried to calm me as he interjected:

"Orest, take it easy! As I've told you before, Christal is just digging to see if he can find anything which shows that you did something wrong. He has nothing and everyone knows it. I'm sure that he only did this to try and keep the investigation alive because he's obviously at a dead end. I wouldn't worry about this if I were you."

It was comforting for me to hear Murphy's response and I was satisfied once again that Murphy was right. On the surface, there was nothing that should have concerned me about what Christal was doing. The problem was that Christal was devious in his investigation. Now I laboured with the sickening feeling that he might lay the criminal charge even if there was no evidence to justify it. I was also concerned that there was a new player in the game: Bill Pinckney. I had understood that files didn't change hands from one Crown

Prosecutor to another unless there was a reason. I didn't want to jump to conclusions but Christal's remark had a sinister element to it.

I calmly proceeded to explain Christal's latest remark to Murphy and to gauge his response:

"Patrick! Before Christal left, he told me to arrange for you to contact Bill Pinckney at the Special Prosecutions office on this. He said that Eileen Nash is on vacation and he is now reporting his findings to him. Isn't it strange that the file would now be moved from Eileen Nash to Bill Pinckney?"

Murphy sounded confused by the situation and his personal sentiments became evident from his comments:

"Well, it is unusual for the file to be switched since a file like this would take a lot of time for a Crown Prosecutor to become acquainted with it. I would assume that Pinckney is just looking after the file while Eileen Nash is away. Pinckney is the head of the department so it's unlikely that he would make any decisions on this. He'll probably just hold it in abeyance until Eileen Nash gets back so she can decide what to do on this file. I'm sure there's nothing to worry about but I'll give Pinckney a call. If there's anything to report, I'll call you. Otherwise, we'll just have to wait until Eileen Nash gets back from vacation to review this with her. Don't worry about anything, Orest! I'll call you if I hear anything further."

On completing this telephone call, I reclined in my chair to relax. As the shock began to subside from my body, I reflected on Murphy's comments. Everything he said was correct and it was logical that nothing would happen until Eileen Nash returned from vacation. It would be unusual for any other Crown Prosecutor to interfere or even look into one of her files unless there was an emergency. There was certainly no emergency on this investigation which had extended almost five years after the actual transaction took place. I resolved in my mind to follow Murphy's advice and not pre-occupy myself with needless worry.

I suddenly realized that my wife had not left the house yet. I rushed upstairs to tell her the news in the hope that it would brighten her day. Pat had managed to diffuse the commotion with the children by sending them out into the backyard. This provided us with a short reprieve of solitude to share our feelings and to calm each other. As we sat in our family room and enjoyed a cup of tea, I tried to impress Pat with the positive items that Murphy had stated. It all sounded so good but the reality was that this whole investigation did not go away. It did not die as we hoped and it was still proceeding ahead. Nothing had dissuaded Christal from spending more time on it, even if his efforts were fruitless. There was still no assurance that a criminal charge of fraud would not be laid against me.

As we sat together resting on the couch, I had to battle the recurring signs of disillusionment. I again examined the dismal prospect that Christal might lay the fraud charge. I shuddered as I considered the obvious result of such a development on my law practice and my family. Once again, I had to live in fear of becoming a victim in Christal's senseless marauding. The frightening feature of this whole scenario was that nothing had hampered him in his devious pursuit. It now seemed that nobody could prevent him from laying the charge even if it was irresponsible for him to do so. Because Christal held a coveted position, he could be confident that anything he did would be defended by the Police department. Their public relations officers would insure that his actions were heralded as falling within the proper fulfillment of his duties as a police officer. The prospect of what could happen was now overwhelming. Although I fought to keep these thought out of my mind, I knew that my worst nightmare could still come true.

Those precious moments of rest and solitude disappeared quickly, forcing us to return to our schedule of activities for that day. I comforted Pat before she left and assured her that we had nothing to worry about. However, both of us now knew better as we silently harboured fears of this unmentionable horror. As Pat gathered the children and then disappeared out the door, I returned to my work with all the determination that I could generate. I forced myself to shake off these scary concerns and proceeded to complete a number of urgent tasks scheduled for that day. It was obvious now that I could do nothing more except wait. I focused my thoughts on the positive things that Murphy had said and I convinced myself that Murphy would call with good news.

Patience is said to be one of mankind's greatest virtues. This must be so because so few people can demonstrate this virtue in their daily lives. This virtue is continually tested by our ability to wait for events to happen. As children, we are forced to wait for everything. One would presume that as we grow and mature, each of us develops more of this great virtue of patience. However, it is my conclusion that although some people can demonstrate patience better than others, few people ever enjoy waiting. Instead, most of us choose to struggle to appear virtuous by subverting the frustration that we feel in having to wait.

As each day passed, I found myself anxiously waiting for some word from Murphy. However, I was determined not to show my concern or anxiety to Pat and the family. With the passing of time I allowed myself to conclude that if anything bad was going to happen, I would have already heard about it from Murphy. It was easy to console myself with such unrealistic rationales since the converse was unthinkable. Perhaps it was simply too horrifying to contemplate. I refused to dwell on the prospect that my worst nightmare might come true. Instead, I forced myself to think positively about the resolution of Christal's investigation.

After a week of intense waiting, I returned to my office on August 8, 1989, and listened in shock to a message from Murphy on my telephone answering machine:

"OREST, PLEASE CALL ME AS SOON AS YOU GET IN. I'VE GOT SOME REALLY BAD NEWS FOR YOU AND I REALLY MUST TALK TO YOU."

At first I told myself that the "bad news"could be anything. Even if it was about Christal's investigation, it could simply have been that some evidence had come forward that needed an explanation. I wanted to believe that there was still hope but I knew in my heart that my worst nightmare had come true. I couldn't accept it and I wouldn't even consider it until I heard it from Murphy.

As I sat at my desk in shock, I tried to assess what I should do. I resolved that I would say nothing to Pat until I knew what Murphy was calling about. I knew that I had to telephone Murphy but I had to fight my recoiling body to force my fingers to dial his number. His receptionist advised me that he was out and that he would call me in the morning. I tried to relax and to clear my mind of these dreadful thoughts. Finally I resolved that whatever the bad news was, I would have to deal with it in the morning. Until then, I was not going to upset my wife with my fearful concerns.

I soon realized that I wasn't going to accomplish anything further so I left my work on my desk and went upstairs. All that was left for me to do now was to take some time to relax and to pray. Above all, I needed the strength to face tomorrow. With my feelings of high stress, it was unrealistic for me to expect to get any rest that night. All the horrors of the past replayed continually in my mind with no resolution in sight. I knew how important it was to maintain a calm and confident exterior to comfort my wife and family. However, my inner feelings were in turmoil as I suppressed fears of imminent doom. I was actually relieved when I heard the morning alarm so that I could rid myself of the night demons that robbed me of my sleep.

The following morning, I felt exhausted but I was determined to find out if everything was as bad as I expected. Knowing that Murphy's call might come early, I completed my morning routine quickly so that I could be ready at my desk if his call came through. As I sat there in momentary reflection, I concluded that this had been the worst year that I could remember. It was August 9, 1989 - just two days before my wedding anniversary. Sadly, there was so little that had happened in the year that I could recall with joy. My parents had both died just six months earlier. First my father died after a lengthy struggle with cancer. We had only started our grieving when my mother died unexpectedly just two few months later from complications relating to knee surgery. Two months later, Pat had a breast tumour removed and was being monitored for recurrence. The shock of these events robbed us all of our emotions as we began to cope with the emptiness and uncertainty that was created.

Now I faced the unwanted responsibility of administrating their estates and dedicating time to resolving those problems. As with any typical family estate, there seemed to be an endless stream of complaints and demands from everyone. Just six months earlier, my legal practice and my family received my total energies and attention. Now, these personal responsibilities were being displaced by the demands of administrating these two estates. The worries and concerns relating to Christal's investigation simply added unbearable pressure to an already difficult situation. I concluded that it would take a miracle from heaven for me to survive all of this without a mental breakdown or a family disruption.

As I surveyed the work spread out on my desk, I realized that my legal files required immediate attention. I knew that I would be getting telephone calls from realtors and clients demanding to know when their transactions would be completed. Although I was experiencing a personal crisis, I knew that there would be no sympathy from the outside world. I therefore pushed myself to continue my work even though every nerve in my body was now frayed with tension. I knew that any work that I completed would have been a miraculous accomplishment.

At that moment, it occurred to me that in these types of circumstances, many people simply quit and walk away from everything. After all, in situations of high stress, nobody can be faulted for giving up the fight. I knew that it takes a phenomenal amount of inner strength to continue to labour against formidable odds. Conversely, the solution of giving up or running away becomes so appealing when all hope is gone. However, in my heart, I knew that I could never give up or run away from this or any other problem.

As I reflected on my situation, I knew that I had done nothing wrong. Surely it had to be evident to everyone that I had not been involved in any wrongdoing. If Christal was able to abuse his position and lay a charge in this case without evidence of any wrongdoing, then it would be my responsibility to prove to everyone that I was innocent. The burden of doing so might be difficult to endure for me and my family but it was surely the right thing to do. My parents had always taught me to face responsibility and not to shy away from my obligations.

As I worked through my files, the telephone rang. My heart began to pound wildly as I wondered if my waiting had ended. As my trembling hand picked up the telephone receiver, I heard Murphy's voice. His sombre tone was unmistakably different. There was no humour, no laughter and no cheerful comments. Instead, he spoke in a soft, sympathetic voice:

"Orest, I don't know how to tell you this! I spoke with Eileen Nash yesterday and she told me that Christal has laid a charge of fraud against you."

As I listened, my heart sank with grief. For a few moments, I could hardly speak. Although I had dreaded the thought that this could happen, I still had not prepared myself for the horror of my worst nightmare coming true. My mind became blank as if frozen in time. I could only hear myself instinctively utter the words of disbelief:

"How did this happen, Patrick?"

His voice showed all the recognizable signs of anxiety and disappointment as he laboured to explain what he had learned:

"Well, it seems that Christal waited for Eileen Nash to go on vacation. While she was gone, he took his whole file to Bill Pinckney. Christal knew that Eileen Nash was not prepared to prosecute this file. She told me that she was satisfied that there was no evidence that you had done anything illegal. That's why he waited for Eileen Nash to go on vacation. When she wasn't around, he took it to Pinckney. He was complaining that Eileen Nash wouldn't prosecute this file and that he had done all this work and gathered all this evidence. Finally, Pinckney agreed to direct a prosecution without reviewing the evidence."

As I listened in disbelief, I could not believe that anyone could manipulate the system the way that Christal had succeeded in doing. Although I had heard stories of devious conduct by police officers, I would never have dreamed that any police officer would go to such extremes. Christal must have really wanted to charge me with fraud to take such measures. I now feared that such a desperate police officer could employ devious tactics to manufacture or suppress evidence in my case also. It was hard for me to imagine that any police officer would be so intent on laying an unjustified criminal charge against me simply to gain an advancement for a promotion in the Police Department. However, I was now a victim of this reality. I realized that Christal was not only devoid of feelings but also lacked a conscience.

In my struggle to remain rational and avoid throwing myself into a well of despair, I asked Murphy:

"Why would Pinckney do such a thing?"

I suspected that Murphy would have asked the same type of questions when he heard the news. I was hoping that he could give me some kind of an answer to explain this blatant abuse of the criminal justice system. I realized that I was putting Murphy on the spot. Ordinarily, he would not have answered this type of question for a client. However, this was different. I was his friend and I wanted to know.

As I sat breathlessly waiting in shock, I listened as he explained to me what he had learned in candid conversation with Eileen Nash:

"Well, it seems that Christal and Pinckney are old buddies. I'm told that they've known each other for a long time. Pinckney decided to order this prosecution to proceed as a favour to Christal. He didn't even bother to see if there was anything there to prosecute. Pinckney doesn't care because he doesn't have to prosecute it. Nobody at the Crown Prosecutors Office ever cares if a prosecution proceeds and gets thrown out by a judge in court. Eileen Nash tells me that she now has to proceed with it because Pinckney has ordered it to proceed. Since he's the head of that department, she has to follow his orders."

This all seemed so unfair and so unjust. How could a system of justice proceed in such a reckless and corrupt fashion? How could the Crown Prosecutors act so carelessly in the work that they were assigned to perform? How could anyone stand by and allow a police officer to act in such a devious fashion? Why would the Crown Prosecutors Office simply proceed on a prosecution that was not supported by any evidence? Finally, how could anyone with a conscience stand by and allow a criminal charge to be laid and a prosecution to proceed against a person who is innocent? How could any decent person manipulate the criminal justice system to intentionally devastate me, my career, and my family?

In a lament of resignation, I questioned Murphy in the hope of learning something that might make sense of this whole situation:

"But I didn't do anything wrong! How can they lay a charge of fraud when I didn't do anything fraudulent?"

At this point, Murphy responded with his own brand of standard legal advise:

"Relax, Orest! There's no point in getting upset. We'll have to appear in Court and set this over for a Preliminary Hearing. When we're at the Preliminary Hearing, we'll see what they've got. If there is nothing, then the judge will throw it out at that stage. I don't see this going any further than the Preliminary Hearing. I know that Eileen Nash feels the same way."

Murphy's advice was meant to be comforting but I knew that I would not enjoy any peace of mind until this nightmare was over. Christal had now managed to harass me with search warrants, torment my family with a criminal investigation, and lay a criminal charge which could not be supported by any evidence. There was no way of speculating what he would do to influence witnesses or to manufacture and suppress evidence. Christal was clearly a cop out of control and he had now managed to secure the cooperation of the Crown Prosecutors office in his quest to destroy me. From this time forward, nothing would be the same and I had to adjust to the reality of this tragic situation.

At that moment, I was lost for words. I simply sat in shock and waited for something to happen. Murphy must have sensed my despair and immediately continued with his legal advice:

"Orest, as you know, you have to be formally charged and fingerprinted. Christal was going to arrest you at your house. He wanted to bring you downtown in handcuffs to charge you and then hold you in custody until bail was arranged. He really has it in for you and he wants to show you how he can put you down and humiliate you."

On hearing this, the last shred of energy drained from my body and I felt like I was going to collapse. I began to breathe deeply as my heart pounded in my chest. All I could think of was Christal dragging me downtown in handcuffs to prove his superior authority over me. He had succeeded in manipulating the legal system for his own purposes and had no qualms in hurting or ignoring those that stood in his way. Because he was the law, he could do anything that he pleased with the blessings and support of the Police Department.

Suddenly my emotions erupted like a smouldering volcano as I exploded in protest:

"That sounds ridiculous, Patrick! There's no reason to arrest me! It's obvious that I'm not fleeing the country. Why wouldn't he simply issue me an Appearance Notice? Isn't that how the police treat everyone else in such a situation?"

The question was simple but there was no real rational answer to it. Calmly, Murphy began to explain:

"The only reason he wanted to do that is to be malicious. That's even obvious to Eileen Nash. That's why I got her to intervene. She arranged for me to bring you downtown tomorrow so that you could be formally charged. After you are fingerprinted, you are supposed to be released on an Appearance Notice. Don't worry! I'm going to stay with you until this is finished and you are out of there. I won't let Christal detain you in custody."

The whole thought of what was about to happen was too much to comprehend. As I sat there speechless, Murphy continued with his instructions:

"Orest, I've arranged with Eileen Nash to bring you downtown to Police Headquarters tomorrow. That's August 10, at 1:00 after lunch. Why don't you meet me at 12:30 at the second floor cafeteria of the Brownlee Building. That's right across the street from the police station. We can talk more about this then. When you are ready, we can walk over at one o'clock and get this taken care of."

As he spoke, I listened in a daze. I was only able to murmur an audible "Yes" to his instructions as I sat motionless in my office chair, mortified with shock. Murphy must have sensed my anguish and offered his sympathy:

"Orest, I know that this is hard on you. I'm sure that it would be difficult for anyone. Don't let it get your spirits down. You'll have to do your best to keep your chin up. We'll work on this together. I'm sure that everything will work out fine."

Shaken and still in shock, I feebly managed to thank him for his words of encouragement and for arranging everything with Eileen Nash. I assured him that I would meet him downtown tomorrow as requested. On completing the call, I felt like crying but I didn't have the energy to do so. Instead, I simply leaned over my desk and cradled my head in my hands. After a few minutes, I straightened up and began to take deep breathes to rejuvenate my body. Now, my work had lost all meaning and purpose. I contemplated what my life would be like as this new turmoil began to take shape.

I decided that I wouldn't work on any legal files today since the criminal charge was now an urgent priority. As I stood up, I could feel my body shaking. I focused all of my energy to force myself to climb the stairs to the main level of our home. As I entered the family room, I could feel the warmth of the sun coming through our drawn window blinds. I longed for a few moments of rest in this warm, comfortable environment to escape the reality of my pending doom.

As I entered the room, my wife noticed me approaching and must have sensed the pain and mental anguish that was consuming me. As I made my way to the sofa, she rushed to the kitchen to prepare some tea and soon we were relaxing in this comfortable environment. The children were outside which allowed us to enjoy the quiet solitude indoors. As I stared at Pat, I wished that I could spare her from the pending ordeal that was fast approaching. She could sense that I had bad news but I still found it difficult to explain what had happened. There would be no easy way to explain it and there would be no better time than right now.

I found myself speaking to her using the same words and explanations that I had just heard from Murphy. She reacted in shock and horror in the same way that I must have reacted. The whole conversation had a tone which was strange and unfamiliar. I continued to ramble and repeat myself until I was sure that I had repeated everything that Murphy had said. When I was finished speaking, we both sat motionless and stared at each other in disbelief.

Moments later, shock turned to fright and then Pat burst into tears. As I hugged her to comfort her, my heart was breaking. To witness the devastation that she was now suffering was more painful than anything that I had to endure. Before I could say anything, she asked:

"What's going to happen to us, Orest? Are they going to suspend you from practising law? What are we going to do?"

The question rang in my ears as deafening silence filled the room. I couldn't imagine how we would cope with everything. This criminal charge would not only create public humiliation but would destroy my career as a lawyer. New questions filled my mind. What would I do to earn an income while this whole situation was being resolved? How would we explain this situation to our children, to our relatives and to our friends? How would we handle the fallout of this ordeal? Most important, could we survive as a family until this whole ordeal was over?

There were no answers to any of these questions. While I comforted her, she wiped the tears from her eyes. As I studied the devastated look on her face, I responded slowly:

"Pat, I'm probably going to be suspended by the Law Society until this criminal charge is dismissed. The problem is that the Court process can take up to two years if this goes all the way to trial. In the interim, I'm going to have to find other work. I'm sure that we'll survive this situation but it's going to take a toll on all of us before it's all over."

Pat asked whether I would be contacting the Law Society and I began to describe my thoughts on what I proposed to do:

"I'm going to ask Murphy if we can delay any proceedings by the Law Society to suspend me. I personally think that they won't wait very long before suspending me. They may wait a few weeks and that will give us enough time to finish the files I now have and collect my fees from them. After that, we'll just have to take things one day at a time."

Pat then looked at me and asked with an expression of terror in her voice:

"Orest, are they going to put you in jail after you get charged tomorrow?"

I responded immediately to calm that concern:

"Pat, don't worry about that! Murphy will be with me to make sure that I'm not put in jail. I'll be home for supper tomorrow as usual. Please don't worry about anything! I'll be working on this with Murphy. I'm sure that everything will get straightened out."

Pat's facial expressions told the whole story. Although she gave a sigh of resignation to this drastic turn of events, she now felt the despair that I had fostered for the last eight months. There would be no joy and no hope until this ordeal was over. All we could do was hope our lives would not be shattered by the events that were to follow.

As we both sat in silence, I began to accept the realization that I was about to be charged with a criminal offence. The proceedings themselves carried a stigma in society, whether or not I was ever convicted. All my credibility would be lost. I would no longer be able to conduct a real estate legal practice since such clients would be reluctant to trust me with funds to be held in my trust account. Similarly, my legal advice would hold little credibility and I would find myself languishing for clients in a competitive market serviced by too many lawyers. The harsher reality was that I would also be suspended pending the resolution of these criminal proceedings. If I was convicted of this fraud charge, then the Law Society would disbar me and I would never work as a lawyer again. This was the only career that I had prepared myself for, studied for, sacrificed for and dedicated my life to. It seemed hard to imagine that it could now be wiped out by such an unlikely turn of events in my life.

In a philosophical vein, I couldn't help but wonder: Was this providence and destiny that could result in a favourable change or was it simply a horrible fate that I was to suffer for some unexplainable reason? There was nothing positive about what was happening to me and it was obvious that I would most likely suffer a horrible fate.

Neither Pat nor I could visualize what lay ahead in the days to come. Because we loved each other, we knew that we could lean on each other and endure this ordeal together. As we finished our tea, we both reluctantly agreed to return to our assigned tasks for the day. We silently parted and I returned to my office downstairs but it was difficult to find any enthusiasm for working on legal files. Necessity dictated that it had to be done and so I drew on my remaining reserve of energy to help me through.

As I returned to my work, my thoughts continually lingered back to the prospect of appearing before Christal to be charged and then fingerprinted. I could never have contemplated that such an event could happen to me. I was only glad that my parents were not alive to witness the ordeal of having their son charged with a criminal offence. It was a blessing that they would be spared that trauma and I only hoped that my family would be spared as much trauma as possible.

Depression quickly overtook me and I could find nothing to be optimistic about. It was hopeless to find any positive elements in what was about to happen. I knew that I would simply have to endure the abusive actions of Christal without any comments or gestures of defiance. I was about to enter the criminal justice system from a different perspective. This time I would experience first hand the plights of those who are wrongfully mistreated and charged by the police. There was no time to adjust to this new reality as all of this was going to start tomorrow.

CHAPTER EIGHT

THE POLICE DEPARTMENT

In the entire legal system, the functions and operations of the police department are the least understood and the most secretive. Based on a military model, new recruits are trained like soldiers to follow orders and obey a chain of command. With a difficult working environment offering job assignments that are either boring or fraught with danger, it is no wonder that many officers become disillusioned and resentful. This resentment in turn is most often directed against lawyers who typically flaunt their position and status before the Courts that these officers must attend. Because lawyers are always working to destroy cases that police officers work hard to create, the resulting animosity continues to fester between these two professional groups.

The magnet that draws human interest to police work is the variety of cases that police officers encounter. For that reason, police departments are frequent settings for movie and television dramas. Unfortunately, the reality of the work in the police department is seldom reflected in the glamour of the movie and television productions. As with most situations, too much happens that is kept hidden from the public because of a system that protects the deviant behaviour of some police officers.

In any organization, there will always be individuals who breach the rules and cast a dark light on those with integrity. In recent times, such incidents are now becoming known to the public from the secretive military to the secretive police department. The problem of cover-up arises because of a desire to maintain a good image of the organization with the public. When a situation is made public, these organizations strive to quiet the complaint by engaging their own procedure for resolving complaints. In most cases, these internal investigative procedures are used to white-wash the conduct of the offending officer and declare the officer blameless. Only in extreme cases does the department take the opposite tact of sacrificing and dismissing the officer as a "bad apple".

As in the military, the police department instills a strong emphasis on the comradarie of its members. Although this is helpful to promote a team effort, this also acts as the basis that forces all members to cover the indiscretions of deviant officers. Regretfully, this flaw in the Police Department has become part of the foundation of the organization. For that reason, the Police Department typically ignores any suggestion of identifying and expelling deviant officers before the public is traumatised by them. Instead, the Police Department makes large expenditures to develop public relations and to hire individuals that will handle the media to justify and excuse the misconduct of officers. This reality causes deviant officers to proliferate and advance in this sheltered environment.

I had already experienced the actions of one such deviant officer by enduring Christal's abuse. The time had now come for me to enter the Police Department and to take an inside look at what happened behind their closed doors. Although my introduction to their procedures would be limited (since I was not supposed to be placed in custody), it was an experience that I would always remember.

I have often marvelled at how resilient the human spirit is to adverse conditions. Over the years, I had witnessed clients in my law practice who were faced with personal dilemmas that created unbearable physical or mental hardships for them and their families. Yet many of these individuals were able to accept the consequences that followed with tranquillity. Although the pain was devastating, they still found strength to endure the onslaught of abuse that ravaged their lives. By enduring their plights, they could endure their ordeals with amazing calmness.

As I worked at my desk on the morning of August 10, 1989, I was amazed to find myself concentrating and performing tasks effectively in spite of the turbulent affairs that were developing. In a philosophical manner, I had accepted the events that would take place that afternoon. Now I had resigned myself to the fact that nothing could change those events and that I would survive this situation without physical harm. I felt comfortable knowing that Murphy would accompany me. Fortunately, he had made arrangements to complete this process without a detention in jail or the requirement of posting bail. I suddenly became conscious of my calm state of mind and realized that for the first time in six months, I had stopped worrying about my upcoming ordeal. Instead, I was working effectively in preparation for this new event in my life.

Having completed some of my work, I reviewed the files on my desk and re-organized them for future follow-up. I then went upstairs just before noon to join Pat for an early lunch. We both knew what was about to happen. I assured her that everything was arranged and that there would be no surprises. It was now more important to resolve this situation than to worry about it. Pat then lamented that this whole situation was so unfair and I responded with the idiom: Who said life is supposed to be fair. I knew that this was not comforting to hear but there was nothing else that I could say about our current family crisis.

I finished my lunch quickly and then went upstairs to change into a suit for my fateful meeting downtown with Christal. I decided to leave early and to take a slower drive downtown through my favourite route along the river to the downtown core. I loved Keillor Road in the summer because the lush foliage surrounded and seemed to consume the road. The sight of the river meandering beside the road conjured images of a peaceful and less stressful lifestyle of a century before. Today, I had to settle for a motorized glimpse of this tranquil setting as I piloted my craft downtown. Soon I would be forced to endure the pain of my dreaded nightmare in the heart of our modern concrete jungle.

As I became engulfed in erratic traffic, my thoughts shifted to the many times that I had made this same trip to meet with clients who needed help in their encounters with the law. During those times, my thoughts were focused on the presentations that I would be required to make on their behalf. At no time did I ever dwell on the pain and grief that had created havoc in their lives. Now, I understood the trauma that was haphazardly inflicted upon those people by the feudal attitudes and procedures that society had preserved in the enforcement of the law.

For a moment, I reflected on the medieval practices still prevalent in law enforcement in our country. I recalled the many lectures at law school which traced the laws of our country and that of the United States of America back in historical time to medieval England. I laboured to understand all the relevant developments that made those laws part of our current practice. I now began to understand that although civilization had progressed remarkably in the field of science, there have been slow and perhaps regressive changes in the area of law. After working with the law for a number of years and seeing its effects on the citizens of society, many experienced lawyers candidly admit that the law has in fact regressed. Some lawyers have quit the practice of law because of this disillusionment that the legal system did not deliver justice to the people.

One area of injustice that still creates outrage is the role and actions of police officers. It is still prevalent today to see some of our country's citizens being turned into outcasts at the whim of our overbearing "sheriffs". Their powers enable them to prowl the domain and arrest common people in an arbitrary manner for anything they deem to be an infraction of the law. As in medieval times, the police are protected by the legal system and seldom are forced to account for abusing their positions.

One unfortunate change is the deterioration of the Court system by delays and technical procedures that only lawyers and judges understand. In earlier times, the adjudications were summarily concluded and the punishments were immediate and brutal. The death penalty was imposed for crimes as minor as theft. With advancement in our society, we have become more compassionate and have resisted and abolished the death penalty. However, opinion polls still suggest that the majority of citizens would still prefer to see the death penalty reinstated. Such attitudes are vigorously touted and promoted by police departments who welcome an environment where force can be used to solve the problem of crime. Police departments also lobby for more control and power in dealing with crime and promote attitudes which would see a return of our medieval past.

On arriving at my destination, I parked my car and walked over to the Brownlee Building to await the arrival of Murphy. I had arrived early because I wanted to relax and enjoy a beverage before Murphy arrived. As I began to reflect further on the laws of our country, I began to appreciate the view of many of the legal critics. Some have proclaimed that our legislators have passed too many laws and that now the laws can be so widely interpreted as to make any activity illegal. The result has led to the creation of a climate that is not favourable for business activities and a legal system that is overpopulated with cases involving people accused of technical breaches. The most unfortunate implication is the erosion of our personal freedoms because of the encroachment of laws to control more of our daily activities.

The continual monolithic growth of our legal system truly sums up all that ails our legal system as it has developed over the last century. If one looks back to the simpler times of a century ago, the laws were few and specific. Everyone understood the laws and how they would be enforced. Today, the laws are complex and are not even understood by lawyers who study them. It appears that almost any activity can be argued as contravening a law and this is determined by a subjective interpretation. Any hypothesis can be supported because of the overwhelming amount of cases decided, recorded and interpreted by the Courts. With computers and more efficient technology, it will become possible for lawyers to argue any point of view on any topic. As a result it is now possible to show that any conduct of any person should be subject to punishment in the Courts. In these modern times, it is possible for anyone to be charged and convicted of a breach of the law if the police officer pursues such a legal position.

While I sat deep in thought at a table in the corner and enjoyed my beverage, Murphy approached with a sombre expression on his face. The thoughts that kept me from dwelling on my own personal misfortune now vaporized and left me with the cold, harsh reality of the moment. As Murphy sat down at the table, he looked across at me. His facial gesture expressed his concern for the way I felt at that moment. Murphy then spoke in his comforting manner:

"Orest, we have a few minutes yet before we have to go over to the police station. Do you have any questions about this whole thing?"

Murphy knew that I had a lot of questions and that we couldn't begin to deal with any of them at this moment. However, I wanted to talk and prepare myself for my imminent encounter with Christal so I asked an obvious question:

"Patrick, why is Christal being so malicious towards me? Am I really such a bad apple that he has to be so abusive?"

Murphy tried to respond to my question in a diplomatic fashion to neutralize my paranoia:

"Orest, you're not a bad apple! I think that Christal is just like that. He enjoys putting people down. He's having a wonderful time sticking it to you. I suspect that he really wants to get you on something more. When we go in there, don't do anything to even suggest that you are resisting the process. Also, don't say anything! I've made all the necessary arrangements through Eileen Nash. I'm here to make sure that everything is done the way we had agreed. I'll take you in there and get this done quickly. We'll be out of there in no time."

Murphy then leaned over and spoke in a quieter voice, indicating a more personal question:

"You know, something is bothering me about the way Christal is conducting this investigation. I've known a lot of police detectives who handle files like this as routine investigations. They are always very objective and very cooperative. They never push an investigation where there is nothing for evidence."

I listened intently to every word as Murphy expressed those familiar concerns that had preoccupied my mind right from the beginning. It was comforting to hear that Murphy found Christal's conduct unusual. I was now more satisfied that my feelings about Christal were not simply paranoia or resentment but an actual, objective observation of a police officer acting out of control. Although I wanted to shout my agreement to every word Murphy said, I sat quietly, listened carefully and waited for Murphy to finish. As he continued, I virtually consumed every word:

"That's what I find so strange about this case. Christal is acting different. He's carrying on like this investigation is very personal. He really has it in for you! He has made it known that he hates you and that he's going to nail you on this case. This is really unusual, Orest! Maybe I asked you this before. I just don't understand why he is so mad at you. Tell me this! I really need to know. Did you ever do anything to get Christal mad at you - like sleeping with his wife or shitting in his briefcase or anything at all? There must be something that you can tell me that would make his conduct easier to understand. Can you think of anything?"

For a moment, I sat there in a daze. I couldn't think of anything and I didn't know what to say. Murphy was convinced that this was not just a case of a police officer doing his job. Rather, this was an intentional program on Christal's part to destroy my life. I just couldn't believe that I had made such a mortal enemy out of this police officer. The worst part about it was that I couldn't recall ever dealing with him. I desperately tried to think of anything that might connect me to Christal. Unfortunately, my mind was blank and I couldn't make any suggestion.

Murphy's expression was intensely serious as he waited for my reply:

"Patrick, the same thought keeps haunting me too. I'm sorry but I can't recall ever having any dealings with Christal. I can't even think of any connection that I've had with him at any time. If I did know what his problem was, I would atone for his grievances. There's just nothing that I can think of."

Murphy then sighed in exasperation. As he started to stand up, he indicated that we should leave and get the unpleasant task completed. As we walked over to the Police Station in silence, I wondered what Christal's hang-up was and why he had singled me out to atone for his anger. There were really only two distinct possibilities to explain his unusual motivation in my case. The first was already discussed with Murphy and was based on the premise that I had offended Christal and he was doing this to get vengeance. The other was that Christal was simply pushing this investigation and the fraud charge because of the publicity that it would generate for him. The obvious motivation here was the promotion that could follow from such a high profile case. In either case, it was obvious that Christal was using his position to maintain an investigation and prosecution of a fraud charge for his personal gain and he had obviously succeeded. Soon I would be in Christal's lair where he would force me to endure the ordeal of being charged, fingerprinted and humiliated.

The ultimate irony was that Christal could draw a salary while he conducted himself in this inappropriate manner. Conversely, I would be paying legal costs and suffering losses as a result of his actions. For whatever I had done to offend him, he was now going to enjoy his revenge while I was going to pay dearly for having offended him. Sadly enough, I would probably never know why Christal had proceeded with this malicious investigation. It would be almost impossible to expose him for this impropriety and he would naturally simply deny any improper motives.

As we entered through the front doors of the downtown police station, my eyes were drawn to the large atrium in the centre that seemed to occupy a large part of the building. This impractical open expanse provided the modern aesthetics that were so commonplace in new government buildings. The public was not allowed to enter the atrium and were confined to the reception area. This unfurnished area was designed as a waiting place until a police officer appeared to escort you to his office. The atrium area could only be accessed by police officers and was of minimal use and benefit to them as well. Sadly, the effect of installing the atrium was to create small, cramped and ineffective office space for the police staff. The irony here was that the building was intended to be an architectural showpiece that reflected public pride. Instead, it was a structural blunder that was poorly constructed, poorly designed and ineffective in providing useful office space for the police staff.

As I waited in the reception area, Murphy advised the police officers at the reception desk about our appointment with Christal. A few minutes later, Christal appeared and escorted us to his office. As we entered Christal's office, the small cramped space caused me to momentarily pity the poor working conditions that Christal must have endured as he worked on my file. I began to suspect that perhaps these working conditions contributed to Christal's attitude of bitterness and callousness. I could understand his resentment as he viewed people in the outside world working in more comfortable surroundings. His callousness became a hammer and his resentment caused him to view me as a nail. It was no wonder that I was taking such a pounding.

On entering Christal's office, we all sat down. I could see in Christal's facial expressions that he was gloating over the success that he had achieved in laying this criminal charge. There was no doubt that he had longed for this day to arrive and was pleased that he could now proceed to charge me. He had achieved his ultimate goal and it was obvious that this brought him immeasurable satisfaction. This was a startling reminder that there were people who derived such great satisfaction in bringing misery to others. It was visible on Christal that he felt no compassion or remorse for his actions. On the contrary, he savoured this moment which would almost certainly lead to further rewards in the form of a promotion. I could now appreciate better why police officers with a conscience found it difficult to work with Christal.

Murphy began by asking Christal if he spoke to Eileen Nash and if he understood what had been agreed upon as the procedure that would be followed. Christal acknowledged that he had and he then explained that he would first proceed to formally charge me. Then he would issue an Appearance Notice to me and I would be released "on my own recognizance". This meant that I would NOT be held in custody and that I would NOT have to post any bail. Instead, I would be free to leave on my promise to appear in Court on the date specified in the Appearance Notice.

Christal then positioned himself smugly behind his desk and began his ego-fulfilling process of formally charging me. Usually, a police officer simply delivers an Appearance Notice to an accused person. The theatrical nonsense that I was enduring was seldom employed. However, because of Christal's desire to personally humiliate me, this theatrical exercise became a suitable compromise to the harsher procedure of being placed in custody.

As Christal opened a neatly positioned file on his desk and withdrew a completed form, he stared at me in a demeaning manner. His movements and gestures were methodical and intended to insure that I felt the degradation of being another fallen member of society. Then, in his typically cold and callous manner, Christal began the process of charging me with the criminal offence by saying:

"First of all, state your name to me."

I responded by saying: "Orest Rusnak". Christal then continued:

"Orest Rusnak, I am charging you with criminal fraud. I will read to you the charge and then I will ask if you wish to respond. Orest Rusnak, your date of birth is 1950, January 21, and you reside in Edmonton, Alberta."

As I meekly answered "Yes", I could feel my heart pounding in my chest. My ears were ringing as this horrifying procedure changed my status in society from a trusted and respected citizen to a despicable outcast. In the Courts, one may relay on the axiom that "One is deemed to be innocent until proven guilty". However, in society and especially the business community, anyone charged with a criminal offence (especially the charge of fraud) was to be avoided. Such an outcast could only hope to function by hiding this "skeleton in one's closet". My whole body suddenly felt weak but I had to finish this ordeal. There was no way out except to persevere.

Christal continued by reading from the document that he held:

"You are charged with - Count 1: Between the 1st day of July, 1984, and the 1st day of April, 1985, both dates inclusive, at or near Edmonton, Alberta, did by deceit, falsehood, or other fraudulent means unlawfully defraud Heritage Savings & Trust of property, money or valuable security, to wit: money of a value exceeding$1, 000.00, contrary to Section 338 (1) (A) of the Criminal Code of Canada. Do you understand the charge?"

As Christal stared at me with a triumphant glare, I again quietly responded: "Yes". Christal then continued with his monologue:

"Do you have anything to say? ..."

Before Christal could say anything further, Murphy interrupted him by saying:

"He has nothing to say."

Christal then looked at me with a smug expression on his face and continued by stating:

"Very well, then! I am now issuing to you an Appearance Notice. This Appearance Notice requires you to appear on September 6, 1989, in Provincial Court, Room #65, to enter a plea to this charge. I require you to sign at the bottom to acknowledge that you have received a copy of it."

I stared at the document but my mind was now paralysed with fear. As I tried to assess what was happening, my thoughts were frozen and I wasn't sure what to do next. Nothing in my life had ever prepared me for this moment. I had never handled a case in which I had appeared with anyone else before a police officer to be charged. As I stared at the document, Murphy prompted me by handing me a pen and directed me to sign on a line at the bottom of the document.

As I reached for Murphy's pen, I could feel my whole body weaken but I took a deep breathe to fortify my efforts so that I could complete this task. With trepidation and anxiety, I slowly signed my name to the Appearance Notice. On completing the task, I returned the pen to Murphy without looking up at him. Christal immediately seized the document in his hands, detached a copy and handed it to me.

I could see my hand moving in slow motion as I instinctively reached to take the document from Christal. It must have been obvious to Murphy that I was in a state of shock because he interceded by saying:

"I'll hold on to that for you, Orest."

With a sudden feeling of relief, I handed this dreaded document to Murphy. My body began to feel more relaxed as Christal placed his document back in his file and then closed his file. I told myself that this traumatic ordeal was almost over and that I could make it through. I had resolved in my mind that I would not give Christal the satisfaction of seeing me shattered or devastated because of this situation. It was important to display strength of spirit if I was to fight to prove my innocence in the Courts. In my mind, the justice system was still sacred, despite the continual incidents of abuse that I witnessed. I was sure that I would receive a fair trial, especially since I had a better understanding of the Court system than most people. As I embraced these positive thoughts, my strength slowly returned to my body and I soon felt ready for whatever remained to be done.

Abruptly, Christal rose from his chair, glared at me and ordered in a loud, demanding voice:

"Now, I'm taking you down to the I.D. Section to have you fingerprinted."

At that moment, Murphy and I stood up. It became obvious that we would have to step out of his office first as there was no room for Christal to walk around us in this cramped office. After we all squeaked out of Christal's rat hole, Murphy and I followed him down the hall to another section in the building. As we walked, Murphy spoke to me in a reassuring voice:

"Orest, this should only take a few minutes. I'll wait for you and then we should go for a coffee."

Murphy's words brought instant relief from the pangs of shock that still seized my body. I knew now that this situation would be over shortly and that Murphy would be there to insure that nothing changed at the last minute. As we walked, I suddenly realized that Murphy probably wanted to talk to me about something specific. I was now curious to know what was on his mind.

Moments later, we arrived at another door on the same floor. Christal direct-ed us to wait in the corridor as he went inside to make the necessary arrangements. As Christal disappeared from sight, Murphy leaned over to speak to me quietly:

"Are you O.K., Orest? You looked a little pale and shook up in there."

There was no point in trying to put up a strong appearance with Murphy. I trusted him as my friend and I was comfortable in confiding to him:

"I am pretty shaken up but I'll get through this. I could sure use a cup of tea after this is over."

Murphy then responded in a jovial manner as he tried to lighten the mood of depression that hung in the air everywhere in that building:

"No problem, Orest! I'll even buy."

As I forced a smile, Christal appeared again and then directed me to step inside the doorway. Murphy advised me that he would wait in the corridor and I complied with Christal's directions.

The room itself had the same decor as the rest of the building: concrete walls, ultra modern fixtures and no decorating. If one had to imagine the most dismal work environment, one could easily believe that this building would find its way to the top of that list. It occurred to me that this building was probably a bad joke by the architect and the designers. Otherwise one would have to suspect that it was intended that police officers should hate their work environments. The benefit would presumably be that police officers would instinctively be less sympathetic to those people who they investigated.

This space was also small and allowed for no partitions or private working areas. After waiting for about a minute, a police officer approached me with clip board in hand. First, he asked me to confirm information that he had on a form filled out by Christal. As he asked me to state my name, date of birth and address, I responded to his questions.

Thankfully, this police officer's attitude and demeanour were totally different from Christal. There were no sentiments of hatred or arrogance and I sensed that he did his job with compassion. This police officer was not interested in hurting anyone. He was just there to do the job that he was assigned to do to the best of his ability. It was police officers like this who should be typical of a police force. Regrettably, it was police officers like Christal that made a police force distrusted and resented by the citizens whom they served and protected.

I was then directed to stand against a back-drop so that I could be photographed. Because of this police officer's pleasant attitude, I wasn't revolted by this degrading procedure. The procedure itself was no different that having a picture taken for a driver's licence or passport, both of which I was quite familiar with. However, the realization that this was part of a procedure to identify me as a criminal still made the whole procedure degrading and repulsive.

After the officer took photographs showing a front and side view of my face, he directed me to a counter against the back wall for fingerprinting. Although I had seen various humorous portrayals of this procedure in movies, none of these images could soothe my feelings of despair. I was then asked to remove my jacket, roll up my sleeves and to remove my rings. When I was ready, he took my hand and forced each finger individually against the ink pad. He then placed it on the paper in a rolling motion to get a total impression of each finger. It occurred to me that the procedure itself was really quite interesting. Under different circumstances, I might not have found it objectionable. However, the context here was "for the identification of a criminal". This made the experience simply one more distasteful occurrence in a tediously protracted nightmare.

As the police officer worked quickly to finish this degrading assignment, my body remained limp and without feeling as I endured this situation. When he completed this messy procedure, he encouraged me to wash the ink from my hands at a sink in the corner. I then looked at my hands which were now covered with wet, black ink. As I stared at them, my thoughts immediately recalled the many stories that I had read about "Guilty Hands". Indeed, this was part of the transformation as the system catalogued me as a criminal. The ink was oily and difficult to dispel as I washed my hands repeatedly with soap. I realized that although I might be able to remove the stain of the ink from my hands, the stain of this event would remain with me forever.

As I completed washing and drying my hands, the police officer then asked me if I had any identifying marks or scars on my body. I advised him that I did not but he was intent on recording even the slightest blemish to document me properly. After he marked his form, he told me that he was finished and that I could leave. His manner was sincere and friendly compared to that of Christal to the degree that it caused me to feel inclined to thank him. However, the thought of what I had just endured caused me to conclude that I had nothing to be thankful for. After securing my rings and my jacket, I looked directly at him and in a soft voice said "Good-bye" before turning and walking to the door.

At that moment I reflected on how difficult it must be for a police officer who felt compassion for others to do these types of jobs. Often a police officer knows or at least can sense if the actions of another officer are wrong or unjust. Yet, they must comply and perform their assigned tasks which add to the devastation suffered by innocent people. As outsiders, we tend to believe that a police officer only performs tasks on investigations that he is conducting. Few of us ever visualize those police officers who assist in the process and have no say as to what happens in the investigation.

As I reflected on the work of police officers, my thoughts focused on the many police officers that I knew over the years. A significant majority of them were friendly and compassionate to others. These officers were the fine recruits that would make the difference on any police force. They served as a good example of what a police officer should be. Unfortunately, the rigors of the job soon set in and pressure begins to mount from superior members of the department. Each police officer is forced to complete assigned work in the manner that delivers up criminal charges for prosecution. In such an environment, the caring and compassionate police officers are out of place. To survive, they must either develop a callous attitude or feel displaced in a workplace that offers limited opportunities for compassionate work. It is no wonder that the police officers with compassion usually become disillusioned, develop ulcers from stress and seek early retirement or quit before retirement.

Once outside the door, I walked to Murphy who was now leaning against a wall in the corridor. He soon noticed me and motioned for me to follow him out. As we left the building, I felt my body start to relax and the tension that was suffocating me now started to dissolve and fade away. As we briskly walked towards the Brownlee Building, I remarked to Murphy:

"Boy, am I glad to be out of there!"

Murphy looked around to make sure that there was nobody close enough to hear our conversation. He then spoke to me in a hushed but sincere manner:

"Orest, I didn't want to say anything in there. However, the reason I stayed until you were finished is that I could sense that Christal was going to have you put in custody. If he did that, he would have forced you to appear tomorrow morning in court to get bail."

For a moment, I wondered if Murphy was joking and I looked at him in disbelief. Then, unmistakably, the expression on his face told me that he was serious. I felt my fingers twinge as I contemplated the horror of being abruptly shuffled into the cell area. Once in custody, I could be detained at the whim of the police. The following morning, the police had to allow those in custody to appear in Docket Court. This would then be my opportunity to ask a judge to order my release if bail was granted and posted. The whole experience could easily take a few days. I couldn't believe that this horror story could have taken such a dreadful turn of events. Moments later, I fell into a momentary shock as I focused on what Murphy was saying.

This latest revelation of Murphy's was in direct contradiction to what I understood before we entered the police station. As I began to collect my thoughts, I asked:

"Patrick, that doesn't make any sense! You said that you had worked out an arrangement with Eileen Nash on this. How could Christal act contrary to that and place me into custody?"

Murphy then continued his explanation: "I did make an arrangement with Eileen Nash and Christal did acknowledge that he knew about it. However, when you are inside that police station, Christal is in charge - not Eileen Nash. He can do anything he wants to do. If he decided to throw you into custody, there is nothing that anyone could do about it. By the time he processed the paperwork, there wouldn't be any time to get you in front of a Justice of the Peace. You would find yourself in Court tomorrow morning pleading to the charge. That would have been very underhanded for Christal to do. Luckily, I was tipped off by a friend that Christal has done that type of thing before. I'm convinced that he would have done that today with you if I hadn't hung around. With me hanging around, he knew better than to try that kind of stunt. If he had tried anything, I would have gotten Eileen Nash down there and then we would have gone over his head to straighten this out."

As I listened to Murphy, I laboured with the disbelief that anyone could be so openly and blatantly deceitful. It was almost unbelievable that Christal would actually believe that he could carry out such an improper stunt with immunity. Obviously, he was confident that he would not be chastised or sanctioned by anyone for such a blatant impropriety. It was frightening to comprehend that a police officer like Christal could expect to get away with such disreputable conduct and not even be concerned about any consequences. Incredibly, Christal and others like him were well known for such stunts. Yet, they knew that they could try these tactics and then justify them as a normal part of their work.

Murphy's comments put me in a mortified shock. My mind was confused as I struggled to understand why Christal would do such a malicious thing to me. Finally, with disbelief, I asked:

"Why would Christal want to do such a rotten thing to me? What does he have to gain by tormenting me?"

Before he could respond, we had entered the Brownlee Building and were now nearing the cafeteria entrance. We secured our beverages and then walked to a secluded table in the corner so that we could continue our conversation. As we sat down, Murphy immediately began his reply:

"You know, Orest, I hate to dwell on this because I know it's hard on you. However, I think you should know what's going on in your case. Christal really wanted to put you in jail and to force you to go to court to get bail. You can be sure that at your appearance in Docket Court, he would have had the news reporters from the newspapers, radio and television tipped off so that they could run stories on this. Christal would have loved to get some press coverage out of this. You see, he's the type who really wants to make this into a high profile case so it can boost his career in the Police Department."

As I sat silently and shook my head in disbelief, I decided that I would have to think this all over before discussing it further with Murphy. However, he had now touched on another topic that had come up in my conversations with my wife: would there be any mention of my criminal charge in the news. It was obvious from Murphy's comments that there would have been if I had been arrested but that didn't happen. I looked at Murphy and blurted out my question to get his reaction:

"It seems that I should consider myself lucky that I haven't been arrested and I don't have to appear in court until September 6. Do you think that the news media will find out about this situation and report it?"

As I waited for his response in momentary silence, I could feel my heart pounding in my chest. I dreaded the thought of a news story and the effect that such publicity would have on my family. I had also hoped that I could conceal any knowledge of this embarrassing development so that I would be able to continue to work at my law practice. I also hoped that this whole thing could be resolved prior to the Preliminary Hearing, just as Murphy predicted. Otherwise, I hoped that I could get a favourable decision at the Preliminary Hearing and then none of it would matter anymore. If I could only get one good break, maybe everything would still turn out fine.

Without hesitation, Murphy responded with his assurances:

"I don't see how that could happen, Orest. Nobody knows about this right now except you and I and Eileen Nash and Christal. Unless Christal notifies the news reporters, there is no way that they can find out about this. As you know, these kinds of charges are normally reported when a person makes the first appearance. It's unusual for a charge to be reported as news before it comes to Court so none of this will become news immediately. Also, I managed to arrange your appearance for the afternoon on September 6. It's not likely that any news reporters will wait around to see what's on the afternoon docket. So I wouldn't worry about that at all."

Murphy then quickly finished his coffee and started to rise from his chair, saying:

"Orest, I need to run to take care of another matter. If you feel O.K. now, I'll leave you here. I'll be speaking to Eileen Nash as this thing proceeds. I'll get copies of any documents that she is going to rely on at the Preliminary Hearing. Nothing more will happen before your appearance in Court on September 6. Take care of yourself and say hello to Pat for me."

I thanked him and watched him slip away down the stairs. Because I felt totally drained, I sat there and finished my hot chocolate. The hot drink made me feel a little more refreshed but I knew that I wouldn't be able to work on any of my legal files today. I slowly got up and proceeded outside to my car for my journey home before the rush hour traffic started. I knew that my wife would be anxious to hear from me and I felt that this was a time that we needed to comfort each other.

As I drove home, I realized that all my emotions and feelings had left my body. Everything had now been stripped away by the malicious acts of Christal, leaving behind a devastated shell that I would have to heal and rebuild. As I entered the doorway to our home, Pat immediately came to greet me and to ask how everything went. At that moment, I couldn't describe to her my feelings of the horror that I experienced. Instead, I simply told her that it was just the same as we've seen on television. Pat then offered to get me some tea so that we could console each other before supper.

As we continued our quiet conversation, Pat suddenly interrupted by asking:

"Will there be anything about you being charged on the radio or in the newspapers tomorrow?"

In response, I confidently gave her the explanation that Murphy had just finished relaying to me. It made sense to me and it seemed to satisfy Pat at that moment. At least that was one worry that we wouldn't have to contend with. We sure needed a reprieve from all the turmoil that kept coming relentlessly into our lives. We spoke of taking a break in September after the kids were back in school. We needed some time to work on feeling better about everything in our lives once again. We certainly didn't need any more turmoil in our lives.

As we finished our tea, Pat asked if I intended to do any work in the office. At that moment, I felt fine but I had no desire to concentrate on anything related to legal matters. She then mentioned the plans that we had made a few weeks earlier to go out that evening to celebrate our wedding anniversary. We both agreed that it would be a welcome change from the depressing developments earlier in the day and so we both proceeded to get dressed for an evening out.

For the moment, I believed that everything would return to normal for a while and that there was no need to worry.

On our evening out, we tried to put our problems out of our minds. We knew that there would be no more surprises for another month until I would have to appear in Court. We could not imagine the horror that awaited us the next morning as we woke to find the news of this criminal charge broadcast for everyone to hear. After struggling with that crisis, I had to endure the appearance in Docket Court. The task that followed was the tedious labour of recording all the details of my encounters with Christal to assist Murphy in preparing for the Preliminary Hearing. Having completed that task, I was now ready to meet with Murphy to review this report and to prepare for Court.

CHAPTER NINE

THE CROWN PROSECUTOR

In the United States of America, they work in the District Attorney's Office. In Canada, they work for the Attorney General or the Justice Department. In the United States, they represent the State in each criminal case. In Canada, they represent the Crown. Their titles are different but their jobs are the same. They prosecute criminal charges in Court.

In making comparisons, there are as many differences as there are similarities. The American counterpart will typically oversee and direct the investigation of crimes. The Canadian Crown Prosecutors rarely become aware of a file until the criminal charge is laid. In the United States, the accountability is to the people because the District Attorney is elected. In Canada, the main influence on the Crown Prosecutors Office is exercised by the Police. Although the work they do appears on the surface to be the same, the environment in which they work is significantly different.

The job of the Crown Prosecutor is to represent the interests of society by securing convictions against people who have committed crimes. The premise of our criminal justice system is that justice can only be achieved if two opposing positions are presented and decided by an impartial judge. This procedure is called "the adversarial process" and is dependent on both sides presenting the case to the same optimum standard. Of course, this process can only produce fair results if the judge remains totally impartial and unbiased. Unfortunately, the Crown Prosecutors are usually more experienced than the defence lawyers and enjoy a favourable bias from judges. This results in an imbalance that is often impossible for an accused person to overcome.

In a criminal case, the Crown Prosecutor must first present sufficient evidence to show that the accused person committed the crime. The Defence lawyer then presents the rebuttal on behalf of the accused person but is not required to present any evidence if they so choose. Although an accused person is "presumed innocent" and the Crown Prosecutor must prove guilt "beyond a reasonable doubt", these legal requirements are seldom obstacles. A Crown Prosecutor often can secure a conviction based on testimony from witnesses that arouses suspicion about the conduct of the accused person. Furthermore, the results in a Court room are often based on the assessment of the theatrical performances of the two lawyers. In such a contest, the Crown Prosecutor often has more experience and therefore has an obvious advantage.

In order to ensure an accused person has a fair opportunity to defend himself in Court, the law now requires that the Crown Prosecutor provide information on the evidence that will be presented in his case. This information is called "particulars" of the Crown Case. However, Crown Prosecutors were notorious for hiding evidence that they knew could prove the innocence of the accused person. Most recently, the Supreme Court of Canada has ruled that if the Crown Prosecutor fails to disclose any information that might be useful to the Defence Lawyer, any conviction that results may be set aside. This ruling will hopefully create more cooperation by the Crown Prosecutors but some Defence lawyers suspect that it may simply make Crown Prosecutors more careful in making sure that such evidence is carefully hidden.

The repetitious work of the Crown Prosecutors force them to confront complainants, victims and police officers on a continual basis. In a short period of time, the Crown Prosecutors typically become callous and indifferent to the fates of those that they prosecute. Some Crown Prosecutors develop a zealous attitude about scoring convictions and pressing the judges to impose harsh sentences. Instead of seeking justice, they pursue a mission of penalizing all those that come before the Court. Instead of being a voice of moderation, they openly advocate radical courses of action to implement their own personal solutions to society's problems. In doing so, these Crown Prosecutors actually become a major flaw in the criminal justice system.

During the short time at the beginning of my legal career when I handled criminal files, I had many occasions to deal with Crown Prosecutors. Although some were professional and understanding, many were belligerent, snobby and unapproachable. These Crown Prosecutors invited adversarial confrontations and flaunted their positions with indifference. On the whole, the attitude seemed to arise from the fact that they did not have to account to the voting public, whose interest they represented in the Court room. All too often, this has been identified by legal scholars as a fundamental weakness in our criminal justice system.

Now that the criminal charge was laid against me, the Crown Prosecutors Office was officially in charge of my file. The critical decision of whether this case proceeded would now be made by a Crown Prosecutor and not the Police. In their discretion, a decision could be made to withdraw the charge or discontinue its prosecution at any time. Now it was the Crown Prosecutor who would have the greatest effect on the resolution of my criminal charge.

Amid the confusion of work and family life, I was able to complete my notes on my encounters with Christal. After a few re-scheduled dates, my meeting with Murphy was set for late October. I was told that he had received copies of documents from Eileen Nash, the Crown Prosecutor assigned to my case. I was anxious to see what had happened in the investigation that could even remotely justify the laying of a charge against me.

As I drove my car on the familiar route to Murphy's office, I tried to quell my nervous anticipation by reflecting on the warmth of the afternoon sun on the last fleeting days of autumn. At this time of year, each day was a glorious reprieve from the onslaught of another Canadian winter which would soon alter our outdoor activities with snow and cold winds. To me, these beautiful autumn days were precious. I treasured each day for providing a reprieve from the need for heavy coats and winter boots to defend against winter's rampage.

Perhaps I was at the perfect time in my life to contemplate the passage of time. I was quickly approaching my fortieth birthday and this was the typical milestone for everyone to reassess their lives in the light of their fading youth. At the age of forty, one is unquestionably into middle-age. The natural aging process on the human body brings about concerns for health and necessary changes in lifestyle. Another reason for reflection is the horror stories that abound of the different forms of mid-life crisis that cause changes in marriages and careers. Once you turn forty it seems that suddenly everything in life becomes so fragile. This feeling of uncertainty is unavoidable regardless of whether any disruption occurs in the lives of the new mid-lifers. In my life, this criminal charge had now become my mid-life crisis which would change my career, shake up my life, destroy my calm perspective and alter my relationship with my relatives and friends. As I pondered how my situation was affecting my family, the same recurring concern flashed through my mind: WOULD MY FAMILY SURVIVE THE TURMOIL THAT HAD NOW CONSUMED OUR LIVES?

Even if I was fortunate in being able to resolve the situation at the Preliminary Hearing in the way that Murphy predicted, I worried that the shock waves from this earthquake might devastate my home life. The thought of what my family was enduring left me with the feeling of hopeless despair. I wrestled to resolve it through a careful analysis of the events that transpired. There was only one logical solution to this ongoing dilemma - to resolve this matter quickly.

As I glanced through my notes and the other papers in my file, I began to grow increasingly anxious about my meeting with Murphy. I knew that I was early but I hoped that perhaps Murphy might be able to see me before my scheduled appointment. As I opened the door to Murphy's office, I listened for the sound of Murphy's voice. All I could hear was the dull drone of office equipment and the voices of his secretaries. I quickly proceeded up the stairs and soon found myself in Murphy's reception area.

With the sound of cheerful greetings from Murphy's secretaries, my spirits lifted and I began to relax. I responded to them in a calm voice that disguised the turmoil that agitated me. As we chatted momentarily about the beautiful autumn weather, his receptionist confirmed that Murphy was on the telephone but would be able to see me shortly. I then walked over to the seating area, picked up a magazine and I sat down. I wasn't interested in reading anything but the magazine provided a temporary distraction that would prevent me from becoming nervous or upset.

As I glanced through the magazine, my thoughts drifted to the documents that Murphy had received from Eileen Nash. I tried in desperation to visualize the types of documents that would be included in that file. There would probably be documents relating to the registration of documents at the Land Titles office as these were public documents. However, these documents would only describe the closing of the transaction and would provide very little useful information. The key documents would come from the Heritage Trust file and these were the documents that were important for me to see.

As questions and comments raced through my head, I suddenly heard a shuffling noise from Murphy's inner office. I looked around as Murphy appeared and walked towards me. With a broad smile on his face, he called out to me:

"Hi, Orest! Nice to see you again. Have these ladies been giving you a rough time?"

Murphy had a natural instinct for taking the rough edge off a difficult situation. His secretaries played their roles so well that it was obvious that this type of verbal exchange was used often to lighten the mood in the office. As I mentally scrambled to respond to his cheerful dialogue, his secretary came to my defence:

"No way! We like Orest. He's a nice guy, not like some people around here."

Murphy liked this kind of jesting and seized the opportunity to do some friendly jousting with his staff:

"It figures! I seem to be the only one who gets abused around here."

By this point, everyone in the office was smiling as they each competed to retort to the banter. In the midst of this frolicking, Murphy signalled for me to join him in his meeting room. I found myself smiling at the light-hearted exchanges between Murphy and his secretaries and I began to relax in the warm environment that had been created. As I sat down in the meeting room, I noticed Murphy coming through the door with two large binders and a file folder.

He placed the binders and file folder on the desk, reached back to close the door and then immediately explained:

"Orest, these binders were sent to me by Eileen Nash. I understand that Christal organized all of the documents that he had into binders. Eileen Nash simply made a second copy of everything for me. Instead of identifying specific documents which she intends to use, she simply sent me everything that she received. All of this was provided on my request for disclosure of particulars."

I looked at the thick, oversized binders in disbelief as I tried to rationalize what could possibly be in them that would be relevant to the case. Because I was rendered speechless, Murphy was prompted to remark:

"Orest, I went through the binders. There is nothing that shows that you did anything in this transaction that is illegal. I spoke to Eileen Nash and she basically agrees with my assessment. As far as I can see, there is no evidence of fraud by anyone in the transaction. If they want to prove that someone made a false statement to Heritage Trust, then the charge should have been laid against Garmaz who took out the mortgage and against the broker who arranged it. I wouldn't worry about the stuff in these binders if I were you."

I felt partially relieved as I continued to gaze at the binders. After a momentary pause, I slowly responded:

"Patrick, I'm glad to hear that your assessment is still so favourable. I'm just surprised that they put together so many documents on a case that was nothing more than a simple real estate deal. I've seen less documents on some very complicated commercial files. With these documents, you would think that this deal involved the sale of a mega mall!"

Murphy nodded in agreement. With his experience in real estate, he understood what I meant. As I finished speaking, Murphy again interjected:

"Orest, there is very little in there that is even relevant to the real estate deal. Christal has dredged up as much paper as he could to make this look like a real complicated fraud case. His tactic is to make it so confusing that a judge might assume there is something wrong because he doesn't understand it. Even Eileen Nash is having difficulty on some of these things because she has never been involved in real estate transactions. At least she isn't confused about what must be proven and so she knows that there isn't the type of evidence to prove that you did anything fraudulent."

On hearing Murphy's comment about Eileen Nash, I was prompted once more to ask about the prospect of resolving the criminal charge:

"If it is so obvious that there is no evidence of fraud on my part, is it possible that Eileen Nash might discontinue these proceedings before the Preliminary Hearing?"

Murphy's serious expression foretold his answer to my question but I listened intently for any glimmer of hope:

"Orest, it's really not up to her at this stage. Pinckney is directing her to prosecute this case. However, once the Preliminary Hearing is completed, she can prepare a report on this matter to Pinckney to show him that there is no evidence of fraud. Then a decision can be made to stay the proceedings or simply withdraw the charge. Right now, there is no point in raising that question with Eileen Nash because the question is decided. The best thing for us to do is work on preparing the defence case for the Preliminary Hearing."

I knew that Murphy was right in his assessment but I wanted to be sure what the options were at the Preliminary Hearing:

"Patrick, you've already assessed the documents and discussed this case with Eileen Nash. Do you feel that this case can be resolved at the Preliminary Hearing?"

At this point, Murphy spoke up in a positive and confident voice:

"If this is all the evidence that they have, your criminal charge should be dismissed or withdrawn at the Preliminary Hearing. I'm sure that Eileen Nash isn't hiding anything and I believe everything that she has told me. They don't have any evidence that you did anything wrong. In fact, there is no clear evidence of fraud on anyone's part. With a case like this, the judge will certainly dismiss it at the Preliminary Hearing. I personally can't imagine this case going beyond the Preliminary Hearing. If this case were to go to trial, there is no way that anyone could find you guilty of anything on this kind of evidence."

Murphy's words were encouraging. However, I was not prepared to relax or to assume anything until this whole ordeal was over and the criminal charge was dismissed. I then asked him about the work that had to be done:

"I'd like to go through all the documents and give you my impressions of them and any recollections that they might stimulate. Did you want me to work on them in the meeting room here?"

To this inquiry, Murphy gave an immediate and unequivocal response:

"No! I'd like you to take the binders home with you and go through the documents carefully. If there is anything that you recognize that may be helpful, let me know. We'll go through the documents together on your next visit to my office, just prior to the Preliminary Hearing."

What Murphy was suggesting sounded ideal. I wanted to carefully review each document and I could do that more easily at my home office. I was delighted with his suggestion and confirmed my willingness to assist him.

I then reached for my briefcase and removed my file with the report of my dealings with Christal. As I handed my notes to Murphy, I explained:

"These are my notes on my dealings with Christal on this case. I tried to be as accurate as possible. I have included all of my dealings with him with as much detail as I could provide. I assume that you'll want to read this over before we discuss it. Perhaps we can conduct a review of this total case on our next meeting."

Murphy glanced at my report before looking up to respond:

"That's a good idea! I'll read this over when I have more time. We can meet when you've checked all the documents in these binders. Why don't you set up a meeting when you're ready to meet again. We can set it for a Saturday morning when we can discuss this without interruptions."

I was happy with Murphy's suggestion and I immediately confirmed:

"Great! I'll phone your secretary to set up the meeting. Thanks for your help. Call me if anything develops in the interim."

Murphy then placed my report in his file, rose from his chair and said goodbye. I then gathered up the black binders under my arm and walked out. After calling out a farewell to Murphy's secretaries, I headed down the stairs and was soon outside and at my car.

While I struggled to open the car door and maintain a grip on the awkward binders, I reflected on the unusual situation that I found myself in. Although everyone freely admitted that there was no evidence, I was still charged with a criminal offence. Now I would be judged at a Preliminary Hearing as to whether I should go before another judge at a trial. Ironically, the Crown Prosecutor and my Defence Lawyer both agreed that there was no evidence that I did anything illegal. Yet, there were two binders filled with documents that would be used to mislead the judge into believing that there was evidence of wrongdoing. The baffling question now was: HOW DOES ONE PREPARE A CASE FOR THE DEFENCE WHERE THERE IS NO EVIDENCE OF ANY WRONGDOING?

When I finally opened the car door, I dumped the binders and my briefcase on the car seat. As I drove away, I began to reflect on the comments that Murphy made on the tactics of Christal. Since there was no real evidence of wrongdoing, Christal was employing the common tactic of confusing the Judge with irrelevant documents. By overloading him with a barrage of paper, the Crown Prosecutor would argue that there must have been something wrong in the deal. At first glance, the tactic seemed hopeless but Murphy did comment on an obvious weakness among judges in general. Many of them knew nothing about real estate deals and could be persuaded to believe that there might be something wrong or illegal. In the final assessment, I would have to prepare a defence against the evidence assembled by Christal even though there was no evidence of wrongdoing. It was becoming painfully obvious that the real onus in my case was not on the Prosecutor to prove that I had done "something wrong". Instead, the onus was on me to prove that I had done "everything right".

As I drove home, I began to assess the task of evaluating each document. It was obvious that only some of the documents would be of any concern. It would be necessary to isolate them and then to feature them in a report to Murphy. It was comforting to know that none of the documents showed any wrongdoing. However, I was still concerned that any suggestion that I did anything improper had to be addressed and rebutted.

On arriving home, I knew that my wife and children were already there. I decided to put these concerns out of my mind and to enjoy a quiet evening with my family. The multitude of documents in the two black binders would have to wait until tomorrow when I would have time to start a thorough review and begin the formulation of my report.

CHAPTER TEN

THE MORTGAGE BROKERS

In today's real estate market, mortgage brokers are becoming as common as real estate agents. However, their role in completing real estate transactions is misunderstood by the general public as well as by the Courts. Although licensed by the government, their conduct is largely unregulated and this gives rise to some of the greatest abuses in that industry.

Like a real estate salesperson, the mortgage broker generates income primarily from fees paid by clients. Although purchasers can apply directly to a financial institution for financing, many prefer the convenience and expertise of a mortgage broker. Sadly, most mortgage brokers have little expertise and many of them have little interest in the financial concerns of their clients or the lenders aside from the fee to be earned.

As in any unregulated industry, the mortgage brokerage business is rift with incidents of disreputable conduct. This serious problem stems from a lack of training for the members and no control over the conduct of mortgage brokers generally. The natural result is improper tactics being employed by many mortgage brokers and exorbitant fees being charged for handling mortgage applications. For that reason, it is a common attitude among mortgage brokers to present only favourable information to lenders in the hope that a loan will be granted before something negative comes to light. If a discrepancy is discovered in the information provided by a mortgage broker, the tactic used is to deny having any knowledge of it. Some mortgage brokers even follow the practice of destroying the contents of their completed files as a form of protection. This insures that a later police investigation would not reveal evidence of their collusion in misleading a mortgage company.

In my real estate transaction, the mortgage brokers had become the unknown variable. It was obvious from the criminal charge that the mortgage company was claiming that a false representation had been made. There were two mortgage brokers involved and either one of them, or perhaps both of them, had submitted false information to secure the mortgage approval. The challenge now was to discover what had really happened and which one was responsible for any wrongdoing that might have occurred.

As I struggled to clear my desk of some routine work from my law practice, the two black binders projected an ominous presence. Although I wanted to start work on the binders immediately, I knew that would be counter-productive since my attention was being continually interrupted by pressing legal work. Therefore, I decided to treat this research as one of my priority files and schedule that work so that it didn't compromise my other obligations.

As I worked into the afternoon, I determined that I would be able to set aside my other work and spend an hour to simply conduct a fast preliminary review of the documents. This would provide me with a quick impression of the work to be done and the documents that might be of interest for a more thorough review. The binders were thick four ring binders stuffed to capacity with photocopied documents and each one was assigned to a numbered tab that served as a divider. At the front of the first binder was an index that identified each document by the number of the tab divider. It also disclosed what the document was and how it was obtained.

I was anxious to see what was in the documents so I began to quickly flip through the dividers and briefly glance at each document. Many of the documents were typical for a real estate transaction of this nature. I briefly glanced at each document, scoured it for anything relevant and quickly moved on to the next one. I was anxious to find something that would yield some information on how the transaction proceeded but nothing looked familiar. It occurred to me that almost all of the documents pertained to the real estate dealings of the Garmazs. Very few documents pertained to my purchase or resale of the property in question. I then opened the second binder which contained comparatively fewer documents. Most of these were copies of cheques and bank records with only a few of them actually pertaining to me.

The documents in the first binder were essentially documents from the Heritage Trust file and included mortgage documents and correspondence. The only other documents appeared to come from the realtors file and included copies of the agreements executed in the purchase of the property by my company. It suddenly occurred to me why Murphy and Eileen Nash could see no wrongdoing on my part in this entire transaction. The documents showed that I was not involved in applying for or obtaining the mortgage from Heritage Trust. My involvement was only in the initial purchase and resale of the property. The party that was primarily involved in dealing with the mortgage company was Stephen Garmaz and it was obvious that any wrongdoing had to be as a result of something that he did. Yet, it was strange that he was NOT charged with any criminal offence and that I was.

I began to ponder how a person like Stephen Garmaz could apply for and obtain a mortgage and then remain blameless. After all, if a false representation was made to the mortgage company, he had to be involved in making it. Suddenly, a thought flashed in my mind that offered the only logical explanation to this puzzle. I had always been bothered by the wording of the charge in the Search Warrant. It stated that I had arranged and caused the Garmazs to make a fraudulent misrepresentation to Heritage Savings and Trust. At the time that I received the Search Warrants, I couldn't make any sense out of any of it. Now, the wording seemed to take on some meaning.

It was quite obvious that Stephen Garmaz must have known that he had done something improper. Because of the police investigation, he had to shift the blame to someone else. That "someone else" was ME. His scheme to avoid any responsibility worked because of the desire of Christal to charge a lawyer rather than an anonymous employee of IBM. With the threat of a criminal prosecution, Garmaz was ready to say whatever was necessary to satisfy Christal and to avoid any possibility that he would be prosecuted.

Slowly, my mental picture of what happened began to form. I began to reflect on Stephen Garmaz and to evaluate whether this new assessment of his character was correct. I hardly knew Stephen Garmaz. I only dealt with him on this transaction and met him through an introduction by a former client. When I first contacted Stephen Garmaz, he appeared so friendly and anxious to do a real estate deal "as long as he could make some money on it." On our first meeting, he explained how he had purchased properties before with the assistance of my former client and then quickly resold them. He was so keenly interested in buying and selling properties and making money in the real estate market. Above all, he was proud to say that he had a clean credit rating and knew how to arrange and qualify for high ratio mortgages. As we discussed the proposed real estate deal, he was so confident about proceeding with the deal that I was sure that the transaction would close without any problems.

I was still reluctant to accept the conclusion that Stephen Garmaz had deliberately lied to Christal about my involvement in the transaction. After all, I had never had any problems or disagreements with Garmaz and the transaction was so straightforward. After the closing, the property was resold which resulted in Garmaz making a profit with no reason to complain. I could only conclude that the pressure of the investigation by Christal caused Garmaz to agree with whatever Christal wanted to hear. Using Garmaz as his pawn, Christal could try to make a case against me.

As I continued to analyze the basis for the criminal charge, it became increasingly clear that there were no real documents that proved any wrongdoing. The whole basis of the criminal prosecution was that a false representation had been made to the mortgage company at the time of the mortgage application. Typically, such information is verbal in nature and comes directly from the mortgage applicant. In a case like this one, a mortgage broker handles the mortgage application. He interviews the mortgage applicant, fills out a mortgage application form, obtains confirmation of the information and then submits it to the mortgage company loans manager. There would certainly be no documents that showed that I made any form of representation. However, one real possibility was that Stephen Garmaz made the representations and then somehow tried to suggest that I was the culprit who did it. I was now convinced that the mortgage brokers were the key to the mystery of what really happened and what went wrong.

I then became curious as to exactly what representations were made to Heritage Savings and Trust. Quickly, I began flipping through the tab dividers in the first binder which contained letters on the letterhead of Heritage Trust. As I glanced through the letters, I noticed references to the property that was mortgaged by Garmaz and then resold. After the resale, there was a default in the mortgage payments resulting in a foreclosure action on the property. Ultimately, Heritage Trust applied to the Canada Mortgage and Housing Corporation

("CMHC") who had provided an insurance coverage against any loss in the event of a foreclosure. From the letters, I determined that CMHC had refused to pay the loss of Heritage Trust. The apparent reason for this refusal was that the manager who approved the loan had failed to conduct any verification to determine that there was a downpayment on the property being purchased. This "downpayment" is a reference to the monies invested into the property by the purchaser in addition to the monies being borrowed from the mortgage company. The verification would show the source of the cash being invested, or alternatively, the property being given in trade if such was the case. This failure to verify the downpayment was clearly a negligent act on the part of the Heritage Trust loans manager and certainly explained why the claim for the loss was refused by CMHC. However, it did not explain what the representation was that the loans manager relied upon.

As I continued my review of the Heritage Trust letter, I located a Heritage Trust memo dealing with the loss and written by John Chubb to his supervisor. The memo confirmed that John Chubb had made a thorough review of the Heritage Trust file and determined that there were no documents that showed any reference to a verification of downpayment. According to Chubb, the loans officer who made the mortgage loan had received no documents to verify the downpayment. From this letter, it was obvious that there was no representation and no wrongdoing but simply negligence by the loans manager.

The memo contained an unsettling closing comment which went to the root of the reason for the actions of John Chubb in proceeding with a complaint to the police. It confirmed that CMHC was correct in refusing insurance coverage since the loans manager had failed to verify downpayment. The memo then concluded that Heritage Trust would have to treat this file as a loss because of the failure of the loans manager. As a closing comment, Chubb stated that "the best we can do is make life uncomfortable for certain people involved in the deal".

It was shockingly apparent that John Chubb was intent on using the criminal justice system to harass anyone involved in the transaction. This form of reaction would over-shadow the reality that the loss resulted from obvious negligence by the loans officer at Heritage Trust. Obviously, Christal had not seen this memo or perhaps he simply chose to ignore it. It is the normal practice for the police to avoid becoming involved in civil collection claims and this file was nothing more than a civil claim. However, Christal obviously had his own motivations for proceeding with the investigation and laying the criminal charge against me. Therefore it was logical that he would intentionally ignore Chubb's motives in this quest to pursue an investigation on a file that would surely advance his career.

As I reflected on John Chubb, I recalled my acquaintance with him from the time that he was still a mortgage broker with his own firm. As a mortgage broker, Chubb used questionable tactics to arrange mortgages to generate brokerage fees. When the economy began to slow down, his mortgage brokerage business was one of the first to dissolve. Through his sales ability, he was able to promote himself enough to get a position as a mortgage officer with Heritage Savings and Trust. This move enabled him to leave his failed business for the security of a monthly salary. To preserve his new found security, it was necessary to prove himself to be qualified and indispensable to hide his inexperience. This prompted Chubb to take steps on files that others at Heritage Savings and Trust would have viewed as inappropriate. It was this motivation that prompted Chubb to initiate a criminal investigation on this file that had already been accepted and treated as a loss attributable to negligence. Undoubtedly, Chubb's actions on this file to institute a criminal investigation caused his superiors to believe that he possessed the administrative abilities that would benefit their company. Ironically, before these criminal proceedings would be concluded, Chubb's manipulative actions would eventually expose him as an undesirable leech and his employment would be terminated.

After glancing through other documents, I located a statement of Stephen Garmaz that described just how devious Chubb was prepared to be in collecting the loss on this mortgage loan. The statement of Garmaz described a telephone conversation from Chubb in which Chubb demanded that Garmaz write a letter for him. His letter was to be used by Chubb as confirmation that Garmaz had cash money that he used to complete the purchase of the mortgaged property. When Garmaz advised him that this was not true, Chubb argued with him and remarked: "Who is to say that you didn't win the money gambling." Chubb insisted that if he could get the letter as requested, he would submit it to CMHC and get them to pay the insurance claim. Then he wouldn't cause any trouble for anyone on this file. Garmaz became concerned about this unusual request by Chubb and advised him that he would think about it and call him back. Ultimately, Garmaz refused to provide a false letter or become involved in such a deception.

As I pondered what I had just read, I realized that Chubb was willing to pull any stunt to collect the loss from CMHC, even if it was illegal. No doubt, Chubb wanted to show his superiors at Heritage Trust that he was capable of handling files where others had failed to collect losses for the company. It was shocking to realize that a person like Chubb could hold a position with a trust company and conduct himself in a manner that was improper and even illegal. It was obvious from his actions that he held no concern for any ethical or moral standards of behaviour and conduct. It was as if Chubb enjoyed immunity from criticism because of the position that he now enjoyed and that anything that he did would never be challenged. I felt disgusted by the attitude exemplified by Chubb. However, I now understood why a file like this would be selected and pushed into a criminal investigation.

From a further reading of Garmaz's statement, it appeared that Garmaz then decided to consult with his lawyer. The legal advice he received was that writing such a letter to assist Chubb to improperly receive money from CMHC would be fraudulent. Garmaz was therefore advised not to comply with Chubb's demands. As a result, Garmaz refused to provide Chubb with a false letter and Chubb then proceeded to have a criminal investigation instituted by the police.

As I considered the actions of Chubb, it occurred to me that Christal did not consider these actions of Chubb which clearly were an attempted fraud. These disclosures could have formed the basis of a criminal prosecution against Chubb. It was obvious that what Chubb had done was clearly illegal but a decision had been made to ignore this improper behaviour. This decision further demonstrated the bias of Christal to ignore any wrongdoing on the part of other people relating to the mortgage loan. He did this to gain their cooperation in his quest to build a case against the lawyer who he selected as the target in his investigation. Christal acted as if it was his absolute discretion to select who would suffer the wrath of the criminal justice system. His decision was to "nail a lawyer" and grab the publicity that such a case would generate for his career.

As I continued to glance through some of the other documents, I realized that there was nothing more that could enlighten me on what had transpired. I knew that I would have to conduct a careful review of each individual document as part of the conscientious evaluation that was necessary. I realized that I would have to schedule more time for such a slow, painstaking review and then prepare the report that Murphy expected. The only other evidence was the statements of the witnesses and this was something that Murphy still expected to receive from Eileen Nash. For the moment, I had work to do. I was intent on making a strong effort to complete it in the best format that was possible.

In progressing to assess the mound of documents provided by the Crown Prosecutor, I hardly took notice of the arrival of the Christmas season. No matter how busy and pre-occupied I might be, this season always provides a welcome distraction from the work and worries of everyday life. Aside from the merriment and goodwill that is touted by everyone, the children remind us all of the special magic of Christmas. As adults, we can only reminisce on our youth when we view and experience this magic with youthful eyes and hearts. This season is indeed an excellent opportunity to reflect on the blessings that one enjoys and to rejuvenate the human spirit with hope for the new year to come.

Because the Preliminary Hearing was to be held early in January, it was necessary to schedule a meeting with Murphy during the Christmas break. This was a crucial meeting to review the evidence that we assumed would be tendered and to discuss the special procedures in Court. This procedure was referred to by trial lawyers as "briefing the case for Court." This process involved a careful, painstaking evaluation of all of the documentary evidence that we had assembled. The difficulty that we faced was that the preparation of our defence could only be based on our prediction of the evidence that the Crown Prosecutor would most likely present in Court. The amount of experience of the trial lawyer did not necessarily shorten this procedure but it did make it easier to evaluate what evidence might require rebuttal.

In setting up an appointment for a meeting with Murphy, the typical problem arose of finding time in his busy Court calendar when he was free for a meeting that would last three hours. To accommodate this, Murphy had recommended a meeting starting at eight o'clock on Saturday morning. A week-end meeting guaranteed that we would not be interrupted by telephone calls from other clients or urgent messages from his staff. The relaxed routine that I usually enjoyed on Saturday mornings with my family had to be sacrificed for this priority. As the day of our meeting approached, I felt nervous with anticipation of what I might hear from Murphy. I prepared my final comments and organized my documents to enable Murphy to easily review my report.

As I drove to Murphy's office, I was hardly cognizant of the harsh winter conditions that had developed which made movement outdoors temporarily uncomfortable. All my thoughts and energies were focused on this critical meeting. I needed to gain a deeper understanding of what would happen during this first hearing of the evidence by the Courts. I wondered what further discussions that Murphy had with the Crown Prosecutor and what his assessment of my case now was.

As I pondered this, I witnessed Murphy's arrival and began to prepare myself to face the rage of winter outside. I hastily bundled up and then forced myself out of the car into the frosty chill waiting for me. As I responded to a warm greeting from Murphy, we both walked briskly to the front door of his office and hurried inside.

While Murphy was brewing tea and securing clean cups, we talked about our families and the festivities of Christmas. We both acknowledged the exhaustion and our increasing difficulty of enduring the activities that had become a family tradition. These activities result in the "hangovers" that linger from day to day caused by over consumption of food and drink. With every passing year we become more anxious to see our lives return to a normal routine as the season ends. However, we both mused that this never seemed to dampen any enthusiasm for celebrating each new Christmas season.

Murphy soon finished brewing the tea and we both sat down and began the process of briefing this case for the pending Preliminary Hearing. The room began to feel warmer with the help of the portable heater and the hot tea we were sipping. It was going to be a long meeting and we both understood the ramifications of the task at hand. As with any Court hearing, the most important task was the preparation before the appearance in Court.

The first order of business was for Murphy to review my notes and copies of documents. In these, I noted the relevant references to issues that might be raised at the Preliminary Hearing. As Murphy read my summary notes and glanced through the documents, I interjected with commentary to assist him in quickly assessing each of the items. While we reviewed each item, Murphy made notes for his later reference and I made notes of the points we discussed. The process was slow as we wanted to be careful not to miss anything that might provide credible evidence which might verify that I did nothing illegal. On concluding his review of my notes, Murphy shifted back on his chair, removed his glasses and commented:

"Orest, you were right to identify these documents in your summary. I'm sure that many of them will be put in by the Crown at the Preliminary Hearing to show what happened with the loan that Heritage Trust made. It's obvious, though, that there is nothing in these documents to show that you had anything to do with arranging that mortgage. If there is going to be any evidence that the

Crown can use to tie you into this case, it will have to be the verbal evidence of the Crown witnesses."

Murphy's comment reflected my conclusion on this matter. This prompted my inquiry:

"Patrick, did you get any information from Eileen Nash regarding any statements that they have from witnesses that discloses what their evidence will be at the hearing?"

Murphy replied in a manner which signalled that he was anticipating this question:

"Yes! I received a statement a few days ago from her. It sets out Christal's interview with the mortgage broker who arranged this mortgage. His first name is Walter and he has a long unusual last name. I'm not sure what nationality it would be but I know it's not Irish!"

At that moment, Murphy smiled. It was his familiar tactic to lighten the serious mood with jesting. He then signalled that he would fetch it from his office. When he left the meeting room, I tried to relax and conform to the lighter mood that Murphy was trying to create. However, my thoughts were riveted to the name of the mortgage broker as I frantically searched my memory to recall if I had ever dealt with him at any time. Unfortunately, I had no memory of any mortgage brokers in this transaction. I could only hope that there was something in his statement to Christal that might trigger my memory.

Moments later, Murphy returned to the meeting room carrying an open file as he read from a document he was holding in his hand:

"His last name is "Pev-ce-vi-ci-us. That must be a Greek name, I would guess. Does that name sound familiar to you, Orest?"

I was certain that I didn't recognize the name and answered without hesitation:

"No, Patrick! It's possible that I may have dealt with him in the past since I've dealt with lots of different brokers through my legal practice. However, I can't recall that name nor any specific mortgage brokers from this transaction."

Murphy sat down again, put on his reading glasses and began to glance through the documents. He then glanced up at me and explained:

"I've read this statement over a few times already. It's obvious to me that this guy doesn't remember anything about this deal. He worked for a company called Premier Mortgage which arranged mortgages. He apparently arranged this one with Heritage Trust. However, he couldn't recall anything until Christal started prodding him to admit certain things. He doesn't remember you at all and he doesn't really remember anything about the deal. It's obvious that he is going to make a lousy witness for the Crown. However, they will have to call him to try and show how this transaction developed."

Murphy's comments were reassuring, but I didn't have to be told that many witnesses change their stories from their initial statements to the time that they give evidence. It was obvious from Murphy's comments that Christal was using his influence on this witness to gain his cooperation. I had already seen Christal's tactics in action when he questioned me. He had no qualms about using force or improper methods to coerce a witness to identify documents or to answer questions on which he had no recollection. It then occurred to me that if this witness was concerned about the way he arranged this mortgage, he might be willing to say anything that Christal suggested. In that way, this mortgage broker could avoid being charged for doing something improper in arranging the mortgage. Christal made it obvious that he had singled me out as the target for persecution. All the mortgage broker had to do to avoid being implicated in the investigation was to say whatever Christal suggested to implicate me.

As I contemplated this dismal prospect, I tried to assure myself that it was premature to form any conclusions on what might arise at the Preliminary Hearing. From my early experiences as a lawyer representing clients in Court, I knew the effect that police officers could have on influencing and shaping the evidence of witnesses. Most witnesses were susceptible to such influence from police officers. It was also typical for witnesses in such cases to have a personal interest in the actual outcome of the case. Naturally, a witness was more likely to be influenced if he was concerned about being implicated because of the manner in which he conducted himself in the case.

Because of these factors, a Judge is left with the dilemma of deciding which witness he believes the most. Often, this evolves into a determination of which witness he believes the least. Furthermore, if the judge is not impartial, it is easy for him to selectively choose the evidence which fits his personal views of the events of the case, whether supported by any persuasive evidence or not. In the result, the hearing is less about the search for truth than it is about the game of hiding, exposing, exaggerating or manipulating the truth.

For the first time, I realized that my former experiences with the court system served as a disadvantage to me. In contrast to people with no legal training who appeared before the court for the first time, I knew the horror stories that could arise. I would naturally allow these past experiences to add to the stress that I would have to endure. Although it was important for me to predict the type of evidence that might be presented by the Crown, I knew that it was counterproductive to anticipate a "worst-case-scenario". Therefore, I resolved to adopt a positive attitude in assessing the possible evidence of the Crown. I was determined that I wouldn't dwell on the negative possibilities until such evidence was presented in Court.

My thoughts were interrupted as Murphy continued with his comments on the documents that he received from the Crown Prosecutor. As Murphy glanced through his file he removed two other documents and remarked:

"Eileen Nash also sent me these two pages which are photocopies of documents that Christal got from a different mortgage broker. According to Nash, that mortgage broker had nothing to do with this mortgage from Heritage Trust. They are going to call the broker to testify as to his contact with you and the Garmazs. The broker's name is Mark Denman with a company called Inter-Group Mortgage. Do you remember having any dealings with him on this deal?"

This new revelation caused a wave of panic to sweep through my body. I frantically searched my memory for any possible familiarity with that name. Finally I responded to Murphy in a slow, thoughtful manner:

"No! I have no recollection at all of that name. I know of Inter-Group Mortgage because that company has been around for a long time. I have recently done legal work on mortgages that were arranged by Gordon Sills from that company. However, I can't remember any dealings with a guy by the name of Mark Denman. What sort of documents did he produce?"

Murphy looked at the documents and then responded:

"As close as I can determine, one document is an interim agreement. It appears to contain your signature and the signature of the Garmazs. The property described in it is the residence of the Garmazs. There is a clause that says that this deal is subject to the purchase by the Garmazs of the acreage property which they had agreed to buy. Do you remember that as being part of the deal?"

I listened to Murphy's description and then glanced at the document. Although it was difficult to recall anything about it, the whole thing had a strange familiarity that impressed me at that moment. As I gazed at Murphy, I reflected on the difference between the human mind and a computer in recalling information. Unlike a computer, the human mind never completely erases anything and never recalls anything with complete accuracy. I desperately groped for details to visualize how this document might have came to exist. Slowly, I responded to Murphy in a cautious manner:

"I vaguely recall that this is how the deal first started. Garmaz was interested in living on the acreage in the beginning but later changed his mind. This agreement was then discarded. I'm sure that our deal actually proceeded on the basis of a second mortgage instead of a down payment and there was no trade involved. Why are they bringing this up when this has nothing to do with the real estate deal or the mortgage with Heritage Trust?"

Murphy listened thoughtfully, then removed his glasses and leaned back in his chair. Drawing on his experience, he began to describe his thoughts on the Crown's case and the reasons behind the procedures that they might employ:

"First of all, they lead this type of evidence at a Preliminary Hearing because they don't know if there is any relevance and it doesn't really matter to them. Their job is to put in any evidence that they have and to let the Judge decide if there is enough to set this case for trial. It's obvious that this evidence is way off base and has nothing to do with the Heritage Trust mortgage. However, they'll put it in anyway even if it doesn't have anything to do with the issues in this case."

Listening to Murphy's comments, I realized that this whole procedure was nothing more than a game or an exercise for the lawyers in the Crown Prosecutors office. After all, to them this was just one more file on their desks. The ramifications would only be felt by the person on trial. To a Crown Prosecutor, the less time spent on a file, the more time that was available for idle chatter and coffee breaks to relieve the monotony of their work. These lawyers are conditioned to the reality that there was no reward for exerting oneself more than necessary since the pay cheque always remained constant. The fact that time might be needlessly wasted in court was not a concern to Crown Prosecutors. Nor was it their concern that their protracted proceedings would be costly and painful for the person who anxiously waited for a criminal charge to be resolved. Murphy reflected for a moment and then continued with his personal assessment:

"The other thing to remember is that in a case like this, Eileen Nash knows that there is nothing really for evidence. Anything remotely connected is going to be put into evidence so that she doesn't look so bad in front of the Judge. If the document has no value as evidence in the case, Nash will use it to try and confuse the Judge. She will try to make it look like there is some evidence to consider even if there is none."

Murphy's last comment left me feeling uneasy as I attempted to comprehend this latest revelation of the tactics that could be used by the Crown Prosecutor. It was discomforting to hear that a Crown Prosecutor would introduce evidence that was not relevant because of a lack of desire to make a decision to exclude it. However, I was alarmed to hear that a Crown Prosecutor would intentionally introduce a document that was NOT relevant to confuse or mislead the Court. Such unethical conduct was always frowned upon as being improper and deserving of the highest sanctions by the Court and by the Law Society. I had no doubt that Murphy was speaking authoritatively based on his extensive experiences, both as a Defence Lawyer and a Crown Prosecutor. Murphy's comments had now introduced a whole new spectrum of concerns for me. For the first time, I was forced to confront the darker side of Court room antics.

While all these new concerns raced through my mind, I questioned Murphy further:

"Isn't there any procedure that we could use to insure that this document is correctly represented to the Court? Shouldn't we present evidence to properly describe what happened and to show that this document is totally irrelevant?"

Murphy quickly responded to calm my fears:

"Orest, you're getting way ahead of the situation at hand. The reason we are proceeding with a Preliminary Hearing first is to see exactly what evidence they may have. I am currently satisfied that there is no evidence. I'm going to argue at the end of the Preliminary Hearing that the criminal charge should be thrown out because there is no basis on which to send this charge to trial. If they raise anything that persuades a Judge to send it to trial, we'll call evidence at the trial to explain what happened. In any event, nothing should change in your life and therefore we should take the time to hear all the Crown's evidence at the Preliminary Hearing. I'm completely satisfied that this is the best way to handle this whole matter."

I then responded with a concern that was nagging at me from the beginning:

"I agree with your comments, Patrick! However, this procedure seems to be taking so long. This whole thing is so upsetting for me, for my wife and for my law practice. I just wish that I could get up in court, give my evidence and then get this resolved quickly. I don't know if I can wait to see this matter drag on through the Preliminary Hearing and then wait for a trial."

Murphy consoled me by responding sympathetically:

"Believe me, Orest! I understand how you feel. However, there is no real urgency to push ahead with a trial right now. By my assessment, this criminal charge will be thrown out at the Preliminary Hearing and there will be no trial. Stop worrying! Tell your wife to stop worrying. This will get resolved but it will take a little time. In the meantime, you still have your law practice. My best advice is to keep busy and don't dwell on this case. Leave this in my hands and concentrate on your law practice and raising your family."

I truly appreciated Murphy's kind words of encouragement and I knew that he was right with respect to the procedures we were following. The long delay in getting a case like this to trial was simply a fact of life in the Court system. The problem was that too many of these types of cases had found their way into the court system. The true solution was to resolve these types of cases without involving the court system. Many excellent proposals to revise various criminal offenses or to resolve them by arbitration have been proposed to achieve this objective. Unfortunately, such reform would require enlightenment and cooperation by politicians, judges, lawyers, police, and the public. To date, this has proven to be an insurmountable obstacle and remains the primary reason for negligible reform in the Justice system.

After acknowledging Murphy's considerate gestures, we both moved on to discussing the list of witnesses that he had received from the Crown Prosecutor. As Murphy read the name of each witness that was expected to be called at the Preliminary Hearing, we discussed what evidence we could predict the witness would be giving. As we continued our review, it occurred to me that we had the witness statement of Walter Pevcevicius and I asked Murphy if we had any others. Murphy immediately responded:

"No! We don't have any other statements from witnesses. That's really strange since there are usually all sorts of statements in these kinds of cases. When I spoke to Eileen Nash, I was told that she did not get any other statements from witnesses. I suspect that Christal is holding back on this evidence. It's probably part of his tactics to try and keep his case from evaporating. I know that there are other witness statements. I suspect that those have said things that would obviously clear you of any suggestion of wrongdoing. I'm going to keep after Eileen Nash to see if we can get all the other statements. I should warn you that I've seen cops just bury evidence and there's little that anyone can do about it. What we need is a law with more teeth to prevent this kind of conduct by police officers and Crown Prosecutors."

Ordinarily, I should have been shocked by what Murphy was saying. However, Murphy's comments seemed to fit so well with the conduct that I had already experienced regarding Christal. At that moment, I stared at Murphy in amazement and we both resigned ourselves to the fact that this whole investigation was handled in the same manner. The only thing that would now surprise us was to see Christal actually tell the truth about anything when he gave evidence in Court under oath. The grim reality was that as an experienced Court witness, he would be versatile in colouring his statements to convey exactly what he wished the court to hear in order to justify his conduct. Christal understood that this case would not be adjudicated on the basis of the truth but rather on the basis of what the various witnesses wanted the truth to be.

We continued with our assessment of witnesses and then slowly concluded our preparation for the Preliminary Hearing. When we glanced at the time, we realized that it was after eleven o'clock and we both agreed that we should conclude this meeting. As we picked up our files, Murphy remarked:

"I'm going to go over everything again before the date that we have to appear at the Preliminary Hearing. I'll call you to discuss any questions that may arise. I don't think it will be necessary for us to meet again unless you want to. Otherwise, we'll get together at nine o'clock in the morning on Monday, January 15, in the Court House cafeteria. If you think of anything that you want to discuss before then, please give me a call. We can talk on the phone or even get together for a meeting over coffee."

I thanked him for the invitation and stood up to leave. Moments later, I said good-bye and left. As I drove home, an uneasy feeling lingered within me as I tried to rationalize the conflicting thoughts that flashed through my mind. Murphy's assessment was clear and emphatic: THERE WAS NO EVIDENCE AND I SHOULDN'T WORRY. I resolved again to adopt a positive attitude and to allow him to handle this matter as we discussed. He was right when he said that the best thing for me to do was concentrate on my work and family. However, nothing could prevent the horror of this situation from filtering into every thought and into every moment in my life. Not even my subconscious dreams could shut out the lingering menace that Christal had created. I could only comfort myself with the reality that I would soon be able to face this nightmare in the Court room and eradicate it from my life. I silently prayed that the Preliminary Hearing would bring an end to this dark chapter in my life.

CHAPTER ELEVEN

THE PROVINCIAL COURT

T he Provincial Courts have always been regarded by some members of the judiciary as the "inferior" courts. This is in contrast to the Queen's Bench Court or the Appeal Court which previously were called THE SUPREME COURT of the province. In the criminal justice system, the Provincial Courts are the entry level of all criminal charges. These courts also hear and adjudicate all minor criminal and quasi-criminal offenses. Only the "serious" and "important" cases may be heard in the superior courts of the province. In those cases, it must first be determined at a hearing in Provincial Court that there is sufficient evidence to warrant a trial in Queen's Bench court. This hearing is called a "Preliminary Inquiry" or a "Preliminary Hearing"

In practical terms, the Provincial Courts are the "workhorses" of the Criminal Justice system because they handle a disproportionately larger amount of cases in year-round sittings. The Provincial Judges are usually more experienced with criminal cases as they often handle such cases exclusively. They are regarded by lawyers as generally much fairer in their assessments of criminal cases than the "superior" judges in Queen's Bench Court. This situation has created the practice among Criminal Defence lawyers of directing clients to Provincial Court if they are likely to be found guilty. Those cases with little or no incriminating evidence are taken to Queen's Bench Court because of the benefit of a Preliminary Hearing. That was the reason that Murphy chose to hold a Preliminary Hearing in my case with a trial in Queen's Bench Court.

The Provincial Courts had changed dramatically in the fifteen years since I began working as a lawyer. Fifteen years earlier, the Provincial Courts were crowded into a two-storey building that had formerly been a police station. The City Jail was in the basement and there were two smaller Court rooms in the basement which heard traffic offenses. The Main Floor and Upstairs housed the Criminal Court rooms, the Clerks Offices and offices for the Provincial Judges and Crown Prosecutors. The whole set-up was uncomfortable and barely adequate for the purposes that it served. The Provincial Judges dressed in business suits and were barely distinguishable from the lawyers who appeared before them. It was only when they mounted their elevated perches to adjudicate the cases of the masses that their authority became pronounced.

In contrast, the "superior" judges occupied a new monolithic structure across the street that conjured an image of foreboding consequences, both from the outside and from within. The dress uniform of "superior" judges was a specially tailored legal gown with a flashy red trim that gave them an untouchable air of distinction. The Court rooms were panelled in expensive wood that dulled the senses to life outside. These Court rooms had no windows and the perches were much loftier and overbearing than the modest setting of the Provincial

Courts. These Superior Court rooms left no doubt for anyone that this was the Supreme Court and that these judges were the reincarnation of God himself.

The disparity between the Provincial Judges and their superior brethren ultimately resulted in pressure from the legal community on the Provincial government to improve the status and working conditions of Provincial Judges. The Minister then made a political decision that it was in the taxpayers' best interest to elevate these lowly Judges to a new level of greater distinction. It was rationalized that the additional money spent to do so would be justified by an improved Criminal Justice system. The metamorphosis began with a dramatic increase in the salary of Provincial Judges. These Judges were also provided with specially tailored gowns featuring a purple trim to magnify their importance. A new Provincial Court facility was built as an annex to the monolithic superior Court complex with expensively appointed offices and Courtrooms for these previously neglected Judges.

Unfortunately, this new increased expenditure of taxpayers' money did little to improve "justice" in the Criminal Court system or to accelerate the disposition of cases. Instead, the effect of this new-found importance for Provincial Judges only made them more aloof and removed from those people who appeared before them in the Court room. Furthermore, the general public now found themselves appearing before a more prestigious Provincial Court and felt more alienated by the threatening presence of this new environment. The Provincial Courts had now ceased to be a "Peoples Court" where ordinary citizens felt comfortable in bringing forth their cases. Instead, it was now an imitation of the superior courts and magnified all the flaws of those courts.

Curiously, the only opposition to these changes came from the "Superior" Judges because they were opposed to "their" building losing its monolithic appearance. The idea of sticking an annex on the side of it to accommodate the inferior Provincial Judges was particularly upsetting to them. Additionally, these "Superior" Judges also voiced opposition, although less forcefully, to the proposed status upgrading. They felt that it would create an appearance of a loss in their "Superior" distinction as the image of the Provincial Judges improved. It was interesting to see the politicians ignore the demands of these privileged "superior" icons in their decision to create another class of elite Judges.

As the world ushered in the New Year of 1990 with fanfare and euphoric optimism, a singular event kept me in apprehension. Each day brought me one day closer to my Preliminary Hearing which would determine if the criminal charge against me would be committed for trial. In rapid succession, the days disappeared as the fateful day of my Hearing approached.

When the day finally arrived, I could no longer hide the nervous anxiety that was plaguing my life and disrupting all my thoughts and activities. I was weary from lack of sleep and exhausted from battling this endless turmoil in my life. Like a zombie, I stumbled through my morning routine before leaving for the Court House.

As I neared the entrance into the Court House, I comforted myself with the thought that I would soon be at the cafeteria where I could obtain a hot beverage. I knew that I was early and I wanted to enjoy a few moments relaxing before Murphy arrived for our briefing. As I rounded the corner, I hoped that I wouldn't meet anyone who would engage me in conversation since that would naturally lead to questions about my presence in Court. What I needed was to be alone for a few minutes to relax and I prayed that I would be afforded that blessing.

In the cafeteria, I immediately recognized the faces of some lawyers who typically had their morning coffee meetings there before proceeding to Court. These coffee cup meanderings had become a standard ritual for many lawyers. It afforded them the opportunity to exchange stories, jokes, and most importantly, gossip that was unavailable through any other medium. The peculiar irony of these inappropriate gossip sessions was that these lawyers inevitably breached the confidentiality of their clients and their responsibility for ethical conduct. Yet they willingly, and even gleefully, engaged in gossip and rumour mongering at the expense of their clients and fellow lawyers.

Sadly, many of these lawyers were so consumed by their work that they had no meaningful social life. Their only escapism was to laugh at and ridicule others who they felt were less fortunate. Because this activity reflected the darker side of the legal profession, it held a strange attraction for newcomers. These "Wanna Be" lawyers willingly attached themselves to this circle of friends in the hope that such comradarie would one day help to distinguish them as esteemed lawyers in the legal fraternity.

As I glanced around the room, I determined quickly that Murphy had not arrived. I secured a hot chocolate and sat down at an isolated table in plain view of the entrance. After a few minutes, I felt more relaxed. As a distraction from the thoughts that haunted me, I began to look around the room at the activity at other tables. As I studied the scene, I began to gain a new perspective on the work of lawyers from a client's point of view. Some of the tables featured lawyers talking to their clients about their cases. I expected that this would soon be the scene at my table. The expressions and actions of the lawyers and the reactions of the clients was enough to tell the story of these solicitor and client relationships.

It was painful for me to watch these lawyers give their impersonal advice while disassociating and distancing themselves from the sorrow and misery of their clients. The only beacon of hope that these clients had was elusively hidden in the fog of the Criminal Justice system. Many of these clients would never see justice or even know why it eluded them. The adage that a lawyer earns his money from the misery of his clients has its origin in these types of circumstances. After studying the distraught faces of the clients, I had to admit that there was a significant amount of accuracy in that description.

On checking my watch I noticed that it was almost nine o'clock and I began to feel some concern that Murphy would be late, or worse, that he might not make it for some reason. I began to panic as I contemplated this possibility. I was not prepared for an adjournment or a delay for any reason. A few minutes later, I was relieved to see Murphy appear in the doorway. As soon as he saw me, he acknowledged me with a nod of his head and a smile. He then headed for the coffee dispenser and the cashier before coming to join me.

As Murphy approached my table, he smiled and remarked:

"Hi, Orest. Did you get what you wanted for Christmas?"

I knew that Murphy was trying to lift my spirits and relax my fears and concerns. I understood his intentions and I appreciated his gestures and his concern for me. For that reason, I wanted to respond with warm and witty jesting. However, this whole situation was consuming me emotionally and I could only respond with the sentiments that burned in my mind:

"Well, Patrick! What I wanted for Christmas was for this Criminal charge to be resolved. Instead what I got was socks."

Murphy always waited for an opportunity to inject some humour and this was the best shot he was going to get. Spontaneously, he retorted:

"Well, at least you'll have warm feet this winter."

Murphy then lit up with laughter and forced me to smile as well. This brought a temporary reprieve from the anguish that I was silently harbouring. It was these moments that made me grateful to be in Murphy's company during this traumatic time in my life. As we chatted briefly about the joy of the Christmas season, it was hard to imagine that we would soon be involved in a battle to eradicate the criminal charge that had traumatized my life.

After a few minutes, Murphy was ready to tackle the topic of the pending Court proceedings:

"Well, Orest, I have reviewed everything pretty thoroughly. Now, I'm ready to proceed. I'll be speaking to Eileen Nash this morning about the witnesses that she will be calling and the order that they will be called. As the Hearing moves along, we'll have time to talk and I'll answer any questions that you have."

As Murphy finished his remarks, I interjected:

"Is there anything that I can do to assist you in these proceedings, Patrick?"

Murphy responded benevolently in acknowledging my gesture:

"Orest, in these types of proceedings, there really isn't anything for an accused to do except sit back and listen to the evidence. I would like you to make notes of all of the evidence. Let me know if there is anything that you think should be covered in the cross-examination of any particular witness. Other than that, we'll just have to see how this whole thing unfolds in court."

Suddenly Murphy began to rise from his chair. I glanced at my watch and noticed that it was ten minutes before the time set for the commencement of the court hearing. Murphy then suggested:

"I guess we'd better get over to the Court room and get ready to proceed. I'd like to have a few minutes to talk to Eileen Nash before we get started. Is there anything else that you'd like to discuss?"

I nodded that there wasn't and I grabbed my coat and briefcase. We both carried our cups over to the conveyor belt that carried dirty dishes to the kitchen area. Moments later we were out the door and on our way to the elevator.

As I walked with Murphy, I was surprised that I now felt at peace. I attributed this to having released control of my destiny to Murphy. Whatever was to happen, it was now beyond my ability to change anything. I was merely a spectator in the events that would unfold before me, regardless of the significant ramifications that they would have in my life. My emotions were totally drained and I now simply moved along like a robot under the control of the system, ready to endure whatever consequence might result.

On entering the designated Court room, I sat down on the back bench. Meanwhile Murphy walked over to the lawyers table which faced the Judge's elevated perch. While he removed the files from his briefcase and placed them on his table, he cordially exchanged greetings with the Crown Prosecutor. Nash was exchanging remarks with Christal but this ended abruptly as she turned away from him, leaving Christal to slink to a bench and sit down. She then rose from her chair and approached Murphy with a large black binder in her hand.

Although I had only glanced at Eileen Nash during my first Court appearance, I now was able to make a more careful observation of her. Her stature was short, thin and abnormally scrawny. Her hideous black outfit must have been specifically chosen to provide an unattractive and stark contrast to her deathly pale-white facial complexion. Nash's ghoulish appearance could have given new meaning to the phrase "Scared Straight". Her dyed black hair and her abnormal skin colour were reminiscent of the character of Morticia in the movie, "The Addams Family". However, her facial expressions were cold and unfriendly which made her unappealing for black comedy. Her most noticeable and detracting facial feature was her long, bent, crooked and protruding nose. It accentuated the cold and sinister image that she portrayed and made her an excellent casting choice for a witch in a children's play. The image that she projected was an unsettling vision in this uncomfortable setting.

It is an accurate observation that many lawyers are unusual characters in appearance as well as personality. Some of the best remembered lawyers who garnered their share of notoriety had unusual mannerisms, unorthodox approaches and unsightly clothes. A notable example was that of Clarence Darrow, an American criminal lawyer whose rumpled, unlaundered business suit became his recognizable trade mark. Also, the current popular television show of Matlock portrays a quirky, folksy, sloppy, unfashionably dressed criminal lawyer. In that manner, this program is a more realistic portrayal of criminal lawyers. This can be contrasted to the equally popular television show of Perry Mason, who is presented as neat, articulate, well groomed and fashionably dressed. Nash did not fit any recognizable mold and was instead a unique and very unusual character. It was easy to conclude that much of her image was intentionally developed to project that ghoulish image before the courts. For a moment, I wondered why anyone would chose to project such an unlikable image. I concluded that perhaps this evolved because of her self-perception of doing dark and sinister work which caused misery, pain and anguish to those people whose cases she prosecuted. Often, lawyers begin to shape their images to conform to the work that they do and this would certainly explain why Nash chose to project the image that she did.

As Murphy and Nash exchanged remarks and glanced through the large black binder that Nash presented to Murphy, the Clerk approached them to ask if they were ready to proceed. The Clerk was wearing a black robed outfit similar to the outfit worn by lawyers in trials in the Queen's Bench Court. This outfit was in contrast to the civilian dress clothes worn by the Court Reporter who sat at the table next to the Clerk. This new dress code for Clerks was also a measure implemented by the Provincial government. This change was also intended to upgrade the physical status of Provincial Courts to make these Courts more meaningful to the general public. Sadly, this new dress code made the atmosphere of the Provincial Courts more unapproachable and removed in the perspective of the average person. Ironically, these "improvements" actually worked to diminish a valuable attribute that the Provincial Courts formerly had.

The role of the Court Clerk and the Court Reporter were both remnants of the old English Court system that was adopted in Canada during our colonial inception. These archaic procedures and roles remain in the Canadian Court system only because of custom and tradition rather than necessity. The Court Reporter's job is to record every word that is spoken during the Court proceedings for the "Court Record". Initially, this was handwritten in shorthand hieroglyphics by the Court Reporter. However, in the last fifteen years, I witnessed the transition to a portable shorthand typing machine. This is then transcribed into a type-written and certified-accurate transcript for the use of the lawyers and judges. From the advent of tape recorders, Court Reporters have always used them as a back-up for easy reference. With the advances in technology, audio recording has eliminated the need for Court Reporters to sit in court and record everything in shorthand in addition to making an audio recording. In fact, some court proceedings such as circuit courts have always relied on audio recordings only.

Similarly, the role of the Court Clerk is unnecessary. It is largely confined to bringing the Court file into Court, marking exhibits and generally running errands for the judge. During the majority of the court time, the Clerk sits at her table and tries not to fall asleep from boredom. Obviously, the tasks of the Court clerk could be handled by the judge complimented by a system for calling the Clerk's office if anything is required in Court. Although this would create a significant savings of taxpayers money, judges have opposed such proposed changes because they enjoy the luxury and prestige of these "servants" in the Court room.

With a nod, Nash and Murphy acknowledged to the Clerk that they were ready to proceed. The Clerk immediately disappeared through a door at the back of the Court room which emptied into a hallway leading to the Judges' offices. Pursuant to the established procedure, it was expected that a Judge would wait in his office until advised that everyone was ready for his arrival. This was necessary because court proceedings rarely started at the scheduled time. Furthermore, it was unthinkable that a judge should be kept waiting even for a few seconds outside the Court room. Only after being advised by the Clerk that all parties were ready to proceed would a judge actually leave his office to go to the Court room. Everyone could wait for a judge to arrive but the judge would wait for nobody.

I witnessed a good illustration of this sacred rule in the old Provincial Court Building before Judge Ken Plomp. Plomp was appointed as a Provincial Judge in the days when the Provincial government was appointing retired police officers to the position because of a shortage of qualified candidates. Plomp had actually taken time off from his work as a Provincial Judge to attend Law School in 1972. However, he found the concepts of law too difficult to understand so he dropped out of Law School. Ironically, he was not qualified to advise anyone on the law but the Government still employed him to judge whether people had contravened the law. This is a good illustration of the fact that an aspiring judicial appointee doesn't necessarily need to know anything about the law to be a Judge.

On one memorable occasion, Plomp became agitated because he had to wait outside the Court room while the Crown Prosecutor organized the cases to proceed. Suddenly Plomp barged into the Court room, convened Court and began calling cases in random order. When the Crown Prosecutor was unable to respond, he arbitrarily dismissed the criminal charges. Even cases that were proposed to be adjourned were suddenly resolved with a dismissal of the charge. It became a glorious day for anyone whose case was on that Docket. Presumably, this was a message to all Crown Prosecutors that this Judge would wait for nobody!

As we waited for the judge to arrive, Murphy motioned that he wanted to speak to me and then asked that I sit near the front and closer to him. I complied by settling into a seat in the front bench directly behind Murphy. The wooden benches themselves were contoured more for appearance than comfort and were in sharp contrast to the cushion padded chairs provided to the lawyers, clerks and judge. These benches served the purpose of providing the general public with a cold, hard and uncomfortable place to sit while observing the proceedings. It was a compelling conclusion that these benches were intended to communicate the message to those who sat in them that the justice to be dispensed would also feel the same.

Suddenly, the silence of the Court room was shattered as the back door opened and the Clerk announced in a loud voice: "ORDER IN COURT!". Behind her trailed the judge who immediately climbed the steps to his elevated perch and plopped himself into his oversized high-backed leather swivel chair. As he looked down on the lawyers before him, both of them greeted him with "Good-morning, Your Honour" and quickly bowed their heads in a customary gesture to show respect. The judge then acknowledged their greeting, opened his notebook and looked to Nash for her remarks about the case to be heard that morning.

The judge was E.D. Stack, one of the more experienced judges on the Provincial Court bench. He was tall with rugged facial features but outwardly friendly and amicable. He was known to be patient and courteous to everyone and had a good reputation for listening to submissions and evidence without prejudging anyone. Murphy admitted later that he was confident that we would get a fair hearing from Stack. Murphy was also satisfied that there was a good likelihood that Stack would throw the criminal charge out if we could demonstrate that there was no evidence on which to commit the charge for trial in Queen's Bench Court. It all looked so promising!

As is customary in all Court cases, Nash and Murphy identified themselves and the case for the Court record. Nash began by identifying herself and the case before the Court. Murphy then rose to his feet to identify himself and to acknowledge that I, the accused, was present in Court. In doing so, he directed Stack's attention to me by pointing his finger at me. This simple formality really put everything into perspective for Stack. In effect, it communicated that I was on trial to prove that I was not the "dirty, rotten scoundrel" that the Crown Prosecutor was about to prosecute. In those few seconds, I was reduced to the humbling position of an outcast of society who had erred in his judgement. I would now be examined to determine what fate would befall me. Gone was my expectation that I would be treated as being "innocent until proven guilty". Instead, it was painfully obvious that I and my lawyer would have to satisfy this Judge that I was not deserving of any consequence or sanctions from the Court.

Nash then proceeded to explain to Stack that she had prepared binders that contained photocopies of documents that would be introduced into evidence. A large black binder was handed to Stack and Nash then explained that the tabs in the binder were numbered with the Exhibit Numbers that she proposed should be assigned to each document. While Nash paused, Murphy acknowledged that he had no objection to the proposed procedure. Nash then continued by stating that she was ready to start the Preliminary Hearing. At that moment, she advised Stack that she wished to make an opening statement with a brief description of the evidence that she would call during the Hearing. This was supposed to assist Stack in understanding the evidence that he was about to hear. Although this procedure is common in jury trials to assist the lay people on the jury, it was unusual in Preliminary Hearings before judges. However, Stack nodded in agreement and Nash proceeded with her statement.

As I listened to Nash's description of what she proposed to prove as the facts of what happened in my real estate transaction, I was shocked and flabbergasted. The statements of Nash were nothing short of pure fiction and appeared to be specifically crafted to cast the darkest possible shadow on me. Her speech was intentionally designed to effectively set the stage for my execution. I had to wonder who her script writers were and if her imagination hadn't been permanently damaged from watching too many soap operas.

As I glanced at Murphy, I noticed that he had stopped making notes and was staring at Nash. His expressions confirmed that he was also having difficulty believing that Nash was actually saying such things about my case. Although these theatrical performances are standard in television Court room dramas, there are totally inappropriate in an actual Court room and very unusual in a Preliminary Hearing. Obviously, Nash was aware of what evidence she actually had to put before the Court.

In contradiction to the reality of the case, she was telling a story of devious manipulation that might have been taken out of a best-selling fiction novel. The story was completed by her description of me as a criminal genius who seditiously masterminded every move of every individual. Nash then stated that she hoped to demonstrate that everyone in the transaction had unwittingly become a part of my incredible plot to arrange a mortgage on property which I didn't intend to own. Nash's comments were stunning and shocking as everyone listened intently. I might otherwise have been intrigued by the story if I wasn't being so maliciously defamed by it.

As Nash continued her narrative, Murphy glanced at me with an expression of disbelief. He then nodded his head which conveyed to me that he would handle this situation. As I listened to Nash complete her narration, I wondered if Stack would even bother to listen to the evidence. After all, it was now obvious that he was dealing with a devious and dangerous criminal who should be reprimanded by the courts. Why would any judge have to spend any time worrying about this case. With this much suspicion, he could simply say that he felt that this matter should be set for trial and not worry about guilt or innocence. The real question now was whether Stack, after hearing such a description of improper conduct, would want to expend any energy listening to evidence that might vindicate me.

The full speech only lasted a few minutes but it seemed much longer to me. As soon as Nash completed her remarks, she immediately declared that she was calling her first witness, Detective Don Christal. I sat there dazed from the shock of her narration. I began to slide into depression as I realized that my lawyer would not even be given the chance to respond to Nash's lies, exaggerations and fictions. How could there be any justice if the proceedings were one-sided? I wondered why Stack didn't give Murphy a chance to comment in response to Nash's remarks. These queries would remain unanswered as everyone ignored these shortcomings of the Criminal Justice system.

We were off to a bad start and it was too late to deal with the damage that was done. It was obvious now that Stack's opinions and assessments would be formed from Nash's perception of the evidence. He would naturally view everything in the context of this initial description of what happened. Therefore, it would be difficult to dissuade Stack from reacting to what Nash was pressuring him to accept as fact. His opinions would be formed before Murphy could present our case. He would be biased toward Nash's position irrespective of how impressive our position was.

Moments later, Christal was on the stand and giving evidence about the exhibits that appeared in the Exhibit binder. As each document was handed to him, he identified it as a document that he had seized and the source of each document. Each document was then marked as an Exhibit by the clerk and identified in the binder for the convenience of the others in Court. As I sat and watched this tedious procedure, I reflected on Murphy's predictions of the likely approach to be used by the Crown Prosecutor. Her tactic was to create suspicion to make it look like there was evidence of wrongdoing on my part. The best way to do this was to paint a dark picture of my conduct and to introduce documents that might reflect on my involvement in the transaction. The fact that the documents were irrelevant to a charge of fraud did not appear to be important to Nash. If it looked confusing to the judge, then maybe he would accept the Crown's theory, no matter how irrational or inconceivable it might be.

This approach, of course, was not a fair way to present the case. However, nothing that Christal did in the investigation had been fair. Also, there was no rule that the Crown Prosecutor had to be fair. After all, she was now attempting to validate the actions of the police officer. If it meant that Nash would have to use desperate tactics to do so, there was nobody who would fault her. Nash admitted to Murphy that she didn't have a case and she knew that there was no fraud. Even so, that would not prevent her from using every tactic that she could to maintain the criminal charge. In this case, that meant hampering our efforts to have the criminal charge thrown out at this initial stage of the criminal proceedings.

Making notes of this evidence was difficult because I didn't have an Exhibit Binder and I therefore didn't know exactly what the exhibits were. I could feel my nervous system erupting with frustration as I watched Nash and Christal cleverly weave the web that was intended to entangle me in the court system. Helplessly, I watched as they used their moments of live presentation before the judge to their maximum advantage to colour the proceedings and manipulate the system. I realized that this was merely a well-practised game for them which each of them had played so many times before in other court proceedings. The tricks and the ploys were all there. Although it must have been obvious to Stack and Murphy, they accepted it as part of the game with no reaction of shock or disapproval. I knew that Murphy and I would have our hands full as we attempted to fight off the suggestions that were being so effectively embedded in Stack's mind.

Christal continued his identification of the documents that appeared in the Exhibit binders for approximately one hour. At this juncture, Nash indicated that she would be adjourning her examination of Christal. She then stated that she would be calling him as a witness after the other Crown evidence had been presented. Murphy then rose and acknowledged that this was satisfactory and Stack ordered a short adjournment to allow everyone to take a coffee break. At this point, the Clerk called out "Order in Court". Everyone stood up as Stack stepped down from his perch and slipped out the back door of the Court room.

Although I tried to catch Murphy's attention, he had walked over to Nash's table to talk to her. I waited until he came back to his table before I called to him. As Murphy walked over to speak to me privately, I blurted out to him with pent-up frustration:

"Patrick, what Eileen Nash said was totally false! There was so little that resembled this case. It was a total fabrication! How can she tell such lies in Court and get away with it?"

Murphy looked at me sympathetically and responded:

"Orest, I know it's not accurate and so does Judge Stack. This opening statement by the Crown Prosecutor is just her description of what she hopes the evidence will show. Naturally it's inaccurate. After all, nobody knows what the witnesses will actually say. A Judge doesn't pay much attention to these statements and they won't have any effect on his decision. So, don't let that bother you."

Murphy may have been prepared to let this situation slide but I was very upset and I wanted something done about it. I pressed Murphy with a further comment:

"I understand what you're saying. However, the statement was made to influence the decision of the judge. I have no doubt that Judge Stack was influenced by what he heard. Everything that the witnesses say now will be heard in the context of what Eileen Nash described. Isn't there something you can say as a rebuttal? Can't you at least object to what she said on the basis that it's totally inaccurate and inflammatory?"

Murphy listened thoughtfully and then noticed that Nash was about to leave the Court room. He blurted out as he began to move away to catch up to Nash:

"I don't think it's a good idea to say anything right now. It will focus too much attention on it. We'll get our chance to respond after the Crown's evidence is all in. At that time, we can put everything into perspective. I've got to speak to Eileen Nash right now but we'll talk more about this later."

As I watched Murphy quickly leave the Court room, I realized that this hearing was not simply a situation in which the judge would objectively analyze the evidence before him. This was going to be a dirty dog fight and the stakes were high for Christal and for me. Nash was poising herself to be Christal's "Red Baron". Their objective was to win this part of the battle by using whatever underhanded tactics that they needed to employ. If they could make me look dirty, it didn't matter whether or not I had done anything illegal. The bad impression of the judge might be enough to have the charge against me committed for trial in Queen's Bench Court. At that point, Christal would be vindicated and I would be involved in the battle of my life.

I sat there feeling stunned as I watched Christal gather up his files and arrogantly walk out of the Court room. I realized that I was doing battle in his arena and that he was far better prepared for this battle than I was. My only hope was that my lawyer could wage a strong enough rebuttal to show the judge that there was no evidence of wrongdoing on my part. I now knew that I was in for a rough ride. I simply had to maintain a calm composure if I was going to be helpful to Murphy.

CHAPTER TWELVE

THE CROWN WITNESSES

One of the procedural requirements of our Criminal Justice system is that the Crown Prosecutor is first required to put before the Court sufficient evidence to justify a conviction on the criminal charge. The actual amount of evidence needed is typically determined by the pre-disposition of the judge to convict the accused person. Frequently, the biased or cynical pre-disposition of the judge allows a Crown Prosecutor to secure a conviction on speculative theories and inconclusive evidence. In such a case, all that is really required is to convey to the judge that the accused person is believed to be guilty by the police and therefore should be found guilty.

Evidence before a Criminal Court is introduced through the verbal testimony of Crown witnesses. These involve police officers and public citizens who are served with a Court Notice called a "subpoena" which requires the person to appear before the Court to testify. If that person refuses to attend or testify, he is inevitably declared to be in contempt of Court and put in jail. In this manner, Crown Prosecutors have forced innocent people, family members and even spouses to testify in Court against their wishes. It is not uncommon to find people in custody who forgot about a subpoena and who are forced to sit in jail waiting for the next trial date while the accused person is free on bail.

The idealistic view of Crown witnesses is that they are called to testify in fulfillment of a public duty to assist the Court. In fact, only occasionally does a Crown witness give impartial evidence and a fair and accurate account of what they observed. The more typical situation is the Crown witness who is motivated by a personal vested interest in the ultimate outcome of the criminal proceedings.

It is not unusual for a Crown witness to testify for the sole purpose of placing the blame on the accused person in the hope of excusing or disguising any improper conduct of the witness. Often the key Crown witness will be offered an exemption from prosecution for evidence that implicates and convicts another party of the criminal offence. Although such arrangements are justified by police and Crown Prosecutors as being necessary to secure convictions, the motivations of these witnesses are never disclosed. The effect of this arrangement is that the evidence is presented in a polished and unblemished fashion with the skilled preparation of the police investigator and the Crown Prosecutor. As a result, the Crown witness knows exactly what to say to insure that the accused person is convicted and the Crown witness can enjoy the promised immunity.

Another motivation of many Crown witnesses is simply to justify their role or conduct in the circumstances surrounding the crime and the resulting investigation. The police officer is motivated to give evidence which will prove the guilt of the accused person to justify his decision for laying the charge. The other Crown witnesses will want to distance themselves from any wrongdoing by convincing the Court that any fault lies with the accused person. With the counselling from the police and the Crown Prosecutor, the necessary evidence to implicate the accused person is put before the Court to satisfy these motivations.

Perhaps the most common motivation of Crown witnesses is the desire to punish somebody for a crime. This sentiment is understandable for a victim but is also a salient factor in the actions of police officers and other Crown witnesses. Those who are not victims are driven by a desire to combat crime in the hope that their efforts will create a safer society. When the police charge an accused person, the Crown witnesses modify their recollections and present their testimony to conform to the conclusions proposed by the police. A conviction of an accused person is seen as a necessary outcome of a Court proceeding. In this way, a punishment can be rendered for the crime and the community can become a safer place to live.

Unless the Crown witness is a police officer, he usually has no experience with the Court system. The experience of appearing in Court presents unique problems because of the unusual process that each case follows. Ultimately, it is these very procedures that create frustration and disillusionment for the general public. The most aggravating aspect of any court proceedings is that each case is subjected to delays, adjournments and long rest breaks. No court proceedings ever start before nine-thirty or ten o'clock in the morning. Lunch breaks are typically two hours long and few court proceedings ever continue beyond four o'clock in the afternoon. Ideally, there are two hours of court time in the morning and two hours of court time in the afternoon. However, there is the mid-morning and mid-afternoon break which is supposed to be for fifteen minutes but may last as long as thirty minutes. Then, when the court is actually in session, there are procedural delays which result in the entire process being slow and cumbersome.

This procedure of procrastination requires lawyers to adapt to a "coffee culture" because they spend so much time taking coffee breaks with clients and other lawyers. Because of the monotony of these extended delays in the court proceedings, the favourite pastime among Court room lawyers is the exchange of gossip which is naturally focused on other lawyers or clients. Because such gossip, especially as it relates to clients, is unethical, lawyers will huddle together to hear whispered accounts that will relieve their boredom. Sadly, many lawyers enjoy hearing stories of ill-fate suffered by other lawyers or clients as it elevates their own self-esteem and makes their depressing work somehow more bearable.

For a member of the general public who by misfortune finds himself engulfed in these strange proceedings, a feeling of alienation is inevitable. The surroundings are cold and uncomfortable. The situation is stressful and emotionally traumatic. The lawyers, clerks, and judges are intentionally distant from the individual affected. It is little wonder that anyone whose case comes before the courts ultimately remembers it as a distasteful and disappointing experience. For this reason, it is said that the statute of the goddess who holds the scales of justice is blindfolded, partly because the sight of the way these proceedings are conducted would disgust her.

Because the Court rooms are locked during each adjournment, I had to wait in the outside vestibule areas. This provided a change from the Court room but also made the waiting much more tedious. As people shuffled to and from Court rooms, I glanced at the faces of these victims of the Criminal Justice system. For each face there was a personal story of anguish, pain and sorrow. It suddenly occurred to me that I had seen such expressions before on countless faces as I walked in and out of court to represent clients. Regretfully, I never once took the time to reflect on the torment and heartache that these people felt. They were helpless victims in a system that showed no sympathy for those who became entangled in it. Now, after working as a lawyer for sixteen years, I was seeing the whole process and the people in it from a different perspective. What I saw was now very disturbing!

My impatience began to mount until Murphy suddenly appeared through the doorway with Nash. As they entered, they both remained engrossed in their conversation. When Murphy noticed me, he concluded his remarks to Nash and walked over to talk to me. As he drew nearer, he began to explain:

"I'm sorry I couldn't talk to you earlier but I had to speak to Eileen Nash. I needed to ask her about the witnesses that she intended to call today. We have to go in right now but is there anything that you wanted to ask before we start up again?"

At that moment, I had a multitude of questions and I wanted to get Murphy's candid opinions. However, I knew that this was not the moment for me to do so. Reluctantly, I shrugged my shoulders and responded:

"That's fine, Patrick! We can talk during the lunch break."

Murphy nodded and smiled. We then both turned and walked into the Court room to face the drudgery of sitting in our uncomfortable seats while Nash paraded out more Crown witnesses. These proceedings never attract any spectators because of the slow procedural nature involved. For lawyers who have endured an endless array of these types of proceedings, the challenge is to remain alert in spite of the monotony. Also, the Defence lawyer is expected to respond to the Crown's evidence by asking relevant questions which might demonstrate the weakness or futility of the Crown Prosecutor's efforts. The boredom is most noticeable on the judge who must attempt to make notes and appear to be interested without participating in the efforts of bringing out any of the evidence from the Crown witnesses.

As we entered the Court room, the Clerk immediately left to advise the Judge that all parties were ready to proceed. Moments later, the Clerk reappeared with her announcement: "Order in Court!" After Stack positioned himself on his elevated perch, Nash proceeded by calling her next Crown witness, Nadia Foster. Foster and her husband sold the acreage property to my company. She was called as a witness to identify the agreements that were entered relating to the sale. She admitted that she had no dealings with me and that all communications were made through her realtor, Doug Hawryluk.

Foster was noticeably apprehensive about being in Court and her testimony was short. The main fact in her testimony was that this transaction happened six years earlier and that she couldn't remember much about it. When Nash completed her examination of Foster, she asked her to answer Murphy's questions. After a brief pause, Murphy rose to his feet while studying the notes he had just made. Then with one hand, he awkwardly removed his glasses, creating the impression that he was still pre-occupied with his thoughts. In a low voice, he began his cross-examination of Foster. Murphy's approach was to re-affirm the fact that Foster could not recall anything very well. She also confirmed that her husband had no contact with the purchaser of their property.

After a few more questions, Murphy announced to the Court that he had nothing further to ask. Stack then asked Nash if she had any further questions arising from Murphy's questions. When Nash confirmed that she didn't, Stack advised Foster that she was excused as a witness and thanked her for coming. This procedure was a standard practice before the Court and was followed for each witness in these proceedings.

The next witness called was Doug Hawryluk, the realtor who arranged the transaction. Hawryluk had known me for a long time and I was not only his friend but his lawyer. He appeared uncomfortable when he entered the Court room. I concluded that he was troubled by the sterile, cold environment and the idea that he was giving testimony on a criminal charge that he openly confided to me to be unfair. His testimony consisted of identifying documents and describing the sequence of them. His comments about discussions and events were prefaced by his admission that he could not possibly remember what happened in this routine transaction six years ago. Murphy's cross-examination was again very short and didn't raise anything of interest.

The testimony of both witnesses was routine and only necessary to identify documents relating to the purchase of the Foster property by my company. At the conclusion of Hawryluk's testimony, Nash asked Judge Stack to adjourn the proceedings to the afternoon. Stack seemed enthusiastic to do so and immediately announced that the proceedings were adjourned. After Stack quickly exited, I waited for Murphy to collect up his files into his briefcase and then we both left the Court room together. As we reached the outside waiting area, Murphy suggested that we could have a discussion at 1:45 in the afternoon. He suggested that we would then have a good opportunity to chat before Court resumed at two o'clock. Murphy explained that he needed to make some telephone calls so I decided that I would run some errands downtown and have a quick lunch at one of the cafeterias nearby.

I was back at the Court House early for my meeting with Murphy. To utilize this time productively, I sat down in the outside waiting area and took some reading material out of my briefcase. The waiting area was empty except for a few lost souls such as myself who were forced by circumstance to wait in these uncomfortable surroundings. In spite of my best efforts, my mind was continually wrestling with feelings of apprehension as the minutes ticked away. I found it impossible to relax or to focus my mind on any thoughts other than the pending proceedings. Questions and fears flashed through my mind randomly and soon my mind began to show a nervous reaction to this overload of stimuli. I decided to clear my mind of all these concerns and to focus on the questions that I would discuss with Murphy during our imminent meeting.

The main question that I had for Murphy was whether he had learned anything from Nash about my case that might offer any hope for a resolution of this matter. Generally, a defence lawyer will have "off-the-record" conversations with the Crown Prosecutor to see if there is some hope of clearing up the charge and to learn more about the Crown's case. I knew that Murphy would be reluctant to discuss this with me since any information he got from Nash would be given on the condition that it wouldn't be repeated to anyone. However, this wouldn't keep me from asking. I was sure that Murphy would give me some kind of indication of what was about to happen and whether there was anything hopeful in what Nash said.

As I continued to evaluate the questions that I wanted to ask Murphy, I looked up and saw him approaching. Murphy smiled broadly and then remarked:

"So there you are; off in the corner! I was hoping that you were here so that we could have more time to talk. Let's see if we can get into one of these conference rooms. That way, we'll have some privacy."

The conference rooms were located outside of each Court room on each side of a walk-though area leading from the waiting area. They were specifically designed to provide an area for private conversations between lawyers and their clients. Each conference room was small and furnished with a standard table and four chairs. Occasionally, one of these rooms would have a telephone available for lawyers to make urgent telephone calls.

As Murphy checked the conference rooms outside of the Court room that we were attending, he found them to be locked. He then asked me to check the other conference rooms outside the adjacent Court rooms. A quick check of the other conference rooms confirmed the same situation. We were soon standing in the middle of the vestibule area wondering where we could hold our meeting. Murphy was exasperated and his frustration showed as he remarked:

"Isn't this ridiculous? Just because a cop got horny and couldn't keep his prick in his pants, we all have to suffer with this stupid situation."

Murphy's comment left me in a state of disbelief as I tried to rationalize what he was trying to tell me. What I heard was certainly unusual for Murphy since he normally avoided profanity and seldom even joked about sex. My look of astonishment must have been obvious to Murphy because he immediately inquired:

"Didn't you hear what happened in this Court House, about two weeks ago?"

I nodded to Murphy that I hadn't and then he continued with his explanation:

"Oh, I thought you knew! Everyone around the Court House has been joking about it. The reason these conference rooms are locked when the Courts are not in session is because an Edmonton police officer was caught having sex in a conference room with one of the clerks during the noon recess break. The police officer was here to testify in court. While he was waiting, he started flirting with one of the clerks in the Clerk's office. They both got hot and excited and decided not to wait any longer. Instead of sneaking off to a hotel across the street, they decided to get right at it in one of the conference rooms. Naturally they were discovered and the story quickly spread throughout the Court House."

As I listened to Murphy's incredible story, I realized that this scene would be perfect for an episode on a television soap opera if it wasn't so incredible to believe. Who would actually believe a police officer and a clerk having a sexual romp in the Court House during a break in the Court proceedings? After all, these two people were involved in law enforcement and were discovered committing a criminal offence by performing an indecent act in a public place. The biggest irony of the situation was that the public place in question was the Court House which was supposed to be revered as the temple of justice and righteousness by the visiting public.

It suddenly occurred to me that it was odd that nothing was ever reported in the newspapers. Obviously, this gross breach of conduct was being silenced by the administrators of justice. As I shook free from the feeling of disbelief, I asked Murphy more about the incident:

"Patrick, that is unbelievable! I've heard some wild stories but this one has to be an award winner. What I don't understand, though, is why weren't criminal charges laid against the two people involved?"

By this time, Murphy was showing his frustration and it was clear that he was upset with this entire situation. His response revealed an obvious tone of anger:

"That's my point, Orest! I guess the police and the Crown Prosecutors don't see anything wrong with two people getting horny and having sex at their workplace. You can be sure that if it wasn't a cop who was engaging in a sexual act in a public place, there would have been a criminal charge laid. What bothers me is that those conference rooms are for the use of lawyers and their clients. Just because a police officer and a Court Clerk sneak into one of these rooms to have their lustful fling, we lawyers now lose the right to have access to these conference rooms when we need them. It just doesn't make any sense! Instead of punishing the two people who did something wrong, the Court administrators ignore them and punish the lawyers who had nothing to do with their actions. Some of the things that happen around here are so ridiculous that you wonder if they have a clue as to what they're doing."

As I listened to Murphy fume in frustration, I began to appreciate his disgust over this inconvenience. Pondering this bizarre story, I was quickly able to put it into perspective and my feelings of disbelief quickly disappeared. In the sixteen years that I had worked as a lawyer, I had heard numerous amazing stories emanating from the corridors of the Court House. The shenanigans of the judges in their private offices could easily create several volumes of non-fiction literature if any judge had a reason to write about it. These paragons of virtue in the Court room often revealed their licentious desires once out of sight in their secluded offices. The stories would trickle out through discreet accounts of Court Orderlies or senior lawyers who enjoyed privileged access to judges. Ironically, these stories were never to be repeated and that was the joy of re-telling them in the lawyers' gossip grapevine.

Lawyers have also created a history with some of their own interesting escapades in the Court House. Stories of lustful adventures have featured such exotic settings as the library, the women's locker room and even a Court room. It had always remained a mystery to me as to how these settings could arouse anyone to that degree. However, the simple explanation was that some people harbour the strangest fantasies. The amusing irony of this paradoxical situation was the plaque that was erected at the entrance to the Court House. The quote was meant to reflect the solemn integrity of the facility and states: "THE PLACE OF JUSTICE IS A HALLOWED PLACE." Obviously, some people have an unusual idea of what the words "hallowed place" mean.

The reason why these activities are ignored by Court Administrators is attributable to an attitude that such occurrences do not affect the administration of justice. Naturally, a publicized scandal over such an incident would bring immediate action from disciplinary bodies who cherish the fantasy of maintaining "an untarnished image." However, these Administrators and Disciplinary bodies must believe that the discreet indiscretions of certain judges, lawyers and police officers are better ignored to avoid the publicity of such errant behaviour.

It is therefore unusual to see the high degree of publicity that arose surrounding the flirtation and courtship between a Court clerk and a convicted murderer. The story had all the ingredients of a best-selling fiction novel. It featured a Court Clerk who became passionately attracted to a roguish criminal on trial for killing a police officer. The Clerk naturally used her influence to be assigned to his Court room and was in charge of facilitating the Court activities. During intermissions in the murder trial, they openly flirted and the romance quickly mushroomed. Although Crown Prosecutors, Court Orderlies, police officers and Court personnel were all aware of the situation, no concern ever arose over the implications.

On the conclusion of the trial, the roguish criminal was convicted and sentenced to imprisonment but the infatuated Clerk continued to visit him. When she announced her engagement to marry him, an outcry arose about the possible compromise to the integrity of the Court. Even politicians denounced the situation as being totally improper and requiring some immediate action. The Court

Administrators did their best to deny any problems but ultimately relented to pressure and moved the Clerk to a position that did not involve Court responsibilities.

All of these incidents dramatically emphasize the attitude of the Court Administrators to hide or deny anything that might necessarily focus unfavourable attention on the Court system. A member of the public could not expect to receive such leniency to excuse such behaviour when standing before the Court. However, the judges, lawyers, police and clerks can escape sanctions for such conduct in order to avoid scandalous revelation about the Court system. One might call this a "double standard" but the reality is that in the Court system, the people who make the rules are not bound by any standard.

Sensing that our time was quickly elapsing, I remarked:

"I agree with you totally! It's easy to see that common sense is not the basis for making decisions in our legal system. That alone goes a long way to explaining why decisions are made the way they are. Anyway, I guess we'd better find a spot where we can talk. Did you want to sit down in the corner of this reception area or would you prefer that we go elsewhere?"

Murphy then shrugged his shoulders in a gesture of accepting the reality of the situation. We both knew that the legal system functioned primarily by the decree of bureaucrats who sometimes acted irrationally. They could do so because they didn't have to answer to anyone for their decisions or justify these totalitarian ordinances with common sense. There was no appeal procedure and no point in complaining. It was best to simply accept this inconvenience and work around it. Murphy stared at the chairs in the corner of the room and then remarked:

"No, Orest! Let's go down to the cafeteria. It will be more comfortable down there. We can sit there at a table with a coffee and discuss things easier than here."

As we walked to the elevators and rode down to the basement to access the cafeteria, we talked about the silly rules that determined how the Court House was operated. Murphy lamented on how little input lawyers actually have in the administration of this Court facility where lawyers spend so much time working. Instead, the facility was controlled exclusively by senior government bureaucrats. Many of them resented lawyers and therefore imposed arbitrary rules that created inconvenience and hardship for them. Because there always was so little sympathy for lawyers in bureaucratic circles, their objections and complaints are summarily dismissed. All of this contributed to a more difficult working environment for lawyers and so much unnecessary strife.

On entering the cafeteria, we both secured our beverages and sat down at a table to discuss my case. I began with my endless collection of questions that I wanted to fire at Murphy. I decided to ask first about his earlier meeting with Nash:

"Did Nash confirm to you what witnesses would be called in these proceedings and what other evidence we might expect?"

Murphy must have anticipated my question because he immediately responded:

"Well, in terms of evidence, we talked about the Exhibit Binder that we are now using in this Hearing. The documents in that binder are being used to support the Crown's case. I had a chance to look them over and there are really no surprises. I am still satisfied that Nash has no evidence that you did anything wrong in this transaction."

I felt comforted to hear these encouraging comments. As I began to relax, Murphy continued his commentary:

"Regarding witnesses, Nash is giving me a list of witnesses that she intends to call at this Preliminary Hearing. The mortgage broker who now lives in Toronto is scheduled later in the week. Nash is concerned that we finish with him that day so that he can return without staying over night. The main evidence is going to come from that witness and from Garmaz, of course. The other witnesses are there to help fill in gaps in the story of how the deal came about. There won't be anything important from those witnesses. In any event, this is a Preliminary Hearing so we can just sit back and see what the Crown has for a case. If there is any evidence that raises a concern, we can prepare our rebuttal and present it at the trial."

Murphy's comments about the witnesses were similar to what I had assessed. Because of my inexperience in these types of proceedings, I relied totally on Murphy's observations. I now felt reassured that I had not overlooked any important aspect of how these proceedings would be conducted. As Murphy completed his comments, I immediately addressed another concern:

"Tell me! What is your experience with Stack as a Judge at a Preliminary Hearing? Is he the type of Judge who will dismiss the charge if there is no evidence or does he have a reputation for automatically setting these cases over for trial?"

Murphy's expression suddenly changed. As he thoughtfully gazed at me, his answer was slow and laboured:

"Actually, Orest, Stack is hard to follow on these cases. I'm told that he has dismissed charges but I've also seen him convict in cases where there was questionable evidence. Some judges are hard to read. I think that in a case like this, he should dismiss the case. I'm certainly going to argue that he should do that but it's hard to say how he'll react to this case once he's heard all the Crown evidence. As you know, there are some Judges that are very picky about Crown evidence and are inclined to dismiss if the Crown case is weak. There are other judges who automatically send everything for trial to Queen's Bench. Stack doesn't fit into either category and so it's impossible to know how he'll react."

As Murphy finished speaking, he gulped the rest of his coffee. I glanced at my watch and realized that we would have to start walking back to the Court room. I quickly asked Murphy a question that lay festering in my sub-conscious. It was the grim reality that I now faced continually as I struggled to resolve this awkward, stressful dilemma:

"Before we start back, I need to ask you this: Do you think that my professional status of a lawyer will affect Stack's decision? Do you think that will be a factor as to whether he dismisses the criminal charge or merely leaves it to be resolved in Queen's Bench?"

As soon as I said that, it became obvious to me that this question was one that Murphy was hoping he wouldn't have to answer. Both of us were all too familiar with the way that the charge had arisen. It was common ground that I was being prosecuted because I was a lawyer and a definite target for Christal and his cronies. We both knew that judges like to frown on lawyers who fail to exemplify the highest ideals. For this reason, it was disastrous for a lawyer to be accused of any misdeed - even that of overcharging a client. A lawyer charged with fraud had certainly fallen from that fabricated and exclusive pinnacle that lawyers and judges like to imagine themselves on. Although I wasn't guilty of any wrongdoing or fraud, I was certainly guilty of being a lawyer accused of fraud and this in itself would warrant a different consideration by the legal fraternity.

After pausing for a few moments to solidify his thoughts, Murphy responded thoughtfully:

"That is not supposed to be a consideration in this case because you acted as an investor when you purchased and resold the acreage property. If you were charged with defrauding your client of money from your trust account, that would be different and your status as a lawyer would be the relevant factor. I don't think that Stack will decide this case on whether you're a lawyer or not because that is really irrelevant in this case."

What Murphy said was true and it was an obvious assessment of this case. However, I was still dissatisfied with his response because it didn't address the true issue that I had raised. I prodded Murphy again for his assessment:

"You're absolutely right, Patrick! The fact that I'm a lawyer is irrelevant in this case. However, Nash referred to it quite strongly in her opening comments. I'm sure she is going to use the fact that I'm a lawyer as an element to influence Stack's decision. Do you think that Stack may be reluctant to dismiss the charge against me because I'm a lawyer?"

Murphy shuffled to gesture that he was getting up to leave as he responded to my question:

"I really don't know, Orest! It's hard to read Stack on that question. It's hard to say if that would influence him in this case. It shouldn't make any difference to him but he might decide not to make any decision. Often there are Provincial Judges who simply take the easy way out by setting the charge over for trial in Queen's Bench. If he does that, it doesn't mean that we have to worry about the Crown's case. We will still be in a good position to prepare our case so that the criminal charge is dismissed at trial. I wouldn't worry about it at this time. I am going to argue strongly that this case should be dismissed at this stage. However, if it is set over for trial in Queen's Bench, we'll simply go to trial and get it kicked out there. Most of the judges in Queen's Bench are pretty good and this type of case would get thrown out without any argument. However, I can't imagine this case not being thrown out at this time. So stop worrying! Just sit back and let me handle this for you. Let's get going. We can talk more on the way upstairs."

With these words, Murphy abruptly ended our conversation as we walked briskly to return to the Court room. I prepared myself to sit through more witnesses and relive more of the apprehension that I had experienced earlier this morning. My only comfort was the fact that Murphy was so positive about the case. Everything that he described conformed to my understanding of these proceedings and I agreed with him on his assessment of the evidence. I realized that I would have to be patient and to continue to objectively evaluate the evidence as it was presented.

The Court was soon in session again after undergoing the usual formalities. As her next Crown witness, Nash called John Gulayets who owned a local insurance agency. His company had placed insurance coverage on the acreage property that the Garmazs had purchased from me. I had never met him but I was acquainted with the insurance agent who worked for him and placed the insurance coverage. Gulayets gave evidence that his company had placed the insurance coverage for Garmazs and that the Garmazs had been referred to their company by me. The evidence itself bordered on being irrelevant. It was presented to identify a document which confirmed that insurance coverage was arranged to enable Garmaz to satisfy a financing condition required by the mortgage company. Murphy did not even bother to cross-examine this witness.

Nash then called Prit Paul, who was being tendered by the Crown as an "expert" witness. He was to give testimony on the value of the acreage property that was sold to Garmazs and financed by the mortgage company. Paul spoke with a heavy foreign accent because English was his second language and he had learnt it only recently after immigrating to Canada from India. Everyone in Court laboured to understand what he was saying since his speech was quiet and his pronunciation of words was often unclear.

Paul advised the Court that he had only recently began appraisal work and was still working to complete his accreditation in Appraisal work. He had prepared an appraisal at the request of Heritage Trust while in the employment of a registered appraiser in May of 1988, approximately four years after the property was financed by Heritage Trust. Paul was now giving evidence to identify the appraisal report that he had prepared and to justify his "expert" opinion in it.

Paul explained that he had obtained a copy of an appraisal report prepared by Peter Pilip, a registered appraiser, which was done in September of 1984. That appraisal report declared the value of the acreage property to be $230,000.00. Paul admitted in his testimony that he was not able to view the entire property. Also, he admitted that he could not verify the changes that occurred in the property since 1984 and that he had only worked with the barest of information relating to the real estate market at that time. Nevertheless, Paul was testifying that he would only appraise the value of the property at $115,000.00, being one-half the value that Pilip had appraised. Paul's appraised value was consistent with the low foreclosure value that Heritage Trust also put on the property when they repossessed it. It became obvious that Paul had testified primarily to validate these unusually low values.

As I listened to Paul's testimony, I began to wonder if it was a staged practical joke. Based on their incredulous expression, I inferred that Murphy, Judge Stack, and even Nash had a hard time accepting Paul's opinion as something that could be taken seriously. The problem was that Nash did not understand real estate transactions and more specifically, she did not understand how appraisers did their work. Otherwise, she might have decided not to call Paul as her "expert" witness.

Just like in the legal field where a lawyer can find some case authority to argue and support any legal position that he must represent, the same is true of property values in the appraisal field. Obviously, Pilip had approached the appraisal of this property from the position of a purchaser of property who was attempting to locate mortgage financing for it. Pilip would have examined comparable properties that sold for similar values and used them to justify his opinion. Paul, on the other hand, was instructed to prepare an appraisal for a mortgage company that had just repossessed the property. Therefore, Paul chose the comparable sales that most suited his client, namely the lowest and worst comparable sales. In the end, neither appraiser had done anything other than express and justify his opinion of value. However, Nash was now creating a ridiculous situation by trying to convince Judge Stack that Paul's appraisal opinion should be accepted as the true value of the property. In doing so, she hoped that Stack would conclude that there was something wrong and improper with Pilip's appraisal opinion.

Murphy's cross-examination emphasized Paul's lack of experience and his difficulties in judging the real estate market in 1984 with the data he had. Paul was obviously well-rehearsed and tried to justify his appraisal but he had to admit the flaws that were obvious. As a parting admission, he agreed that his appraisal was merely his opinion and Pilip was entitled to form his own opinion.

As soon as Paul was excused, Peter Pilip was called as the next Crown witness. Pilip was now retired and spent his retirement in Edmonton where his children and grandchildren lived. I had been acquainted with Pilip for about twelve years and first met him a few years before this transaction occurred. On the occasion when he performed appraisals for me, I had conversations with him over coffee about his children, his retirement, his travels and his various endeavours in the development business. Pilip was truly a wonderful, kind, understanding and compassionate man who exhibited the highest standards of honesty, decency and integrity. I immediately felt sympathy and compassion for him as I watched him enter the witness box to be criticized, humiliated and degraded by Nash. All of this would be done intentionally by Nash in her misguided attempt to discredit Pilip so that Paul's opinion of value might be accepted and relied upon by Judge Stack.

Pilip's testimony began with his explanation that he had worked as a registered and accredited appraiser for over twenty years. He explained that every financial institution accepted his appraisals and had high regard for his appraisal opinions. In response to Nash's questions, he identified his appraisal report, confirmed how he had prepared his appraisal and explained why he had reached the conclusions of the appraised value. Pilip spoke in a kindly fashion and looked like a grandfather who was advising his adult children on how appraisal work should be done. His answers were clear and direct and resonated with wisdom. He carefully answered each question with enough of an explanation to demonstrate that he was a seasoned professional in the appraisal business. I was pleased to see that Pilip could effectively respond to even the sarcastic references that Nash directed at him without losing his composure or becoming angry.

Murphy's cross-examination focused on the fact that Pilip had prepared this appraisal report with no input or direction from me. The appraisal was researched and compiled in a manner that he had always followed and the conclusions were based solely on his research. Pilip then concluded his remarks by stating that he still stood by the conclusions in his appraisal report. As both lawyers completed their questions of Pilip, he left the witness box with the same dignity and class that he had exhibited when he entered. I only hoped that he wouldn't have to repeat this ordeal again at a trial.

Nash then advised the Court that she wished an adjournment and Judge Stack agreed. As the Judge left the Court room, Murphy walked over to me looking confident and pleased at the way the proceedings had gone. Not wanting to speak in Court, we slipped into the conference room outside the Court room. As I closed the door behind us, Murphy began to comment:

"You can see that Nash is not very pleased with the way the case is going. She was getting very frustrated in there. She's struggling to put something in as evidence but there's simply nothing there. Both appraisers have their own opinion of value. Even if there was something questionable in Pilip's appraisal, he's still entitled to his own opinion. Nash has definitely got a problem on this issue."

I was pleased to hear Murphy's remarks. My thoughts questioned why it was important to even lead this kind of evidence since it had no relevance to anything that I had done. I decided to get Murphy's comments on this:

"Patrick, I agree with your assessment! There is nothing in that testimony that shows any wrongdoing by Pilip and there is no suggestion that I did anything improper? Why do you suppose this evidence was even put before the Court?"

Murphy sat back in his chair and peered across the small table at me. After a short pause, he began to explain:

"It probably doesn't make any sense to you because you have never prosecuted a criminal case. I have and therefore it makes a little more sense to me. First of all, she had to call Pilip as a witness because she had to identify that appraisal as an Exhibit. Otherwise, I'm sure she wouldn't have called him. Secondly, her tactic with Prit Paul was to show that his value is correct and that there was something wrong and even fraudulent in the way that Pilip did his appraisal. As you saw, Pilip was able to answer her questions. Best of all, he declared that he stands behind his appraisal value so Nash hasn't demonstrated anything that was done wrong. Thirdly, she called Pilip and that insurance agent simply to show that you referred the Garmazs to both of them and to try and connect you in some way to what they did. On this last point, it's clear that you didn't do anything that can remotely be considered improper. The best way to sum this up is that Nash went fishing for evidence and came up empty-handed."

I always found it interesting to hear Murphy's description of the events from his experience and perspective as a Crown Prosecutor. This gave Murphy a helpful advantage in anticipating the tactics that would be employed in the Court room. The procedures followed in the Court room are supposed to create a level playing field for the two parties so that two equally-matched parties could participate in a good, clean fight. In Court, the more that a lawyer can understand and anticipate about his opponent's strategy, the better equipped the lawyer is to prepare and present a case for his client.

The theory of the adversary system is that if two lawyers present the best possible case for two opposing positions, the judge, as a neutral observer, can make a well-informed decision on the resolution of the issue. The problem with this system is that the Crown has the advantage of being better prepared with lawyers who primarily specialize in specific types of cases. Defence lawyers seldom prepare to the same degree or specialize in the same way. Furthermore, the Crown Prosecutors can usually count on a favourable bias from the judge and can rely on numerous technical advantages when presenting and arguing their cases. For these reasons, a Defence lawyer is at a distinct disadvantage in the Court room. Politicians who promote and applaud the judicial system as being fair with equal advantages to both sides fail to understand this fundamental reality.

As I contemplated the inequities of the Criminal court system, I comforted myself on one main premise: if there was no evidence of wrongdoing, then surely the criminal charge against me would be dismissed. No matter what the Judges's bias and no matter how unbalanced the system was, I could still expect to be vindicated. After all, there still had to be a semblance of justice in the legal system. Otherwise it would be intolerable and offensive even to the people whose livelihood depended on the perpetuation of the criminal justice system. I could not accept the idea that it was so corrupted and unjust that each accused person entered the system expecting luck, and not justice, to save him from improper persecution and punishment.

As Murphy completed his explanation, I still felt uneasy about the uncertainty of what lay ahead. However, our recess time had quickly elapsed and since Murphy wanted to call his office, we agreed to talk later. I left the conference room and walked out into the open reception area in the hope of relaxing for a moment before returning to Court. As I walked slowly to the water fountain, I tried to think positively about the days ahead and silently prayed for a quick resolution to this nightmare. While reflecting on the situation, I concluded that the only positive thing that could result from this whole ugly experience was a dismissal of the criminal charge. I couldn't imagine how I or my family would cope if this nightmare actually continued to trial. In such an event, the courts would schedule a trial at least a year away and it would be a more protracted experience than what I was now encountering.

When I returned to the Court room, I saw Murphy motioning to me. I quickly strode over to Murphy and as I got near to him, he stated:

"Orest, they're going to start up again. Nash only has one short matter. She's calling a witness to identify a document and he has nothing more to testify on. This will be over quickly and then we'll be adjourning until tomorrow. Let's get this over with."

I suddenly felt relieved that the proceedings would soon be concluded for the day and that I could then return home. This first day had been emotionally draining and I felt sickened by the way that Nash was conducting the proceedings. The Crown witnesses that she called were now finding themselves on trial for what they saw and did. Nash conducted her tormenting procedures like a medieval torturer who was hardened and immune to the pain and suffering of her victims. If the Criminal justice system had any virtues, they were all overshadowed by the ugliness that I had witnessed today.

In silence, I resolved that I would endure these final moments of anguish and then return home as soon as possible. I knew that I had to focus on positive thoughts and to ignore the distasteful antics that were being performed by Nash to accentuate the horror of these proceedings. My thoughts drifted to being at home with my family for supper. The ugliness around me soon lost its abhorrent appearance. My goal now was to maintain a calm and objective attitude in the Court room and not react to the impropriety that I witnessed.

As anticipated, the Court was soon adjourned to the next morning and moments later we were all out the door. On my arrival home, I already had time to reflect on the court proceedings. I knew that my wife would be anxious to know how everything had turned out. I didn't want to describe my worst fears in graphic detail or dwell on the horrifying prospects that might lay ahead. Actually, there really wasn't anything decisive or even relevant that came out in evidence.

After supper, the children scurried off to their bedrooms to complete homework, read and then go to sleep. Pat and I enjoyed the ritual of sitting in our family room with the simple comfort of a hot cup of tea and warm conversation. As I explained to her in brief detail the evidence from the witnesses, I interjected some commentary from my discussions with Murphy. Pat commented on how ridiculous it was that this case was even being prosecuted before the courts. In the moment of silence that followed, we both wrestled with the apprehension of not knowing what other Crown witnesses might say later in the Preliminary Hearing.

Finally, I broke the silence by trying to comfort her:

"Nash is going to try to show that there was something improper or possibly suspicious about the transaction. However, Murphy says that there is no real evidence of wrongdoing by anyone. On that basis, he's going to ask the Judge to dismiss the criminal charge. Murphy is very confident about that assessment and I've decided that I'm not going to worry about it. Let's just relax and wait for this to take its course. I'm sure that Murphy has analyzed this case properly and we really don't have anything to worry about."

Pat softly agreed and then we changed the topic and tried to put this out of our minds. After reviewing all the developments with the children and the household through the day, we relaxed with some reading and television before retiring early to bed. We found however that it was impossible for either of us to truly relax while these proceedings were disrupting our lives. There really was no way of knowing what effect this ongoing turmoil would ultimately have on our lives.

Each evening provided the same routine, as both Pat and I anxiously wrestled with this tragic horror that had now taken centre stage in our lives. Our normal, quiet lives were now pre-occupied with legal proceedings that were threatening to destroy the happiness and tranquillity that we jealously guarded in our home from the rest of the world. Our lives were now in a war-alert response and we would have to struggle with the anxiety of the situation until the criminal charge was eradicated.

The following day, Murphy met me at the Court room a few minutes before my Preliminary Hearing was to resume. As he neared, he smiled and greeted me cheerfully before leading me into the Court room. On following Murphy in, I noticed Nash scribbling at her desk. She was still wearing the same black outfit which now seemed to appropriately match her cruel attitude of dissecting and destroying people in Court. Her cold facial expression and her stark white complexion caused me to imagine that she might have spent the night sleeping in a coffin. That would explain why she was brought back into the Court room without even changing her clothing. I was also convinced that the coolness of the Court room was being maintained to keep her from transforming into a creature from a horror movie. Her menacing glances at me and her stiff and calculated movements served to further affirm these suspicions.

As soon as Court was back in session, Nash called the next Crown witness, Keith Gilmour, a former manager at Heritage Savings and Trust. Gilmour was middle-aged but his balding head and his diminishing physical stature caused him to look much older than he was. When he answered questions, he was noticeably hesitant, evasive and defensive. One reason for this was his inability to remember what had happened on this specific mortgage file after six years. He could only rely on notes or memos in the Heritage Trust file and there was very little to refer to. Another reason for his elusive testimony was that the initial assessment on this mortgage file was that he was at fault in failing to properly assess the loan application before approving it. It was now imperative for him to place the blame for any loss onto someone else and this prosecution provided the ideal opportunity to do that.

Gilmour had worked as a mortgage broker prior to landing a job with Heritage Trust as a mortgage manager. Shortly before the assets of Heritage Trust and North West Trust Company were merged by the Government of Alberta, Gilmour lost his job but was lucky enough to land a new job with Royal Trust Company. What Gilmour lacked in competence was compensated for in personality. This mainly accounted for his success in landing these cherished jobs with trust companies. Unfortunately, incompetence leads to noticeable mistakes and these ultimately translate into termination of employment. Gilmour's success depended on his ability to hide his incompetence and when discovered, to blame it on something or someone else. It is in these circumstances that Gilmour's mistakes would result in harm not only to his employer but to innocent people who become convenient scapegoats.

Gilmour's evidence was lengthy because he had to describe his total involvement in receiving the mortgage application of the Garmazs and approving it. He was also questioned on his instructions to the lawyer to prepare the legal documents and on the eventual funding of the mortgage loan. During his testimony, he was called upon to identify various documents. This process was time consuming and technically procedural in nature. It became obvious that Gilmour was well rehearsed to present this evidence. His memory of this one mortgage file that he worked on approximately six years earlier was remarkable and as clear as if it had happened yesterday. During the time that elapsed he must have handled hundreds of files and held various positions with Heritage Trust and then Royal Trust. Yet, his answers were precise and positive on exactly what he did and how everything developed. He even seemed to have a phenomenal ability to recall conversations he had with various people even though he had no notes or other documents that would have aided his recollection. This all would have been quite amazing if it wasn't so noticeably manufactured to achieve a desired result.

When Murphy began his cross-examination, Gilmour readily admitted that he NEVER, at any time, dealt with me or spoke to me on this mortgage application. All representations and information came to Gilmour through a mortgage broker, Marcel Notschaele, who represented Stephen and Gayle Garmaz. Gilmour also admitted that he was aware that the property was being purchased from my company and being financed with the mortgage loan approved by him. However, he agreed that I had NO INVOLVEMENT with the mortgage application and he had NO DEALINGS WITH ME as the mortgage only concerned the Garmazs.

Murphy then proceeded to question Gilmour on the issue of why a loss was suffered by Heritage Trust. Gilmour stated that a condition of the mortgage loan was the approval of mortgage insurance from Canada Mortgage and Housing Corporation (CMHC). On payment of a premium on the placement of the loan, CMHC agreed to pay any loss suffered by the lender if a default in repayment occurred which resulted in a loss to the lender. Gilmour then stated that when Heritage Trust realized a deficiency after default and foreclosure on this mortgage, CMHC refused to pay the loss. CMHC took the position that Gilmour did not verify the downpayment in a satisfactory manner. The mortgage broker had apparently represented to Gilmour that the Garmazs were trading their home for the new property and that their home was clear title. Gilmour then admitted that he did not do a search of the title to the Garmaz home to verify that it was in fact clear title. For that reason, CMHC justified their refusal to pay the loss because of Gilmour's failure.

The whole truth now lay there exposed for all to see. It was obvious that this was a case of incompetence that was being covered up by Gilmour and others at Heritage Trust. They were now attempting to lay the blame for the loss elsewhere. If Gilmour had properly investigated the loan application, he would have satisfied the requirements of CMHC relating to the lender's responsibilities. In that event, CMHC would have paid for the loss suffered by Heritage Trust. However, because he failed to do so, Heritage Trust suffered a loss that they could not recover from CMHC. In order to preserve his position, it was necessary for Gilmour and those that took over the file to place the blame on somebody else. The story that was developed was that Heritage Trust suffered this loss because of a false representation that caused Gilmour to approve the loan. However it was now obvious that irrespective of any representation in the mortgage application, the loss was actually attributable to Gilmour's negligence and incompetence.

At the conclusion of Gilmour's evidence, the Court was adjourned to the afternoon. Murphy quickly left the Court room to attend to another pressing matter. As he raced out, we agreed to meet outside the Court room just before Court resumed at two o'clock. However, Murphy arrived late and we hastily walked into the Court room to start the afternoon session.

When Court resumed, Nash called William Patrick, the lawyer who represented Heritage Trust in the legal work and the ultimate funding of the mortgage loan to the Garmazs. Patrick was a tall, slender, middle-aged man who walked awkwardly and appeared shy and apprehensive. His badly fitted suit fit the stereotype image that he portrayed of a bumbling lawyer. He had difficulty looking at anyone directly and preferred to focus his eyes on this file which he brought to Court.

Patrick was noticeably uncomfortable during his appearance in Court, which was strikingly unusual for a lawyer. However, I could understand why he was nervous since he seldom if ever appeared in Court for clients. He was a commercial lawyer who spent as much time as possible securing and completing real estate and mortgage files. Such work was typically completed by his conveyancing secretary which enabled him to have a limited amount of contact with clients. In good economic times, this type of work was the most lucrative work in every law firm. Patrick would have secured the legal work from Heritage Trust through a generous amount of public relations work involving Gilmour and the other senior executives. Such friendship and public relations could be easily compromised if he said anything disparaging about Gilmour or Heritage Trust. Although Patrick was obliged to tell the truth, it soon became obvious that he would not say anything that could embarrass his prized clients.

The art of public relations is a fascinating aspect of the legal business world. It is the primary method of securing large clients and extends the influence of the law firm into the Court room and into every facet of community life. The practice of providing expensive gifts as "polite bribes" to secure work or favours has always been blatantly commonplace in the legal profession. It is done discreetly to avoid the scandalous and offensive stigma that would arise if such practices became publicized. The larger law firms have better finances to purchase expensive gifts for executives of firms, such as paid vacations and paid memberships in golf clubs. Managers of banks and directors of large corporations would expect these types of "gifts" in return for sending work to the law firm. Government work was secured through loyal contacts and contributions to the governing political party.

The most disturbing practices are the "polite bribes" that are routinely given to judges by lawyers. The expensive gifts are used to guarantee that the judges will grant favourable decisions to benefit the benevolent lawyers and their clients. Naturally, a judge would be loathe to accept such gifts from anyone but a close acquaintance who he could trust to keep this arrangement secretive. Since most judges either come from large law firms or have close alliances with lawyers in larger firms, the influence of the large law firms is unassailable before most judges.

Since there is a greater sensitivity about presents to judges, the nature of the gifts must be such that they are easily hidden. Naturally, because the stakes are high, ingenuity can make even the obvious very difficult to prove. For Christmas gifts, it is commonplace for some firms to send a judge a case of his favourite wine or whiskey, delivered discreetly to his home. In return, the lawyers from the benevolent firm can expect to be treated favourably, and indeed royally, when appearing before a bribed judge on any cases or applications that he is adjudicating. However, the influence extends much further, since judges can arrange to adjudicate specific cases where a favour is needed. Furthermore, a bribed judge has influence with other judges who are his colleagues and can exert the necessary influence to help sway a case for the benefit of a benevolent firm. Naturally, there were some judges with higher ethical standards who didn't subscribe to these bribes. However, because these activities could be so discreetly executed, it is a rarity to find a situation where the corruption in the legal system did not influence the outcome of the case.

Patrick was cautious in his testimony and insisted that he didn't want to say anything that he couldn't clearly remember. He would only testify with information found on his legal file. It was however obvious that he did not want to say anything that might cast his former client, Heritage Trust, or Keith Gilmour in a bad light. The only conclusion for this was his fear of reprisal by loss of future work from these sources. This became very clear when Patrick became unwilling to give any evidence on conversations that he had in the closing of the mortgage transaction. He later admitted to me that he did recall some specific conversations with Gilmour that were relevant and even critical to the issues in the case.

In a private conversation after his appearance in Court, Patrick advised me that he actually recalled a telephone conversation with Garmaz's lawyer in which all the information of the real estate closing was revealed to him. He then spoke to Gilmour and was told to ignore what he knew and to excuse any short-comings in the mortgage application since Gilmour was anxious to fund the loan. Apparently, Gilmour was under pressure from his supervisors to make secured loans and he needed to complete this mortgage loan. Patrick then advised me that he would deny these comments if ever asked about them by anyone. For Patrick, it was better to lie under oath and to say that he did not recall any conversations than to testify truthfully about such conversations and risk losing some lucrative work.

Patrick's testimony was also slow mainly because of the need to identify and mark various documents as exhibits in these proceedings. Also, because he was unwilling to testify freely, the Crown had to slowly extract evidence from him. It was even more tedious for Murphy to cross-examine him without alienating him. Ultimately, both Nash and Murphy became frustrated with him and concluded their examinations quickly without extracting much for useful admissions.

As her next Crown witness, Nash called Marcel Notschaele. He was noticeably short, middle-aged and smartly dressed. His presence was that of a confident and successful businessman. He impressed everyone as sincere and knowledgable, leaving no doubt that he was truthful about his evidence. As I watched him enter the witness box, I reflected on his role in this whole mortgage transaction. Notschaele was a mortgage broker who ran a company called Equiplan Mortgage Services which specialized in difficult-to-arrange mortgages. Naturally, he charged a higher fee for such mortgages and received referrals from various brokers.

As Notschaele began to testify, he explained that he had received a referral from Walter Pevcevicius of Premier Mortgage, another mortgage broker, to arrange a difficult mortgage. After reviewing the application, he determined that he could place it with Heritage Trust. In order to confirm his assessment, he telephoned Gilmour, an old friend, and was told to submit the mortgage application. Notschaele then prepared a new application form using his own company forms and simply copied the information from the Premier Mortgage Application form. He admitted that he committed a BLATANT IRREGULARITY by simply printing Stephen Garmaz's name where Garmaz's signature should have appeared on the new application form. Notschaele then forwarded the information to Gilmour and it was immediately approved.

Notschaele also assisted Gilmour in securing the execution of the Commitment Letter and the other legal forms required before the mortgage loan could proceed. One of these forms was required by law to be executed by the mortgage applicant before the lender. Instead, the form was signed by Notschaele on behalf of Heritage Trust even though he had no status or authority to do so. Furthermore, the declaration on the form stated that Notschaele had attended upon the mortgage applicants and explained the terms of the mortgage to them. Notschaele admitted that he hadn't done that and that the declaration was FALSE. However, the fact that these forms were improperly prepared and executed in contravention of the statute law was blatantly ignored by both Christal and Nash. It was interesting that the "false" information which was the root of the fraud to be proved in this case was located on this new form prepared by Notschaele in this inappropriate manner. However, no suggestion ever arose in the prosecution of the case that Notschaele acted improperly or fraudulently.

Of further interest in Notschaele's testimony was the fact that Pevcevicius had lied to Notschaele about the amount of commission being charged so that

Notschaele would accept a smaller fee. When Notschaele learned of the discrepancy, he threatened to cancel the deal. Pevcevicius then hastily agreed to pay him his agreed fee without any records in cash "under the table". Notschaele didn't seem to be embarrassed about this situation and simply stated that he agreed to it and that was how it was done. This testimony of unethical and illegal actions on the part of both mortgage brokers being openly admitted in Court raised serious questions about the value and credibility of the total evidence adduced. On hearing this testimony in Court, everyone reacted with surprise. It suddenly became obvious that if there was any wrongdoing or fraud, these two brokers should have been charged with the offence and not me. However, Christal had obviously chosen to ignore their conduct in order that their cooperative testimony would implicate me.

When Nash had finished her questions, Murphy proceeded to question Notschaele on his primary admissions. Murphy's tactic was to emphasize all the improper steps and actions that were now blatantly obvious to everyone in Court. Notschaele reaffirmed all of his admissions without flinching or even showing concern over these improper irregularities. His attitude was that these types of irregularities and improper actions are commonplace and therefore of no real concern to mortgage brokers.

When Murphy concluded his questions, Court was adjourned to the following day. At that moment, I felt positive about the evidence that was presented and I could see that Murphy was also quite pleased. As we entered the conference room for a quick discussion, Murphy immediately exclaimed:

"Orest, I'm sure you're happy with the hearing so far. This is the Crown's main evidence relating to the mortgage. Already it's obvious that you had nothing to do with the mortgage application. It doesn't really matter what happened in the other parts of the deal. We still have to hear from that other broker, that Wally from Premier Mortgage. I've read his statement to the police and it's obvious that he doesn't remember anything about this deal. The way it looks now, I'm sure that this charge is going to be dismissed. There is NO evidence that you did anything wrong. There is certainly nothing to suggest that you did anything fraudulent."

I agreed with Murphy and was pleased that he felt as positive as I did. I quickly responded to his comments:

"I'm so glad that you feel that way, Patrick! I'm feeling quite apprehensive about getting this resolved. I'm glad that everything is developing as we predicted. I know that you are probably anxious to get going but can we meet to discuss some of the upcoming witnesses tomorrow morning?"

Murphy agreed and we grabbed our briefcases and headed out the door for home. I now felt more encouraged about these proceedings and the situation looked hopeful. There were a number of witnesses who would still testify, but at least the main evidence relating to the Heritage Trust mortgage had now been given. I had every reason to feel confident that this ordeal would be resolved, as expected. I was now looking forward to tomorrow with hopeful anticipation and less apprehension.

CHAPTER THIRTEEN

PERJURY

O ne of the most ridiculous shortcomings of our Criminal Justice system is that it works on the premise that the people who give evidence will tell the truth. To guarantee that a witness will tell the truth, that person must swear an oath to God, or at least to the Court, solemnly affirming to do so. The theory behind this elaborate and ritualistic procedure appears to be that even if a person would otherwise tell a lie, the oath might bind the conscience and force that person to tell the truth. Unfortunately, every case that is brought before the Court contains conflicting evidence which demonstrates that some or all of the witnesses are not telling the truth.

To understand why people tell lies or give false testimony, one must understand some basic fundamental facts relating to evidence from witnesses. Except for expert witnesses who are called to express a professional opinion, all other witnesses are asked to testify on what they observed and what they did. Naturally, these statements will be coloured by their perspective and their personal motives. Those witnesses with a personal interest in the outcome of the case or even a preference as to the outcome will describe their observations and actions to influence the judge and jury to adopt their sentiments. Those facts which are unfavourable will either be conveniently forgotten or described and defended in a favourable manner. Presumably, none of this is perjury because the person is not telling a lie. Rather, the person is simply telling the story from his perspective.

A further problem which alters a witness's testimony is that human memory may fail to retain key facts. As a result, the witness may subconsciously intermingle their belief of what must have happened with the facts that they do recall. Surveys conducted by behavioral psychologists have identified and proven this process of "reconstructing memory". The result may be a description of an event which is drastically different from what actually occurred. Again, the witness is only speaking from recollection and the falsities are not sufficient to be called lies or perjury.

Unfortunately, it is a small step from being innocently mistaken to being intentionally deceptive and committing perjury. In many cases, it is difficult to determine or prove when a witness has been intentionally deceptive and the decisions of the Courts have provided little guidance. In a recent case where a mother sought child support, a judge determined that the mother intentionally lied in Court when she failed to reveal welfare income. On entering the conviction of perjury, the judge showed no compassion and ordered a term of imprisonment.

In direct contrast, some judges have excused blatant cases of perjury. At a recent trial, a judge heard evidence of a police officer who admitted making a false statement under oath in the murder trial of Wilson Neepoose. The lie was later discovered and was one of the factors that resulted in the conviction of Wilson Nepoose being set aside. During the perjury trial that followed, the judge chose to excuse the police officer in spite of his blatant false testimony. The judge reasoned that since the police officer later admitted the truth, he obviously didn't intend to lie in the first place! This case now serves as a blatant example of how police officers can abuse their trusted positions and commit perjury. After all, it's easy for them to assume that they will escape any consequences since the perjury will remain undetected or will be ignored without sanction.

The problems of false testimony, intentional lies and probable perjury are a continual reality in almost every case before the Courts. The main role of the judge is to decide what the truth is and this usually is a determination of whose version of the event he favours. In criminal cases, this choice is usually between a police officer and an accused person. Because of the prevailing bias among judges that most accused people are guilty of something, it is rare for any judge to favour the accused person. Typically, the testimony of the accused person conflicts with that of a police officer and the tendency then is for the judge to accept the police version and assume that the accused person is lying.

Because judges will typically accept the evidence of police officers without doubting it, the predictable consequence is that some police officers will confidently fabricate evidence and testify in a manner that will result in a conviction. These police officers feel that they must justify their efforts with convictions and therefore it is necessary to circumvent the judicial process to incriminate anyone that they believe to be guilty. By putting forth verbal confessions that were never made or giving testimony of actions that can't be proven false, a police officer can provide conclusive evidence for a conviction without risking detection. Although it may become evident to the Defence lawyer, the Crown Prosecutor and even the Judge that the police officer has lied, seldom is the consequence worse than the dismissal of the criminal charge. Most often, the inconsistencies of a police officer's fabricated evidence will be ignored and a conviction entered, thereby vindicating the police officer's actions.

Most police officers become very experienced in presenting evidence in Court and professional in tailoring evidence to generate convictions. Some use this experience to instruct and influence key Crown witnesses on how to present evidence to the Court. Most Crown witnesses are easily influenced by police officers since people generally trust the police and strive to accommodate any request they might make. Some may simply fear reprisals if they don't cooperate with the directions of a police officer. Furthermore, those Crown witnesses that may be implicated in the commission of the criminal offence are always ready to say whatever the police officer suggests. After all, a conviction of an accused person works to vindicate the others who were involved but not charged.

I had never contemplated that false testimony and perjury would be significant factors in my Preliminary Hearing. I had evaluated my case thoroughly and could not visualize any possible Crown witness who would wish to see me falsely implicated on this criminal charge. Sadly, I had failed to imagine the motivations of some of the witnesses and the degree to which Christal would stoop to secure a conviction against me.

The start of the third day of the Preliminary Hearing was not as traumatic as the first two days had been primarily because I was becoming accustomed to the pain and mental shock of the proceedings. I began to appreciate the emotional blanket that Criminal Defence lawyers must use to shelter their feelings from the continual devastation of lives around them. Their situation was no different than that of people who must witness tragic circumstances in their work on a continual basis. To perform such work, a person must become de-sensitized to be able to view the horror without emotion. Similarly, lawyers must insulate themselves from the suffering of those who appear before the Court. To do so, it was commonplace for them to rationalize that the actual horror is the fault of the accused person or the criminal justice system. Ironically, although the actions of many Defence lawyers may in fact contribute to the suffering that occurs in the courts, these lawyers still view themselves as blameless for the misery of their clients.

As I waited outside the Court room for Murphy to arrive, I marvelled at how one isolated, inconsequential real estate transaction had created the chain of events that was now threatening to destroy my legal career. There were countless clients that I had represented in my legal practice who completed similar real estate transactions. Yet, it would be impossible for any of them to comprehend that a consequence like this could arise. At times, I too found this situation difficult to rationalize. I reflected once more on Murphy's comment that if it had been someone other than a lawyer, no charge would have ever been pursued in this case. My downfall was simply that I was a lawyer who was involved in this real estate deal. I became a target because this case offered a career advancement opportunity for Christal. The criminal charge that Nash was now trying to prove before the Court had very little to do with any wrongdoing. Instead, this was simply politics and my name came up at the wrong time.

Sitting in the corner of the reception area adjacent to the Court room, I watched Christal as he engaged in a fervent conversation. I assumed that the stranger who he was instructing would be another Crown witness scheduled to give evidence that morning. Although one expects the evidence of Crown witnesses to be independent and impartial, it is common knowledge that these witnesses are briefed thoroughly to give the evidence that the Crown Prosecutor needs to prove in the case. Usually, this is done by the Crown Prosecutor who has an ethical responsibility not to improperly influence the testimony of the Crown witness. However, in this case, Christal was taking no chances and was doing some coaching himself. Obviously, Christal had a vested interest in this case. It was more important for him to hang around the Court House to influence Crown witnesses than it was to pursue other police investigations.

Suddenly, I noticed Murphy coming through the door at a galloping pace. I waited in the corner for Murphy to get near so that I could talk to him about Christal. Murphy sat down beside me and asked, with a smile:

"Hi, Orest! Now that you've seen how weak the Crown case is, are you ready to take the case over and finish it off yourself?"

Murphy's mood was upbeat and he was obviously very happy with the way the case was progressing. I responded with a smile, although I felt empty inside:

"No, Patrick! You're doing great! I'm not going to mess with it. I would just love to see this finished as soon as possible. Tell me this! Why is Christal allowed to influence the future Crown witnesses? That's equivalent to tampering with their evidence. These witnesses are all intimidated by him and would probably say anything to avoid being charged by him. Why is Nash allowing him to hang around the Court house like this?"

Murphy leaned over so that he could speak quietly and not be overheard:

"As you know, Christal has been excluded out of the Court room on the basis that he is a Crown witness who will be testifying at this Preliminary Hearing. Under such circumstances, he shouldn't be talking to other Crown witnesses. Furthermore, Christal is in the situation where he is currently under oath. He has already given testimony and he will be recalled to complete his testimony and be cross-examined. He shouldn't be talking to anyone about this case or to anyone involved in this case until his evidence and my cross-examination of him is concluded. The fact that he is hanging around the Court room and talking to Nash and the other witnesses about this case is totally improper. Furthermore, you can be sure that he and Nash both know that."

What Murphy said was basic knowledge for any trial lawyer or police officer. Christal and Nash were veterans of the Court house and knew the rules concerning evidence from witnesses. Yet Christal was blatantly ignoring the rules and procedures. Curiously, Nash was not admonishing him but instead was encouraging him by ignoring his conduct. The question on my mind was: "Why was Nash allowing this?". Before I could make any further comment, Murphy continued:

"In my experience in prosecuting cases, I've had many instances where a cop will insist on sticking around to assist with a case even though I tell him not to. It's hard for a Crown Prosecutor to do anything about a cop who decides that he is going to hang around and watch the prosecution of a case. That's the situation Nash is in. There's not much that Nash can do about Christal as he knows how to bully his way around. Supposedly, Christal is answering questions that the Crown witnesses have about the procedures in Court. However, we all know that he is telling them what to say in Court. It's typical for witnesses to incorporate a cop's suggestions into their testimony and soon nobody knows what the truth is anymore. When I prosecute cases, I can tell when a witness has been briefed by a cop. However, as a Crown Prosecutor, my job is to present the case. Even when I know that the evidence isn't right, I present it and let the judge decide. Nash is doing the same thing in this case. Don't worry about Christal! His coaching may look good to him but it's not fooling Stack. It's obvious that the Crown witnesses have been coached and that some are lying. Christal is doing more harm than good and that's only making Nash's job harder. It's my job to demonstrate when a witness is lying and I don't think I'll have any problems doing so in this case."

I looked at the time and realized that we would have to go into court in a few minutes. I decided to limit my questions to the upcoming Crown witnesses.

Murphy answered me directly as he had reviewed some information on the next Crown witnesses to be called in Court:

"On the list that Nash gave me, it appears that the broker from Premier Mortgage who now lives in Ontario will be a witness today. This guy gave a statement to Christal and I got a copy of it. HE DIDN'T REMEMBER ANYTHING AND DIDN'T EVEN KNOW WHO YOU WERE. I wouldn't worry about him. Also the other broker, Mark Denman, will be testifying today. His deal never came together and he never dealt with Heritage Trust. I don't see any problem with his testimony. The other evidence is just filler that Nash has to put in to tie the case together. I don't see anything of concern in their testimony. So let's go in and get it over with!"

I nodded, stood up with Murphy and followed him into the Court room. As I entered, I looked across at Nash seated at her table. I was intrigued to see her in the same black outfit and appearing just a ghoulish as before. The trial must have been tiring for Nash as she appeared to project a more frightening appearance with each passing day. It suddenly occurred to me that she must have been suffering from burn-out. Her automated actions, her sombre expressions and her neglected appearance were all symptomatic of so many other lawyers in distress. It was ironic that while she was cruelly attacking me, she was actually destroying herself. I couldn't help but feel pity for her and I was thankful for her sake that the hearing was to be concluded by the end of the week.

Suddenly, Christal entered the Court room and arrogantly strode over to Nash's table. After whispering some last minute instructions to her, he briskly walked out again. As we began to settle into our respective seats, Court resumed. Nash called as her next Crown witness, Douglas Thompson.

Thompson was a lawyer who I had met in 1983 when he acquired my legal files from my St. Albert law practice. It was at that time that I moved to Edmonton and began a law practice restricted to a few corporate clients. Thompson was quite meticulous and conscientious in his legal work and I referred many new inquiries for general legal work to him. It was during this time period that Garmazs inquired about a lawyer. I recommended Thompson to them and he ultimately completed the real estate deal for them. As Thompson stepped into the witness stand, he exuded an attitude of self-righteousness. With a cold and impersonal manner, he made it clear that he did everything properly. Naturally, he implied that if anything was improper, then it was only because of my involvement in the transaction.

Thompson's evidence was quite predictable since it focused on his legal work on behalf of the Garmazs. Both Murphy and I were able to accurately anticipate his testimony. He admitted that he couldn't locate his file and therefore was testifying from his memory. Surprisingly his memory was better than anyone would expect it to be. It was interesting to hear him testify about conversations he had with Stephen Garmaz confirming details about the transaction. Naturally, all of these conversations justified his actions and showed that he had followed all the requisite steps in concluding the file. He stated that he was satisfied from conversations with Stephen Garmaz that his clients understood and were willing to complete the real estate transaction. It was also interesting to hear him testify about conversations with Patrick during the closing of the transaction. Thompson clearly recalled a telephone inquiry by Patrick about the balance of the purchase price that was being paid by the Garmazs to complete the transaction. Patrick was obviously making a down-payment verification for the benefit of Heritage Trust. This testimony was proof that Patrick had lied when he refused to disclose that he had made this inquiry to verify down payment.

This inquiry was also proof that Gilmour and Patrick knew that there was no trade of property, contrary to Nash's theory of the case. Instead, Gilmour and Patrick expected that the balance of the purchase price was being paid in cash and they wanted Thompson to verify this. Thompson stated that he told Patrick that the balance of cash was being satisfied by a private second mortgage arranged between the parties. Patrick then said that he would be advising Gilmour at Heritage Trust of this arrangement and advising him to withdraw their loan commitment. Thompson stated that he believed that Heritage Trust would likely cancel their loan commitment and that the transaction would not close. He admitted that he was surprised when the mortgage funds arrived a few days later. Obviously, Gilmour had chosen to ignore the advice of his lawyer and proceed with the loan.

This evidence was clear and irrefutable proof that Heritage Trust was not misled in any way. It was obvious that all the details about the real estate deal had been communicated to Heritage Trust through their lawyer, Patrick. When I later telephoned Patrick to ask about this, he confidentially admitted that he specifically told Gilmour about this information from Thompson. According to Patrick, it was Gilmour who insisted on proceeding with the mortgage loan. Unfortunately, Patrick refused to confirm this information to Murphy and instead chose to withhold this evidence to protect Gilmour from blame. To Patrick, it was better to risk perjury in Court than to risk losing a commercial client.

Murphy's cross-examination of Thompson focused on his conversations with Garmaz and Patrick. These were key items in destroying the Crown's theory that I had somehow manipulated everyone in the transaction. Murphy demonstrated that Garmaz knew what he was doing and Gilmour at Heritage Trust had information relating to the way the transaction was actually being completed. It now became obvious just how much Nash had truly exaggerated the Crown case against me in her opening statement to Judge Stack. It was also obvious that she had no proof to substantiate any of her allegations.

On the completion of Thompson's evidence, Nash called Walter Pevcevicius as the next Crown witness. According to earlier testimony, he identified himself as "Wally" and worked as a mortgage broker for Premier Mortgage. Wally was tall and thin in stature and portrayed the slick salesman appearance in his clothing and demeanour. It was Wally who scooped the five thousand dollar commission for essentially referring the mortgage application to Notschaele. The false information about the Garmazs came from Wally's application form. It would be interesting to see how Wally would excuse himself from any wrongdoing since he already admitted to Christal that he couldn't remember anything about the transaction.

As Wally entered the Court room, I recognized him as the witness that Christal was so intently coaching earlier that morning. I couldn't identify Wally and I certainly had no recollection of him in this transaction. For a few brief moments, I sat in silent terror as I listened to his testimony. It was obvious that his evidence had been coached and was well rehearsed. He assured everyone that he recalled this transaction clearly even though it happened so long ago and his file had since been discarded. There he stood, testifying as if this transaction had only happened yesterday and reassuring everyone that he had such a clear recollection of all the events.

As I listened to his evidence, I realized why Christal was being so attentive in briefing this witness and how dramatically Christal had now affected the course of this Preliminary Hearing. It was obvious that Wally was to be the Crown's key witness and their only hope of maintaining a case against me. Furthermore, Wally had arranged the application for the mortgage which was the main issue in this fraud case. If I wasn't implicated in this case, then he could surely expect to be charged with fraud. Wally had therefore agreed to become a "cooperative" witness. Following the coaching of Christal, Wally testified that it was I and not Garmaz who gave him false information over the telephone about the Garmaz property. Wally emphasized that he had dealt exclusively with me and not with Garmaz.

This was a shocking setback for our defence of the case. Murphy immediately realized the importance of attacking Wally's credibility as a witness. Murphy questioned Wally about his initial statement to Christal but Wally explained that his memory all came back later as he thought about the matter. By now, it was obvious to everyone that Wally had developed a better memory of the events than any other Crown witness had. Yet, there was no reason why Wally could recall any details of this case after such a long passage of time. Murphy then challenged Wally on his key evidence relating to the telephone call during which he supposedly obtained false information from me on the Garmaz property:

Murphy: "On the 25th of April, 1989, you couldn't even remember who Mr. Rusnak was?"

Wally: "That's correct."

Murphy: "So how do you know that the person you spoke to on the phone was Mr. Rusnak?"

Wally: "I guess I really don't, when it comes down to it."

Murphy: "And you were acting for somebody by the name of Garmaz?"

Wally: "That's correct."

Murphy: "And you knew Garmaz's address?"

Wally: "That's correct."

Murphy: "And you knew Garmaz's phone number?"

Wally: "That's correct."

As Murphy completed his cross-examination, I felt some relief in knowing that he had achieved a retraction of Wally's evidence which accused me of providing false information to him. The statement was so incredible that it could only have been manufactured by Christal to coincide with the Crown theory. Wally was openly susceptible to Christal's persuasion because of his questionable actions in this transaction. Now the total case of the Crown lay on this one witness whose self-interest was to avoid being charged for impropriety in arranging the mortgage. Wally had been the "perfect pigeon" for Christal to manipulate. After all, Wally's ethics in striking an "under the table" deal with Notschaele would have alerted Christal to the fact that Wally would stoop to anything to serve his own self-interest. The only blessing was that Wally was not a very good liar and Murphy was able to demonstrate the truth in his cross-examination.

The next two Crown witnesses were Darrell Thompson and his common-law wife Juline Boucher. They both testified that they had purchased the acreage property through a realtor, Peter Horn. They then lived in the property for only a short time before releasing the property to Peter Horn. This evidence was essentially only useful in providing details on what happened after the transaction was completed. They did however admit that they had never met me and that they dealt solely with Peter Horn throughout the transaction.

After their evidence was completed, Court was adjourned for the lunch recess. As soon as Murphy approached me, I asked him to join me in the conference room for a few minutes. As Murphy followed me in and closed the door, I immediately remarked:

"That evidence from Wally is a total fabrication. I did not give him any information on Garmaz. He had to get that information directly from Garmaz. There is no way that I knew any of the stuff that was written in his application form. Why was Wally so ready to commit perjury by lying under oath?"

Murphy felt the anxiety of the situation and tried to calm me by remarking:

"It was obvious to the judge that he was lying, especially after I started to cross-examine him. He admitted that he doesn't know who gave him the information that went into the application form so I wouldn't worry about that. Obviously, Christal had something to do with getting Wally to say what he did. As you saw, Wally just isn't a very good liar because he didn't figure out all the angles. In any case, everyone knows that he's a liar and so I wouldn't worry about his evidence. The other evidence didn't affect you in any way so you should just relax and not worry about it."

Murphy then advised me that he had to make some telephone calls and attend to some other matters. I agreed to meet him outside the Court room before two o'clock so that we could talk about the next Crown witnesses. During the two-hour court recess, I had a quick lunch and spent some time in the Court house library reviewing cases dealing with Preliminary Hearings. As with any legal cases, no two cases say the same thing and any argument can be supported by some form of case authority. The general consensus was that the judge at a Preliminary Hearing had to be satisfied that there was some evidence on each of the elements of the criminal charge which could be put before a jury at the trial. At a Preliminary Hearing, the judge did not have to determine if there was enough evidence to convict the person of the crime. It seemed obvious from this research that if there was a lack of evidence on any of the elements of a charge, the charge would have to be dismissed. I felt confident that there was a total lack of evidence of fraud and that my nightmare was about to end.

I was late in returning to the Court room and Murphy was already inside talking to Nash. I passed Christal as he stood outside the Court room briefing yet another Crown witness. The practice of "briefing a witness" is used by all lawyers and Crown Prosecutors prior to the witness giving testimony in Court. The purpose is to learn what the witness knows or has to say so that the lawyer or the Crown Prosecutor can avoid unnecessary surprises. The witness also benefits by finding out the type of questions that will likely be asked in Court. In principle, it is an essential part of the process for preparing a case for court.

Problems arise when these preparations of a witness result in "coaching" the witness on the evidence to be given. Not only is coaching frowned upon and considered improper and unethical, it can be construed as tampering with the evidence of the witness. For that reason, police officers are not supposed to interfere with the Crown witnesses. The involvement of the police officer actually ends when the criminal charge is laid and the Crown Prosecutor assumes conduct of the case. This practice assures everyone that the police will not improperly interfere with the Crown witnesses.

Unfortunately, Christal chose to ignore these common procedures in order that he could influence the outcome of the Preliminary Hearing. It was upsetting for me to see how Christal was abusing his position by influencing Crown witnesses. I felt a desperate desire to do something. However, I had to accept Murphy's advice that there was little that he or Nash could do to stop him. I had to simply put my trust in Murphy and the justice system and hope that Justice would prevail in spite of Christal's interference.

When Court was re-convened, Nash called Mark Denman as the next Crown witness. I soon realized that this was the witness that Christal was coaching outside the Court room. I now assumed that Denman's evidence would also be distorted in the same way as the evidence Wally gave. I could just picture this witness telling the Court that he could remember everything on this isolated, routine file from six years ago as clearly as if it had happened yesterday. No doubt, he would recall me clearly even though we had no dealings since that time. He would also be able to recall conversations and his involvement clearly without the aid of any file or notes. In short, he would be able to recite his evidence flawlessly from the memorized script created from Christal's coaching.

Denman's evidence was just as I had predicted. It could have been damaging to my defence if Denman wasn't forced to admit that he never had any communications with Heritage Trust or the two brokers, Marcel Notschaele or Wally Pevcevicius. He also identified an interim agreement showing the trade of the Garmaz house for the acreage property that Garmaz was buying. This document had come from his file and was not found on the Heritage Trust file. Ironically, all the Crown witnesses had now given evidence that this document was part of the mortgage application that went to Heritage Trust. There was no doubt that the architect of this confusion was Christal. During his investigation, he had introduced this document to each of the Crown witnesses and caused them to believe that they had actually seen and relied upon it. I now understood the horror of how I was being framed by this fabricated evidence. Christal's actions were transparent but I wondered if Judge Stack could appreciate what had happened.

On the completion of Denman's evidence, I was concerned that Nash was succeeding in arousing suspicion with Judge Stack about the transaction. However, there was still no evidence of any actions on my part that could be categorized as wrongful. Therefore, according to my research, there was no evidence to put before a jury at a trial. For that reason, Judge Stack would have to dismiss the criminal charge on the basis that the Crown's case lacked evidence that would justify a committal order. On the evidence presented, there was no basis for a decision to order a trial in Queen's Bench Court.

As the Court recessed for a coffee break, I waited for Murphy to join me in the conference room. As we entered the room, Murphy indicated that he was a little perturbed by the proceedings. Before I could say anything, he remarked:

"As you can see, Orest, they really have no evidence that you did anything wrong, here. Now they're trying to drag in things that are irrelevant to try and show that you had dealings with two different brokers. Denman wants us to believe that even without a file, he can remember back six years and he sure knows how to tell a story. This whole business of Denman's evidence has a terrible smell to it. It's obvious that Christal got a hold of that interim agreement from Denman and then persuaded the other Crown witnesses to believe that they saw it in the application that went to Heritage Trust. But don't worry about that! I'll still get a chance to cross-examine Christal. I'll get him to admit where that document came from and that it wasn't part of the Heritage Trust application. That should clear up that little mystery and leave the Crown's case capsized in the proverbial creek."

I could see that Murphy was in good form and ready to respond to the tactics being employed by Christal and Nash. I smiled at Murphy's comments and was amazed that he refrained from using crude and vulgar remarks. Most other criminal lawyers used it as part of their main vocabulary, except in Court of course. Murphy's comments dissipated all of my concerns about Denman's evidence. At that point, I was feeling emotionally drained and physically exhausted. I looked up at Murphy and asked what other Crown witnesses would be giving evidence today. Murphy thoughtfully replied:

"There are three other witnesses for this afternoon. They will be real short since they are only being called to identify their signatures on the mortgage documents. They acted as witnesses and Commissioner for Oaths on the real estate documents. We should be finished early this afternoon."

Murphy needed to make some telephone calls so I left the conference room to take a walk in the main reception area. When court resumed, the three final witnesses were completed as expected and Court was then adjourned to the next day. As I left, I agreed to meet Murphy the following morning before Court and I returned home to rest up after this ugly experience. Murphy predicted that the balance of the Crown's case would likely be completed tomorrow and we would then know if this case could be resolved without a trial. The waiting would be difficult but I was determined to bravely endure it.

Although a person may be able to train the mind to cope with specific anxieties, it is usually impossible to face an unusual and protracted situation in a calm and rational state of mind. I could easily cope with being in a Court room to observe or handle a case since these were familiar experiences for me. However, the experience of being accused of a criminal act and being put on trial was an improbable situation that could not be anticipated. I could not rationalize or face it with a calm state of mind. Although I tried to maintain a relaxed disposition at home with my family, this ordeal was straining my ability to even function. I therefore withdrew as much as possible from the daily activities at home to rest and relax. My legal practice required my attention but I was able to reschedule and postpone my work while I devoted my attention and energies to this ongoing nightmare. My only hope was that SOON it would be over and SOON everything could return to normal once again.

As I waited outside the Court room for Murphy's arrival on the fourth day of the Preliminary Hearing, my feelings were now numb to the proceedings around me. I gazed at Christal as he carried on his coaching with a gentleman whom I guessed to be Stephen Garmaz. I had only met Garmaz briefly and could never have identified him without assistance. However, I suspected that Garmaz would be more accurate in his recollections when he gave his evidence. After all, he had the benefit of Christal's coaching in reconstructing his memory. As I watched this shameful display of abuse in the Court system, I felt sickened. However, I couldn't react emotionally because I felt totally drained. Instead, I comforted myself with the thought that this whole ordeal would soon be over. All I could do was pray that Judge Stack would agree that there was no evidence to justify a committal order and dismiss the criminal charge.

I was jolted out of my thoughts by Murphy's greeting as he approached:

"Good morning, Orest! I see Christal is up to his old tactics of preparing the Crown witness so that they say exactly what he wants in Court. I never like to see that when I'm prosecuting because cops tend to mess these things up worse than if they left it alone. That witness is going to sound rehearsed and everybody in Court is going to know that. Do you know if that witness is Garmaz?"

While Murphy was speaking, I quickly gathered my thoughts and then responded:

"I think it is, Patrick! I believe I only saw Garmaz once. Maybe I saw him two times during the deal. That was six years ago. But he looks familiar. Is Garmaz supposed to be the first Crown witness today?"

Murphy was peering at Christal and the witness as they carried on a lively, friendly conversation. Then Murphy frowned and turned to me to answer:

"Yes! According to Nash's schedule of witnesses, he is supposed to be the first witness today. Anyway, let's step into the conference room for a minute and then we'll go into the Court room."

On Murphy's suggestion, we walked into the conference room. Before Murphy could say anything, I interjected:

"Patrick, I know this is premature, but what is your impression of how Judge Stack is reacting to the evidence? Do you see any favourable indications that he might dismiss this charge?"

Murphy was cautious in responding but proceeded to give me his confidential assessment:

"There's no way of knowing exactly how Stack is viewing the evidence. It's obvious that he is following it closely but he may chicken out in the end and simply set it over for trial. All we can do is present our argument and hope that he has the balls to turf the criminal charge out."

What Murphy said reflected my worst fears: that this Preliminary Hearing was really a waste of time. Even if there was no evidence, this case could still be set over for trial simply because the judge was too lazy or gutless to make a decision. The Court system gave the Provincial Judge at a Preliminary Hearing an unlimited latitude in setting matters over for trial. Therefore, this was the easiest approach for disposing of these cases. Often, judges feel pressured into making politically correct decisions that do not offend anyone. This is typically true if the case concerns vocal pressure groups. However, for some judges, it is a concern in every trial or hearing. Using this rationale, the safest course for Stack would be to commit the criminal charge for trial in Queen's Bench Court. The justification of the judge is that by doing so, the Crown Prosecutor is not offended and the accused person has the opportunity of defending himself at the trial. The fact that such a decision unnecessarily prolongs the ordeal for the accused is not a consideration. The fact that the costs of such a trial is significant for the accused and the taxpayer are never considered by the Provincial Judge since it really isn't his concern.

It was no wonder that our Court system was becoming more backlogged with cases. This results in delays which cause unjust and unfair adjudications. This situation of delay in adjudicating cases became so outrageous that the Supreme Court of Canada ultimately recognized a need to dismiss cases that had been improperly delayed. Unfortunately, this did little to reform the Court system. For a short time, it granted relief by dismissing cases of accused people who suffered prejudice from delays. However, the Supreme Court of Canada later retracted that position and the hopes of reform quickly vanished.

Murphy and I then spent a few minutes talking about the next Crown witnesses that would be testifying. We briefly discussed our research and assessments on each witness. As our time ran out, we got up and strolled into the Court room. On entering, I glanced at Eileen Nash who was still dressed in the same black outfit and looking more macabre than before. Although Crown Prosecutors have always complained and even threatened to strike to protest their inadequate salaries, one had to assume that Nash should have been able to afford at least one change of clothes. The only other explanation that I could conceive was that Nash's cold body temperature prevented perspiration and therefore she never needed to change her clothes.

As I gazed at Nash, the thought struck me that she looked cold, emotionless and strangely appropriate for the environment in which she worked. Possibly, she had been shaped by the Court system and the multitude of cases that she handled. She now dressed and acted like a trained robot programmed to execute the commands of a higher master. For a moment, I actually felt sympathy for her plight and was glad that I had resisted the prospect of becoming a Criminal lawyer. My current ordeal was not enviable but at least I could leave the Court system once it was over. At least, I could escape before it could suck the life out of me. Nash had not been that lucky.

As we settled into our seats, Court resumed and Nash called Stephen Garmaz as the next Crown witness. Garmaz was tall and slender in physical stature and displayed a noticeable cocky attitude about everything that he did. His over-confidence was partially attributed to Christal's assurances that he would not be charged for any criminal actions in this case. Garmaz was employed by IBM as a technician and his wife was employed as a registered nurse. Together they generated a significant income and used their earning power to deal in real estate. Before I met them, they had bought and sold real estate through a mortgage broker, Dan Hewitt. It was through Hewitt that the Garmazs were educated on the art of applying for and securing mortgage loans and the other essential aspects of the real estate business.

Hewitt, like most mortgage brokers, followed the attitude of only presenting the specific information to mortgage companies that would qualify the applicant for the mortgage desired. Most mortgage brokers work on the premise that mortgage companies usually fail to detect undisclosed information or false entries in the application form. The attitude of mortgage brokers is that if any problem arises after a mortgage is granted, then the fault lies with the mortgage company in failing to investigate the mortgage applicants properly. If false information is discovered on a mortgage application form, then the broker simply insists that he didn't know about it. The mortgage application is then withdrawn only to be tendered to another mortgage company that might accept it.

It is no wonder that mortgage companies follow the practice of checking all information in mortgage applications carefully. However, in the unusual situation where a mortgage company suffers a loss, they are usually able to recover their loss through default insurance with Canada Mortgage and Housing Corporation ("CMHC"). In the unlikely event that the loss is not insured or CMHC refuses to pay, the blame must fall on someone. Usually it is the mortgage manager but in this case, the blame was miraculously shifted to me. Only with the help of Christal could such an unlikely event have occurred and it was now up to us to show how preposterous this was.

It was through Hewitt that I was introduced to Garmaz as someone who was interested in purchasing and financing the acreage property. At our first meeting, Garmaz considered the idea of financing the property and then reselling it but ultimately decided that he wished to purchase it for his own use. As a result, we executed documents that contemplated that I would take Garmaz's residence in trade as the down payment. Garmaz met with Denman who obtained all the information for the mortgage application. When Denman discovered that

Garmaz's residence was encumbered and not clear title as represented to him by Garmaz, the application was refused. As a result, that total transaction was cancelled. Garmaz then agreed to purchase the acreage property, arrange a mortgage and then resell it immediately. I agreed to accept a second mortgage on the property so that Garmaz could earn an immediate profit of five thousand dollars. Our inquiries then located a realtor, Peter Horn who agreed to purchase the property if the mortgages were assumable. These terms were acceptable to Garmaz who then met with Wally Pevcevicius and provided him with the information to secure a mortgage on the property. A mortgage was then secured with Heritage Trust and the transaction was concluded as contemplated.

When Garmaz began to testify about these transactions, he was noticeably cautious. He had to be aware that any alleged wrongdoing would first be attributable to his conduct. His testimony was well rehearsed and specifically directed to support the Crown's position that I was the culprit. His general attitude on all the questions was that he couldn't remember the specific incident or discussions. He insisted that he couldn't even remember signing documents which obviously bore his signature. On the sensitive issues of who provided information to the mortgage brokers, his response was that he couldn't remember doing it and therefore it must have been done by me. Whenever he could, he insisted that he didn't understand anything and that he relied on me because I was a lawyer. This was an obvious ploy since I was such a convenient scapegoat. Who better to blame than the person who was already charged with fraud!

The disturbing part of his evidence was that it had changed from the statements that he had prepared with the assistance of his lawyer to present to the police during the investigation. In the original statements, he admitted that he met with the mortgage brokers. Now that he was giving evidence at my Preliminary Hearing, he close to lie about this. He denied meeting with any mortgage brokers and insisted that I must have met with them. He denied that he provided them his personal information for the mortgage application and claimed that I must have provided it. This was ridiculous since much of the information on the mortgage application form was personal in nature and had to come from Garmaz and his wife. When questioned about that, Garmaz steadfastly insisted that the information must have been given by me since he couldn't remember meeting with any mortgage brokers. Ironically, Garmaz was not aware that Denman had already testified that he had personally met with Garmaz to fill out his mortgage application. Therefore, everyone in Court could easily see that Garmaz was lying in Court and committing perjury. Furthermore, his whole testimony was so unbelievable that he lost all credibility. Unfortunately, in this hearing, his evidence was not being assessed for credibility. Instead, Garmaz's manufactured evidence would be accepted at face value to determine if the case should go to trial.

Garmaz concluded his evidence with his description of a telephone conversation that he had with John Chubb of Heritage Trust approximately two years after the real estate deal was completed. Chubb had telephoned him to advise that he was now administrating the file regarding the mortgage loan made to

Garmaz. Chubb explained that Heritage Trust has suffered a loss when the property went into foreclosure and that he was attempting to collect the insurance claim from CMHC. He wanted a letter from Garmaz stating that Garmaz had money from a gift or some other source that would have been sufficient to complete the real estate deal in addition to the mortgage proceeds from Heritage Trust. Garmaz then advised Chubb that he never had any funds as described since the real estate deal was completed on the basis of a second mortgage. Chubb then insisted that Garmaz provide him with this letter even though it was false. Chubb even threatened Garmaz that there would be dire consequences for Garmaz if he did not cooperate.

This evidence came out as a complete surprise to everyone in the Court room. Nash then proceeded to clarify what had ultimately happened:

Nash: "Did you, in fact, supply the letter?"

Garmaz: "No, I certainly did not. That's fraud. He was quite keen on getting this letter. It really upset me because I didn't expect that to come from someone that is supposed to be, I don't know, honest or ... it was quite an education, anyway. He had said if I had given him this letter, that he would then be able to take it to CMHC, that Heritage Trust would be happy because they would have their money and that CMHC would ... they would be okay and they would not come looking to retrieve their money from me. And I said to Mr. Chubb, "I don't have the money. I have no way of getting any money like that." And he said to me, "Who is to know you are not a good gambler? You could have won the money gambling." So he was very, very interested in getting that letter and sending me up the creek."

Judge Stack was noticeably shocked by what he heard and asked Garmaz to repeat his testimony again to enable him to make proper notes of it. Nash was embarrassed by the testimony because it destroyed the credibility of one of her main witnesses, John Chubb. The testimony of Chubb was important because he was the complainant that caused the investigation to be started by Christal. Usually, the police and the Crown Prosecutors are more careful in their investigations of these cases. Ordinarily they refuse to investigate and prosecute cases where there is an indication that the complaint was made to satisfy personal motives or to achieve the collection of money. Yet in this case, the police and the Crown Prosecutor were prosecuting Chubb's complaint which was obviously filed because Chubb could not collect a loss for Heritage Trust on a mortgage loan. Furthermore it was now clear that Chubb was guilty of an attempted fraud on CMHC and should have been charged for his improper conduct. Instead, all of this was being intentionally overlooked and ignored to pursue a case with higher profile: THE PROSECUTION OF A LAWYER FOR FRAUD.

When Nash completed her examination of Garmaz, she requested an adjournment for the mid-morning coffee break. Murphy automatically joined me in the conference room for a quick discussion. As Murphy closed the door, he exclaimed:

"Boy, was that great! We couldn't have asked for a better break than we just got. Garmaz is very shaky on the stand. He's also lying about obvious things.

Everyone can see that he's evasive about answering questions. He's trying to hide his involvement in the real estate deal. In my cross-examination, I'm going to demonstrate how evasive he really is and nothing more will be necessary."

As Murphy spoke, he displayed a broad smile and seemed to glow with enthusiasm. Garmaz was the Crown's key witness and was expected to deliver the decisive evidence of my involvement in arranging the mortgage. Although he tried to disassociate himself from the mortgage applications, it was transparent that he had to be involved more than he was willing to admit. He had fooled nobody with his attempts to implicate me by claiming that I must have provided his personal information to the mortgage brokers. However, it was important for Murphy to get Garmaz to admit during his cross-examination that he had dealt directly with the mortgage brokers. It was necessary to dissolve his suggestion that I had provided information as alleged in the criminal charge. After all, the test in this Preliminary Hearing was that of "some evidence" of fraud. Murphy's job was to demonstrate that there was no evidence of fraud to avoid a trial in this case.

These proceedings presented an interesting dilemma regarding the "onus of proof" or the responsibility of the accused person to prove or disprove anything. In a trial, the principle of law is that the Crown Prosecutor has the "onus" to prove the criminal charge beyond a reasonable doubt. However, the purpose of a Preliminary Hearing is simply to determine if there is some evidence that would warrant a trial on the criminal charge. The practical reality is that an accused person has the onus (or responsibility) to demonstrate that there is no evidence that would justify a trial. If the accused person fails to do so, he will inevitably be ordered to stand trial on the criminal charge.

I decided not to question Murphy on his approach in cross-examination since I would observe this when court resumed in a few minutes. Instead, I asked him about Garmaz's evidence relating to Chubb:

"Patrick, I'm curious about that evidence from Garmaz about Chubb demanding a false letter to defraud CMHC. Will that help our case in this Preliminary Hearing?"

As I spoke, Murphy lit up with a smile. As he suppressed his laughter, he responded:

"That evidence was enough to bring the house down on the Crown's case. If this was a trial, many judges would stop everything, give the Crown Prosecutor hell for proceeding with the case and then dismiss the charge. Stack is a little more reserved about these things but he was noticeably taken back by what he heard. I'm sure that Stack will keep that evidence in mind when he makes his decision. I'm going to focus on the other evidence and argue the dismissal on the basis that there is no evidence to justify sending this case to trial. That's the safest way to go and I'm satisfied that we've got a good argument for dismissal."

I felt relieved to know that the case was progressing well for us and that Murphy was confident about a dismissal. We agreed to talk later and I left the conference room for a short walk into the reception area. A few minutes later, I returned to the Court room and the hearing resumed. Murphy spent the balance of the morning cross-examining Garmaz on each of the documents he signed. He questioned Garmaz on his testimony that he couldn't remember them or that he didn't read them before he signed them. Garmaz then admitted that he understood what the documents said and that he understood his responsibilities with respect to the mortgage that he obtained from Heritage Trust. Garmaz also admitted meeting with the mortgage brokers but insisted that he couldn't remember any conversations or details of what happened. As Murphy concluded, Garmaz was admitting that he didn't know what happened and he couldn't remember what happened.

After the cross-examination was completed, the Court was adjourned until two o'clock. I felt pleased with the admissions that were extracted during the cross-examination. Although Murphy had other commitments to meet, I pulled him aside in the conference room to confirm his assessment of Garmaz's testimony. Murphy spoke confidently and without any reservation:

"There's nothing to worry about! There is nothing in Garmaz's evidence that we should be concerned about. Nash will call Mrs. Garmaz and then John Chubb this afternoon. I'm not expecting any surprises from either of them. You can relax! We'll just ride this one through and wrap it up. There is no evidence that any fraud was committed by you and Stack has to dismiss the charge. If anyone should have been charged, it should have been Chubb for his attempted fraud on CMHC. Garmaz and that broker, Wally, should be charged for the mortgage application that was presented to Heritage Trust. But I would question if there really is enough evidence to lay charges against Garmaz or the broker from the kind of evidence that we have here. It's obvious from the evidence that Gilmour mishandled the mortgage application and that is what resulted in the loss by Heritage Trust. There's no way that anyone can seriously believe that Gilmour relied on anything in the application form. This must have been obvious to Nash and Christal even if they don't know anything about real estate deals. In any event, this criminal charge against you is really nonsense. It's becoming pretty clear to everyone, especially Stack, that you didn't do anything wrong."

Murphy then advised me that he would see me at two o'clock and scurried off. A feeling of relief descended upon me as I sat back in my chair in the conference room. I took a few deep breathes of air to relax and strengthen myself for the continuation of this ordeal. I then decided to telephone my wife during this court recess to comfort her and to tell her about the progress in the proceedings. Everything was now quiet and I knew that I had a few minutes before a Court Orderly would ask me to vacate the room so that he could lock it. My quiet conversation with my wife helped to calm my nerves and to develop a fresh perspective on my Court case.

During the noon Court recess, I had to run some errands for my clients to the Land Titles Office and to Corporate Registry. Normally, these errands can be quickly completed but I used the extra time to visit with acquaintances and returned to Court at two o'clock. On my arrival in the Court room, I discovered that Murphy had returned before me and was speaking to Nash at her counsel table. I settled into my seat and watched as Murphy and Nash spoke in whispered voices and pointed to documents in Nash's document binder. A few minutes later, their discussions were interrupted as Court resumed for the afternoon.

Nash immediately called her next Crown witness, Douglas Gahn. Gahn was the lawyer who handled the foreclosure of the acreage property on instructions from Heritage Trust after the default in mortgage payments occurred. Gahn testified that the property was owned by Darrell Thompson who had purchased the property from Garmaz. Gahn's evidence was needed primarily to identify documents and to confirm that CMHC had refused to pay pursuant to their insurance coverage on this property. The reason given by CMHC was that Gilmour had failed to properly verify the information in the mortgage application and to verify the down payment in the purchase agreement. He further confirmed that Heritage Trust ultimately secured a judgement against Darrell Thompson for the deficiency loss in the foreclosure action.

As I listened to Gahn's testimony, I marvelled at the contradiction in the position that Heritage Trust had taken. They had obviously accepted Darrell Thompson as the new owner of the property. According to the law, Darrell Thompson had become mortgagor and was personally responsible for the payment of the mortgage debt. This change in ownership also released Garmaz from all further financial responsibility under the mortgage. Any interest that Garmaz had in the property or the mortgage was now the absolute interest of Darrell Thompson. Heritage Trust took legal proceedings to enforce their new position by foreclosing on the mortgage against Darrell Thompson. Heritage Trust also obtained a deficiency judgement against him for the deficiency shortfall that might be realized from the resale of the foreclosed property. Garmaz was no longer relevant to the position of Heritage Trust and there was no reason for Heritage Trust to pursue any recourse against anyone except Darrell Thompson. Yet, this was all being ignored by Nash in the prosecution of this case in the same way as it was ignored or subdued by Christal as he pressed for the criminal charge to be laid.

Gahn's testimony was brief and so was the cross-examination. Nash then called Gayle Garmaz as her next Crown witness. She testified that she had signed documents along with her husband Stephen Garmaz but that she couldn't remember anything very clearly. It was obvious that this was a very traumatic and terrifying experience for her. I could empathize with her as these proceedings must have been as painful and unfair to her as they were to me. She tried to answer questions honestly and fairly but she was clear in saying that she couldn't remember much and couldn't be sure of anything. In contrast to her husband, she answered questions honestly. She admitted that she remembered meeting the mortgage brokers who came to her house although she could not remember what happened. That was easy to understand since this transaction had taken place over five years ago. Nobody could really be expected to remember much about this situation after so many years had passed. She admitted that she cooperated with her husband to purchase and mortgage real estate because of his desire to get involved in the real estate market. She was now prepared to tell what she knew and face whatever consequence might arise. It was easy to respect her for her honesty and I felt sorry that she had to endure these proceedings. I was happy for her when she was finally excused as a witness.

The last Crown witness to be called that afternoon was John Chubb. He was a short, middle-aged, balding man with probing eyes that leered through dark framed glasses. His hair was slicked back in a hairstyle that was popular forty years ago and combed in a pattern to hide the balding spots on his head. He looked like the least likely person that a financial institution would hire to project an image of honesty.

As Chubb stepped into the witness stand, I reflected on the first time that I had met him. Chubb started his career in finances as a mortgage broker and quickly demonstrated that he had the least amount of scruples in arranging mortgages. The story that Garmaz told about Chubb asking for a false letter was no different than the tactics that he used when arranging mortgages for clients. In a mortgage application that Chubb presented for one of my clients, I had to counsel my client to resist making representations that were exaggerated and misleading. Chubb had advised him to do so on the premise that nobody could prove otherwise. Chubb's professed attitude about false statements to mortgage companies was that he used this tactic when the mortgage company had no means of proving that the information was false. Because of his devious tactics as a mortgage broker, he now viewed all mortgage applications as being presented in the same manner.

After a short employment at Heritage Trust, Chubb moved over to North West Trust Company after the reorganization of the two trust companies. He was no longer presenting mortgage applications for borrowers and earning a commission only if they were approved and funded. Now he was earning a good salary for reviewing and approving mortgage loans. It was interesting that Chubb's dishonesty and deceitfulness as a mortgage broker had not seriously damaged his reputation. His tactics had worked favourably for him which resulted in securing comfortable employment. The only glimmer of justice was that North West Trust Company ultimately discovered Chubb's true character and his employment was terminated prior to the commencement of these court proceedings. With his reputation having finally been exposed, Chubb left the finance industry to work in a retail store selling paint. This made me realize that even that industry must have its share of questionable sales practices.

Chubb was unable to give any evidence about the mortgage loan itself as he was not employed by Heritage Trust at that time. Instead, his primary evidence was about his efforts to collect the deficiency loss on the mortgage loan using the CMHC coverage. He quietly denied any suggestion that he tried to obtain a false letter from Garmaz. He confirmed that he pressed Garmaz for a letter but expected it to be truthful. The comment about Garmaz getting the money from gambling was fine with Chubb so long as it was put forward as being truthful. In any event, Chubb wanted everyone to know that he would only be involved in dealing with this claim on a proper basis.

Chubb also stated that the purchase agreement showing that Garmaz was trading his home for the acreage property was provided to Heritage Trust with the mortgage application. He believed that this document was needed to verify the downpayment by the Purchaser. He had no way of knowing if that document was received by Heritage Trust but he insisted that it had to be that document or something else. He could not accept the fact that Gilmour had neglected to secure any verification of downpayment as CMHC had claimed when refusing to pay the default loss.

In general, Chubb's evidence was quite predictable and well rehearsed. Although it provided continuity in the evidence of witnesses, it was not enlightening for anyone in the Court room. During Murphy's cross-examination, Chubb was questioned on his attempted fraud on CMHC. Chubb tried to avoid the issue by advising Murphy that he was not the person on trial. His cocky attitude fooled nobody and the truth was as evident as the grease in his hair.

At the conclusion of Chubb's testimony, Nash advised the Court that the only remaining Crown witness was Christal. She expected his evidence to be brief and confirmed that the Crown would then close its case. It was agreed that the Court would be adjourned to the next morning as everyone was feeling the exhaustion of these protracted proceedings. There was no concern of any difficulty in completing this case on the last day scheduled for this hearing.

As Murphy and I walked out of the Court room, I quickly asked him for his assessment. He commented that he would be preparing his comments for the final argument tomorrow and he would be urging Judge Stack to dismiss the criminal charge. He encouraged me to go home and rest and assured me that this whole ordeal would be over tomorrow.

On my way home, I reflected on everything that had happened over the last four days and silently prayed that this whole ordeal would finally end. My anxiety was at a critically high level. I knew that I could not continue to suffer this torment much longer. It had to end and my only hope was that Murphy's assessment was accurate.

When Court resumed the following morning, Christal was called to the witness stand. His first evidence was to describe the search and seizure of documents from my home. According to Christal, nothing out of the ordinary happened and everything that occurred at my home was quite amicable and cordial. Nobody was even upset about this startling intrusion into our lives. He confirmed that I and my wife responded cooperatively to his demands and acted as if these were everyday occurrences.

Christal chose NOT to mention that when he first confronted my wife with his first Search Warrant, he threatened to kick the front door down if she didn't open it immediately. He also chose NOT to mention that his rude actions and his obnoxious remarks had reduced my wife to tears. Additionally, Christal chose NOT to mention that I was obviously shaken and upset by his intrusion into our home. Furthermore, Christal chose to NOT to mention that he had initially threatened to remove all the files in my office and my computer. He also failed to mention that he was actually proceeding to seize and move every file and document in my office until we satisfied him that we had no documents that he was looking for. All of these obvious facts were now described in the same tainted manner that characterized his entire investigation. Christal knew how to present his evidence to avoid saying anything that could discredit the Crown's case. When challenged on any points of improper conduct, he knew how to explain his recollection without being branded as a liar. Typically, he was walking that fine line of lying in Court but hoping not to be caught or appear suspicious in what he said. Christal made his traumatic intrusion into our home sound like it was a pleasant and joyous surprise for us!

To hear Christal testify made me wonder if he had confused his searches at my home with instances where he had searched his own home for missing documents. This was the only explanation that I could imagine where he could conduct such a search of someone's home and receive such cooperation and loving, sympathetic understanding. Although I was disgusted with the way that he coloured his testimony, I was not really surprised. During this last week, I had watched him influence the other Crown witnesses to colour and bolster their evidence. I already knew that he would lie and commit perjury to succeed at this Hearing to send my case to trial in Queen's Bench Court.

Christal then produced a copy of the tapes that contained the recorded conversation that we had together with a typed transcript of our conversation. These were marked as Exhibits without objection from Murphy. It was our assessment that my statements showed a positive desire to cooperate and were consistent with our position that there was no wrongdoing. Christal also identified some bank documents and other records that demonstrated what happened in the transaction. However, these did little to add information about the mortgage application or the central issues in this case.

On the conclusion of Nash's questions, Murphy then cross-examined Christal. The main question that Murphy wanted to ask related to the interim agreement that showed that Garmaz was trading his residence for the acreage property. Christal admitted that the source of this document was from Denman, who never dealt with Heritage Trust or the two brokers who arranged that mortgage, Marcel Notschaele and Wally Pevcevicius. Then Murphy asked him if he searched the Heritage Trust file to locate a copy of that document and whether he found a copy of that document on the Heritage Trust file. Christal admitted that he did search the Heritage Trust file and that he did NOT find a copy of that document on that file.

This final admission should have conclusively finished the case and called for an immediate dismissal of the charge. It was so obvious that the two mortgage brokers, Notschaele and Pevcevicius, as well as Gilmour and Chubb of Heritage Trust, had all either lied or simply been mistaken. They all stated that they thought they received a copy of that document and relied upon it in the mortgage application. In fact, it was obvious that they couldn't have had that document and that Heritage Trust was never in possession of that document. It was also evident that when Christal got a copy of that document from Denman, he showed it to each of the Crown witnesses. Each of them assumed that they had seen that document and were induced by Christal to believe that they must have seen that document when the transaction took place. As a result, all of these witnesses had lied while testifying either because they wanted to believe that they must have received such a document or because they simply couldn't remember and were induced to believe that by Christal.

What was really shocking was that these key witnesses were influenced to lie in Court because they believed Christal suggestions about that document as being part of the file of Heritage Trust. This may well have been the worst case of evidence tampering that I had ever heard about. I was aware of cases where police officers, through sloppiness or over zealousness, had altered evidence in a case. Very recently, the case of Wilson Neepoose featured a police officer who altered documents and then presented false testimony in Court. Unfortunately, the Courts process numerous other cases in which this prevalent and deceitful practice of police officers is evident.

In most cases, the police officer will only involve himself in this illegal tactic of altering evidence and lying in Court. Christal's actions were more despicable because his scheme involved manipulating other witnesses to give false testimony. It was bad enough that he manufactured evidence by introducing a document that never formed part of the file of Heritage Trust. There was really no need for this document to ever be put before the Court to confuse and cloud the issues. There certainly was no need to influence the evidence of witnesses by showing them that document and inducing them to commit perjury by stating that they had received and relied upon that document.

Although the evidence of Christal was shocking to me, I have since learned from experienced criminal lawyers that this situation of altering evidence is commonplace. What Christal did in falsifying his own evidence about his execution of the search warrants is nothing unusual in criminal trials. Nor was it so unusual that a police officer like Christal would induce witnesses to commit perjury by intentionally or mistakenly giving false testimony in Court.

Over the past twenty years, I have heard of many actual accounts from lawyers, Crown Prosecutors and even police officers detailing how some police officers act in a discreditable manner. Their motivation is to obtain convictions in cases where they have insufficient evidence. Although this common practice is well known to lawyers and judges, they maintain an unspoken understanding that the integrity of police officers is not to be questioned unless the false evidence is blatant and obvious. Even on these rare occasions, the criminal charge may be dismissed but the police officers are seldom reprimanded. As a result, some police officers will routinely falsify or alter their evidence sufficiently to secure a conviction in Court. They know that their evidence will usually be accepted without question, resulting in unjust convictions. This factor alone contributes to the growing resentment and mistrust that the general public feels towards police and the justice system.

What Christal had done was totally pre-meditated, obviously malicious and blatantly improper. Unfortunately, I was the target of this judicial persecution and Christal would avoid any criticism on the basis that he was simply doing his job as a police officer. Although it was possible that he could receive a sanction for such misdeeds, that was unlikely. Christal could avoid blame by saying that the actual prosecution of this case was the responsibility of the Crown Prosecutor. He could point out that Nash had the actual control of the case and all that he did was to assist with the Crown witnesses. No matter how one evaluated it, he knew that he could act in this discreditable and malicious manner and avoid any consequences even if his actions were obvious to everyone in Court.

Sadness filled my thoughts as I reflected on the actions of Christal. It was still hard to comprehend how this one police officer had acted so maliciously to implicate me and charge me with this criminal offence. I consoled myself with the thought that he too must atone for his sins. As Murphy always said: "We must forgive our enemies and ask God to give them a cool place in Hell." I liked Murphy's concept of forgiveness. Judging from his happy disposition, it worked well for him. In Christal's case, I was sure that he had already signed a pact with the Devil. Therefore, there was no sense in me getting in the middle of that arrangement by asking God to intervene.

CHAPTER FOURTEEN

THE COMMITTAL ORDER

After all the lawyers have spoken, the climax of a trial or hearing is the judge's decision, which is commonly referred to as the verdict. In a Preliminary Hearing, the decision is whether a committal order should be made that would require the case to be tried in Queen's Bench Court. It is a natural expectation that judges will be impartial and will make divine decisions that reflect the collective wisdom of society. From an elevated loft that conjures for many the image of God speaking from Heaven, the judge is viewed as invincible, totally knowledgeable and unquestionably just. All the hopes of our civilized and obedient society rest on the assumption that a judge will properly fulfil his role of deciding each case with fairness and propriety.

Sadly, in current times, the general public has had a multitude of reasons to distrust judges and the legal system. Rather than emulating the ideal that has been ascribed to them, many judges choose to ignore their responsibilities and even abuse their position. Cynicism and an unrealistic view of the ideals of society cause judges to make improper decisions which are devoid of any legal justification. Because there is currently no review mechanism for the performance of judges in Canada, this deterioration is never checked or treated. As a result, injustice is simply perpetuated until these judges retire.

One of the most subtle abuses by judges of their position is the blatant actions of some judges to avoid work by making impromptu decisions without giving thorough consideration to the case. To protect the integrity of the legal system, other judges will justify and rationalize these ludicrous decisions. If this wasn't done, the judiciary would be unable to hide the obvious reality that the actions and abilities of judges should be more closely scrutinized. Although lawyers have been reluctant to criticize judges for fear of the resultant ramifications, a recent legal magazine published the results of a survey from lawyers on Provincial Judges in each province. The results confirmed what the lawyers already knew: that there are a few exceptional judges, many mediocre judges and too many bad judges. Although this survey did spark some reaction from the general public, nothing ever resulted to call for changes or a review of this situation.

After a restless night, during which I replayed the events of the whole week in my mind, the fifth and concluding day of the Preliminary Hearing had finally arrived. After evaluating all the evidence, I was satisfied with Murphy's assessment that the charge should be dismissed. Based on my legal research, this case was one where there was no evidence on which a reasonable jury could make a finding a fraud. However, the question that remained was: WOULD JUDGE STACK HAVE THE COURAGE TO MAKE THE DECISION TO DISMISS THIS CRIMINAL CHARGE? The other alternative was that Judge Stack might renege on his responsibilities and simply make a committal order that would refer this case for trial in Queen's Bench Court.

My morning routine was filled with the usual commotion that prevails in family life with children. On this day, it was a blessing as it helped my wife and me to focus our attention away from the nervous anticipation of the verdict that was now imminent. Today, we would find out if we could rid ourselves of the torment that had plagued our lives since Christal's first visit over one year ago. If I lost today in Court, this nightmare would continue to haunt us for the another year or longer as this case slowly progressed to trial in Queen's Bench Court.

As the worrisome prospects flooded my mind, I struggled to dispel my doubts. I knew that I had to place my faith in the justice system and trust it with blind devotion, like the statute of the blind goddess who held the scales of justice. In Murphy's assessment, I was blameless of any wrongdoing. It was therefore immaterial as to what Nash had said earlier to convince Judge Stack otherwise. It was clear from the evidence that there was no wrongdoing on my part and I was entitled at law to be presumed innocent. The Crown was obligated to bring forth proof that I had committed an act that was wrongful and fraudulent In the absence of such evidence, I was entitled by law to have the charge dismissed. Surely, this would be as obvious to Judge Stack as it was to everyone else in the Court room. A fair decision was the least that I could expect from the justice system.

As I drove my car downtown, I could feel the adrenaline racing through my body. This caused me to feel alert and somewhat hyper to the activities around me. To counter this, I turned up the volume of the radio to distract my mind from thoughts of the pending proceedings. I laboured in agony to drive my car on this final journey downtown to confront and eliminate this continuing nightmare. I knew that I had to maintain a calm composure and face this situation without revealing my anxiety which was heightened by feelings of uncertainty.

On reaching the Court House, I proceeded to the cafeteria. On entering, I glanced around the room but I couldn't see Murphy anywhere. Without thinking, I automatically secured a hot chocolate and sat down at an isolated table to wait for him. As I sat there, I began to study the people at the other tables. Some of these were Court House employees on their "pre-work coffee breaks". The discussions at these tables were lively and louder and typically featured the topic that this was the last work day of the week. The excitement was growing that after a few more hours of work, the good times would begin again. These perennial denizens of the Court House felt no anxiety from the proceedings that they worked on and no remorse for the victims that the Courts produced on a daily basis. To them, this was just a job. As soon as it was over, they could go back to their lives. The misery of those unfortunate souls caught within the legal system would be left behind in this building with no concern from anyone that worked here.

The saddest situation was that of the lawyers who sat at the other tables, either alone or in groups of two or three. Many lawyers were having their breakfast or simply a coffee away from their families. Their typical morning routine would be to either reflect on a case or share gossip with other lawyers until court was ready to start. Some of them bore the sad and disillusioned faces of lawyers who had witnessed more misery and pain suffered by their clients than anyone should have. In a strange paradox, these lawyers also became victims and casualties of the legal system.

Sadly, these lawyers eventually became hardened to the realities around them in the same way as medical personnel become impervious to suffering and death that they must continually witness. This is a necessary and natural transformation that enables lawyers to cope with the sorrow generated by the failures of the justice system. In the process, these lawyers progressively lose all feeling as their ability for compassion slowly dies within them. As disillusionment mounts, they begin to question whether they should continue to do their best to obtain a just result. Eventually, they begin to recognize the futility of a system that fails to meet the expectations of the general public. As the lawyer's ability to feel compassion for the plight of a client dies, so does that part of the human soul that makes him a caring and feeling person. In the end, all that is left is a functional robot that continues to perform a task for which he is programmed, without feeling or emotion.

Unfortunately, for most lawyers, there is no escape from the drudgery of the work or the misery that must be continually endured because of it. The early idealism of every lawyer soon fades by accepting the reality that the justice system frequently fails to provide justice. The task of defending clients in a system manipulated by police and Crown Prosecutors inevitably becomes overwhelming. Disillusionment quickly escalates as the lawyers realize that the decisions of some judges are frequently based on their whims, biases and irrational assumptions. The incompetence of many judges leads to decisions based on favouritism rather than a proper consideration and application of the law. Because there are a limited number of reasonable judges, despair accumulates as an increasing number of clients appear before incompetent and irrational judges. In such a case, the lawyer can do nothing as the judge callously tramples on the dignity of the judicial system in dispensing "Wild West Justice." The lawyer is then left to deal with the despair of his client and to rationalize his role in contributing to the tragedy. Ultimately, it becomes too difficult a task to explain and defend the operation of a legal system that fails to meet the needs and expectations of society.

It is no wonder that there is an alarming increase in the number of lawyers who have become disillusioned and are looking for ways and means to escape the distasteful work of practising law. Some are fortunate in being able to specialize in an area of law that allows them to escape the prospect of Court work. However, most practitioners find themselves undertaking some court work to supplement and guarantee income and cash flow that would otherwise not be available to them. Another possible escape is to leave the practice of law and enter a business unrelated to the practice of law. Unfortunately, lawyers in general are poorly trained to operate businesses, including that of their own legal practices. Some lawyers, such as myself, venture into real estate development and real estate transactions. However, the fluctuating market conditions force most lawyers to return to the practice of law to earn a livelihood and support their families. The result of this disillusionment is an increasing incidence of alcoholism and drug abuse for many lawyers which in turn generates a higher incidence of divorce and even suicide. A recent survey described in "The Canadian Lawyer" magazine confirmed that one third of all lawyers are seriously affected by this crisis in the legal profession. Similar government studies reflect that as many as fifty percent of all lawyers are plagued by problems of alcohol or drug use.

As I reflected on the realities that are faced daily by lawyers in the practice of our profession, I watched the doorway for Murphy's appearance. A few minutes later, I was pleased to see him coming in and signalled to him. He acknowledged me and then walked over to get a coffee before joining me. As Murphy approached, I looked at him and noticed for the first time that he too had been shaped by the years of practice in the legal profession. The harsh reality was that the legal system was a gruelling, omnipotent force that left nobody unaltered. Murphy's salvation was his sense of humour and his light-hearted attitude towards the tribulations of life. This not only helped him in his daily endeavours but touched everyone that he dealt with along the way.

As Murphy sat down, his serious mood lightened as he opened the conversation with a friendly inquiry:

"Good Morning, Orest! How are you feeling today, and how's everything with your family?"

These moments of anguish that we suffered were made more bearable by knowing that Murphy cared and was sincerely devoting his best energies to resolving this problem. I felt comfortable with Murphy and I was confident that he would present a good case to the Court to resolve the criminal charge that had paralysed my life. There was no doubt that Murphy knew how I felt so I tried not to complain. Instead, I answered him in a positive and forceful manner:

"The kids are fine! Pat and I are managing to cope with the stress at this time. I just hope that this criminal charge is resolved today. I can't imagine what it would be like to struggle with this ordeal for another year while it winds its way to trial. Do you think that the charge will be dismissed today?"

My question was all too typical for lawyers and I hated to throw it at Murphy. However, I needed to know how he felt as we prepared for the last session in this Preliminary Hearing. Murphy finished a sip of his coffee, paused and then responded like an enlightened visionary making a long-awaited prediction:

"As I've said before, Orest, there is no real evidence of wrongdoing or fraud in this whole case. The one thing that is also very clear is that they have not produced any evidence of wrongdoing on your part. Everything in the Crown's case is speculation. There is clearly no evidence to support Nash's theory that you concocted this real estate deal for the purpose of defrauding Heritage Trust. I went over my notes on all the evidence last night and I've made notes for my final submissions. I'm satisfied that the Crown has got nothing and that this charge should be dismissed. All we can hope is that Judge Stack looks at this case objectively. Hopefully, he won't be frightened off by Nash and her argument that it's such a complicated deal that this case has to go to trial."

Murphy had touched on the root of the problem that plagued every person who is subjected to the criminal justice system: an obvious cynical attitude of judges. Personified in its simplest state, judges have been known to remark to an accused person: "If you weren't guilty of something, you wouldn't be here." Sadly, judges, especially Provincial Judges, who adjudicate continually on criminal cases often lose their objectivity. Either openly or sub-consciously, they begin to pre-judge cases without carefully examining the evidence and considering the law. This attitude unfairly favours the Crown's position since the Crown Prosecutor only has to raise the suspicion of the judge to get a conviction. Often in such cases, the Crown Prosecutor merely confuses or clouds the real issues to be considered in order to satisfy the judge that they have proven their case.

The result of this unfortunate reality is that the burden of proof becomes improperly reversed. The law states that an accused person benefits from the principle that "Every accused person is presumed innocent until proven guilty". Furthermore, the Crown Prosecutor must prove the guilt of the accused person "beyond a reasonable doubt". However, depending on the attitude of the judge, an accused person will actually be "presumed guilty" unless he can prove his innocence. In such a case, any suspicion on the part of the judge usually results in a decision against the accused person. The old adage of "Where there is smoke, there is fire" translates in the criminal justice system to "where there is suspicion, there is guilt".

In cases where the Crown has little or no evidence, the tactic of the Crown Prosecutor is to introduce enough innuendo to raise the curiosity of the Judge. The Crown Prosecutor then simply argues that the suspicious circumstances are enough to justify a conviction. An old joke among Crown Prosecutors, stated in its crudest language, is: "If you throw enough shit at a person, some of it is sure to stick. When you are finished, there is no way that your target will look clean." Therefore, in order to respond to a case, the Defence lawyer must usually present evidence to answer all the suspicion raised in the Crown's case. Moreover, he must prove that his client is innocent beyond any cynical doubt that may be harboured in the mind of the judge. On this basis, it is no wonder that some judges seldom acquit anyone who appears before them.

As these thoughts flashed through my mind, I felt pressed to ask Murphy for his current assessment of Judge Stack:

"I know that you're right in your assessment of the evidence in this case and I'm praying that Stack agrees. Tell me how you feel about Stack and his pre-disposition on these kinds of cases. Do you think that he will look at the evidence seriously and throw out the case? I'm really concerned that he'll be swayed by the garbage that Nash is trying to drag into this case. Do you think that he may simply decide to leave it for a Queen's Bench judge to decide?"

As Murphy finished his coffee, he looked up and replied thoughtfully with a voice full of vitality and conviction:

"I think that he's going to throw the charge out. Stack is the kind of judge that can go either way. He doesn't always favour the Crown and he has thrown cases out. I can tell you this: If this was a trial before him, he would definitely dismiss the charge. I could almost guarantee that! However, this is a Preliminary Hearing and there is always the likelihood that any judge might decide not to bother with it and simply send it upstairs for a trial in Queen's Bench. If he does, we'll get it kicked out in Queen's Bench. But let's see what happens here first. I think he'll dismiss the criminal charge today. Why don't we get going and get this case finished."

As I followed Murphy out of the cafeteria, I reflected on his last words. It really depended on whether Judge Stack was prepared to look at the evidence and make a decision today or whether he was going to "pass the buck" to Queen's Bench. The easy way out was for Judge Stack to refer the case for trial to Queen's Bench. That way, he wouldn't be concerned about the lack of evidence and the volumes of case law that determined how he should decide the case. All I could hope was that he would be motivated to act in this case because of the obvious lack of any evidence of fraud. Then he might feel obligated to make the extra effort of considering the evidence and making a fair determination of the case before him. I wondered if I was asking for too much.

When Murphy and I entered the Court room, Murphy went to his counsel table to set up his files. I quickly settled down on the uncomfortable wooden bench for the last session of this Preliminary Hearing. Christal was in Court talking to Nash in whispered tones at her counsel table. As the minutes passed, I felt my body trembling. It wasn't just the coolness of the Court room but also the anxiety that was now exploding within my body. I took a deep breath of air and then began to focus my thoughts on the positive things that Murphy had just said. I knew that it was important for me to remain calm as this could also affect the proceedings and the decision of Judge Stack.

The Court was soon re-convened and Christal was called again to the witness stand to provide the balance of his testimony (as described earlier). When this was completed, Nash announced to Judge Stack:

"This is the case for the Crown, sir."

At this point, the Court followed the procedure of inviting the accused person to give evidence, if he so chose. It is unusual for an accused person to testify or present any evidence at a Preliminary Hearing simply because that would only confuse the evidence. That would then guarantee a referral of the case for trial and allow the Crown Prosecutor to use that evidence to the advantage of the Crown case. However, the law required that Judge Stack put on record a formal statement which allowed me to respond to the evidence that had been presented.

As I waited breathlessly for this moment to pass, Judge Stack looked at me and then announced:

"Orest Rusnak, would you stand up please."

For a moment, my mind was in a daze as I realized that I now had to confront this ugly ordeal. Murphy turned to me and motioned for me to stand beside him. I slowly stood up and carefully walked forward towards him. Moments later, as I reached the area behind the lawyers' table, Murphy whispered: "I'll answer for you." As I stood beside Murphy and looked up at Stack, it felt like I was looking up to God for judgement in a trial in which I was defending my life. As I stood there rigidly, I could hardly hear the words of Judge Stack. Thankfully, I knew that I only had to last a few more minutes before this part of the ordeal was over. Stack then read out a statement that he kept in his notebook:

"Having heard the evidence, do you wish to say anything in answer to the charge, or any other indictable offence, in respect of the same transaction, founded on the facts that are disclosed by the evidence? You are not bound to say anything, but whatever you do say will be taken down in writing and may be given in evidence against you at your trial. You must clearly understand that you have nothing to hope from any promise of favour and nothing to fear from any threat that may have been held out to you to induce you to make any admission or confession of guilt, but whatever you now say may be given in evidence against you at your trial notwithstanding the promise or threat. Do you wish to call any witnesses or to give evidence?"

I was beginning to feel weak and wanted desperately to sit down again. As I stood there motionless, my mind went blank. A few agonizing moments later, Murphy responded to Judge Stack:

"He does not, sir."

Judge Stack then closed his notebook, looked at us and responded:

"Very well! I will hear what submissions there may be."

At this moment, Murphy whispered to me to return to my seat and I felt relieved to be able to do so. I was surprised that these proceedings had affected me as much as they had. It was obvious that my past familiarity with the Court room in no way prepared me for the traumatic and horrifying ordeal that I was now undergoing as an accused person. At this moment, I was living the nightmare of every lawyer's client. This was as traumatic for me as it was for anyone who was unfamiliar with the Court system. What made it worse for me was that I understood it a little better and I was all too familiar with the shortcomings of the criminal justice system.

As I was returning to my seat, Nash got up and began her submissions to Stack. She was dressed again in her familiar black costume that was only appropriate in the depressing environment of a Court House. Nash began her oratory in a melancholy and eerie voice as if she was trying to set the stage for a grotesque execution. With no surprise to anyone, Nash spouted off a speech that had been rehearsed from the countless prior proceedings that she had handled. Instead of dealing with the actual evidence that was heard by the Court, she emphasized to Stack that the transaction was so complicated. In her mind, it was a suspicious factor that I had incidental contact with various people who were involved in presenting the mortgage application. As she spoke, she made a passing reference to various cases without actually giving a citation or quoting what they said. She gave the impression that it was all standard textbook law and that everything that she said should be accepted without question or further discussion.

Nash then insisted that certain conclusions had to be drawn from the evidence. She contended that because Heritage Trust lost money on the mortgage loan, there obviously had to be fraud to perpetrate such a loss. Furthermore, she insisted that because I initiated the transaction and ultimately made a profit in the real estate deal, this was enough for a jury to conclude that I had committed fraud. She then professed that there was very little that the Crown was required to. prove to justify a committal order in this case. Finally, she insisted that even with the lack of real evidence in this case, the matter should be set over to Queen's Bench Court in any event.

Stack sat on his perch, listening to her speech while refraining from interrupting her with questions. This was a bad sign as most judges will usually ask questions if they disagree with a lawyer. Frequently, a judge will comment if he is unwilling to accept a specific point that is being pressed by a lawyer. I was not comforted by what was happening but this was not the time to panic or to make assumptions. Nothing was decided yet and it was open for Stack to agree with either lawyer. It was therefore important to remain calm and to wait for a decision.

As soon as Nash finished, Stack called on Murphy to make his submissions Murphy began by countering Nash's flippant attack on my involvement in the real estate deal. He pointed out that the realtors, the mortgage brokers, and Garmaz all made a profit in the real estate deal. He then protested that making a profit in a real estate deal was not the test for whether a fraud had been committed. His next point was that Heritage Trust was never deceived by anyone. The obvious reason for their loss was attributable to the negligence of Gilmour in failing to properly investigate the information in the mortgage application form. This was confirmed by CMHC who ultimately refused to pay the deficiency loss of Heritage Trust.

At this point, Murphy proceeded to review the evidence and to point out the false statements that were made in evidence by the various Crown witnesses. After a few examples, Judge Stack interrupted Murphy to agree with his contention but then stated:

"Mr. Murphy, it seems to me, although it's not my function to determine the credibility of any witness or witnesses ...that there are a lot of untruths.

The thing is fraught with it."

Hearing these comments from Judge Stack brought immediate relief to my panic stricken body as I waited in agony for these last few minutes to pass. Murphy was moving along nicely describing the evidence of each witness and emphasizing that there was no evidence of wrongdoing by me. He then pointed out that the initial statements of Nash at the commencement of the Hearing remained unproven. Furthermore, there was no specific evidence of any act of fraud on my part. Murphy's final argument was that there never were any dealings or in fact any connection between me and Heritage Trust in this transaction. This fact made the contentions of the Crown totally unproven. He then elaborated on this point by stating:

"It would take a leap over an abyss as wide as this room by a one-legged man to connect Rusnak to Heritage Trust."

Murphy's remark brought a smile to the face of Judge Stack as he momentarily reflected on the comments Murphy had made. As Murphy sat down, Judge Stack then turned to Nash and asked her if she had any response to Murphy's submissions. Normally, judges don't allow the Crown Prosecutor to have a second chance at re-hashing her comments because every lawyer wants to have the last word. In a case such as this, where the defence calls no evidence, the defence counsel speaks last according to Court procedure. However, a judge can make his own rules about procedure in his Court room and nobody would dare to correct a judge on the procedures that he chooses to implement.

Everything now looked so positive. I was confident that Murphy had convinced Judge Stack to dismiss the criminal charge. My hopes began to sink as Nash stood up once more to re-address the Court on her position. She knew that her case was weak so her main tactic was to convince Judge Stack that it was a complicated real estate deal. She emphasized that he shouldn't try to evaluate the evidence but instead should simply refer it to a Queen's Bench trial judge. Her final position was that although there was no evidence that proved fraud, she insisted that Judge Stack had to draw inferences of wrongdoing. In other words, if there was any unresolved suspicion in his mind, then this case had to be referred for trial in Queen's Bench.

From an objective and legal assessment of the law and the facts, this statement was utter nonsense. However, it was the only thing left for Nash to rest her unproven case on. Nash was hedging her bet on the fact that in a Preliminary Hearing, most Provincial Judges will look for an easy resolution to a case by avoiding any decision-making if possible. This is contrary to the expectation that these judges have a legal responsibility and obligation to carefully review the evidence and make a careful assessment. Unfortunately, the real question in these types of circumstances usually is whether the Provincial Judge is willing to make a decision. Most often, the judge will abdicate his responsibilities and obligations in favour of referring the case for trial to Queen's Bench Court.

As soon as Nash finished her comments and sat down, Judge Stack began to deliver his decision without pausing or adjourning Court to consider the arguments. His reaction was unusual in light of what had transpired over the week. This case involved five days of testimony from numerous witnesses, a large amount of documents, technical case law that had been cited to the Court and lengthy submissions from the lawyers. Normally, in a case of this magnitude, a judge would adjourn the matter to review everything carefully. He would then read his carefully drafted written decision in open Court at a later time. Seeing Judge Stack proceeding immediately without taking even a short adjournment sent a shock wave though my body as I waited to hear each word that he was about to say.

The decision of Judge Stack was short and sounded rehearsed. Many of the comments probably came from the many cases that he had heard in Preliminary Hearings. He incorporated a few comments of each lawyer but refrained from saying anything about the evidence. This was a typical judicial manoeuvre to minimize the opportunity for anyone to criticize his decision in an appeal procedure. Furthermore, there was no reference to any case law or even any description of what he was considering in making his decision.

Suddenly, Judge Stack stopped his speech, looked at me and ordered:

"Mr. Rusnak, would you stand up, please."

The moment that I had agonized over for the last two years had now arrived. I was about to hear the decision of Judge Stack. It would either free me from this ordeal or plunge me deeper into a nightmare that would devastate my family and my career. It was a frightening prospect and my body was momentarily paralysed by the prospect of what might develop in the next fleeting moment.

As I rose from the wooden bench, I felt momentary relief for my sore, aching muscles that endured the pain of a cold and uncomfortable bench over the last five days. Murphy had now stood up and was motioning for me to come and stand beside him so that Judge Stack could give his decision. As I took a deep breathe and began to walk to Murphy's side, I looked at Nash and Judge Stack and the sombre, callous expressions on their faces. They both simply wanted this case to be concluded so that they could close their files and begin to ready themselves for the week-end that was now at hand. Nobody in this cold, sterile and dismal room, aside from Murphy, would feel any happiness for the positive resolution of this charge or the sorrow if the charge was referred to trial. If the decision was wrong or unjust, I alone would suffer. Everyone else would go on with their lives, leaving me to deal with the horror of the consequences.

When I reached Murphy's side, Stack began to speak again. Paralysed with anxiety, my heart pounded as each word tumbled down from Stack's perch. My mind was in a daze but I struggled to understand these critical words which would affect my life so dramatically:

"On the evidence before me, I am satisfied that there is some evidence which ought to be presented to a jury properly instructed. Accordingly, it is my finding that there is sufficient evidence to place you on trial, and you are therefore ordered to stand trial before a court of criminal jurisdiction to be held in the City of Edmonton, in the Province of Alberta."

The Court proceedings were now over. I stood there in shock and tried to analyze what I had just heard. Immediately, everyone began to close their files and prepare to leave the Court room. Suddenly, Judge Stack stated that he wanted to see both lawyers in his chambers. This meant that he wanted to have a few words with the lawyers in a private meeting. These were usually held in a small meeting room located through the back door of the Court room. Both Murphy and Nash followed Judge Stack out the back door of the Court room and I sat down again to wait for Murphy's return.

As I sat there on that cold, uncomfortable, wooden bench, I struggled to understand what had just happened. I wondered how Judge Stack could decide to send a case like this to trial. More to the point, I wondered how Judge Stack could say that there was some evidence of fraud or conclude that there was sufficient evidence of fraud to warrant a trial. What troubled me the most was that Judge Stack did not take some time to consider the evidence and the law before rendering his decision. This was not only his responsibility but what everyone expects from every judge.

After waiting silently for about five minutes, Murphy and Nash finally reappeared through the back door of the Court room. Murphy stopped by his table to pick up his briefcase and we then headed out the Court room to the Conference Room. As Murphy followed me in, he immediately began to explain:

"Orest, I'm really sorry about the way this Preliminary Hearing turned out. I feel awful about this! I know that you were counting on the criminal charge being thrown out. I still feel that Stack should have dismissed it. It was a typical case of Stack not wanting to stick his neck out by dismissing the charge. Instead, he took the easy way out by setting the charge over for trial. If it's any consolation, neither Stack nor Nash feel good about what's happening to you. Stack's parting comment to me was: "If you fly with the geese, you're going to get shot at." That statement seems to describe his attitude about this case. In Stack's view, if you get involved in real estate deals, you run the risk of something going sour. His attitude is that getting charged with fraud and having to go to trial is just part of the game. It's just too bad that Stack took that attitude."

As I listened to Murphy's explanation, I sensed my body going numb with shock. My mind was gripped with disbelief as I struggled to accept the implications of what had just happened. For everyone else, including Murphy, life would simply carry on and this wouldn't upset their daily lives. For me, the ordeal would now worsen and I would have to find new strength to meet this escalating horror in my life. As Murphy spoke, his words seemed consistent with my analysis of this matter. When he finished, I added my assessment to his comments:

"It kind of makes you wonder if he listened to a word that you said. I believe that he had his mind made up right from the beginning."

Murphy understood exactly what I meant and his reaction told me that he had the same thoughts on the matter. Before Murphy could make any further comments, I quickly interjected with an idea that had occurred to me while I was waiting:

"Just a thought, Patrick! If there was no real evidence of fraud in this matter, why don't we appeal his decision? Couldn't we make an application to a Queen's Bench judge to quash this decision?"

My comment must have peaked Murphy's curiosity because he responded enthusiastically:

"That just might work, Orest! There is no evidence of fraud to support Stack's decision. If we can demonstrate that, maybe a Queen's Bench judge might reverse his decision and throw the charge out. That means that the law on that point will have to be carefully researched. If you want to research it, I will be happy to work on it and make the application."

Sadly, this was the most positive thought that could be salvaged from this disastrous turn of events. Nonetheless, I felt somewhat uplifted by Murphy's remarks. I knew that it was important to make the best of this dismal situation so I tried to react positively to his remarks:

"I'd be happy to compile some research on this point and share it with you when it's completed. I'll conduct some research and then we can talk about it later."

Murphy was showing a positive attitude but he couldn't hide his disappointment over Stack's decision. We agreed to get together in a few weeks to discuss this situation again. He then consoled me as we got ready to leave the conference room:

"Remember to keep your chin up, Orest! We haven't lost anything yet. Because of the way the justice system works, almost all cases that go to Preliminary Hearing are automatically set over for trial. There are only a few Provincial Judges with the balls or the interest to dismiss charges at the Preliminary Hearing stage. That's one reason why the courts are so backlogged. If more cases were dismissed or resolved at that point, they could clean up more than half the cases that end up in Queen's Bench. But most judges are too lazy. Typically, they do as little as possible and pass the buck whenever they can. Unfortunately, that's just the way the system work. But don't worry about it! We'll get this criminal charge dismissed at the trial or possibly in that application to quash the charge."

What Murphy was saying about the criminal justice system was all too familiar. I had heard similar comments from so many lawyers who became increasingly frustrated with the system. As lawyers spend more time working in the system, they witness the blatant waste of time and resources as cases are ineptly handled and shuffled around. Instead of being determined quickly to minimize the inconvenience and prejudice to the individuals involved, cases are adjourned or referred to other judges and Courts. Because everyone involved in the criminal justice system receives a government salary, there is no urgency to do more than the minimal amount of work required. Typically, nobody ever takes any initiatives to get cases cleaned up and resolved. Over time, this situation results in more Court facilities being created to handle an escalating backlog of cases with no real progress in resolving them. This in turn creates the fictitious need for more judges, lawyers and court workers.

As I was about to leave, Murphy called out a reminder about the proceedings to follow:

"I'll be getting a letter from Nash advising when we have to appear in Queen's Bench Court to enter a plea to the charge and set it for trial. When I find out, I'll send you a letter. Why don't you go home now and rest. We'll talk some more later."

On bidding Murphy good-bye, I began to walk out towards the exit and then to my car. As I walked, I shuddered as I thought of the way that my wife would react to this horrible news. We would now have to re-live the horror of this nightmare over and over for the next year until I could finally resolve it at a trial. Regrettably, there was nothing positive that I could tell my wife. We would just have to console each other and wait for this ordeal to take its course. If we were lucky, our marriage and family would survive. Everything else that we valued so dearly in our lives might be lost because of this new uncertainty in our lives. We had no way of knowing what lay ahead in this nightmare on the Road to Justice.

CHAPTER FIFTEEN

ARRAIGNMENT COURT

The reality of the situation still eluded me as I grappled with the implications of Judge Stack's decision to commit me to stand trial on the charge of criminal fraud. Unless we could successfully appeal this decision, I would be forced to proceed with a trial on that criminal charge. It would unquestionably become a media event that would be more devastating than anything else that had happened to date. I wondered how I would find the stamina to endure this pending ordeal and how my family would survive such a traumatic event.

Before the Preliminary Hearing, I and my wife could console each other with the assurances and belief that the criminal charge would be dismissed, thereby ending this sickening turmoil. Unfortunately, everything that we hoped for had turned out different. Now, we faced the unanticipated challenge of enduring this ordeal while continually shielding our personal home life from it. The stress that previously only occasionally displaced our thoughts now took on a more ominous appearance and remained as a permanent companion in our sub-conscious minds. Now, more than ever before, there was a mounting urgency to take any steps that might quickly resolve or end these proceedings before they slowly consumed the last remnants of our quiet and private lives.

In dealing with any stressful situation, the best antidote for worrying is to immerse oneself in work. In order to cope with my shock and disillusionment of the Criminal Justice system, I immersed myself in my legal work which had been partially neglected during the Preliminary Hearing. My work enabled me to imagine everything in my life to be normal. Unfortunately, I was always confronted with the reality that my life was now changing and that I had no control over that fate. My legal career, my future plans and even my peace of mind would now become casualties of a process that ignored personal hardship. After all, that played no role in the bureaucratic process that would eventually find me defending myself at my trial. I was casually aware of how these devastating procedures destroyed the lives of those who endured such proceedings. I was now forced to face the reality that these court procedures might devastate me to a greater degree than it would affect others. The unspoken truth was that it was different if you were a lawyer on trial on a criminal matter.

I resolved in my mind that I would have to dispel these images of doom and prepare for the eventual trauma of a trial in the Court of Queen's Bench. These "superior" courts are touted by many lawyers as being a better forum for criminal trials as the judges are presumably less cynical about the publicized crime in the jurisdiction. Because Provincial Judges continually adjudicated cases in criminal court, some became hardened with the attitude that everyone that appears in court must be guilty. Needless to say, it is impossible for anyone to get a fair trial before such a judge. However, because a Queen's Bench judge hears a wide variety of cases, he is presumably not as cynical or biased. The problem is that most of these judges have little or no experience in criminal matters. As a result, their decisions are normally appealed because of blatant errors made at the trial. The obvious conclusion is that one can only get a fair trial in Provincial Court or in the Court of Queen's Bench if one gets a fair judge. Unfortunately, there are only a few in each court that are respected as being fair, unbiased judges. Therefore, justice is more the result of a lucky chance than it is of natural occurrence.

About two weeks after the Preliminary Hearing had concluded, I received a letter from Murphy's office advising me that the date for my Arraignment in the Court of Queen's Bench was on February 14, 1992. I expected to receive this letter and I was aware that the date of Arraignment would come. However, I had not expected it to arrive so suddenly. Worst of all, I wasn't mentally prepared to cope with this new stress that was now casting its shadow on me and my family.

Arraignment is the name of the special court proceedings held in the Court of Queen's Bench for the first appearance of a person charged with a criminal charge. The purpose of these proceedings is for the accused person to enter a plea and for the Court to set a trial date. These proceedings are only held once every two months to ensure that there is a sufficient backlog of cases to require the lawyers and judges to undertake such an inconvenient and archaic procedure. Because of necessity, these proceedings are conducted in an over-sized Court room in an atmosphere of continual chaos. It is distressing to think that any decision of real importance might be made by anyone under such circumstances. Because of the formality attributed to this occasion, each lawyer appearing before the court must be dressed in formal black court gowns. Every lawyer is expected to follow the ritual of making all the requisite bows and gestures of being subservient before the awesome presence of the judge who directs the proceedings from his elevated pedestal. The whole atmosphere is intentionally uncomfortable for everyone except the judge. Unfortunately, these proceedings are very intimidating to those "outsiders" who appear for the first time to experience this "arena from the medieval ages".

After taking some time to adjust to this new reality, I began to visualize how these proceedings would unfold and I resolved to meet this new challenge in a positive frame of mind. After all, it was just a court appearance! These types of court appearances are routine for lawyers and undoubtedly the greatest inconvenience that they must accommodate. I could recall making these types of appearances as a newly admitted lawyer over fifteen years ago. I wanted to believe that there would be no real surprises in what would happen. Still, that was a long time ago and I was now appearing as a person charged with a criminal offence. I knew all too well that there was a dramatic difference in the way that I would be treated in Arraignment Court today.

It is simplistic to say that the need to make an Arraignment Appearance in order to maintain an antiquated practice was ridiculous in these modern times. These vestiges of useless tradition resist the idea of modern advancement. Yet some aspects of the Court system, particularly the filing and storage of files, are becoming more modern with the age of computers and electronics. This dinosaur from another era is actually adapting to a new environment. Still, the actual Court procedures remain unchanged because of a reluctance by judges to adopt more efficient practices.

There was such an obvious need to improve the inefficiency of the Court systems and the archaic customs associated with Court procedures. One good example was the Court appearances to set trial dates: a theatrical exercise in which nothing of substance is achieved. Usually, this Court appearance becomes a forum for the judge to demonstrate to the public the awesome authority vested in him. This forum also provides an opportunity for lawyers to seize another opportunity to feed their egos. Here, they may put on a performance for their clients and play to a larger audience, especially since some of the people might not have lawyers representing them. However, for most lawyers, the effect of these appearances is a waste of half a day in Court to arrange one trial date. The lawyer will accomplish nothing else for the client but the client must pay for this waste of time.

The irony of the situation is that in civil cases dealing with the litigation of monetary claims, the need for a Court appearance to set a trial date has been eliminated. In those cases, the Court follows a policy of allowing the lawyers to arrange a trial date through a trial coordinator. The same practice could easily be incorporated into the criminal court system. However, such a change would rob the actors in the profession of their opportunity to display their most impressive performances. It is no wonder that the courts are so backlogged with cases and are so inefficient in processing them.

This inefficiency was recently recognized by the Supreme Court of Canada as a breach of the rights of an accused person under the Charter of Rights and Freedoms. It was declared that the Charter guaranteed each accused person the right to a trial within a reasonable time and Court delays could not be excused because of a shortage of facilities. With that ruling, thousands of cases were ultimately identified as creating a breach of these Charter rights. The result was to put pressure on the Provincial Governments to process cases faster or see them dismissed to avoid injustice to the people awaiting trial. When it became obvious that the Courts could not adjust to this new expectation, political pressure forced the Supreme Court of Canada to retract its position. In doing so, they essentially condoned the existing situation of inefficiency and abuse of rights that has continually plagued the Criminal Justice system.

After reflecting on my pending appearance at Arraignments, I reluctantly responded to Murphy's request to telephone him and arrange to meet with him prior to the Court date. Murphy was away from the office so I simply left a message with his receptionist. I then made a note in my diary regarding this Court appearance. The process of noting the date brought a reality to the situation that I was still struggling to accept. Soon I would be in Court to enter a "Not Guilty" plea to a criminal charge of fraud. This Court Process was quickly taking the form of a dark, hideous monster in a nightmare that was slowly consuming and destroying me. I knew that the only way to end the nightmare and force the monster to retreat was to directly confront my worst fears.

It was later that afternoon when Murphy called and found me at my desk immersed in my legal work. I had managed to put the thoughts of the Court appearance out of my mind and I hadn't expected a call back from Murphy until the following day. As I answered the telephone, I could tell instantly that he was having a good day because his warm-hearted, jovial disposition always shone through in his greetings. As I answered, Murphy blurted out:

"Hi, Orest! I just heard a joke that you'll like. There was a Crown Prosecutor who went on vacation to the Caribbean. He was cruising around a tropical island in a small boat when he ran out of gas. He decided to swim to shore to get help even though he could see killer sharks swimming around his small boat. But when he jumped into the water, the sharks pulled back and gave him lots of room so that he could swim to shore without any hassle. Do you know why?"

As with all of Murphy's humour, I knew the punch line was cute and that he was probably going to make reference to my situation. I found myself drawn into his story and I wanted to hear the ending so I quickly responded:

"No, Patrick! Tell me why."

Like a professional comedian, Murphy responded:

"Professional courtesy!"

Murphy then laughed. I found myself smiling although it was somewhat painful to laugh. I then responded to Murphy's story with my observation:

"It's a cute joke, Patrick! I'm sure that most of the Crown Prosecutors with the Attorney General's department have a reputation for being sharks in the way they prosecute their cases. I have no doubt that many of them could expect to receive that type of professional courtesy."

Murphy obviously liked my response and was quick to add his own thoughts:

"Actually, Orest, some of those barracudas at the Attorney General's office are so vicious that I would worry for the sharks in a situation like that."

I started to feel better as a result of Murphy's humour. For a moment, we both laughed and then Murphy interjected with his comments on the upcoming Court appearance:

"I talked to Eileen Nash about your first appearance for Arraignment in February. It's obvious that the transcripts from the Preliminary Hearing won't be ready by then. We therefore agreed that this matter should be adjourned to the following Arraignment date, which will be in April. Unfortunately, you'll have to attend the Arraignment hearing in February even though nothing will happen. Your case will simply be adjourned to April. I hope that this won't cause you any problem?"

The situation that Murphy described was so typical of each case that came before the Courts. There was always a multitude of reasons why a case should not proceed. It was always assumed that if the Crown Prosecutor was not ready to proceed, then naturally everyone should agree to an adjournment. The problem was that an adjournment was still costly for an accused person. It was still necessary to appear in Court with the Defence lawyer and the lawyer would naturally bill for his time. However, there was nothing of any practical benefit that could be done about the situation and therefore I reluctantly agreed. As Murphy paused, I sighed and then responded as positively as I could:

"That's all right, Patrick! I hate the idea of making extra Court appearances but I know that they are entitled to one adjournment. There's no point in being difficult with them and so I'll agree that there's no need to object to the adjournment. Do you want me to meet you in the Court room or do you wish to meet me earlier to discuss anything?"

Murphy responded immediately to my question and began to instruct me on how this court appearance would be handled:

"No, I'll see you in the Court room. I'm sure that you're familiar with Arraignments and you know the procedure. I have another matter in Provincial Court that morning so I'll probably be a few minutes late. However, your case is way down the list so I should be there before it's called. If it comes up before I get there, just ask the Judge to put it to the bottom of the list. After we speak to this matter at Arraignments, we can then sit down for a coffee to discuss any questions that you have."

As I listened to Murphy instruct me on the Arraignment appearance, it struck me that he was also detached from my emotional turmoil. For him, it was an incidental moment of another work day. For me, it was a turning point in my life. It was obvious that the Criminal Justice system had even hardened Murphy to the anxiety of his clients. I felt disappointed and partially alienated but I replied without showing any expression:

"Sure, Patrick! I'll see you in the Court room. I would like to meet with you after the Court Appearance to talk about appealing the Committal Order of Judge Stack and applying to strike it out. I've done a little research and I've had some further thoughts on it. I believe that such an application could be successful. If so, that would resolve this matter immediately."

As usual, on topics like this, Murphy responded in a cautious but positive manner:

"I wouldn't be able to express an opinion until after I had done some research but I would be happy to review the cases that you have read. I personally feel that Stack's decision was wrong but applying to quash such a decision is difficult. The reason for that is very few judges understand the law or really take the time to read up on these legal questions. Therefore, few of them are able to evaluate them to make a proper decision. However, if you have some strong cases in your research, it's always worth taking a shot at it."

Murphy then paused for a few seconds. His next comments related to another nightmare that was transforming itself into a ghoulish form in my life:

"Another thing that we should talk about when we meet is this ongoing investigation by the Law Society. Those people are like vultures and they see you as injured prey dying in the desert. Our buddy from Law School, Jim McLeod, keeps calling me on this. It's pretty obvious that he wants to get you kicked out of the profession. I keep pointing out to him that there is no evidence that you did anything improper or illegal but he doesn't seem to care about that. I don't like the way that this is developing. We should talk about what can be done if they move to suspend you."

As I listened, I could feel my heart beating faster and my chest tightening with tension as I contemplated the prospect of a suspension by the Law Society. This new nightmare had been periodically rearing its ugly head ever since the news media broadcasted the fact that I was charged with fraud. Now that the criminal charge had been committed for trial, Jim McLeod could smell the blood. He was in the ideal position to agitate the right people and push for my suspension. Sadly, there was nothing that could be done about this. The Board of the Law Society could suspend a lawyer without a hearing, without notice and without a justifiable reason. Over the years, the Law Society had craftily lobbied the government to amend the Legal Professions Act. The result was to eliminate the various challenges and objections that lawyers had used to appeal such decisions to a Judge. Consequently, lawyers are now more fearful of a persecution by the Law Society than they are of a prosecution in the Courts.

I decided not to ask Murphy any further questions relating to the Law Society and to spare myself the further anguish that could arise from such a conversation. As I hung up the telephone receiver, I realized that I was slowly entering a new part of the legal maze. Each twist and turn brought me face to face with new horrors that I had to resolve. The maze had looked easy to pass through when this horrible nightmare first began. However, I was now beginning to question if I would ever find my way through to safety at the other end. The worst part of the puzzle appeared to be that the longer I remained in the maze, the more tragedies I would suffer as a result of this ordeal.

More than ever before, it became obvious that I had to resolve this situation as quickly as possible. Instead of becoming discouraged and fearful of the future, I decided to adopt a positive attitude. My priority was to work harder on researching the legal questions involved in an application to quash the Committal Order. When the time arrived, I would face the ordeal of my Court Appearance at the Arraignments. Until then, I was determined not to expend any energy dwelling on it.

With work as my distraction, I hardly noticed the passage of time leading up to the date for my Court Appearance. I had already mentally prepared myself and my wife to accept this as just a normal Court Appearance. I was determined to free myself from the stress that paralysed my mental thoughts and stifled my ability to function. My morning routine, which culminates with breakfast with the family, proceeded like any other morning except for the tension that I and my wife endured silently.

After breakfast, I went to my downstairs office to review work that needed to be completed that day and to identify any work that could be completed after my court appearance at Arraignments. The minutes quickly vanished as I rummaged through the files on my desk and it was soon time for me to leave for Court. As I left the house, I tried to calm my wife's fears and to reassure her that this court appearance was just a normal part of the process. Inside, I knew that this simple step in the Court process would confirm to all those involved in the Court procedures that I was a criminal in the assessment of our society. No degree of vindication could ever eradicate that stigma.

As I drove my car down the icy streets on my destination to the downtown Court House, I reflected on the appropriateness of the weather on this dismal occasion in my life. Winter in February is no longer a novel season of magical snow and youthful excitement; it is instead simply a time when it is too cold to enjoy the outdoors. Anyone who can't escape for a winter vacation to a warm climate is now tired of the winter ordeal and longing for spring weather. The only distraction from the boring winter conditions, aside from winter sports, is Valentines day. Everyone celebrates it with zestfulness only to relieve the boredom and symptoms of depression that are so prevalent. The reasoning of the inhabitants of this cold climate is that if you had to remain indoors and struggle to remain warm, romance ignites the sparks that bring the most heat to your body.

Having arrived early at the Court House, I proceeded to the library to complete some research. I also needed to secure copies of cases that would assist in the legal brief that I was preparing for Murphy's assessment. The Court House library contained the most extensive public collection of legal books and provided an environment that was ideal for my research. The facility was noticeably under-utilized and was maintained by the government. It was mainly used as a resource for the lawyers from small firms who could not afford to own their own libraries stocked with expensive volumes of legal books. With the advent of computers, most lawyers may soon access this legal literature from the comfort of their own offices. However, at this moment, I still had to content myself with this traditional approach to research. I mused as I considered how quaint it would be to be remembered as part of the old breed of lawyers who actually did legal research from books.

Most often, it was too easy to lose track of time while researching. Suddenly, I realized that it was ten minutes before the scheduled Court time of ten o'clock. Instinctively, I simply left all my research books on the table and rushed out the door. The books I was using were intentionally left on the desk to be re-shelved by the librarians. I had learned during my articling year that these librarians insist on re-shelving books since they do this job better than lawyers. This traditional practice justified the jobs of extra librarians in an under-utilized library. It also provided lawyers with the privilege of avoiding the menial work of re-shelving the books that they used.

The elevators were especially busy since all of the Courts are typically scheduled to start at ten o'clock. I patiently made my way through the crowd of people jammed in the corridor by the elevators and then headed for the Court room designated for Arraignments. This Court room was unusually large and specifically designed to hold and process large numbers of people. It was only used for specific functions such as Arraignments, installation of judges and jury selections. Such events generate an atmosphere of confusion and pandemonium and are therefore fondly referred to as "carnival events". The prevailing attitude was jubilant since nothing of significance would result from these proceedings. Instead, these occasions provided an opportunity for lawyers to socialize and to display their social skills in the presence of their clients.

Of prominent significance was the "Prisoner's Box" that was guarded by two Court Orderlies. It was slightly elevated and located to the right side of the large tables used by the lawyers. The Prisoner's Box was capable of holding at least half a dozen prisoners at once. It's design featured a simple, straight-back wooden bench enclosed on four sides with a four foot wall. It was built of expensive oak wood and featured a door which could only be opened by the Court Orderlies. It was designed to display to the public the unfortunate people who come before the Court to be formally charged with a crime.

The purpose served by the Prisoner's Box is to hold the accused person in custody while the Judges and lawyers deal with his case. The Prisoner's Box protects the people in Court from the accused person and prevents him from escaping. However, in a recent case, a prisoner demonstrated how easy it was to jump out of the enclosure and escape while the Court was in session. The prisoner, while still in handcuffs, was actually able to get outside of the Court House before finally being apprehended on the street. This incident proved that the Prisoner's Box is actually a useless feature in the Court room and doesn't even prevent prisoners from escaping.

As I gazed at the Prisoner's Box, I marvelled at how different this occasion was for lawyers as compared to that of the accused people. For the lawyers, this truly was a carnival, complete with laughter and entertainment. For the accused people, this was a degrading experience intended to shred every semblance of decency and self respect from their individuality. It was hard to understand how a country that valued the freedoms and rights of every individual would still utilize such an archaic facility as a Prisoner's Box. It was clearly improper to subject anyone who hadn't been judged guilty of anything to such an inhumane and unnecessary humiliation. The mockery of the accused person served no legitimate purpose and only helped to bolster the egos of those judges who revel in demeaning people that must appear in Court.

Concerns about the propriety for the use of a Prisoner's Box in Court is now receiving attention from legal reform advocates. Its use is also being challenged. In a recent decision of the Newfoundland Courts, it has been declared to be a breach of the rights of an accused person under the Canadian Charter of Rights and Freedoms. However, many judges and bureaucratic administrators still oppose the abolition of the Prisoner's Box. Therefore, the process for eliminating them from the Court room will be significantly delayed. Naturally, it will take continual pressure from those who advocate human rights and meaningful reforms to change this situation.

Typical in these types of proceedings, Court was not convened until fifteen minutes beyond the appointed time. This practice was followed to allow the judge an opportunity to finish his morning coffee. It also insured that all the stragglers were in court and ready so that "His Lordship" could proceed without any delay. As I waited for Court to convene, I continually glanced around the Court room in the hope of seeing Murphy's arrival. I then remembered that he would be late and that my matter might have to be delayed to the end of the proceedings. The minutes passed slowly as I endured this tedious situation. I now began to appreciate the anxiety that every accused person must feel as they await the determination of their fates before the Courts. For lawyers, a delay is a temporary inconvenience but for an accused person it is an eternity of despair and anxiety.

As I waited, I wondered why the indignity and stress caused to accused people by the procedures and delays of the criminal court system are ignored by civil rights proponents. Indeed, these demeaning procedures and constant delays are the "punishment" that accused people must suffer for having been charged with a criminal offence. Occasionally, this "punishment" has been recognized by judges, lawyers and society as being a sufficient punishment for the actual crimes. Unfortunately, an accused person must endure the "punishment", whether or not the crime is actually proven. There is currently no recourse or compensation for the hardship and losses suffered by an accused person if the criminal charge is dismissed. It is strange that people expect an accused person who endures such a punishment to actually feel lucky and grateful if a criminal charge is not proven.

In response to this prevailing injustice, some accused people have been applying for Court costs and other monetary compensation. In some cases, formal apologies have been made by the Justice Department to vindicate the accused person for such unjust treatment. As an example of this, Donald Marshall was able to successfully gain a monetary settlement for his improper conviction and incarceration for murder. Currently, David Milgaard is pursuing a claim against the Saskatchewan Government for the 23 years that he spent in jail before his murder conviction was set aside. One can only hope that a formal procedure will be established soon to give this recourse to all people who suffer losses through improper incarceration.

Suddenly, the Court Orderly called out: "ORDER IN COURT!". With a flurry of movement, Justice John Agrios entered the Court room, all decked out in his black and red judicial robes. As all the lawyers solemnly bowed to him, he arrogantly deposited himself into his chair on the majestic perch dedicated to him. Although many judges in Queen's Bench can be characterized as being arrogant and superior in their attitudes, Agrios had distinguished himself in this regard. He had a reputation in the legal community for his actions in demeaning those lawyers who had not found favour with him. Conversely, he openly extended privileges to those selected lawyers who he liked or who were properly connected to his "favoured" legal firms. Most lawyers tried to avoid his Court room whenever possible to insure a fair hearing for their clients. There was no doubt that if my case was heard in his Court room, I would be presumed guilty with no chance of proving myself innocent. I considered myself lucky that on this occasion, I was simply making an appearance before him to adjourn these proceedings to another date.

The first names to be called were for accused people in custody. These cases moved slowly as many of them were still arranging lawyers or applying for adjournments. In each case, it was necessary for Agrios to make a ruling or to answer their questions. Agrios found this to be a tedious procedure as he much preferred to rush through these proceedings. As each name was called, I continued to look around for Murphy. The minutes ticked away and the names continued to flow as my mind began to chant: "WHERE IN THE WORLD IS PATRICK MURPHY?"

When Agrios finished with the accused people in custody, he proceeded with the rest of the cases in the order as set out on the docket list prepared by the Clerk's office. As each name was called, I knew that mine would be coming up soon so I began to prepare myself to speak to the Court to request an adjournment of my case. I carefully prepared the words in my mind, knowing that at any moment my name would be called. The request was simple as was the procedure but I was concerned about a critical variable: Agrios. Nothing precluded him from making any number of requests or inquiries and his commentaries would certainly not be complementary. I wished that Murphy would appear so that we could simply deal with this case in a simple, direct manner. However, it was beginning to look like Murphy was not going to show up in time.

My mind was now numb as I waited in suspense for my name to be called and I didn't even notice Douglas Vigen approaching me. As Vigen neared me, I looked up while he sat down beside me to whisper a message:

"Murphy asked me to tell you that he's going to be delayed in Provincial Court. He asked me to appear with you. You're going to be entering a plea and setting a trial date today, right?"

For a moment, I was startled to think that Murphy wouldn't be able to show up. Even worse, I was concerned that Vigen didn't know what had transpired or what needed to be done. I quickly advised Vigen in a whispered voice:

"Doug, that's wrong! Murphy told me that my case would simply be adjourned today because the transcripts are not ready yet. Apparently, this was agreed upon between Murphy and Eileen Nash. Is there any possibility that Murphy can be reached to confirm what should happen?"

A feeling of desperation swept over me as I waited for Vigen to react to my question. Vigen then suggested, in a whispered voice:

"Look, Orest, would you mind if we just put your case over to 1:30 this afternoon. Murphy has another case that I'm going to ask the Court to adjourn to that time. Murphy will be in this Court for the afternoon sitting and he will be able to speak to your case then. If that time is convenient for you, I'll ask for your case to go over to that time, also."

Vigen's suggestion sounded like the best course of action and so I agreed. Vigen then got up and walked over to Murphy's other clients to speak to them. A few minutes later, my name was called. Vigen stood up and walked to the lawyer's table to advise Agrios that Murphy was in Provincial Court on another matter. He then asked if my case could be adjourned to 1:30 in the afternoon and

Agrios agreed. Without anything further being said, Vigen walked over to me and whispered:

"That's all for now, Orest! Come back at 1:30 and Murphy will be here to speak to this case with you."

I thanked Vigen, got up and left the Court room. For the moment, my ordeal was in remission. I now had two hours to complete some errands downtown before I had to be in Court again. As I left the Court House, I tried to console myself that this emotional ordeal was almost over and that my Court appearance would be completed quickly that afternoon. The emotional roller coaster ride that I was on had now entered a slow and calm phase. I would have time to gather my composure and focus on other matters before the ordeal resumed.

I returned to the Court room fifteen minutes before Court was scheduled to resume in the hope that I could speak with Murphy prior to my court appearance. What Vigen told me about his instructions from Murphy concerned me. It sounded like Murphy had changed his mind about adjourning the matter and was now ready to proceed. Expediting these proceedings was always a good idea but it bothered me that this had arisen without any communication to me about it. I then reflected on the fact that the biggest complaint of clients in general was that their lawyers did not keep them informed of developments in their case. Now I was feeling the same frustration on this situation.

After checking inside the Court room to see if Murphy had arrived, I sat down in the reception area. It was simply a large, open waiting area beyond the elevators that provided access to each of the Court rooms on that floor. As I sat on leather-cushioned, contemporary benches, I watched the elevator area carefully to be sure that I spotted Murphy when he arrived. I was intent on speaking with Murphy as soon as possible and I didn't want to miss him. All I needed was a positive assurance on what would take place inside the Court room before the anxiety that was suffocating me would dissipate.

After waiting for ten minutes, I began to ready myself to go into the Court room and wait for Murphy there. I definitely did not want to be out of the Court room when my case was called. I could not even contemplate the horror of being absent from Court, failing to respond to my case and having a warrant issued for my arrest for failure to appear. I was far too familiar with the procedures of the Court and this was one situation that was not going to happen to me even by accident. As I got up and began to move towards the Court room, I saw Murphy coming out of the elevator. He gestured a greeting and as he walked towards me, he called out:

"Hi, Orest! I'm sorry I couldn't make it this morning but I had a trial in Provincial Court that didn't end until noon. I saw Vigen for a minute and he said that your case was put over to this afternoon. I hope that this is not too great an inconvenience?"

Murphy sounded so sincere and sympathetic to my plight that I knew that his sentiments came from the heart. I could see that our time was limited so I responded quickly:

"No problem, Patrick! I'm wondering, though, if my case is going to be adjourned as you mentioned earlier? Vigen suggested that you wanted to proceed today to enter a plea and get a trial date."

Murphy looked surprised for a moment and then responded with his usual smile:

"I'd be ready to start the trial this afternoon, Orest, but Nash isn't ready. She likes to do things by a certain procedure. In her world, you wait until you get the transcripts before you set a trial date. There was no point in being difficult so I agreed to an adjournment on your case. The Court automatically grants these requests on the first appearance anyway. Your case will therefore go over to the April Arraignments. Do you feel that will be a problem for you, Orest?"

By now, I was feeling foolish for bringing the matter up again but I truly felt confused by Vigen's remarks. I realized that time was slipping by and that we had to go inside so I quickly responded:

"That's fine with me, Patrick! I just want to get this over with and get on with my life. I guess we'd better get inside and deal with this adjournment."

As I finished my remark, Murphy began to move quickly and responded with instructions:

"Orest, I have another client who is also appearing this afternoon. You can go in and have a seat. When your name is called, just follow my instructions. I'll get you out of there quickly."

With that remark, Murphy turned and spotted his other clients at the far end of the reception room. As he walked off to meet with them, I walked into the Court room and sat down to wait for Court to reconvene. As usual, the Court room was buzzing with inaudible chatter from various points in the room as lawyers exchanged remarks with clients or with other lawyers. After a few minutes, Murphy entered with his other clients and directed them to be seated. He then went to speak to the Crown Prosecutor to identify his cases. A minute later, he was seated with a few other lawyers as they waited for Court to reconvene.

As I waited quietly and looked around the room, I was amazed to notice the difference in the activities from the morning. If the morning was the "carnival", then the afternoon represented the "morning after the carnival". All that remained to be done was the clean-up, as the major entertainment and festivities were gone and the celebrities had all now left. The atmosphere was sedate and relaxed and everyone seemed anxious to finish and go home. My sentiments were exactly the same and I couldn't wait for this extended ordeal to end.

My thoughts were once again abruptly shattered by the call of the Court Orderly: "ORDER IN COURT!". As the lawyers shuffled to their feet for their ritual bow, the commotion in the Court room came to a stop. As Agrios settled into his lofty perch, the Crown Prosecutor started calling names to complete the Arraignment List. While I waited, I focused on the matters before the Court and tried to relax as much as possible. I now knew that nothing eventful would transpire but it was important to get through this moment and move on with this case.

Suddenly, my name was called by the Crown Prosecutor and my turn had come at last. Murphy immediately rose to identify himself to the Court and then signalled for me to come to the front. My heart began to pound in my chest and I began to feel weak and light headed. I knew that I had to complete this ordeal in a respectable manner so I slowly rose to my feet and walked through the public seating area towards the front of the Court room.

As I came closer to Murphy, he motioned for me to step into the Prisoner's Box. For a moment, I was SHOCKED that this was going to happen to me. It made no sense for me to be put in custody like a dangerous criminal simply because I was charged with a criminal offence. I began to realize what is really meant by the legal doctrine that all accused people are treated equally before the law. What is meant is that all accused people are treated like they are guilty of a criminal offence and humiliated by being put on display in the Prisoner's Box.

Without emotion or reaction, I walked into the Prisoner's Box and faced Agrios who scowled down at me from his elevated perch. As I entered into the Prisoner's Box, the Court Orderly closed and locked the door behind me. He then stood there in a manner suggestive of the fact that he was guarding me from "His Lordship" who now sat in judgement of me. Murphy meanwhile walked over to the Prisoner's Box to be near me as the Clerk read out the criminal charge:

"Orest Rusnak, you stand charged that at Edmonton, in the Judicial District of Edmonton, Alberta between the 1st day of July, A.D., 1984 and the 1st day of April, A.D., 1985, did by deceit, falsehood or other fraudulent means, defraud Heritage Savings and Trust of money of a value which exceeded $1,000.00 by causing a false mortgage application to be submitted to Heritage Savings and Trust contrary to the Criminal Code. How do you plead to this charge?"

Murphy immediately spoke up and responded for the Court Record:

"He reserves his plea, my Lord."

Murphy then walked over to the lawyer's table and proceeded to address Agrios on this matter:

"My Lord, Eileen Nash is the Crown Prosecutor on this file. I have consented to her request that this matter be adjourned to the April Arraignments to give us a chance to receive and review the transcripts from the Preliminary Hearing."

In his typical summary fashion, Agrios then quickly remarked for the Court Record as he made an endorsement on the file:

"Very well, then! This matter is adjourned to the April Arraignments."

With that remark, the Court Orderly opened the door to the Prisoner's Box and signalled for me to leave. As I walked out, Murphy grabbed his file and followed me. As we walked to the back of the Court room, he whispered:

"Orest, wait for me outside. As soon as I'm finished here, we'll go for a coffee and talk."

I was happy that Murphy remembered our scheduled meeting and I quickly acknowledged:

"That would be nice, Patrick!"

As soon as I walked out of the Court room, I felt relief from the anxiety that gripped my body moments earlier. This ordeal was over for the moment and I hoped that the anxiety would be easier to endure as the case progressed in

Queen's Bench Court. Now I could relax and look forward to having a comfortable meeting with Murphy prior to rushing back home before the rush hour traffic started.

About ten minutes later, Murphy came out of the Court room with his other clients trailing behind him. He then said a few parting words to them and they left for the elevators. Murphy then signalled to me and waited until I walked over to join him. Our first stop was the basement and the Lawyer's locker rooms where Murphy changed from his Court gowns to his suit jacket and street clothes. The Lawyer's Locker Room was crammed into a small empty room in the Court House located two floors below ground level. It contained the maximum amount of lockers and barely the minimum amount of space for walking or changing. With cramped conditions and low ceilings, the air barely circulated and smelt with perspiration, all of which added to the atmosphere of this dingy room.

Because of over-crowding, often two or more lawyers stuffed their Court gowns into one small locker. It was also typical of most lawyers to only launder their shirts once a year, if even that often, and to leave the outer vests and gowns unlaundered. As a result, some lawyers continually appeared in Court with wrinkled and untidy Court gowns which ultimately became their recognizable trade marks in Court. Sadly, this could be avoided by utilizing space better so that lawyers aren't reduced to being treated like rats in a sewer.

A few minutes later, Murphy and I were on our way to the cafeteria, renowned as the breeding ground of lawyer's gossip and other less-intellectual pursuits. This was the place to find out who was in trouble with the Law Society, who had just been kicked out of a law firm and even which lawyer tried to commit suicide. These valuable facts could then be exchanged for even more gossip in discussions with the rest of the legal fraternity on the telephone. I had no doubt that my name would have been a highlight on a number of occasions in this fervent exchange of smutty revelations.

If the gossip on lawyers was exhausted, then the conversation could focus on shocking or amusing cases featuring the lawyers' current clients. The only professional allowance made for the clients was that occasionally the names might be kept confidential. In this environment, ethics and propriety took a back seat to the lustful pursuit of tacky tidbits of information and gossip.

As we entered the cafeteria, we both got our beverages and then headed for a table where we could talk privately. Murphy was in a good mood and his light-hearted disposition soon allowed me to relax. My tense muscles began to loosen and the anxiety that had held me in its grip earlier in Court quickly disappeared. As we both began to settle into our chairs, I shocked Murphy with this comment:

"Well, Patrick! Now that I'm officially charged, I guess that I'm well on my way to becoming branded as a criminal of our society. If it were up to Agrios, we could have rapped this up today without waiting for a trial. By the look on his face, he was ready to convict and sentence me without hearing from anybody."

Murphy was slow to react and stared at me to determine if I was serious. He then responded:

"Orest, Relax! You know that this is just part of the procedure in this Court. All of this means nothing! I know this is difficult for you but you can't take any of this personally. Regarding John Agrios, I'd have a hard time finding any lawyer who has anything nice to say about him. Not only is he rude in Court but he's not even a good judge. Most of the time, he doesn't know the law and just makes decisions to suit his whims. Mind you, I try to get along with everyone but many lawyers just avoid him like the plague. Don't let this bother you! Believe me, all of this is just the normal procedure and doesn't make any difference at the time of trial."

I knew that Murphy was right in what he said but I was still concerned about the obvious attitude displayed by Agrios. I decided to push Murphy for his feedback:

"I agree with you, Patrick! I won't complain any further about the court procedures. However, I'm really concerned about Agrios and his disposition. If we get a judge like him at my trial, how can we possibly expect a fair hearing?"

Murphy's jovial attitude subsided as I pressed my concerns. He then looked at me and responded in a serious tone:

"You know quite well from experience that there are judges who don't listen to anyone and just do as they please. If you end up with a judge who loves to convict people, then nothing you say will convince him to throw out the charge. That's why I always elect Judge and Jury just to be on the safe side. If you get a decent judge who will listen to the evidence and make a fair decision, then often you can have the trial changed to drop the Jury. But even with a jury, there are judges who try to influence the jury to bring in a guilty verdict by making suggestive remarks during the trial. For that reason, getting a fair trial really depends on the judge that you get. With a judge like Agrios, you would want the jury. You would hope that the jury had people with minds of their own who could see things for what they are. Anyways, don't worry about that now. We'll have plenty of time to prepare for that and to deal with those questions as the trial date gets nearer."

Murphy's comments about the attitudes and biases of judges was standard knowledge to lawyers with similar court experience. I could vaguely relate to these comments and recognized immediately that it was a candid and accurate assessment of a harsh reality. However, his comments about jury trials was disturbing as one expects a fair and impartial decision in a jury trial. This question was one that I would have to probe later. I therefore resolved not to worry about that situation and to concentrate on the work that needed to be done. I decided to raise the topic that was now my new hope for resolving this nightmare:

"Okay, Patrick! Let's leave that for another time. Let me tell you about the research that I've done to date. From my reading of the cases, there is no evidence on some of the key elements that need to be proven to get a conviction for fraud. According to these cases, we can apply to the Court of Queen's Bench to get an order in the nature of certiorari to quash the charge."

As I spoke, I showed Murphy photocopies of some of the cases that I had researched. He slowly glanced at each of them to get a better impression of what I was describing. He then answered with noticeable enthusiasm:

"That's right! These are the cases that Eileen Nash made a reference to at the Preliminary Hearing. They describe the elements of fraud that must be proven by the Crown. There was no doubt in my mind that the Crown did not have evidence to support some of the elements in the fraud charge. Stack really should have thrown this charge out. I think that an application to a Queen's Bench judge is worth a shot. We certainly have nothing to lose. If we get a judge that will listen to us, then this charge could be thrown out at this stage."

Murphy's response was encouraging. I then proceeded to tell him about another legal argument that I discovered while researching:

"I also looked into the question of the long time delay between the date that the transaction took place and the date that the charge was laid. That was a period of five years. From the evidence we heard at the Preliminary Hearing, none of the witnesses can remember anything clearly. It's pretty obvious that some witnesses are lying and some are just making up evidence to make themselves look good. Also, most of the files of the witnesses have been destroyed. All of this creates a prejudice to me in presenting a defence to the criminal charge. According to the cases, we have the right to apply to a judge to ask for a stay of proceedings because of this prejudice. The cases are based on the Canadian Charter of Rights of Freedoms which requires a trial within a reasonable time. I'm convinced that a good argument could be made for a stay of proceedings."

Again, Murphy slowly glanced at the cases that I was handing to him. As I finished speaking, he remarked:

"I've read some of the cases from the Supreme Court of Canada on this point and I know that they are taking a firm position on trial delays. It would be a good idea to include those arguments as an alternative position in an application to a Queen's Bench judge. Depending on who we get, the judge may like that argument better than our argument on the lack of evidence. That's because some judges hate to be critical of the decisions of other judges. There are some judges who are more academic and these types of arguments really get them excited. Why don't you put together a legal brief on these cases and then we'll meet at my office where we can tear into these cases and get a handle on them. We'll need an affidavit in support of the application and you should start preparing one in a draft form that we can talk about."

Murphy's words were very encouraging and perhaps the only real progress that I had made on this case all day. I now felt more enthusiastic about resolving my case by getting an application before a judge to rule on these legal questions. I therefore resolved to prepare a legal brief that was appropriate for the most important legal case of my whole career as a lawyer.

CHAPTER SIXTEEN

THE COVER UP AND THE CONSPIRACY

During my childhood, my only image of a lawyer came from watching Perry Mason on television. Like most viewers, I developed the profound vision that a lawyer was someone like Perry Mason who saved the lives of his clients by figuring out who the mystery murderer was. Knowledge of the law was secondary because success in Court depended on finding clues and analyzing evidence in a manner that the police and the prosecutor failed to do. The Courtroom was a giant stage where all the interested parties gathered and served as the ideal forum to demonstrate to everyone, beyond any doubt, the innocence of the accused person and the solution to the murder mystery.

It was easy to assume that to be a good lawyer, one simply had to possess the investigative mind of Sherlock Holmes and dedicate all of your time to one case. Because Perry Mason never researched the law or argued legal principles in court, I assumed that the law was only relevant as it pertained to court procedures. The law appeared to be irrelevant in the preparation and presentation of a case on behalf of a client. Sadly, the general public rarely sees anything different on television or in an actual Court room. In reality, most criminal cases are actually resolved in an arbitrary fashion without careful consideration of the law by either the lawyers or the judges.

Reality is a shocking contrast to the fictional characters and stories in a television Court room drama. The fictional character of Matlock typically earns a fee of one hundred thousand dollars for each case. He manages to solve the murder mystery and successfully conclude each case within a week only to start a new one the following week. His charm in the Court room is strong enough to subdue an obnoxious judge or to extract a confession from the most devious predator. One cannot help but believe that even the most incriminated accused person has nothing to fear since a lawyer can always find the right facts to prove innocence beyond doubt.

The real world is a sharp contrast from the fictional and entertaining world of television. Few criminal lawyers ever earn the type of fees that our television hero charges. In fact, most criminal lawyers depend heavily on legal aid cases for the minimal earning supplement that it provides. A typical criminal case can take a few years to conclude and a lawyer must handle a large caseload to generate a reasonable income. Because of the necessity to make court appearances and meet with clients, lawyers struggle to find time to research the law on their cases and cannot possible make time to investigate a case personally. Few lawyers ever use private detectives and instead depend on the information received from the Crown Prosecutor which is based on the police investigation of the crime. In the final analysis, the most that a Criminal lawyer can offer a client is his ability to cross-examine and discredit Crown witnesses and his ability to argue defences based on technicalities in the law. In the real world, a client has good reason to worry about the fate awaiting them in the Court room.

When I first entered law school to train for my career as a lawyer, I was amazed to hear the law professors say that it was the law and the legal principles that were the paramount consideration in presenting cases in court. For three years, I undertook the fascinating study of case law that defined the general underlying principles of the law. The lawyer's craft was to recognize the subtle distinctions that would distinguish when a Court would grant a remedy in a case or would rule in favour of a specific application. In the minds of the law professors, there was a clear and uncontradicted way for every case to be decided. If certain facts appeared in a case, only a certain decision could be made by the Courts. We were assured that judges always knew the law and followed the law without exception, bias or favour. I now marvel at how naive we all were to have believed that at the time.

After graduating from law school, I was fortunate to enter articleship for one year with Rostyk Sadownik, who was best known in the legal community for his cantankerous and crude mannerisms. Short and heavy in stature, he resembled a ferocious pit bull terrier in appearance and tenacity. On the social scene, he was a country boy who never quite fit into the big city. Although he tried, he was too much of an individual to blend into the snobbish society of the elite city lawyers. He rebuked the role of a sophisticated upper-class socialite and instead chose to be a tough, crusty street fighter who loved a good time.

Although Sadownik was very demanding and overbearing, he was a good teacher who believed strongly in understanding and applying the law properly. He was not only well-read on the law but considered it imperative to research and know the law before entering the Court room on even the most routine cases. His philosophy was that if you knew the law and your position was right, then you could argue it successfully in Court. If the Judge disagreed, you could simply appeal to the Court of Appeal. If they disagreed, then you could take your argument to the Supreme Court of Canada. To Sadownik, the law would always vindicate those who studied and believed in it. The ultimate in life was to seek justice and to use the law to help clients in distress. Having dedicated his life in that way, he has won respect and recognition by tilting enough legal windmills to be regarded as Alberta's Don Quixote.

Under Sadownik's guidance, I developed strong research talents and a deep respect for the legal system. I enjoyed the challenge of presenting cases that featured difficult legal questions for consideration by the Court. In those early years, I was comfortably naive about the realities of how judges decided cases and the practicalities of appealing decisions when a judge ruled adversely. I was to learn over the years that judges often ignore legal argument and decide cases in a manner that justifies their pre-determined assessments. After selecting case law that best supports the desired decision, judges can simply declare that the facts of the current case are the same as the case law selected. By making the "facts" fit the case, judges can negate the possibility of successful appeals of their decisions.

As I continued in the practice of law, I encountered too many situations where the decisions of judges were influenced by bias for lawyers that they favoured. Such experiences are common for trial lawyers and most often define their strategy in Court. Trial lawyers in general proceed into Court knowing that it is not as important to be right in law as it is to appear before a judge who likes you more than the other lawyer. The more experienced clients understand that if their lawyer has the ear of the specific judge, then they can obtain any remedy that they may ask for.

On reflection, I realize now that I should not have clung to the naive attitude that being right in law was a solution to my ordeal. However, at the time, it gave me real hope and comfort that my criminal charge could be resolved in a predictable manner if it was presented to a fair judge. I reasoned that if there really was no evidence that I did something that was fraudulent, then a Judge had to dismiss the criminal charge because THAT WAS THE LAW. I further rationalized that in civil cases, it was more typical for a Judge to choose a favourite lawyer and grant him the decision that he wanted for his client. However, this was a criminal trial and I assumed that judges would be more concerned about insuring that their decisions were proper and made according to the law. I just wouldn't accept the thought that a Judge could ignore a properly-researched legal brief that proved that a criminal charge should be dismissed.

I now faced the greatest challenge of my legal career involving the most important case that I would ever work on. I was determined to use all of my legal skills in preparing the finest legal research brief. I also knew that I would have to thoroughly review all the evidence and investigate any questions that arose from the evidence. Although I lacked experience in the criminal courts, I certainly had the appropriate skills for legal research. The law would be the basis on which the application would be argued in an attempt to reverse the decision of Judge Stack. I felt confident that I was ready for this challenge and I enthusiastically embarked on it with renewed hope.

In order to conduct the necessary legal research, it was necessary to make a number of trips to the Court House Library to read an endless number of cases. The challenge was to limit my research to the specific issues arising from the specific legal issues in my case. Each case usually referred to decisions in other cases, all of which set out the distinctions of the legal principles that would be described in my legal brief. The process involved making volumes of notes and photocopying dozens of legal cases. I then drafted a summarized statement of all these cases that clearly and succinctly described the law and how it was applied to specific fact situations. The work itself was tedious and the progress was slow. I was encouraged by the legal cases which clearly described the evidence that was required to be proven by the Crown. It was clear that the criminal charge should have been dismissed by Stack. I was excited about the prospect that the law vindicated our position and we could prove that we were right.

I was satisfied with my research of the law but it was now apparent that there was something terribly wrong with the evidence. Murphy's comments about a conspiracy between Christal and Pinckney in the laying of the criminal charge peaked my suspicions. I was now inclined to believe the old adage that when you find a rat, you can expect to find a pack of rats. By suppressing evidence to protect a key Crown witness and fabricating evidence to bolster the Crown's case, Christal had crafted a criminal prosecution out of his malicious plot to incriminate me. However, what intrigued me was his blatant actions to ignore the criminal activity of the key Crown witnesses and effectively provide them with immunity for their testimony. Such an arrangement had to involve the Crown Prosecutors office and would have been sanctioned by the senior members of that department. It was obvious that Pinckney would have participated in this "arrangement" but other officials in a more senior position would also have condoned it. As with any situation, finding all of the rats usually proves to be impossible.

When you have a problem with rats, it's important to first assess how the problem arose. Although Christal was an obvious rodent, he certainly was not the "King Rat". To find the King or the others, I first began to evaluate the performance of these rodents. From the first time that Christal arrived at my home with a Search Warrant, he openly resorted to slimy tactics and openly abused his position. He had tricked me at the outset by arranging a meeting at his office only to secure and execute a Search Warrant on my home at the same time. It was clear that he expected me to be away from my home when he arrived so that he could go through my files while I was absent. He had no qualms about using force or being abusive to my wife as she pleaded with him to wait for my return. From threatening to break our door down to making improper searches of my legal files, there was no limit of what he might do. From arrogantly flaunting his power to being abusive in his comments, Christal was the ultimate portrait of a cop high on power and out of control. It was fair to assume that the other rats in his pack would possess the same type of attributes.

It was important to consider that the type of trickery that Christal used was not new or unique in criminal investigations. There are those police officers who resort to trickery in their misguided missions to trap unsuspecting targets and obtain convictions against them in Court. The problem with such stunts is that they are admittedly improper and can result in a dismissal of any criminal prosecution arising from such a tainted investigation. Even Christal was obviously concerned about the impression that the Judge would have about the way he conducted himself. Although he reluctantly admitted his trickery, he insisted that he showed the highest respect for me and my family as he conducted his search. He denied that he threatened to kick the front door down and he insisted that nobody was upset by his intrusion into our house. Christal had intentionally chosen to lie in Court to bolster the integrity of his conduct. There is no clearer manifestation of a rat than one that hopes to be accepted as a respectable rodent.

The manipulation of Court procedures by Christal was just as blatant as the trickery that he employed during our first encounter. In order to prolong his investigation and keep his file open, he had to show that he was still conducting this "important" investigation. To accomplish this, he swore false affidavits claiming that he needed to search my office for documents that he knew did not exist. This intentional harassment and abuse of Search Warrants was done on the pretext of obtaining more evidence. The manipulation that he practised continued into all facets of the case and ultimately affected everyone in the prosecution of the case.

Christal's most treacherous actions became evident in his planned conspiracy to secure the necessary approval of the Crown Prosecutors office to lay the criminal charge against me. Having been told by Eileen Nash that there was no evidence to justify a criminal prosecution, he conspired with Bill Pinckney to subvert this process. As he dragged out his investigation, both he and Pinckney waited for the opportune time to act. The occasion ultimately arose when Nash took her summer vacation which allowed Pinckney to intervene and give the authorization. The conspiracy worked and Christal once again succeeded in his devious and nefarious objectives.

Unfortunately, many blatant cases of misconduct similar to this are being discovered and exposed in the criminal justice system. Usually the impropriety is not discovered or proven when the case is first brought before the Courts. This results in accused people being improperly abused in the legal system and then wrongly convicted of criminal offenses. Many of these cases are never exposed or corrected but some recent cases demonstrate how innocent people can suffer from such conduct. In the recent Canadian case of Donald Marshall, the general public was shocked to realize how injustice can afflict innocent people as a result of conspiracies involving the police, Crown Prosecutors and even judges.

In that case, Marshall was wrongly convicted of murder and served over ten years in prison before the injustice was finally exposed. A special inquiry ultimately confirmed wrongdoing that involved the judges in various Court hearings as well as improper conduct by police and Crown Prosecutors. Each of the parties acted wrongly in securing the conviction of an innocent man and in covering up the improper actions of Court officials. The inquiry concluded that several parties acted in a conspiracy to effect the injustice that was suffered by Donald Marshall. Even more tragic, however, are the countless cases of such conspiracies where innocent people are victimized and then never vindicated or compensated.

The conspiracy moulded by Christal was not confined to the laying of the criminal charge but extended to developing the evidence of key Crown witnesses and inducing them to testify in the manner he desired. The inducement was transparent since each of the key Crown witnesses could have been charged for a variety of misdeeds that were clearly revealed in the evidence before the Court. By offering and arranging immunity from criminal prosecution, Christal could expect in return their fullest cooperation in providing evidence that would incriminate me. With that inducement, these witnesses became susceptible to anything Christal suggested and testified without hesitation on events of which they originally had no recollection.

It is a much easier challenge than one would expect for a police officer to alter or reconstruct the memory of a witness. One factor that favoured Christal was the long passage of time since the original event because the witnesses had little or no actual memory of it. With no clear memory to clash with what was suggested by Christal, each witness would subconsciously develop "reconstructed" memory based on what they were told or shown as the facts. Those witnesses that were motivated to protect themselves from prosecution easily accepted the bait and joined the other fish. Those witnesses that were less implicated were innocently subdued by their desire to help the cause of justice. Their belief and trust in police officers made them easy prey for Christal as these witnesses began to believe that they "remembered" what Christal stated as having happened so long ago.

These cases of false memory or reconstructed memory are common problems in evaluating evidence from witnesses in Court. Although some witnesses are intentionally deceptive and lie in Court, the witnesses who unintentionally reconstruct their memory to vindicate themselves are far more common. However, the most pervasive problem in Court relates to witnesses with a manufactured memory that was developed through instructions from police officers, Crown Prosecutors, lawyers and other interested parties. In most cases, the false testimony that results may not be construed as perjury if the witness failed to appreciate that what was said was false or if the witness did not intend to lie. In such cases, the witness is as much a victim of the criminal justice system as the person on trial.

The development of false memory is now recognized by mental health professionals and extensive medical studies have now confirmed such cases in a variety of circumstances. This condition is now known as the "false memory syndrome" and an international organization known as the False Memory Syndrome Foundation is working to educate people and identify cases. Typically, the false memory is induced by a person in authority and trust such as a therapist or police officer. Once false memory is induced in the victim, most will defend their false memory and refuse to admit that they are mistaken. For those victims that ultimately seek treatment, the hardest realization is the pain and suffering that resulted to others because of the false memory.

The false memory induced by Christal involved the belief of several witnesses that a specific document showing the purchase of the Garmaz residence was actually provided to Heritage Trust. THE ADMISSION BY CHRISTAL WAS THAT THERE WAS NO SUCH DOCUMENT ON THE HERITAGE TRUST FILE. Yet, Christal knew that he needed to prove a false representation to support a criminal charge against me. By showing this document to key witnesses and suggesting to them that they must have handled it, Christal succeeded in convincing those witnesses to adopt this false fact into their reconstructed memory of the event. Thus, Christal was able to fabricate evidence and create enough suspicion to implicate me.

The tactics of developing false memory in witnesses, fabricating evidence and substituting suspicion for fact are commonly used by police when they have no evidence but desire a conviction for a crime. Some aspect of this conduct is common in too many cases that come before the Courts and are not exposed to prevent an improper conviction. The most notorious examples can be drawn from publicized murder cases such as the recent revelations in the David Milgaard case. There was no real evidence that Milgaard committed the murder so the Crown Prosecutor instead developed his case on suspicion. Because Milgaard's friend couldn't provide him with an alibi, the Crown Prosecutor relied on this to argue that Milgaard had opportunity to commit the crime and no proof that he hadn't. With only suspicion and a hysterical community demanding that the case be solved, the Crown Prosecutor was able to convince a jury to enter a conviction against Milgaard.

Although appeals were taken by Milgaard, the Appeal Courts chose to uphold the conviction even on questionable evidence. Only because of a persistent investigation by Milgaard's mother was an inquiry finally ordered by the Federal Justice Minister over twenty years later. The Supreme Court of Canada was directed to review the evidence and elected to hear new evidence before concluding their inquiry. Their decision ultimately set aside the conviction of Milgaard as they felt that the new evidence adduced warranted a new trial. The Crown Prosecutor then elected not to proceed with a new trial but continued to maintain that Milgaard was guilty of the crime. Sadly, Milgaard had already served almost his total prison sentence for the crime. Furthermore, it now appears that he will always be plagued by the stigma of this crime and will never be vindicated. Instead, he will simply become one more victim of injustice in the Canadian criminal justice system.

Perhaps the most blatant form of abuse in the criminal justice system is the perpetual problem of some police officers telling lies in Court. Because police are unquestionably trusted by judges, they know that they can exaggerate, leave out details or phrase comments to suit their objectives. However, some police officers go beyond acceptable boundaries and tell blatant lies and alter the evidence in their cases. Christal did this when he lied in Court about his tactics in executing the initial Search Warrant at my residence. He also lied when he said that he did not have a mortgage file on a prior deal concerning Garmaz and instead kept the file concealed in his briefcase. These lies were blatant acts of perjury but Christal knew that he could lie and then escape all repercussions.

These types of tactics of police officers was exposed in a recent murder case of Wilson Neepoose. The police officer was discovered to have altered a document and then lied in Court about it. Another Crown witness had also lied and this was sufficient to set aside the conviction. Perjury charges were then laid against the police officer for his false testimony in Court. To the amazement of the general public, the verdict in the perjury trial was "Not Guilty". The judge noted that the police officer knowingly told a lie in Court but then ruled that he was Not Guilty because he didn't intend to lie. This verdict can only be explained as one more instance where the Judges will act to protect police officers even when they blatantly abuse the process of the Court. Anyone else in the same situation would have likely been convicted and sent to jail to set an example to the general public of the Court's disdain for those that commit perjury.

Christal's brazen actions to use improper tactics and his conspiracy to fabricate evidence made me wonder if I would ever discover the truth. I knew that Christal and the Crown Prosecutor had not presented all the evidence to the Court and that there was an obvious cover-up in this case. There were missing pieces in the evidence and I knew that the only hope for me was to conduct a little investigation of my own. I felt apprehensive about this challenge since the critical facts would probably be difficult to uncover. I was also not equipped with the necessary skills to effectively do this investigative work. However, I knew that I had to at least try to uncover some of this missing evidence.

I began by studying my notes from the Preliminary Hearing and focused on the evidence that was NOT presented by the Crown Prosecutor. There were some serious, unresolved questions that had peaked my curiosity: Was there really a merger between Heritage Trust and North West Trust Company? What ultimately happened to the Acreage Property? Who actually suffered the loss after the foreclosure action? Was there really any loss suffered in this case? Suddenly, I was convinced that evidence was being intentionally withheld on this point as I recalled the evidence of John Chubb. He had testified at the Preliminary Hearing that Heritage Trust had been merged with North West Trust thereby combining them into one company. This occurred in March of 1987 which was approximately the same time that Heritage Trust was refused coverage on their loss on the acreage property by CMHC. I recalled the news coverage on the re-organization of these two trust companies by the Alberta Government. I was sure that there was no information of a "legal merger" that was reported. This led me to suspect that Chubb was hiding the real facts and that there was more to the story of what happened than Chubb or the Crown Prosecutor had chosen to reveal.

I started my investigation with a visit to Companies Branch, the Provincial registry for all incorporations. On speaking to a supervisor, I was informed that each trust company is incorporated by an Act of the Legislature of the Province. Therefore, a trust company did not fall under any of the rules of their department. Instead, trust companies were administrated by the Department of Alberta Treasury which monitored the operations and reserves of each trust company continually.

My next move was to track down the right people in Alberta Treasury. After a few days of telephoning and waiting for return calls, I finally found the right department and received a cautious response for cooperation and assistance. I made an appointment to meet with the official at Alberta Treasury and was able to confirm at that meeting that there had been NO merger. I now had proof that Chubb had lied in Court when he testified that there was a merger of the two trust companies.

I was then provided with copies of the Order in Council that approved the re-organization plan that simply transferred assets and left the corporate structure of the two trust companies intact. In the re-organization, some of the assets of Heritage Trust were transferred to North West Trust Company and the balance were transferred to 335674 Alberta Inc. Heritage Trust was left with no assets but the Government of Alberta then transferred sufficient funds to pay off all the debts of both trust companies. There was no information about which assets were transferred to North West Trust Company and I knew that I would have to find that out on my own.

I suspected that the acreage property that was mortgaged by Garmaz had been transferred to North West Trust Company under the re-organization plan. After all, Chubb had testified that North West Trust Company had lost over one hundred thousand dollars when it liquidated that property. I was curious to see what monetary value was shown on the transfer documents when the title was transferred from Heritage Trust to North West Trust Company. After all, it was possible that the acreage property might have been transferred at a lower value and then resold by North West Trust Company at a higher value, thereby creating a profit and not a loss for North West Trust Company.

The answer to this mystery could only be found at the Land Titles Office, the Provincial Government Land Registry Office for Northern Alberta. All documents and old titles to every property were stored on microfiche and a photocopy could be obtained on payment of a nominal fee. As with any government service, patience is essential and waiting is mandatory. I had a copy of the title to the property showing Heritage Trust as the owner after the foreclosure action was concluded. I used it to order a copy of the Transfer of Land that would show where it was transferred next. When I finally got a copy of the Transfer document, I was stunned on learning the rest of the story.

I am told that the thrill of any investigation is the discovery of surprises in areas where you least expect them. In my amateur investigation, I was hoping to discover something that could be helpful. I never expected to stumble upon a cover-up that would prove my suspicions about a conspiracy in this case. Not only did it prove that Chubb had lied in Court about everything but it also proved that the whole prosecution was nothing more than a sham and an abuse of the Court process.

As I stared at the copy of the transfer document, I began to consider the implications of my discovery. The Transfer of Land proved that the acreage property had never been transferred to North West Trust Company. Chubb had lied when he said that the property was taken over by North West Trust Company and that it suffered a loss on the resale of the acreage property. Indeed, North West Trust Company had suffered no loss because it had nothing to do with the acreage property. This was a critical part of the Crown's case and the lie was necessary to implicate me. The question now arose as to who else was involved in this cover-up.

There was no question that Christal would have known about this since he had the Heritage Trust file and also had conducted extensive title searches on the acreage property. Nash and Pinckney would also have been aware of this since they had all the information that Christal had assembled. They all would have participated in the conspiracy to cover-up and suppress this evidence from the Court. The question now was how many others in the Crown Prosecutors Office and in the Government had knowledge of and were involved in this cover-up and conspiracy.

It was crucial for me to investigate further and to confirm some of my other suspicions. I now realized that I had unmasked the tip of an iceberg and that the majority of my discovery still lay hidden from me. The transfer document showed that the acreage property had been transferred to 335674 Alberta Ltd., a privately incorporated company used in the re-organization of the two trust companies. I now needed to learn how the Government of Alberta actually completed this re-organization and what really happened to the acreage property.

The next move was another visit to Companies Branch to search the registry file for the company 335674 Alberta Inc. This company was incorporated by John Karvellas, a lawyer with the Cruickshank Phillips law firm in Edmonton. Strangely, Karvellas was named as incorporator and director of the company and there was no mention of any interest by the Government of Alberta. I suddenly got the uncomfortable feeling that my inquiries would stop with him and I could only hope that he would be sympathetic to my request for information.

Because Karvellas was a senior lawyer in that law firm, it was impossible to meet with him unless you made an appointment first. It seemed to be an understood and unwritten rule with senior lawyers in large law firms that nobody could see them by dropping in uninvited. After all, these senior lawyers had to maintain the image of their important position. Having anticipated this, I telephoned his office for an appointment and was immediately questioned for the precise reason why I felt that Mr. Karvellas should take time to see me. As I explained the situation, I was repeatedly interrupted to clarify what I was saying by his secretary as she struggled to make notes for her boss. She then abruptly advised me that she would review this matter with Mr. Karvellas and then follow his instructions about setting up an appointment for me.

I now realized that it would be much harder than I anticipated to get information about the acreage property after it left Heritage Trust. As I recalled, there was little debate or criticism in the Legislature over the re-organization that took place. Very few details were ever published in the newspapers and very little was actually known about this Government bailout. The only thing that the general public was told was that the Don Getty Government would spend a significant amount of taxpayers' money to salvage two insolvent trust companies and turn them into one that was financially solvent. What was interesting is that this same Government refused to do the same for Principal Trust and instead allowed all its investors to lose millions of dollars. It was evident that the information that I needed was carefully suppressed or covered up but I knew that somebody had the answers and I was determined to get some type of answers.

A day later, I received a telephone call from John Karvellas who expressed his regret that there was nothing that he was permitted to tell me about the re-organization. He advised me that because he acted as the lawyer for the Government, all the information that he had was confidential and could only be released with the requisite consent of his client. Having hit a solid barrier in my quest for information, I began to ask him general questions about the way that the re-organization worked. I solicited his response on the basis that the general plan was public knowledge and therefore not confidential.

Karvellas was straining his limits as he candidly explained to me that his role was to incorporate a private company that was owned by the Government. This private company in turn owned the shares of both Heritage Trust and North West Trust Company. Because it was not a public corporation it did not have to reveal any information to the general public or the Government members. The reason for this strategy was for the private company to take title to all the real estate assets where a loss was anticipated. The properties were then liquidated at prices that assured a quick sale and the monies accounted to the Alberta Treasury Department.

I then asked him if this private company made any efforts to collect any deficiency losses relating to the initial mortgage loans on the foreclosed properties. Karvellas responded that he didn't treat the properties as having any deficiency losses and that no claims were made against anyone relating to properties that were transferred to the private company. According to Karvellas, the Government had paid off all the losses of Heritage Trust and was simply interested in liquidating the remaining tangible assets and closing the books on Heritage Trust. No collection actions were ever contemplated and none would be taken.

Having extracted this information from Karvellas, I then described what had transpired with the acreage property. He confirmed that the land and everything relating to the mortgage loan would have been transferred to the private company under the re-organization plan. He expressed surprise at hearing that a criminal investigation had proceeded on that file since nobody had authorized the necessary complaint from the private company. However, he insisted that there was nothing that he could do about it since he was now treating this as a closed file. As a closing comment, he encouraged me to talk to some of the former executives of Heritage Trust to get the inside information on what happened on this particular property.

After hanging up the telephone, I made notes and reflected on the implications of what Karvellas said. According to what he said, the mortgage loan file on the acreage property should have been turned over to him on behalf of the private company, 335674 Alberta Inc. Instead, Chubb had improperly removed it from the Heritage Trust offices and fed his personal ambitions by pursuing a criminal investigation on that file without proper authorization to do so. Karvellas also confirmed that there was no claim made for any loss and that the private company and the Government were taking the position that there was no loss incurred. This implied that if there was no loss incurred, then there was no basis for prosecuting a fraud charge.

These revelations were getting more promising with every inquiry but I still needed that elusive witness that could be produced in Court to give testimony. This was going to be difficult. I had to find someone who had been in a high management position with Heritage Trust and could reveal this information without prejudice to himself. Because many of the senior managers moved over to North West Trust Company on the re-organization, I began my inquiries at their head office. Through my inquiries, I was able to locate the former

President of Heritage Trust who was now the Vice-President of North West Trust Company. Because of his privileged new position, he refused to discuss any issues arising from the failure or re-organization of Heritage Trust. As I expected, the wall of secrecy that existed when the trust companies were re-organized would be my greatest obstacle.

My only chance was to find somebody who was in management at Heritage Trust and was then laid off during the re-organization. As I scanned through the photocopies that I had from the file of Heritage Trust, I uncovered a memo from Ross Pillott. A telephone inquiry to North West Trust Company confirmed that he did not work there. This was my hopeful lead and I began my search for him in the telephone directory to get his home telephone number. After a few unsuccessful tries, I found him and a meeting was set up for later in the week.

Pillott was now working in his own construction business and we met at one of his job sites. He naturally had no recollection of the acreage property or what happened on the Heritage Trust file. I began to ask him general questions on the operations of Heritage Trust and was most interested in how the default mortgage loans were categorized prior to the re-organization. Pillott explained that all loan accounts at Heritage Trust were categorized as either income producing accounts or non-income producing accounts for accounting purposes. When a loan went into default, it was simply categorized as a non-income producing account and that designation remained until the file was closed and it could be determined what profit or loss was realized. In a property foreclosure, the account would remain active until the property was sold and all efforts were exhausted in collecting the deficiency balance.

I then provided him with some information on the acreage property based on documents that I had secured. Pillott confirmed that the mortgage loan relating to the acreage property would have been a non-income producing account. This meant that it would have been an active file at the time of the re-organization since the property was not sold and no final decision was made on the collection of the deficiency loss. Therefore, no loss or profit would have been realized or recorded by Heritage Trust on that mortgage loan account. He also affirmed that the intervention of the Government with its re-organization would have eliminated any prospect of a loss on that loan account. The effect of the re-organization was that the Government purchased all the non-income producing accounts from Heritage Trust and transferred them to the private company, 335674 Alberta Inc. Therefore, no profit or loss would ever be realized by Heritage Trust or any other company with respect to that mortgage loan account.

As we talked about the re-organization of the two trust companies, Pillott began to give me his insights into the politics behind the scenes. According to Pillott, Heritage Trust had a reserve problem but it also had a strong asset base. It therefore submitted a proposal to Alberta Treasury that would have allowed it to resolve its problems and continue as a viable trust company. In stark contrast, North West Trust Company was actually rendered insolvent because its President, Larry Rollingher, bled off all its good assets and put them into his private company.

Pillott and the senior management of Heritage Trust had clearly expected that North West Trust Company would be wound up and that Heritage Trust would be allowed to continue to operate and remain viable. What they didn't anticipate was the hidden variable in politics which was the ability to draw the favour of the Premier. Since Rollingher and Premier Don Getty were good friends, the improbable became reality as the Government stepped forward with barrels of cash to intervene where no intervention was necessary. This same Government had no problem watching the investors and creditors of Principal Trust languish from the results of liquidation. However it acted with haste to pour unlimited funds into the rebuilding of North West Trust Company.

The re-organization was strange and had the effect of covering up all the prior transactions that led to the fiscal problems of the two trust companies. Ironically, all the good income producing assets were stripped from Heritage Trust and put into North West Trust Company to make it a viable trust company once again. The Government money was used to buy up all the non-income producing accounts and to transfer any lingering assets to a private company for a secret liquidation. What was amazing was that there was no reaction from fiscal critics about the way the re-organization took place or to the secrecy of the whole situation. It was the best cover-up operation to ever be executed in open view of public criticism and it basically slipped by unnoticed.

Sadly, this bailout with taxpayers' money was only one of many similar bailouts, loans, and financial fiascos that were typical of the Getty years in Government. In one decade, Don Getty was able to transform one of the most affluent provinces in Canada into one of the most debt-ridden provinces. In the process, countless friends of Getty secured financial help and billions of dollars were lost on these Government forays to assist business ventures. The legacy of the Getty years will be a huge Government deficit that will take years to bring under control. Instead of leaving our children with a Heritage Trust Fund, we can now expect to leave them with a Heritage Budget Deficit.

Now that I had uncovered these facts, I became more alarmed at how Christal had conducted his investigation. I could now understand that he had manipulated the situation right from the beginning to develop an opportunity for himself to charge a lawyer with fraud. In the course of my law practice, I had met or heard accounts of many people who had committed deeds that were improper and despicable to further their own personal interests. However, Christal was clearly the worst example that I could think of. He had pursued this investigation when he knew that there was no loss to anyone. There was no complainant and there was no victim. His actions to charge me and have me convicted of fraud were solely to feed his ambition to gain recognition in his department. The only word that could sum up his actions in this case was DIS-GRACEFUL.

Having assembled all my research, I proceeded to complete my legal brief for Murphy. In doing so, I used a format that could be converted to a Written Submission for use in Court in this type of application. I also proceeded to draft an affidavit setting out my evidence on the application. Although the written transcript of the evidence from the Preliminary Hearing would automatically form part of the material before the Judge, an affidavit had to be sworn by me to set out the facts on which the application would be argued and adjudicated. Naturally, all of the new facts that I had learned from my investigation could only be introduced through this affidavit. Furthermore, the affidavit was important to demonstrate the prejudice that I had suffered. That would justify the need for intervention by the Court to prevent injustice by ordering a Stay of Proceedings in my case.

In drafting the affidavit, I knew that I could use this opportunity to put forward government documents that demonstrated the facts that I had discovered relating to the two trust companies. In addition, I needed to establish evidence that Christal had been callous, malicious and vindictive in his investigation for our application for a stay of proceedings. Even though the police and the Crown Prosecutor are required to prove that they didn't act improperly, the Court still looks for evidence of improper conduct. This requirement would be easily met as all of Christal's actions had been consistent. He demonstrated a clear attitude by his conduct that could only be described in these words.

As I worked on my materials, I became convinced that there was sufficient evidence for a judge to grant a stay of proceedings on the criminal charge. Our other argument was that there was no evidence to prove the elements of fraud and the law that I researched conclusively showed that. It was now a matter of completing the materials and meeting with Murphy to review them. Ultimately, Murphy would have to finalize them and then proceed with this application. I felt excited about the prospect that this situation might soon be resolved and my life could once again return to normal. I had no way of anticipating the devastating set-back that I would imminently suffer.

CHAPTER SEVENTEEN

THE LAW SOCIETY

The month of March is a glorious month in a climate that endures such a long winter. Not only are the days noticeably longer but also warmer. Although the midday sun tempts us to take out the bikinis and summer clothes, it is still too early to put away the warmer winter clothes. However, the first official day of spring also falls in March. After enduring winter weather for four months, it is encouraging to see signs of relief from the ongoing drudgery of snow and ice. It is a month of extreme contrasts featuring colder weather with occasional storms and warmer weather with melting snow, mud and slush. Children really enjoy it while adults simply endure it and pray for a quick transition to warm, dry spring weather.

With the warmer weather usually comes a rebirth in the interest of home buyers and this in turn stimulates the real estate, banking and legal business. This new business activity is a welcome relief to law firms since the winter season can create a dramatic reduction in legal work and fees for any law practice. I was particularly relieved to see the arrival of new files that would result in immediate fees to cover expenditures that became due at that time. One of the most significant was the Professional Fees for membership in the Law Society which were payable at the beginning of March. Failure to pay on time resulted in immediate suspension of the licence to continue a law practice.

Similar to most previous years, my Law Society fees were sent to the Calgary office of the Law Society just prior to the deadline date. I was always apprehensive that one of these years, my cheque wouldn't get there on time and the Law Society would embarrass me with a suspension. In such cases, a notice is sent to every practising lawyer advising that a particular lawyer is suspended for non-payment of fees. This was the type of publicity that I really didn't need at this time to add to all my other problems.

I should have become accustomed to seeing my most dreaded fears transforming into reality. Still, I was truly shocked when I actually received a telephone call from the Law Society:

"I'm phoning from the offices of the Law Society in Calgary for Mr. Orest Rusnak. Is Mr. Rusnak in?"

For a moment, I sat at my desk in disbelief as I listened to the voice on the telephone. I couldn't recognize the female voice and I just couldn't believe that my Law Society fees had not reached their office in time. I first tried to compose myself quickly and then attempted to resolve the problem:

"Yes, this is Orest Rusnak. If you are phoning about my Law Society fees, I definitely mailed them. You should have received it."

I was interrupted at that point by the female voice as she continued:

"Mr. Rusnak, this has nothing to do with your Law Society fees. I'm the secretary for Mr. Oman. Mr. Oman asked me to telephone you to tell you that you have been suspended by the Law Society pending an investigation into complaints against you."

For a moment, I sat at my desk in shock as I struggled to understand what had happened. I was aware that the Law Society was also investigating my fraud charge and I had even had communications with the Law Society investigator, Jim McLeod. McLeod had been a classmate in my Law School class. He was much older and enjoyed the perk of receiving a full salary from the Royal Canadian Mounted Police force during his attendance at University. The Police force funded his University education on the expectation that McLeod would use his Law degree to compliment his investigative work on the police force. Instead, McLeod left the Police force shortly after graduation for the more lucrative prospects of private practice. However, he soon found that his abrasive personality didn't fit well with the clients of the law firm where he was employed. With a little influential help, he secured a more suitable job featuring a comfortable and guaranteed salary working as an investigator at the Law Society offices. The work that McLeod performed for the Law Society was not really that of a lawyer investigating allegations of improper conduct. Instead, he chose to handle the files like a police officer searching for evidence to prosecute lawyers accused of professional misconduct. When the Law Society hired McLeod to do their police work, it prompted a fellow classmate, Adam Germain, to later remark at a class reunion: "ONCE A COP, ALWAYS A COP."

McLeod wasted no time in distinguishing himself at the Law Society offices with his zealousness for exercising his new found authority over solicitors that he chose to investigate. Any limitation that a police officer had in conducting an investigation was now irrelevant in McLeod's investigations. After all, a lawyer did not have the right to be informed of anything and McLeod was not limited in what he could do in an investigation. McLeod introduced a new era of fear and harassment to the history of the Law Society and now an investigation by the Law Society was more threatening to a lawyer than any investigation by the police. Indeed, what the Law Society created was their personal version of the Gestapo police to investigate, harass, and eliminate lawyers who were out of favour with the ruling hierarchy.

The fundamental principles of a Law Society investigation are based on the premise that these investigations do not involve the police and no information is released to the public. Only if an investigation reveals that a criminal offence has been committed will the police be asked to investigate. McLeod changed all that because of his close affiliation with various police officers. He used his police access to increase the abilities of the Law Society investigator to implicate lawyers targeted by his investigations. To McLeod, a simple complaint of discourteous conduct could easily become an investigation into a major conspiracy to disgrace the Law Society. This task of disrupting or destroying a legal career was made easy as there were always the dissatisfied clients in every law practice. These unhappy clients needed little persuasion to give statements that the lawyer under investigation acted improperly and caused them hardship and losses that could have been prevented.

It was the close relationship between McLeod and the police forces that enabled McLeod to become aware of the investigation by Christal even before any criminal charge was laid. It was this close relationship that caused Patrick Murphy to believe that McLeod had assisted Christal in the criminal investigation. Murphy's suspicion was that McLeod encouraged Christal to pursue the criminal investigation and the laying of the criminal charge to assist McLeod in his Law Society investigation. Because we could never gain access to the Law Society file that McLeod created, we were never able to confirm that theory. However, Murphy was adamant in his belief and I was satisfied that Murphy had a reasonable basis for making such a strong accusation.

During McLeod's investigation, I was asked to provide him with a letter explaining the particulars of the fraud charge. That request and my responding letter were the only proceedings that had taken place to date on that matter. If there was to be an investigation by the Law Society, I should have first received a notice with details of a specific charge. Because I had not received any formal notice, I was satisfied that no further steps were being taken. It was Murphy's advice to me that McLeod's investigation would not be the subject matter of any Law Society proceedings until the criminal proceedings were resolved. What confused me was that a decision to suspend me had already been made and therefore this matter had already been considered and decided in my absence.

After a short pause, I began to respond to the secretary at the Law Society offices with questions to clarify what was happening:

"I don't understand what is happening here. I didn't receive any notice of any hearing regarding any proceedings to suspend me. The last communication I had on this matter was my letter to Jim McLeod to provide particulars which was sent about two months ago. I haven't heard anything further on that matter and I didn't receive any notice regarding any hearing. Did Mr. Oman talk to my lawyer, Patrick Murphy, about this matter?"

The secretary responded quite abruptly as she tried to quickly complete her assigned task:

"Mr. Rusnak, the Law Society does not have to give you notice of any hearing regarding a suspension. The Benchers of the Law Society have the right to suspend a member at any time without a hearing. The Benchers just concluded a meeting and this suspension was directed by them. You will receive a letter advising you of that decision but your suspension takes effect immediately. A date for a hearing will be set later and you will receive notice of that. When your hearing is held, a decision will be made whether the suspension should continue or be lifted. Right now, I am preparing a notice to send to the legal profession regarding your suspension. Can you tell me who is going to act as legal custodian of your law practice?"

As I listened to her speaking, I began to realize that there was nothing that I could say that would resolve this matter with her. I felt totally unprepared to deal with this latest disaster in my life and I couldn't think of what I should do next. I needed a few minutes to collect myself and to develop some thoughts on how to resolve this situation. In a final effort to gain a reprieve from this disturbing conversation, I responded:

"As you know, I work alone in my law practice. I only have a few clients and a few files. I will talk to Patrick Murphy about this. As you know, he represents me on my legal matters. Can I call you back to confirm whether he is prepared to act as legal custodian of my law practice?"

The secretary from the Law Society confirmed that she would wait for my telephone call and as my shock heightened, I said good-bye and hung up the telephone receiver. As I collapsed into my chair, I tried to collect my thoughts on what I should do. I had been a lawyer for seventeen years and had relied on my legal practice to earn an income to support my family. My law practice always provided a sufficient, although sporadic, income which we relied upon throughout all those years. Now, my law practice was about to disappear. I had no idea what I would do to earn a livelihood since the only thing I was trained to do was be a lawyer. I had no idea how I would support my family and I suddenly felt lost and helpless.

I knew that this latest set-back would be very devastating to my wife. She had such a hard time dealing with each of the devastating situations that arose. The only positive aspect of our current financial situation was that Pat chose to return to work two months earlier. Her income was helpful in meeting our monthly financial obligations. My only hope now was to use my experience and knowledge to perform some consulting work for some of my former clients and earn an income in that way. Under these circumstances, these alternate incomes would be our only salvation in surviving this desperate situation.

After a few minutes, I forced myself to act and started by telephoning Murphy to inform him of this development. Murphy was gone to court so I spoke to his secretary and explained that I needed to speak to him urgently. His secretary assured me that she would get a message to him and that he would call back shortly. As I hung up the telephone, I quickly analyzed what had to be done to wind up my legal practice. I began to jot down on paper some notes describing the status of the work on each of my legal files.

As I worked, I reflected on how my personal circumstances had changed since I first began my legal career over seventeen years ago. When I first started my law career, it would have been impossible for me to believe that one day I would be prosecuted for fraud and suspended from the practice of law. Yet I was now fully engulfed in just such a nightmare. As the sorrow and despair of this current crisis began to overpower me, I began to understand the feeling of complete helplessness. I had witnessed businessmen, doctors, and lawyers who acted irrationally when faced with the prospect of losing their professional careers or businesses. Some drowned themselves in alcohol and drugs, some emptied their trust accounts or stole from their companies and some even committed suicide. Invariably, their actions only added to the grief of their families and friends. I immediately resolved that no circumstances would ever cause me to feel such mental depression as to consider such a frightening prospect. However, I now knew that I would always think differently of those who were weak and vulnerable to succumb to such desperate actions.

I worked frantically to determine which files would be closed or returned to clients and which needed more attention and had to be referred to Murphy's office. It was typical for me not to appreciate how much work I had in progress. I had become accustomed to handling my workload in a routine fashion and never evaluated it in the context of my total work commitment. As I flipped through my files, I secretly hoped that none of my clients would call until I could confirm that Murphy would undertake them. I would then be able to explain the transition to my clients with specific instructions. In the midst of this flurry of activity, the telephone rang. I reluctantly reached to answer it only to hear Murphy's voice straining with deep concern:

"Hi Orest! This is Pat Murphy calling. I was just talking to my secretary. I understand that you need to speak to me urgently. What's wrong?"

At that moment, I wanted to vent the rage and frustration that was erupting within me. I wanted to tell Murphy that everything was "wrong" and that I couldn't handle any other "wrong" things in my life! However, I realized that none of this was his fault and that he had worked hard to try to resolve this situation for me. Furthermore, Murphy had always shown such genuine concern and empathy in everything that he did for me. I decided that it was important for me to show him that I understood and appreciated that.

I took a moment to calm myself and then responded to his question:

"Patrick, I'm sorry to bother you like this! I just got a telephone call from the Secretary for Oman at the Law Society offices. She called to inform me that I had been suspended by the Benchers yesterday. I just don't understand how they can do that. There was no reason for them to suspend me. They did that without giving me any notice or even a chance to explain my side of the story. Did you hear from anyone about this suspension?"

Murphy sounded surprised as he responded:

"I'm very sorry to hear about that, Orest! I hadn't heard a thing from McLeod or anyone else at the Law Society. My last communication was that letter of response to their inquiry for an explanation of how the fraud charge arose. I assumed that they would simply wait until your trial was concluded. After all, you are entitled to be considered innocent until proven guilty even by the Law Society. But you know, the Law Society can do anything they like. Still, this is really so unfair and so unnecessary."

For a moment, I felt dazed as my tension continued to grow. Murphy's comments had so succinctly described the general sentiment of most lawyers involved in small law practices regarding the actions of the Law Society. A lawyer in a small firm or independent law practice needed good connections to be favoured by "the Benchers". The word "Benchers" described the Board of Directors of the Law Society and consisted of lawyers primarily from large law firms. Those elite members of the legal profession who held the position of Benchers could flaunt their authority over the other members of the legal profession. Their power extended to their ability to exempt their favoured colleagues from sanctions for misconduct. If a lawyer was not well-connected, he could expect the Benchers of the Law Society to be harsh in the manner that ethical conduct rules were enforced. For that reason, any time that I received an inquiry came from this tyrannical authority, it was never welcome news. The dreaded reality for most independent lawyers was that if there was a complaint, then you had a reason to worry. The Law Society could act arbitrarily and without any notice and one could expect to be reprimanded even if there was no basis for the complaint.

The situation was totally different for lawyers in large law firms who enjoyed the secret privilege of immunity from investigations relating to complaints. This privilege evolved from the control exercised by large law firms through mutual cooperation in electing representatives to the governing Board of Benchers. Because of this dominance of control, a lawyer in a large firm could count on a private procedure where all complaints were quickly and quietly resolved with the intervention of the firm's representative to the Benchers. In contrast, a complaint against an independent lawyer or a lawyer from a small firm who was not favoured by the Benchers knew that all complaints would be scrutinized by McLeod followed by an investigation, a hearing and sanctions.

This cooperative network between large law firms also created a private procedure for resolving complaints between lawyers of two large law firms. This procedure guaranteed that no complaints regarding these lawyers would ever be sent to the Law Society. Instead, it was an understood procedure that if such a complaint arose, then the complaint was arbitrated by representatives of the two large law firms. In contrast, if the complaint was against a lawyer from a small law firm, then the understood practice within this cooperative network was that all complaints were forcefully advanced to the Law Society. Such complaints were then prosecuted with vigour as it was in the collective interests of this manipulative network to eliminate the competitive services offered by small law firms.

This antagonistic attitude and class structure in the Law Society has fuelled a growing resentment between large and small law firms. In response, some independent lawyers and small law firms have formed an association to make a unified stand against the injustices of this upper class of lawyers. In order to gain some representation for the forgotten independent lawyers, this organization is advocating a consolidated support for electing specific candidates to the Board of Benchers. This Association has become a quiet voice of discontent crying out in the wilderness. Interestingly, this movement has sparked criticism from the large law firms who obviously feel threatened. They have arrogantly pronounced that there is no need for independent lawyers to band together. In a typical totalitarian response, they have even criticized the character of the organizers in the hope of discrediting them. The signal was clear that any real changes that could guarantee fair treatment to all lawyers would be opposed by those that wanted to retain control in the Law Society.

An example of how this cooperative network has succeeded in controlling the Law Society is easily demonstrated by a comparison of two similar and astounding cases of unprofessional and discreditable conduct. The first case involved George Perdicaris, an independent lawyer in Edmonton who was not favoured by the Benchers of the Law Society. Although Perdicaris had found himself as the subject of minor complaints to the Law Society, he had always escaped any significant consequence. Many times, the complaint became the subject of a full investigation, a hearing and then a reprimand or sanction. However, the complaint that ultimately upset his career arose from an attractive female client seeking a divorce. She had complained to the Law Society that Perdicaris had made a proposition to her to exchange sexual favours for legal services. According to the complainant, when she advised Perdicaris that she didn't have sufficient money to pay the legal fees, Perdicaris showed his benevolence to accommodate her by making this proposition.

To Perdicaris, this seemed like a good arrangement as he was newly divorced and probably needed the companionship. However, the client was indignant that Perdicaris would think that she would lower her standards that dramatically to spend her intimate time with him. On receiving the complaint, the Law Society happily proceeded with an immediate investigation followed by a hearing before the Benchers. In an expeditious manner, Perdicaris was found guilty of the complaint and the Law Society ordered a three year suspension as a punishment. Most observers agreed that a reprimand was in order but it was common ground that even a short suspension was excessive in this case. The three year suspension was ridiculous and could only be rationalized on the basis that the Benchers really wanted to get rid of Perdicaris.

A similar and comparable case involved Don Goodfellow, who had always enjoyed the image of being part of a favoured large law firm. He enjoyed a good and friendly relationship with all the established Benchers of the Law Society and had even served as a Bencher himself. When Goodfellow's larger law firm dissolved, he immediately was welcomed at the Calgary offices of Milner & Steer. His entry into this large, prestigious law firm was heralded as a welcome addition since he was friends with all the senior lawyers and could bring some large corporate clients with him. However, shortly after he joined, he became enamoured over a young attractive secretary in his new office. When his flirtatious advances failed to attract her, he became a predator and cornered her in the photocopy room during an office party. During the encounter, he grappled with her, pulled her clothing off and shed his, and began directing her on how she was to gratify his lust for her. The commotion attracted others at the party who were then able to restrain him from molesting her further.

It was blatantly obvious to the partners at Milner & Steer that this incident had the potential to become explosive and injure the fine conservative image of this prestigious law firm. It was therefore decided that the partners would conduct an immediate in-house investigation and resolve everything quietly. The secretary was easily appeased with satisfactory compensation and the guarantee of stable employment. When it was discovered that Goodfellow had a history of sexually harassing and assaulting his female employees, it was determined that Goodfellow had to leave the law firm. Goodfellow was forced to agree to move out quietly on the understanding that nothing more would be said about this incident. This assured him that no complaint would be made to the police and no investigation would be made by the Law Society. However, the story ultimately circulated in answer to inquiries about Goodfellow's sudden departure from Milner & Steer. It was no surprise that the Law Society ignored the stories and the incident even passed unnoticed by the vigilant investigator of the Law Society.

The comparison of these two cases demonstrates effectively how complaints of the Law Society are handled and the blatant inconsistencies in the Law Society investigations. Every small practitioner quickly learns the advantage of being favoured by the elite representatives of the legal profession who control the Board of Benchers. Those who are not favoured know that any complaint can lead to devastating ramifications for a promising legal career. Unfortunately, there is currently very little movement for change. As long as these investigative procedures can be controlled and manipulated by the cooperative network of large legal firms, there will always be disparity in the way that complaints are resolved.

Over the last few years, the Law Society has implemented changes that have brought even more hardship to independent lawyers. Rather than making the entire complaint process more balanced, the Benchers have increased the scrutiny of the unrepresented masses. By boosting the powers of the investigator and giving McLeod an open reign on selected targets, they have unleashed even more hardship on the independent lawyers. Most recently, the Benchers have opened the disciplinary hearings to the public so that news reporters could attend and report on the proceedings. The result is that the news reporters can get the story first hand instead of through their informants. However, this did nothing to affect the protected lawyers since they had no fear of being exposed or appearing in these public disciplinary hearings.

I was all too familiar with this disparity between the two classes of lawyers. It was clear that the odds were against me to get my suspension set aside. In a desperate and final attempt to cling to the hope that this dismal situation could be rectified, I pleaded with Murphy:

"Patrick, help me if you can! I would really appreciate if you could make some inquiries to find out why the Benchers held a hearing without notice to me and then suspended me. I was also wondering if the Law Society might consider cancelling the suspension and instead impose conditions on my law practice. I really don't have any other source of income so I don't know how I would generate an income to support my family. If there is anything that you can do, I would really appreciate it."

Instinctively, I knew that there was little likelihood that the Law Society would act to change their decision. I was therefore pleasantly surprised when Murphy responded positively to my suggestion:

"I'd be happy to make some calls on this, Orest. I'm going to be back at my office this afternoon and I'll call Peter Royal. He's the current Chairman of the Discipline Committee and he would have been the one who implemented this suspension. He's nothing like Ed Molstad was and I don't particularly care for Royal. He's young, arrogant and acts like his shit don't stink. But there's no harm in calling him up and talking to him about this. There really was no reason for them to suspend you at this stage. If you agree to work under my supervision, maybe they'll go for it. In that case, at least you'll be able to work as a lawyer and earn some money to support that large family of yours."

Thankfully, Murphy was able to visualize everything clearly and always maintained a positive attitude on resolving problems. For the first time since I heard the news of the suspension, I felt optimistic that perhaps some arrangement could be made. Suddenly, I felt some relief from the stress that had tightened its hold on my nervous system and clouded my thoughts all morning. With this breath of fresh air, I responded to Murphy with some enthusiasm:

"That would really be a salvation to me if we could arrange that, Patrick! Please call Royal as soon as you can. I'll stay close to the telephone to hear from you after you've talked to him. In the interim, I'll continue to clean up my office. By the way, Oman's secretary asked me to advise her who the custodian of my law practice would be. Would you be prepared to take over my files? They are mainly real estate files but I have a couple of collection files."

Murphy was gracious about my situation and responded sympathetically to my inquiry:

"Of course! I'll do anything to help. If your files have to be completed at my office, then I'll take them over and complete them. But don't start doing anything on that until I let you know about my conversation with Royal. I'm sure we can get some type of arrangement going that will resolve this matter and keep you working as a lawyer."

I then thanked Murphy for his concern and hung up the telephone. My spirits were uplifted by the hopeful prospect that this dismal situation could still be resolved. What Murphy had suggested was reasonable. All that I could hope was that the Law Society would take a reasonable attitude towards this situation. I knew from experience that it was asking too much for the Law Society to take a reasonable approach on anything that involved the plight of an independent lawyer with no influence. However, I still hoped that everything might be different this time. I decided to call Oman's secretary at the Law Society offices to confirm that Patrick Murphy would act as the custodian for my law practice. I then returned to my work of reviewing my files as I waited for that telephone call from Murphy that would determine my fate.

It was late in the afternoon when Murphy finally called. At once, my nervous tension erupted as I struggled once again to subdue my emotions. After greeting Murphy, I stopped breathing as I waited for him to describe his telephone conversation with Royal:

"I finally got through to Royal. He explained that Jim McLeod put the pressure on him to have you suspended and then recommended that to the Benchers. Royal's attitude is that there doesn't have to be any real evidence that you did anything wrong since they don't follow the rules of the Courts. You know, they would never do this if you were with one of the big firms. Unfortunately, since you work in a small law practice, they have no qualms in kicking you out of the profession. It's their sick way of trying to curb the competition. I did make the suggestion that you be allowed to practice under my supervision and he agreed to consider that. He has also agreed to meet with us tomorrow at one o'clock in the afternoon at his office to discuss this further. Will you be able to attend that meeting?"

I was instantly relieved and felt some excitement over the possibility of working out an accommodation with the Law Society. Without hesitation, I quickly responded:

"Patrick, I'll make myself available anytime and any place to try and resolve this situation. Would I be able to meet with you before our meeting to discuss how we should handle this meeting with Royal?"As I completed my response, Murphy interrupted to answer my last inquiry:

"I was about to say that we should meet beforehand. Maybe we could have a quick lunch near his office. We can discuss this whole thing at that time. Why don't you meet me outside Royal's offices at twelve noon. From there, we can just walk to a restaurant near his office."

I now began to relax once more as I accepted this latest news from Murphy. I was sure that we would somehow persuade Royal to recommend a change to the decision of the Benchers. With renewed enthusiasm, I confirmed to Murphy that I would meet him as requested and then we both said good-bye.

It had been an exhausting day with emotionally charged events that left my body totally drained of all energy. I now had to prepare myself to explain this situation to my wife who would be arriving from work shortly. I knew that she found it especially hard to understand the injustice and unfairness of all of the events that had happened to me. This latest development would only create more stress and difficulty for her and there was nothing I could do to change or improve that. My greatest problem was that I really didn't understand the injustice or unfairness myself. I began to wonder if all of this was part of a destiny or a master plan that I wasn't supposed to understand. All I could do was to pray that I would have the strength to persevere and to work diligently in resolving this dismal and hopeless situation.

It was difficult to preoccupy my mind as I waited for the appointed time of my meeting with Murphy outside Royal's office. The hardest task was to talk to clients who had called and to avoid talking about the files or what had to be done. Until we spoke with Royal, I wouldn't know if I could still continue to work on my legal files in some capacity or whether these files had to be turned over completely to Murphy. As I waited to meet with Murphy, I felt exhausted from the nervous energy that ravaged my body and stripped me of all feelings and emotions.

I tried to comfort myself with the thought that my concerns would be considered by Royal. As I watched the minutes slowly pass, I mentally rehearsed what I would say to Royal to convince him to intervene on my behalf. I convinced myself that this was an appropriate case for him to use his authority to rectify an erroneous decision by the Benchers. After all, it was bad enough that I wasn't allowed to attend the hearing in which the decision had been made to suspend me. What was even worse was that there was no procedure to appeal the decision of the Benchers or to have it reconsidered. Although this meeting with Royal was a poor substitute for the original meeting before the Benchers, I reasoned that at least someone with some authority would hear from me. I prayed that this meeting would be enough to get this situation properly resolved.

Murphy was late, but unfortunately, that was a normal trait for most lawyers. When he did arrive, we immediately walked to a nearby restaurant and ordered a light lunch. At that moment, the last thing that I needed was something to eat. What I really needed was to discuss the Law Society proceedings and our imminent meeting with Royal. Murphy described in careful detail his discussions with Royal which offered some new insight of how the suspension actually resulted and the actual role of Jim McLeod. It was now apparent that McLeod had successfully achieved a new recognition for his ability to ruthlessly purge the legal profession of wayward lawyers. McLeod's self-appointed mission was to eliminate those lawyers that he felt were potentially harmful to the image of the legal profession. Like Hitler's vision of a pure society, McLeod had his own vision of the lawyers who belonged in the profession. He was now carrying out his Master Plan to eradicate those lawyers who didn't possess those pure and elite attributes. The only hopeful sign was that Royal was interested in meeting with us to hear my explanation and to consider Murphy's proposal. This wasn't much but it was the only hope that we could cling to for resolving this devastating situation.

Murphy and I were both careful to insure that we finished our lunch early and arrived at Royal's office a few minutes before the appointed meeting time. As Murphy announced himself, Royal's secretary was notified. A few minutes later, she appeared and told us that Royal had left for Calgary that morning. She further commented that Royal did not have anything marked in his calendar regarding a meeting. Murphy then asked if she could contact Royal in Calgary but she insisted that she did not know exactly where he was. She advised us that she only knew that he was attending more Law Society meetings. As our hopes sank, Murphy left his name and telephone number. Royal's secretary agreed to pass on the message and inform Royal about our office attendance. Murphy's disappointment mirrored mine as we both turned and left the office.

As soon as we got outside the office, Murphy remarked with disgust:

"How do you like that? ROYAL LIED TO ME! He acted like he was prepared to listen to us and he agreed to meet with us. Now, it's obvious that he had no intention of even being here when we arrived. I don't think I've ever been treated this badly by any other lawyer. Talk about discourteous! If I had done this to him, I'm sure that he would push to have me disbarred. But he can do this and nobody can do anything about it."

As my last hope vaporized into thin air, I struggled desperately to respond in a strong and positive manner:

"I guess there is no chance of resolving this problem right away so I'd better start arranging to get my files over to your office. Do you think that we have any other choice in this matter?"

Murphy was quite upset but he was trying to accept what had happened and to deal positively with it. After a few moments, Murphy responded:

"At this point, that's probably the best way to handle this. Just bring over the files when you're ready and I'll arrange for my secretary to complete any work that needs to be done on them. If I get a chance to talk to Royal, maybe I can still arrange for you to work with me on your files. Let's just wait and see."

That was how my legal career ended. NO hearing, NO notices and NO opportunity to defend myself. After seventeen years in the legal profession, I suddenly became an ex-lawyer who was removed from the profession. All the unfinished work in my law practice would be forfeited and I would exit from the profession under suspicious and disgraceful circumstances. I was now someone who lawyers would avoid. I would only be remembered in the delicious rumours that would be shared over coffee to the secret delight of more righteous lawyers. This was hardly the way that I intended to retire from the profession but that was now my destiny. My only hope was to ultimately win my Court case but there was no assurance that a dismissal of the charge would allow me to be re-instated. With the Law Society, there really were no definite rules and therefore one couldn't count on anything with any certainty.

I thanked Murphy for all his efforts and his concern for me as we parted and walked to our cars. During my drive back to my home, I realized that nothing further would transpire. Soon, the notice of my suspension would be arriving at the offices of each lawyer, making the news official. The only blessing was that this would not be reported in the news media.

In the week that followed, I worked to transfer my active files to Murphy's office and to close out and deliver inactive files to my clients. Murphy never did get a call back from Royal and his assessment of Royal proved to be correct. It was obvious that Royal never intended to meet with us. As I completed the task of cleaning up my files, I began the dismal task of finding work without training for anything except being a lawyer. The education and the experience that I possessed proved to be inconsequential and in some respects, a detriment in seeking other employment. Ultimately, similar work experience and specific educational training were the only factors being considered. Everywhere, the buzzword was "hiring freeze" which translated into no employment opportunity. Ultimately, I would find myself working as an independent consultant, which provided a minimal opportunity for generating an income. At least it provided an avenue which allowed me to work while waiting for my criminal charge to be resolved.

It was now imperative that the application to quash the decision at the Preliminary Hearing was successful in resolving this matter quickly. If it was not successful, I would have to wait for a trial and that would necessarily take another year. In the interim, I worked diligently to advance the preparation of the legal brief for the application and prayed for a speedy resolution of this matter.

CHAPTER EIGHTEEN

CERTIORARI

T he most serious problem with the law of our country is that it is NOT plainly written. This means that it does NOT lend itself to an easy understanding by the general public or even the legal professionals who must interpret, advise and adjudicate upon the law. The result is a general dissatisfaction by the general public since each citizen desires to know what laws affect him in society and how to govern oneself to comply with the laws. It is this illogical and unnecessary circumstance that has manifested itself into a major irritant with every citizen. Naturally, this creates an inevitable reaction of disgust when a citizen is accused of being in contravention of one of the many laws, by-laws or regulations that seem to control every activity in society. This situation is made worse by the attitudes of the courts that failure to know the law is never an excuse for being in breach of it.

I have always marvelled at the irony that leads to the creation of the many new laws that evolve from our elected governments on an annual basis. The citizens of the various communities elect representatives to the Legislative Assembly or Parliament to decide upon new laws that would benefit the constituents. Unfortunately, very few of these elected representatives have any knowledge or training to determine the implications of these proposed new laws. In fact, the draft legislation that is ultimately presented to the Legislative Assembly or Parliament is worded in such a manner that many of the elected representatives have difficulty in understanding or explaining it.

The reason for this situation is that the new proposed laws are actually drafted by lawyers who use their abilities to describe situations with words and phrases that are never used by the general public. As a result, laws are not drafted to be understood by the general public or their elected representatives. Instead, laws are worded to comply with the terminology that accords with the banter of the legal community. In this way, this continual problem with the laws of our country is methodically perpetuated. This system of creating laws also creates a greater need for citizens to seek advice from lawyers to interpret the law. There is therefore much justification in the conclusion that legislation is really a process whereby lawyers create work for lawyers at the expense of the general public.

It is a common criticism that most statute laws, by-laws, and regulations created by the elected legislative bodies are confusing and difficult for most people to understand. However, the law which the general public least understands or is least aware of is the "unwritten law" of Canada, known as "The Common Law of England". To most people with no legal training, the words "common law" describe a relationship between an unmarried man and woman who are living together in a relationship resembling marriage. In order to easily describe this type of relationship, the slang expression of "common law" was implemented and is still the normal phrase used today. Although most lawyers accommodate this improper slang usage of the phrase, some judges are less accommodating. I had once witnessed one judge reprimand a witness who used that expression to describe his relationship with a woman. The judge scolded the witness with these memorable words: "I don't know what your relationship with that woman is but I can tell you that it is NOT Common Law."

The Common Law of England is a throwback in time to the medieval ages in England. In those feudal times, the spoken decrees of the King and his judicial representatives settled disputes between parties and granted remedies that could only emanate from a supreme being such as the King. These judicial decisions were recorded by the "judges" with an explanation of the circumstances and the reasoning for the decision. As new cases arose, the judicial appointees of the King followed the practice of deciding similar cases in the same way. This procedure resulted in the practice of arguing "precedents" or similar cases to persuade a judge to rule in favour of a particular party. Essentially, a party could present his case with the argument that his circumstances were the same as a previous case and therefore he was entitled to the same remedy. Unfortunately, this practice quickly replaced the original common sense procedure that could easily be understood by the general public. This new practice of following precedents ultimately required people who had studied these laws. Soon the need for lawyers evolved to offer advice or argue cases that involved disputes between members of the general public.

To complicate the Common Law of England even further, each remedy or principle that was applied by the judiciary was given a name to describe it. Since the language of the literate elite was Latin, the Common Law became deluged with Latin expressions that only lawyers who carefully studied and researched the Common Law could understand. This unfortunate development made it impossible for the citizens of the general public to understand the Common Law. Furthermore, because the remedies were difficult to understand, the judges who were not conscientious lacked an understanding of these remedies and simply refused or avoided granting such remedies. The challenge for a client was to find a lawyer and then a judge who understood the law well enough to obtain the appropriate remedy.

Because first year law courses in Law Schools essentially deal with the historical basis of the various areas of law, these primary courses involved a study of the Common Law of England prior to 1870. These medieval laws were ultimately adopted as the law of Canada after Confederation in 1867. Although many of these principles are seldom used after law school, one of the most popular and useful remedies is that of certiorari, (pronounced SIR SHIR OR I). The word itself is Latin and translates to mean "to quash". This remedy is used widely by the Courts in criminal matters to set aside the decisions of a lower court. In Civil Court, this remedy is commonly used to set aside the decision of a board or tribunal. Nevertheless, this remedy is scarcely used. Although the application of this remedy has been adequately defined and adjudicated upon by the Courts, the majority of judges and lawyers seem to avoid relying upon it. The main reason for this is a failure on the part of judges to comfortably understand it.

Unlike many lawyers who resist the inconvenience of having to research the law in preparing their files, I enjoyed researching the law. To me, it was a treasure hunt. As I read cases, I found clues of other cases that could provide a strong foundation for the position or argument which I wished to advance. Occasionally, I reached a dead end with one argument and found that there was insufficient case law authority to support that position. When that happened, I had to abandon that argument and develop a new position that could be supported by case authority. As my crusty mentor, Rostyk Sadownik, had often growled: "The reason that a client hired a lawyer was to retain someone who knew the law." In his mind, a lawyer had to research and prepare each case and then present a good legal argument to achieve the result desired by the client. I had always subscribed to this philosophy in my law practice and found that it was the most satisfying way to work on legal files.

After my suspension by the Law Society, I had more opportunity to conduct legal research and to prepare a better draft of a legal brief for the argument on the certiorari application. As I continued with my research, I discovered more legal arguments that supported my position that Judge Stack had erred in his decision. The difficult challenge was to simplify the arguments and the legal brief so that it was easy to understand and could be easily presented in argument to the Judge hearing the application. Through experience, all lawyers learn that to be persuasive with judges, you must simplify arguments. A legal presentation which is lengthy or filled with complex principles is almost certainly doomed to failure.

In addition to my legal research, I was now working as an independent consultant and struggling to secure work from prospective clients. My financial circumstances had become more desperate so I was now very anxious to complete my research so that the application could proceed as soon as possible. I continually had to struggle to maintain a positive outlook on my diminishing situation. Although my wife encouraged me to continue the fight to vindicate myself, I knew that she too was having difficulty coping with our desperate personal situation. The future now looked so uncertain. It was difficult to imagine that everything could be resolved and that our lives might return to the normal, quiet lifestyle that we once enjoyed.

In the midst of this flurry of research activity, I received a letter from Murphy reminding me of the Court Appearance at the April Arraignments to set the trial date. I telephoned Murphy's office to confirm that I would meet him at the Court room. I also left a message for Murphy that I wanted to meet him after our appearance. This now became my deadline for completing my research and legal brief so that this application could be reviewed by Murphy and then filed at the Court House. With this goal in mind, I worked with renewed enthusiasm to complete this project. After that, I could free myself to devote more time to my consulting work while I awaited the outcome of this critical Court application.

APRIL SHOWERS BRING MAY FLOWERS. This short and simplistic saying describes the hopes and aspirations of people who live in the Northern temperate climate and must endure winter conditions that can last six months each year. Although the first official day of spring comes in March, it is the month of April that truly guarantees warmer weather. It is then that precipitation usually falls to the ground as rain instead of snow and causes the final vestiges of ice and frost to disappear. This in turn stimulates the wild flowers, grass and leaves to grow. The general spirit becomes one of renewed hope as everyone witnesses the rebirth of life in the world of nature. This moment in nature's cycle always causes me to have renewed faith in my ability to meet the challenges that life presents.

On the morning of the Arraignment Hearing, I was pleased with my efforts in finalizing the draft copies of my legal brief and affidavit. I actually felt eager during the drive to the Court House as I anticipated my meeting with Murphy. There would first be the appearance in Arraignment Court but this would now be a repeat experience to the earlier one in February. Although I knew it would be unpleasant, I was mentally prepared to endure it. Because of that prior experience in Arraignment Court, I was now more confident and worked at my home office later with the expectation of arriving at the Court room after the Arraignment Hearing had convened.

As I drove to the Court House, I felt unusually calm and relaxed about the imminent court appearance mainly because I was so pre-occupied with thoughts of my meeting with Murphy. While I plodded along to my destination, I revelled in the warmth and brightness of the sunshine which made this a glorious day to be outside. Nature seemed to reaffirm my hopes that my crisis would soon be resolved and that the darkness in my life would soon disappear like a cloud hiding the sun.

On my arrival at the Court House, I quickly proceeded to the Court room assigned for Arraignments and was pleased to see that the proceedings had just convened. My case was far down the list so I had time to compose myself. Murphy was nowhere to be seen so I assumed that he would be late because of another Court matter. As I sat at the back of the Court room and watched the proceedings, Murphy walked into Court and looked around hastily. On recognizing me, Murphy waived for me to come outside. I then rose to my feet and exited from the Court room.

Murphy greeted me with a cheerful remark and then proceeded to explain what would transpire during this court appearance:

"I just had a chat with Eileen Nash. Basically, all we will be doing today is entering a NOT GUILTY plea to the criminal charge and then setting a trial date. After we complete that, we can meet downstairs in the cafeteria for our meeting."

At that moment, I was grateful that I had concluded my research because I now understood that our procedure today in Court would affect our legal position in applying for the remedy of certiorari. I quickly interrupted Murphy to advise him of my research:

"Patrick, setting a trial date is fine with me. However, according to the case law, entering a plea today would waive my right to apply to the Court to grant a certiorari order to quash Stack's decision. We therefore can't enter a plea to the criminal charge today. Can a trial date be set without a plea being entered?"

Murphy looked surprised when I raised this point of law, making it obvious that he wasn't familiar with that case law. Murphy reacted in his typical accommodating style:

"That's an interesting point, Orest! I'll look at those cases later when we sit down over coffee. I'd better call Eileen Nash to ask her if she is prepared to simply set a trial date now. If this case goes to trial, you can enter your plea before the trial starts. Why don't you wait for me inside the Court room. I'll speak to Nash and also get changed into my Barrister's clothes. I'll see you in a few minutes."

I acknowledged Murphy's request and returned again to the Court room to wait for my case to be called. As the cases before mine were slowly dealt with, I waited patiently while gazing at the lawyers slumped in their chairs as they waited for their client's names to be called. It seemed absolutely ludicrous that a lawyer who was educated and trained to rendered specialized services in conducting a trial had to sit all morning to appear with a client to set a trial date. Such matters could easily be handled by the lawyer's secretary and the Court clerks if the judiciary allowed it. More appropriately, such procedural matters would more effectively be set through telephone or computer communications. Instead, we all sat in boredom as each case was called before the Court followed by the ceremony of Arraignment to set the trial date.

Because of my distraction, I didn't notice Murphy enter the Court room. I looked around in surprise when I heard his whispered voice next to me:

"Orest, I spoke with Eileen Nash and she agreed to proceed on that basis. There will be no plea today; just the setting of the trial date. Your case should be coming up soon. When your name is called, come up to the front and we'll get this done quickly."

I nodded in agreement as Murphy finished speaking. He then stood up and walked to the area in front of the metal fence that separated the general public from the judicious area. After a slight bow of his head to the Judge, he sat down in one of the leather chairs reserved for lawyers as they waited for their cases to be called. As I looked around, I noticed that Eileen Nash had entered and taken a seat in the same area. I was amused to see her still in the same black outfit, which I assumed to be her professional trade mark. Her black robes now made her outfit more suitable in this environment of agony and suffering. As I glanced at the forlorn expression on her face, I surmised that when misery and melancholy produced a child, they called it Eileen Nash.

Suddenly, I heard my name called by the Clerk and I knew that my waiting had ended. At that moment, I simply wanted this monotonous ordeal to be finished. As I walked to the front of the Court room, Nash and Murphy both acknowledged for the Court Record that they were the legal counsel on my case. When I reached the front of the public seating area, I was directed into the Prisoner's Box once again. As I stepped inside, the door was closed behind me by the Court Orderly. I faced the Judge and the Clerk again read the criminal charge to me as she did during my first appearance. As soon as she finished, Nash spoke up:

"My Lord, Mr. Murphy has advised me that he will be making an application to the Court of Queen's Bench for an Order of certiorari relating to the committal order of Judge Stack. Because of that, I have agreed with him that no plea will be entered by Mr. Rusnak today but I would like to set a trial date. If the application is unsuccessful, then the plea can be entered on the commencement of the trial. Regarding trial time, I anticipate that this trial will take two weeks."

Murphy then acknowledged to the Judge that he was in agreement with what Nash had said. The Judge then asked the Clerk to confirm the next available Court dates for trial. The Clerk looked through her Court calendar and a few moments later, she announced: "January 10 to 24, 1992". Both Murphy and Nash acknowledged that the dates were satisfactory and then the Judge ordered that my case be adjourned to January 10 to 24, 1992, for trial. At that moment, the Court Orderly opened the door to the Prisoner's Box. I slowly disembarked and then walked toward the back of the Court room.

As I left the Court room, I noticed Murphy following me out. He then asked me to wait for him in the cafeteria while he went down to the locker room to change to his business clothes. I proceeded to the cafeteria, purchased a beverage and sat down at a table that offered some privacy. Murphy was delayed so I knew that he must have stopped to call his office. I was almost finished my beverage before he arrived and joined me. As he sat down, he immediately began to talk about our court appearance:

"Orest, it's a good thing that you did your research and caught that point about not entering a plea. When I told Nash about it, even she wasn't sure at first. She had to check and then agreed that we were right. Well, at least that is over and we won't have to make any more court appearances at Arraignments. It there is one thing I hate, it's sitting around and doing nothing just to set a trial date. It would be nice if they adopted a better system."

Murphy's sentiments echoed every lawyer's assessment of this blatant waste of time. To voice agreement with his remarks, I stated:

"I totally agree, Patrick! It's such a ridiculous waste of time that it's really a bad joke. The problem is that everyone pays for it. Lawyer's can't charge for all their time, clients have to pay for the unnecessary appearances, and the taxpayer foots the bill for a procedure that is senseless and fruitless. What is really sad is that nobody seems to be too interested in changing it so the system just carries on."

As I completed my remarks, I began to pull my file out with the drafted legal brief, the photocopies of the legal cases and the draft of the affidavit. I then described the general context of my notes dealing with the Application for the Orders of Certiorari and the Stay of Proceedings. As I quickly showed Murphy the legal brief, I pointed out the research that I had done on the most recent cases decided by the Supreme Court of Canada. These cases defined when an Order for Stay of Proceedings should be granted to prevent injustice from the prejudicial delay of Court proceedings. Murphy acknowledged that he had read some material on the new case law that was founded on our Charter of Rights and Freedoms. He then confirmed that he believed we had a good basis for making the Court application. Then, after a quick glance at the drafted Affidavit, he remarked:

"Orest, you really did a great job on this material! I'd like to take it back to my office to study it more carefully. Why don't you call my office at the end of the week so that we can set up a time to discuss the research and the affidavit. At that time, we'll discuss what changes should be made and how we should approach this. When we get everything sorted out, I'll get this application filed and set a date for it to be heard."

I felt encouraged by Murphy's optimistic remarks. However, I felt apprehensive about how this matter would be set for hearing. I decided to confront Murphy with my concerns:

"Patrick, I'm glad that you like the legal brief and that you feel that these are good arguments to present to a Judge. I'm concerned, however, about this application ending up before a Judge who is lazy or who doesn't understand the law or one that doesn't care how he decides the case. You and I both know that there are too many judges like that in Queen's Bench Court. If we get a judge like that, it won't matter how good our arguments are because he'll simply avoid making any decision. That kind of judge would simply sluff off this case and dismiss our application. You'd never get a lazy judge to read all this material and make a proper decision. To get a fair hearing, we would have to get a Judge who likes researching and writing legal decisions. Is there any way that we can arrange for such a Judge to hear this application?"

Murphy responded spontaneously in agreement as he acknowledged my concerns:

"You're absolutely right! The key to this type of application is to make sure that it is heard by a judge who likes the academic challenge. If we get a lazy or burnt-out judge, it's useless to try and convince him of anything. I would think that Daisy MacDonald or Ronny Berger would really get excited with an application involving a Charter argument. There's a few others who would be good on this one as well. I think I'll speak to Nash about this. I'll suggest to her that we both approach one of those judges and ask them to hear the application. That way, this won't be a waste of time. At least, we'll get a fair hearing even if the Judge doesn't agree with our application."

I was relieved to hear Murphy's comments and confirmed that his proposal to approach Nash was acceptable. After all, it was quite obvious that this was a specialized application. Under these circumstances, it was appropriate to arrange for the application to be heard by a judge who was qualified to understand and decide it. There was no reason for Nash to disagree with Murphy's proposal. After all, it was equally important to her that the judge hearing the case did not arbitrarily grant the application without fully appreciating what he was doing. It all made good sense and Murphy was adamant about the importance of arranging for this matter to proceed before a competent judge. I therefore felt content in letting Murphy handle this matter in his own way and to wait for his instructions on what should be done in processing this application.

Murphy then gathered up all of my material and placed it in his briefcase. He confirmed that he would review all the legal research and the draft affidavit before we met to discuss this matter in depth. I agreed to telephone his office during the following week to arrange an appointment for our meeting. As we concluded our conversations, Murphy rushed off to another commitment and I also left to run some errands downtown. Everything was now in place to proceed to the next step in these proceedings. Making the final corrections and then filing the documents at the Court House would be a simple step. At last, Murphy would present this case to a judge using the law as our shield against this unfair prosecution. Now I awaited the moment when I would see justice work. I was confident that the law would vindicate me this time.

It was almost two weeks later that Murphy and I met to review my legal research brief and my drafted Affidavit. Our objective was to test the foundation of this application to a Queen's Bench Judge regarding the decision of Judge Stack. We carefully examined and debated the merits of the various legal arguments supporting the premise that there was no evidence to justify a committal of the criminal charge for trial. Murphy seemed to prefer the other legal arguments under the Charter of Rights and Freedoms. His conclusion was that it would be obvious to any judge that there had been an inordinate delay in bringing the case before the Courts. The law was clear that the Courts should order a Stay of Proceedings to prevent prejudice and injustice in this situation.

As we spoke, I referred Murphy to other research which supported the arguments in the legal brief and answered his questions. While we worked our way through the legal brief, we engaged in the customary game of Devil's Advocate. Murphy seemed to enjoy assuming the position of the Crown Prosecutor and anticipating all of those arguments. The only weakness in the game was that Murphy couldn't really empathize with the Devil's position and we really needed Eileen Nash for that.

As Murphy completed his review of the documents, I agreed to make the changes that he requested. Once the documents were ready for his final review, Murphy agreed to quickly finalize them so that they could be filed with the Clerk of the Court of Queen's Bench of Alberta. Because this matter had become such an important priority with me, I dedicated my immediate attention to completing the changes. A few days later, I met with Murphy to conduct a final review. Murphy was satisfied with the changes and I executed the Affidavit in his presence. He then agreed to file the documents immediately and to obtain a hearing date. On leaving Murphy's office I was exhilarated with confidence that soon there would be a hearing before a Queen's Bench Judge. I would soon know if my ongoing ordeal would be resolved.

Setting a date for the application would be the next order of business and perhaps the most critical part of this application. Murphy had already advised me that he would be taking a trip to Ireland during the summer. Another relevant factor was that most Queen's Bench Judges are away on vacation during the summer. Therefore, we both agreed that it would be preferable for this application to be heard before the end of June. As the weeks passed, I began to telephone Murphy's office to confirm the hearing date but his secretary repeatedly advised me that she was unable to obtain anything from Murphy. Finally, I spoke to Murphy and was advised that he was having difficulty getting a suitable date that was convenient for Nash. He therefore decided that this application would have to be heard in the fall sittings of the Queen's Bench Court. Although I was disappointed, I knew that setting hearing dates between lawyers and Judges could involve frustration because of conflicts with other court dates. This was especially true in our case because the primary consideration was for this matter to be set before a specially selected Judge. It would be a total waste of time to proceed with this application if the Judge was not competent or open to consider the special arguments that formed the integral part of our application.

The warm weather that summer introduces comes to an end just as quickly as it starts. With the arrival of September, a difficult transition was made as everyone returned to work in earnest following the summer vacation season. I now visualized with excitement the prospect of attending Court before a Queen's Bench Judge to obtain a just remedy to the injustice that prevailed in my case. I felt confident that my glorious day in Court would arrive soon. All my sacred beliefs in the legal process which I took to heart during my law school training would soon demonstrate the majesty of the law as it trampled injustice.

I continued to follow up with Murphy to confirm the hearing date of my application. Unfortunately, he was hard to catch and his secretary had no information on the date which he was arranging with Nash. As September drew to a close and October brought on the Halloween season, I finally was able to discuss the situation with Murphy. Again he explained that he was having difficulty setting a date which was convenient with Nash. In a few more weeks, the Halloween season had passed and still no date was set. We slipped into the colder weather of November when I reached Murphy and he was able to confirm that the application would be heard in December. I started to feel concerned that Nash was manipulating this application but I put my faith in Murphy to be vigilant against any of her ploys.

It was a relief for me to finally hear that the application was set to proceed in Chambers and that we could soon expect to see a resolution of this matter. Although this application was being heard six months later than I originally expected, I was simply relieved that it was finally proceeding. I understood the delay since Murphy was being careful to insure that this application was heard by a Judge who would give us a fair hearing. I wasn't too concerned that the trial date was also approaching quickly because I was so confident that our Court application would resolve this whole situation and end this difficult ordeal.

As the time approached for the hearing of the application, I continued to ask Murphy who the Judge was that would be hearing this application. Murphy finally explained that there was a possibility of a few different Judges. He reassured me that he was confident on getting a judge who was good on these types of legal arguments. He agreed to inform me with more details as we got closer to the hearing date. He then suggested that we meet on the Saturday prior to the hearing date to make one final review of the case law and legal principles to be argued. However, on the day before our scheduled meeting, Murphy phoned to advise me that he would prefer to simply review the file on his own. He asked if we could meet instead on the morning of the date of the hearing to simply discuss any fine points in the legal argument. He sounded confident on this file and I now placed all my faith in his judgement. My role was only to assist him as he required.

On the date of the hearing, I arrived at Murphy's office at ten o'clock in the morning, just as he had requested. This allowed Murphy the opportunity to meet with other clients before our meeting began. On my arrival, Murphy was in his office returning some telephone calls and I was asked to set up in his meeting room. I quickly arranged the copies of the legal briefs and the photocopied legal cases for Murphy's review. As I worked, I struggled to control the nervous excitement that was now rushing through my body. Soon I would get Murphy's impressions of how this application would proceed. As the minutes slowly passed, I glanced at the various cases that would be relied upon in the legal argument. For a moment, I tried to imagine how the application would be presented to the Judge but my inexperience in Court made this a futile effort.

As my thoughts wandered, I suddenly became aware of Murphy's voice as it became more clearly audible. My mood lifted as I realized that he was coming to the meeting room. A moment later, Murphy opened the door and stood there smiling as he exclaimed:

"Well, Orest, this is the big day for the showdown with Eileen Nash! I guess you are pretty anxious to see this concluded so we better get busy. Just let me get some tea and then we can work without interruptions."

As Murphy returned and settled into his chair, I decided to ask him a question that had been constantly on my mind:

"Patrick, which Judge will be hearing our application, today?"

Murphy hesitated for a moment and then responded with an element of surprise in his voice:

"Oh, Orest! I thought you knew. We got Dea for this application."

Those words rang in my ears. I sat there motionless and in shock. As I struggled to collect my thoughts, I wondered how this could have happened. Finally, I blurted out my reaction to what I just heard:

"Oh my God! Not Dea! How could this have happened? We're just going to waste our time today. He's not going to listen to a word that you say. Why would you agree to go in front of Dea?"

Murphy now reacted to my response defensively, although it was obvious from the tone of his voice that he understood the sentiments that I had just expressed:

"I don't think that Dea is that bad. I've had good luck in front of him a few times. I think there's a chance that he might just kick this charge out."

At that moment, I could not control my frustrations any longer. Before Murphy could continue, I interrupted him:

"Burkey Dea! Are we talking about Burkey Dea? There's no way that he's going to listen to this application. I've seen Burkey Dea in Queen's Bench Chambers. He's totally irrational! Everyone knows that he's the laziest Judge on the bench. For him, it's an inconvenience to take time from his social schedule to listen to applications in Chambers. How can you say that we will get anything resembling a fair hearing out of Burkey Dea?"

As I stopped speaking, the silence that filled the room created an uncomfortable atmosphere and Murphy moved quickly to fill the void by calmly placating me. This scene of calming an excited client is commonplace for lawyers. Murphy was as accustomed to doing this as any other lawyer. Once I finished ranting at Murphy, I regained control of my reactions and remained silent to avoid an argument with him. As I sat in my chair, I began to cope with the realization that this application was an exercise in futility. As a mood of desperation swept over me, I listened to Murphy explain:

"Orest, I'm sorry about this but I didn't have any choice. When I set this application down for hearing, I had to choose a late date to accommodate Nash. At that time I had no idea who was scheduled for Chambers on that week. It turned out that Dea was one of the Judges and that's how we got him. Now what you are saying about Burkey Dea is true but you should know that the Crown Prosecutors have just as much trouble with him as do Defence lawyers. Personally, I think we have a good chance today. We will have to keep everything very simple so that Dea doesn't have to do much reading. That way, he will feel comfortable with making a decision. I think it can be done in your case because it's really quite simple and straight forward. That's basically why I feel we have such a good chance with Dea. Besides, we have to proceed now so we might as well give it our best shot."

I quickly realized that Murphy was doing his best to comfort me. However, I understood the reality of the situation and nothing he could say would appease me. Appearing before Dea, it was obvious that we could expect one of two reactions. Because Dea was prone to being lazy, he would probably find a quick and simple way to dispose of the application. The other possibility was that Dea might act irrationally and either grant or refuse the application without any legal justification. In either case, our advantage of being able to argue the case law and win this case on the merits of the law was gone. Dea was not the type of Judge who made decisions based on the law. Instead, we had to appeal to his ego and hope to win favour with his irrational and impatient attitudes. Unfortunately for us, Murphy had not presented Dea with any expensive Christmas presents this year so Murphy could not expect to be on Dea's "Good Lawyer List".

It wasn't necessary for me to explain any of my conclusions to Murphy since we both understood the dynamics of what motivates Judges to make decisions. It was a reality that every lawyer understands and is clearly "the Human Flaw" of the Justice system. The flaw is not just that many judges are incompetent, irrational, biased and corrupt. The flaw extends to the code of silence that lawyers must observe to avoid being ostracized by the judiciary or chastised by the judges and the Law Society. Although such situations exist to some degree in every professional body, the worst by far is probably the legal profession.

It is interesting that judges are now perhaps the last "sacred cows" of our society. For that reason, there appears to be a general reluctance and a recognizable fear of criticizing them. An interesting analogy is that judges in many respects now exercise the type of power that the monarchy of medieval times enjoyed. They can not only create laws or disallow them but can also arbitrarily grant or deny rights at their personal whim. They are not controlled by any Legislative body other than their own private club and are perhaps the most powerful people in our society. Furthermore, once appointed by the political party they courted, judges are beyond the control of anyone and their powers are often exercised in a dictatorial manner.

Not only can judges make arbitrary decisions and demand unconditional compliance, they can also expect everyone to defend their decisions. Even judges are loathe to question the actions of other judges. Because of self interest, lawyers are fearful of the implications of criticizing judges. Instead, most choose the safer course of defending even the most improper conduct of judges. Even those members of the general public who find themselves before judges are afraid to criticize judges for fear of repercussions. Those who do criticize are quickly denounced as outcasts whose opinions are contrary to the interests of society. The occasional criticisms that surface from journalists and the academic community are quickly countered by friends of the judges to maintain the integrity of the judiciary. As a result, judges enjoy a position of total immunity from criticism as they rule over their domain.

Lawyers must especially be fearful for the clout of a judge. A Contempt of Court Order and immediate imprisonment can result for the slightest sign of disrespect. A lawyer must be careful on how to voice an opinion that a judge was wrong in a decision. The proper protocol is that a lawyer may "respectfully disagree" with a judge but a judge is never wrong. This lesson has been brutally communicated to a few lawyers who dared to stand up for their clients in Court. The only escape from a Contempt of Court Order is for the lawyer to make a sincere apology in Court and hope for leniency. Judges also frequently report lawyers to the Law Society for immediate disciplinary action. Needless to say, such a complaint will inevitably result in severe sanctions since the Law Society Benchers cherish their friendly relationships with all judges.

The irony of this immunity from criticism that judges enjoy is that the very people who witness the impropriety of judges are effectively silenced by the legal system. Lawyers can't speak out because of fear of reprisals. Even when the "Canadian Lawyer Magazine" did its first survey on good and bad judges, there was pressure mounted by the judiciary to stop its publication. Ultimately, the magazine persevered but one wonders if they will continue to withstand the pressure mounted by the judges on the lawyers who act as advisors to the magazine.

Another example of this immunity from criticism was the appointment of Jack Major as a judge of the Supreme Court of Canada. Aside from the usual criticism that Major was only selected because of his political support to the party in power, there was also the criticism of his suitability. It was widely expected that a woman would be appointed to strengthen the Court on its views of women's issues. Major did not represent the interests of any visible group in the Country. For that reason, he could only be seen as purely a political appointment that brought no new perspective to the Country's highest court.

The most demeaning criticism came from the academic legal community who pointed out that Major lacked the necessary experience for such an appointment. In his short term as an Alberta Queen's Bench Judge, he only heard a limited number of cases and garnered a limited amount of recognition for his ability to adjudicate. The criticism was quickly quelled and Major in fact used every opportunity to ridicule his critics for their criticism. At his swearing in ceremony, he was praised for his wit and sense of humour which clearly proved to be his only outstanding characteristics. Unfortunately, the only thing that wasn't needed in that Court was the ability to laugh at other people's misfortunes.

The ultimate horror in going to Court for every lawyer and client is the prospect of facing a "bad" judge. We couldn't have done much worse than Dea. I began to suspect that perhaps the tactics of Eileen Nash in delaying the application were intentional and that having Dea on the application was no coincidence. In spite of what Murphy said, I knew that he was unhappy about presenting this application before Dea. Unfortunately, Murphy was right about the fact that nothing could be done to change the judge now. There was no time to delay the application as the trial date was now only one month away. We had to proceed and hope for the best. I reluctantly agreed with Murphy and we turned our attention to the work at hand. Our review continued through the lunch hour and finished shortly after one o'clock. Murphy then announced that he was ready for the application and we both started to collect and organize the documents.

While I finished assembling all the Court material, Murphy slipped into his personal office to make some telephone calls. When he returned, we grabbed our briefcases and headed out the door. Murphy and I had agreed to ride downtown in my car and I offered to bring him back to his office after our Court Appearance. During our trip downtown, we casually chatted about how the case should be presented to Dea to avoid irritating or upsetting him. As we neared the Court House, Murphy suddenly suggested:

"Orest, I was thinking that maybe it would be better if you did not appear in the Court room with me. It's my feeling that if there is only me and Nash for Dea to look at, I can keep his attention better. It's my impression that Dea gets distracted easy. He'll probably open up a lot more if Nash and I are the only ones in Court with him. Do you have any problem with doing it that way?"

At first, I was surprised that Murphy would ask me not to be present on this application. After all, this was something that was important to me and I had every right to be there. Murphy pressed the point that he was trying to develop a better atmosphere for his presentation of this application. He was adamant that he needed an empty Court room with no possible distractions. Naturally, I understood that the two lawyers and Dea could say things that they might not otherwise say if there were spectators in Court. If the party involved in the case is in Court, there is usually a performance by everyone to demonstrate how the legal system works. If the Court room is empty, these pretences are dropped and the atmosphere is more relaxed. Because I trusted Murphy's judgement, I reluctantly agreed with his suggestion and I also agreed to meet him in the cafeteria when he was finished.

After I parked the car, Murphy and I walked to the Court House and then parted as he headed for the Court room and I proceeded to the cafeteria. After getting a beverage, I proceeded to a table in an isolated corner where I could complete some reading while waiting for Murphy. The time passed slowly as I tried desperately to focus on my reading but I couldn't ignore the nervous anxiety that reeked havoc within me. I had experienced so many moments like this since this wretched nightmare had begun and now I frantically wanted it to be over.

The application was scheduled to begin at two o'clock and it was after three o'clock when Murphy showed up in the cafeteria. As he approached me, he displayed a large smile on his face. I watched him as he drew nearer and I silently prayed that he had good news for me. Murphy's smile could mean that he had good news for me or it could mean that he was trying to generate a good mood to discuss some really bad news. On reaching the table he sat down and began to speak. In a momentary flash, the suspense was over:

"Well, Orest, we lost! Dea wouldn't go for any of it. I thought that I had a chance on the certiorari arguments until Nash got up to talk. At that point, he made up his mind that he was just going to dismiss that application and not bother with it. On the Stay of Proceedings, he simply said that he wouldn't deal with it. His decision was that I should present it to the trial judge before the trial starts. I wanted him to at least give us written reasons but he wouldn't go for that. He simply gave a short statement from the bench and that was it. I'm sorry, Orest, but at least we can still use the Stay of Proceedings argument at the trial. Maybe it will work then."

At that moment, I felt numb and emotionless. I quietly agreed with Murphy and we then grabbed our briefcases and headed for the door. Murphy continued to talk about the case and his submissions to Dea. In my dazed condition, all I could do was listen and murmur some words to acknowledge what he said. I just couldn't accept the fact that we could be right in law and still lose because a Judge didn't want to take the time to consider our application. This really was not news to me as I had the same experiences on applications that I had argued for clients. Still, it certainly was not fair or just and I felt bitter. This was not Justice and I was entitled to a better hearing on my application. Finally, I queried Murphy:

"Patrick, if Dea was wrong in law for dismissing our application, why don't we appeal his decision to the Court of Appeal? Certainly those judges would see things differently and maybe they will give us a more just decision. What do you think of an appeal?"

At this point, Murphy answered with hesitation that signalled his desire to take some time to consider this matter:

"If we were to appeal this decision, we would have to adjourn the trial date. You have a good point about doing an Appeal. Off the cuff, I'd say that if its what you want, then an appeal should be made to the Court of Appeal. However, I would have to consider this carefully before I could give you an answer as to whether I recommend an appeal or if I believe that it would be worthwhile to proceed with an Appeal. Why don't you let me look this over. We can talk about this at the beginning of next week."

Everything had turned out badly but Murphy still gave me hope that something could be done to resolve the problem. I knew in my heart that an Appeal was the right thing to do but now there was the problem of the trial date that would have to be cancelled. If that happened, the new trial date would have to be rescheduled and delayed for one more year. I wasn't sure that I wanted to wait that long to see this matter resolved but I really wanted to get a fair hearing on this application.

After I dropped Murphy off, I confirmed that I would call him at the beginning of the week to discuss this whole matter. At that moment, I felt totally drained as I headed for home. I didn't know how I would be able to tell Pat the disappointing news and I didn't really know how I would personally come to terms with it. For the moment, I was still in emotional shock. It would take time before I could comfortably deal with the reality of what had occurred. I now felt adamant that I wanted the Court of Appeal to consider my legal argument on the certiorari application. However, for the first time, I began to accept the dismal reality that this case might have to be resolved at a trial. This was an unsettling prospect but one that I now obviously had to prepare for.

CHAPTER NINETEEN

BETRAYAL

The relationship between a lawyer and his client has historically been revered as one of utmost trust. In legal texts, it is referred to as the "solicitor-client relationship" and is the subject of countless court decisions. From early English law, it has been recognized that a lawyer cannot properly advocate a client's position unless he holds the client's total trust and confidence. Because lawyers usually represent strangers in Court, the trust must be based on the rules of conduct followed by the legal profession and recognized by the Courts. The administration of justice is based on the premise that a client may unequivocally rely on the existence and protection of this sacred trust of lawyers.

In accepting a case, a lawyer undertakes to represent the client to the best of his abilities and to secure for the client the best remedies that the law affords. At no time may a lawyer allow personal interests to interfere with or affect his representation of a client's interests. To do so would put the lawyer in a "conflict of interest" which would jeopardize the client's case and the legal position that might otherwise be available to the client. When complaints arise of a conflict of interest, lawyers are typically reprimanded by the Law Society unless the lawyer has persuasion with the Benchers.

One of the principal features of a solicitor-client relationship is the absolute privacy of any communications between them. A client may discuss and disclose anything to a lawyer without fear that the information or admissions will ever be disclosed to the prejudice of the client. This protection to the client is called "privilege" and only the client can give specific permission to the lawyer to disclose that information. Such information can never be disclosed by a lawyer in Court nor can it ever be used as evidence against the client.

In Canada, the trust in a solicitor-client relationship is more sacredly guarded by the Courts than that of doctor-patient, husband-wife or even the priest-confessor relationship. In the Courts of the United States, all such communications are usually disallowed in evidence against an accused person. However, in Canada, the law does allow the Crown Prosecutor to force a spouse to testify against an accused in spite of the objections of the spouse and accused. Similarly, the private communications to doctors, psychiatrists, psychologists, and even priests have been ordered to be revealed by the Courts.

Fortunately, it is a rare occasion when a spouse, physician or priest has been summoned to Court to reveal such discussions by an accused. However, it is shocking for most people to find out that the Courts do not fully recognize the sacred nature of such communications. In contrast, the solicitor-client relationship is protected in an absolute manner and such a relationship has been deemed to exist in even the most informal meetings between lawyers and possible clients. As always, the Court protects its own sacred principles but is casual in ignoring the other sacred relationships that exist in society.

Because of this sacred trust that must be absolutely maintained by a lawyer, a client typically expects a lawyer to act in the client's best interests. Most clients fail to recognize that lawyers will often make deals that will compromise a case and even sabotage a client's prospects of success. In fact, lawyers are notorious for using their information to conduct discussions that the client would not approve. By the time that a client finds out about the betrayal of trust, it is too late to act. Instead, a client is forced to accept the situation, knowing that he had been "sold out" by his lawyer.

Having worked as a lawyer for over seventeen years, I intimately understood the fine distinctions that had to be made in honouring the trust of my clients. Now I was the client and my total trust was in Murphy to represent my interests to the full limits of the law. Murphy was also my friend and I felt that I understood his weaknesses and strengths as a lawyer. It had never occurred to me that he might subordinate my case to his other self-interests.

It was hard to believe that the Christmas season had arrived again, marking two years since Christal first visited our home with his first Search Warrant. Since that day, this ordeal had continually escalated into a horrific nightmare and none of Murphy's efforts had prevented the progressive devastation of my legal career and my life. Now, we had suffered yet one more setback in failing to halt this travesty of injustice during the court application. Ironically, I still struggled to maintain a positive outlook in spite of what I had already witnessed.

Although I always embraced the Christmas season as a time to rejoice and reflect on the blessings of life, it was different this year. I found it difficult to focus on the joyful activities all around me because I was so preoccupied with my legal dilemma. I now wrestled with the question of whether I should appeal the decision of Judge Dea to the Court of Appeal to get a proper hearing on the merits of the application. To do so would result in an adjournment of the trial date and this was something I dreaded. If my appeal was not successful, this adjournment would needlessly postpone this case yet another year.

As I pondered this situation, I reflected on the atrocious delays in the Criminal Justice system. It was commonplace to hear commentaries about unnecessary delays from politicians, judges, and lawyers. They all agreed and endorsed the principle that: JUSTICE DELAYED IS JUSTICE DENIED. Yet, every case that came before the Court was necessarily delayed because of the inefficiency of the Court systems. Furthermore, each level of the Court system operated at its own pace, without reference to the operations of the other courts. This created further inefficiency in the general operations of the Court system. Sadly, these delays in justice resulted in obvious cases of denial of justice. However, such cases were routinely treated as unavoidable. For that reason, everyone tended to ignore the injustice that resulted.

A week after the Court application, I arranged to meet Murphy at his office. We were now pressed for time and had to discuss the next steps that should be taken in resolving the criminal charge. On arriving at Murphy's office, I was told by his secretary that he was with a client in the meeting room so I sat down in the waiting area. The atmosphere in the office was festive and active as everyone was trying to complete certain work that needed to be finished before the Christmas break. As I glanced through a magazine in the reception area, it occurred to me once more how much my life had changed. Although I knew that one day this ordeal would all be resolved, nothing could be done to rectify the pain and humiliation that I and my family had to endure.

As thoughts of Christal's actions flowed through my mind, I reminded myself that this was the Christmas season. As a good Christian I knew that I had to be able to forgive Christal for his actions and the hurt that he inflicted upon me and my family. At that moment, I wondered if anyone who had suffered like this could truly forgive those that caused such pain and agony. Suddenly, I heard Murphy's voice as he opened the door to the meeting room and came out. On seeing me, he immediately welcomed me:

"Hi, Orest! Sorry to keep you waiting. Please have a seat in the meeting room. I just have to arrange a new appointment for these people and then I'll join you."

I acknowledged Murphy's request and made my way into the meeting room. As I sat down, I began to remove my file and writing pad from my briefcase for our meeting. Murphy suddenly appeared in the doorway and in a moment had closed the door and sat down with me. Murphy must have noticed that I was unusually quiet and as he sat down, he began to inquire:

"How are you doing, Orest? Are you and your family enjoying the Christmas season?"

At that point, I couldn't control my depression and I decided to share my personal thoughts with Murphy:

"Patrick, this whole situation is wearing on all of us. The children have been shielded from most of this but I and Pat are really feeling depressed about it. It seems so unfair that Christal could devastate our lives by pushing to lay a criminal charge that is unfounded. It seems so wrong that he can do something so malicious and his actions are now being condoned by the Courts and the legal system. I know that I shouldn't dwell on this. After all, a good Christian must forgive his enemies. But I must say that I have difficulty forgiving Christal for what he did to me."

Murphy listened to me attentively and as I finished my remarks, he responded in his jovial and sincere manner:

"Orest, you're too nice a guy! I never forgive my enemies and you shouldn't forgive Christal for what he did to you. This charge should never have been laid and you should not have lost your legal career. You have every reason to hold Christal and Jim McLeod and even Pinckney responsible for the ordeal that you have suffered because of them. As far as being a good Christian, I know that I'm a good Christian and I pray all the time. When it comes to my enemies, I pray that they get a nice, cool place in Hell. You should do the same."

Murphy's remarks brought a smile to my face as I queried whether he was joking. Murphy responded by steadfastly insisting that this was his philosophy in life. Murphy proclaimed that he had a strong faith, that he believed in the power of prayer and that this approach was the best way to deal with one's enemies. As Murphy concluded his remarks, I thanked him for his comforting words and then raised the dilemma that I had been wrestling with:

"Patrick, I'd like your opinion on what should be our next step in the criminal proceedings. I've considered the idea of appealing the decision of Judge Dea. I'm convinced that an appeal has a good chance before the Court of Appeal. The problem is that if we go that route, the trial date will be put over. Then it will take another year before the new trial date comes up. If we don't succeed at the Court of Appeal, this whole process will be delayed for one more year. I'm tired of this ordeal and I just want to see this whole thing resolved as soon as possible. What is your advice on this?"

Murphy leaned back in his chair and then slowly began to speak:

"I think that you should take this case to the Court of Appeal. I have thought about your case and I feel that it's just too bad that Dea didn't take a better look at it. However, that's what the Court of Appeal is for and it's your right to get their decision on this. As far as the trial date is concerned, that's just part of the process. If you set a new date right now, you will have enough time to do the appeal before the trial date comes up. I would suggest that you go to the Court of Appeal and accept a later trial date."

Murphy looked to me for my nod of approval on his advice. He then assumed a more serious expression and began to speak again:

"Orest, there's something that I wanted to discuss with you relating to your case. I just found out from Eileen Nash that you filed a complaint against Detective Christal. Now I know that he treated you badly during his investigation but you should have talked to me before you filed a complaint. I would never have let you do that if you had asked my advice."

For a moment, I felt confused about Murphy's position. The complaint process dealing with the conduct of police officers had nothing to do with the legal system. My complaint was about Christal's conduct toward me during his investigation. Murphy was aware of how Christal conducted himself and agreed that Christal had acted improperly. My complaint documented over a dozen specific breaches of conduct committed by Christal which included deceit, corrupt practices and unnecessary exercise of authority. If there was ever a case for discreditable and unethical conduct, this case with Christal was certainly a prime one to investigate.

What I really didn't understand when I filed the complaint was how such complaints were handled and how the disciplinary system is used to vindicate the conduct of police officers at the expense of their victims. The actual complaint procedure for a police officer's misconduct is similar in most jurisdictions in Canada and is restricted to a procedure defined in the Police Act or similar legislation. A complainant must provide a written complaint to the Chief of Police. If he chooses to investigate it, the Chief of Police appoints a senior police officer to interview witnesses and prepare a report for him. The Chief of Police then decides whether to reprimand the police officer or simply dismiss the complaint. The complainant doesn't get to see this report or even make comments or submissions about the contents of the report. Since most complaints are dismissed, the only recourse is to then appeal the decision to a specially appointed board called the Law Enforcement Review Board. This Board conducts a public hearing to determine if it should affirm the decision of the Chief of Police or send it back to him for further consideration.

It should be no surprise that few complaints ever make it through this extremely-biased review system. In fact, the real purpose of this process is to eliminate the recourse that the general public would otherwise use. Because of this procedure, a complainant is denied the opportunity to request the government and their elected representatives to intervene in such matters. Because this elaborate system exists, a person who has been abused by a police officer has no recourse but to ask the police to intervene and to side against one of their own. Most people who have undergone a humiliating experience with a police officer would seldom want to deal with another police officer on the same police force to resolve the problem. In fact, most victims of police abuse correctly assume that they will get little sympathy or understanding from the police officer investigating a complaint against one of his friends and colleagues. Furthermore, most complainants are intimidated and fearful of repercussions for taking such a position against a police officer. Most victims are too frightened or intimidated to present their complaint to another police officer. As a result, many legitimate complaints about serious breaches of conduct are silenced by the threatening structure of the complaint procedure.

Of those complaints relating to police misconduct that are made, most are summarily dismissed with a letter from the Chief of Police. These letters are professionally crafted to make the complainant feel responsible for any hardship that resulted from police intervention. The tone of the letter clearly implies that the police acted correctly even if they acted arbitrarily and improperly. A complainant is typically influenced to believe that nothing was improper and that nothing will be done to deal with the abuse of the police officer. Regretfully, these letters seldom express any remorse for the hardship of the complainant or the victims. On the contrary, an apology is seldom extracted from the Chief of Police unless a legal action is taken to sue the police for damages in civil court for the abuse suffered by the victim.

In those cases that show blatant misconduct which may create problems for the police force, the Chief of Police usually adopts a different tactic. Rather than just dismissing the complaint with a well-crafted letter, he will instead acknowledge the complaint and appoint an investigator to prepare a report. This investigator is not an impartial person who will fairly evaluate the facts but rather a senior police officer with training on how to develop a file that will repel further criticism. The investigator interviews witnesses but writes each statement in his own words to soften the statements and to support the police position as much as possible. When the report is prepared, it is provided to the Chief of Police only and the complainant gets a final response many months later. Invariably, the complaint is dismissed with a well-crafted letter and in cases of serious breaches, a token sanction may be imposed on the offending police officer to appease the complainant.

In recent times, the news media has exposed a growing number of cases that demonstrate how this protective practice has shielded police officers from disciplinary proceedings. A recent well-publicized case in Alberta clearly demonstrated how such blatant cover-ups and manipulations of the complaint procedure occur. In that case, a constable with the Royal Canadian Mounted Police detachment in Leduc, Alberta avoided disciplinary action because of an effective police effort to "close ranks" to protect him. The constable, Peter Adams, admitted that he took a female suspect into his police car, forced her to perform oral sex on him and even tried to have sexual intercourse with her before releasing her. The constable felt that the victim would excuse his misconduct because he was prepared to overlook the fact that he might have charged her with impaired driving. When the victim filed a complaint, the police simply ignored it and no disciplinary action or suspension was made. In fact, the police officer was allowed to continue working on the pretext that nothing improper had happened.

Although the victim persevered and brought the information before the Crown Prosecutor's office, the police resisted the directive to lay a charge against Constable Peter Adams. Ultimately, three criminal charges of sexual assault, taking a bribe and obstruction of justice were laid by the Special Prosecutor who reviewed the file. When the criminal charges were finally laid, the police implemented the complaint procedure on their own initiative to conduct an intensive investigation of the victim. This investigation focused on the victim's past relationships to assemble evidence to support the Constable's contention that the victim was sexually permissive and had initiated the sexual encounter. This evidence was then provided to the lawyer representing the Constable in Court to assist the defence in having the charges dismissed.

This case demonstrated not only how the complaint procedure is misused and abused but also how a victim can be made to look like a criminal in such an investigation. In that case, the police worked together to cover-up the actions of a member and used the complaint procedure improperly to justify an investigation of a victim. Ultimately, by humiliating and discrediting the victim, the police were able to vindicate the police constable of criminal charges. They effectively proved how the process for investigating complaints against police officers is misused. As a result, the discreditable conduct and abuse of power of police officers that should result in reprimands and dismissals is effectively covered up. The victim is ultimately left disillusioned and without recourse while the police officer confidently continues his work and abusive practices.

Because I knew that the complaint procedure for police misconduct had nothing to do with proceedings in Criminal Court, I couldn't understand why Murphy was concerned with this. If I had suspected that this complaint procedure could influence my Court proceedings, I would have naturally discussed it with him. At this point, it was still a big mystery for me and I felt confused as I stared at him.

Murphy had paused as he re-positioned himself in his chair and looked at me with the painful expression of a father comforting his dying son. I remained silent as I could sense that Murphy had something of a pressing nature that he wanted to tell me. Suddenly, Murphy began to speak again as I listened intently:

"As you know, I've been on my own in this law practice for the last ten years. It's very competitive out there but I'm lucky because I get asked by the Crown Prosecutors office to do a lot of ad-hoc prosecuting for them. They call me when they need someone to fill in for a Crown Prosecutor. The rate of pay is pretty good. The reason they call me is because I get along real well with everyone at the Crown Prosecutors office. They all like me and trust me just like someone working out of their office. I also get along real well with all the police officers and this also helps me to get more prosecuting work. That's why, when I defend a case, I always do it in a way that doesn't offend the Crown Prosecutors or the police in any way. Usually, if I plead my clients guilty, I can get them a good deal on sentencing. You can do that if you've got a good relationship with the Crown Prosecutors and the police. To me, it's more important to get along good with the Crown Prosecutors and the police than it is to get into an argument with them just to prove that my client is right. Do you follow what I'm saying, Orest?"

As I sat there in silence, my mind raced frantically to anticipate where Murphy's comments were leading. I knew that he did some prosecuting for the Crown Prosecutors office but I had simply assumed that he would never let that interfere with the way that he handled my case. It was obvious now that Murphy's relationship and commitment to the Crown Prosecutors office was closer than I ever realized. I suddenly felt sickened by what I imagined was the true reality of my situation.

The basic principle that operates in any Court proceedings is that two skilled advocates argue their cases before an impartial judge who then has the benefit of considering two well-presented opposing views. In a criminal case, the Crown Prosecutor is assisted by the police and generally presents the best case that the evidence will afford. An accused person hires a Criminal Defence lawyer who he believes is not only experienced but also prepared to fight to prove that the Crown Prosecutor and the police are wrong. This usually involves a vigorous cross-examination of police officers and argumentative rebuttal of the comments of the Crown Prosecutor. It is a Criminal Defence lawyer's primary responsibility to present the best case possible for the client, regardless of his feelings for any other parties involved in the case, especially the police or Crown Prosecutor.

It was now obvious from Murphy's comments that he was compromised by his continuing work as an ad-hoc Crown Prosecutor and was unable to defend my case the way other Criminal Defence lawyers might. Although there was perhaps no actual conflict of interest, it was now obvious that he was not fighting to press my defence as well as he should have. As this realization gripped me, I suddenly felt betrayed. I had trusted Murphy so deeply with the most important case of my life and he wasn't handling it properly. To use an analogy,

Murphy was like a boxer who was supposed to go into the ring to win the fight for me. Instead of using all his skills to destroy the opponent and win, my boxer didn't want to hurt them so he simply went through the motions of fighting. His gestures and appearances were intended to satisfy me and the audience while he ultimately forfeited the fight and the chance of winning. Similarly, in my case, Murphy maintained his friendship with the Crown Prosecutor and the police by sacrificing my case.

Suddenly, a sadness filled me as I considered the implications of my new awareness. Murphy was my friend long before this situation arose and I trusted him. I didn't want to believe what was obviously unfolding before me so I responded with determination to probe for the truth:

"Patrick, I know about your ad-hoc prosecuting. As far as I can see, that has nothing to do with my complaint to the Chief of Police regarding Christal's conduct. You said yourself that Christal had acted improperly and that he was a cop out of control. I feel that it's important to have him investigated to keep him from abusing his position further. None of this should make any difference to my case before the Courts or to any work that you do in the future."

As I finished, Murphy simply stared at me with a look of exasperation as he shuffled in his chair. He then responded in a slightly louder voice which showed that his emotions were becoming aroused:

"You obviously don't understand how these complaints against cops are handled and dismissed. For one thing, all the cops will stick up for each other. They always do! Mark my words! They'll do an investigation and report that Christal did nothing wrong and all the cops right up to the Chief of Police will back Christal in every way. Also, if you think that anyone at the Crown Prosecutor's office would speak up against Christal or any other cop, you're dreaming. I know how they handle these things. Wait and see! No matter how they feel about Christal, they'll all say that he did everything right and that he's a perfect cop. They'll back him on everything. Believe me! I talk to the Crown Prosecutors a lot and I know how they operate."

Murphy's expression now changed to that of painful agony as he paused to collect his thoughts. In a softer tone, he continued:

"This whole thing with the complaint puts me in a bad spot. I have no choice but to agree with the Crown Prosecutors and back their position that Christal did nothing wrong. I know that it puts me in a bad position with you but I won't risk losing the work that I get from the Crown Prosecutor's office. Any other lawyer would do the same thing in this situation. I have to consider how this whole thing is going to affect me and my legal work. After all, I have a family to support with this legal practice so I can't afford to get the Crown Prosecutors office upset with me. Besides, I really have no problem with Christal and when they come to interview me, I'm just going to say that he was fine by me."

I listened to Murphy in stunned silence and was unsure of what I could say in response to all of this. I was now feeling abandoned more than betrayed. Murphy was steadily pulling away from me and casting me off into the Sea of

Uncertainty to face my problems on my own. Before I could say anything, Murphy warned:

"There's one more thing that you should be aware of. Christal is now getting Eileen Nash fired up to nail you on this charge and to make an example out of you. I've heard a reliable rumour that the Director at the Crown Prosecutor's office is using his influence through the Attorney General's office. HE'S TRYING TO ARRANGE A JUDGE WHO IS GUARANTEED TO CONVICT YOU. Since nobody knows who will be assigned to your case, there's a good chance that he can pull that kind of stunt off. If he does, you'll need to go to trial before a jury and not before a judge alone as we once hoped. In any case, you're going to need a real experienced criminal lawyer who does a lot of large cases before juries. Your case is going to turn into a real nightmare and you'd better prepare yourself."

As his words tore into me, I remained speechless as I pondered the effect of what Murphy had just said. I knew that he didn't exaggerate and it was obvious that he was also somewhat shaken. He almost sounded frightened as if he was aware of a monstrous plot to destroy me and was afraid that he might get drawn into it. In my wildest dreams, I couldn't imagine anything like Murphy was suggesting so I decided not to over-react. Instead, we had to calmly develop a course of action to resolve this problem. Before I could say anything in response, Murphy continued:

"One final concern I have is that we've been friends for a long time, and I would feel awful if you were convicted at the trial. The way it looks, the cards are getting stacked against you. It would be easier on me emotionally if you hired another lawyer to handle this case at trial. It seems that this is the right time to make that type of change and I think that it's the best move for you to make."

I could see that Murphy was agonizing over this situation and I decided to "ease his pain". Murphy had been a good friend and I wanted to maintain that friendship. It he felt that he wasn't able to continue handling my case, I would never consider asking him to do so. Without hesitation, I responded to his request and tried to reassure him of my sentiments:

"Patrick, I understand your position. I also appreciate everything that you've done on this case. Unfortunately, this case hasn't gone as well as either of us wished. If you feel that I should get another lawyer, that's no problem. I hope that you'll still be able to help the new lawyer with your assessments which I'm sure he'll want. Don't worry about me! I'm sure I'll be fine."

As I spoke, Murphy showed a little smile and then proceeded to share his thoughts on the next step to be taken:

"I've been thinking about how we should proceed on having the trial postponed and I have an idea. I'm sure that I can have this case added to the next Arraignment list so that we could arrange for a new trial date. I'll be able to withdraw off the record at that time which will clear the way for another lawyer to take on the case. However, as you know, the Judge sitting at the Arraignment Hearing will only let me withdraw if we can present a proper reason for doing so. One reason that we could present to the Judge is that we disagree on the direction that we should follow in this case. We can use this appeal to the Court of Appeal as our basis for disagreement. I would suggest that you file the Notice of Appeal personally and not through my office. When we speak to this matter at Arraignments, I'll advise the Judge that you want to proceed with the Appeal and I'm advising you against it. That would form the basis of a legitimate conflict between us on how to proceed on your case. That would be enough to allow me to withdraw as your lawyer and will also be a good reason to request that the trial be re-scheduled. If that is fine with you, I'd prefer to go on that basis. I really don't want to take the position that we are arguing about anything but it's okay to disagree on how a case should proceed. Do you have any other suggestions on this?"

As Murphy paused, I sat speechless and tried to concentrate on the instructions that he had just given me. My mind was blank as I certainly had not prepared myself to deal with any of this. What he described seemed like an effective way for us to deal with all the matters that had to be resolved. After making some notes, I slowly began to respond:

"Okay! I'll get that Notice of Appeal filed immediately and I'll let you know when that is done. In the meantime, you can arrange for this case to be put back on the next Arraignment list."

As I sat there dazed and completed my notes, Murphy responded to a call from his secretary and left the meeting room to deal with an urgent matter. After collecting my notes and file, I wished everyone a Merry Christmas before putting on my winter coat and proceeding out the door. As I walked to my car, I was still in disbelief at the way this meeting had gone. I realized that I now had to start again to arrange a new lawyer and to brief him on this case. None of this was comforting and I was concerned that this was just one more set-back that I just didn't need. Instead of moving forward to resolve the criminal charge that plagued me, I now had to start again. Worst of all, this would be distressing news for my wife. I wondered how I could reassure her that this would get resolved in a positive manner. This was definitely a low moment for all of us and it would be difficult to participate in the merriment of the Christmas season with this latest set-back on our minds.

I was also not pleased with the prospects of having to appear at yet another Arraignment hearing. Not only were these hearings a total inconvenience but were also a humiliating experience for an accused person. If any of the lawyers or judges who paraded before the Court had to experience this humiliation just once, no doubt there would be an outcry for more respectful treatment of accused persons. However, this was just one more agony that I would have to endure in silence on the road to resolving this ordeal.

As Murphy had suggested, I filed the Notice of Appeal on my own behalf. After serving a copy on Eileen Nash's office, I delivered a copy to Murphy for his file. Murphy arranged for our appearance at the next Arraignment hearing date and we agreed to meet at the Court room to speak to the list. Murphy confirmed that he had already talked to Nash about this and that she had no objections to this. All I wanted now was to get this done quickly so that I could put this out of my mind.

Because of my prior appearances at Arraignments, I was now more casual and relaxed about this procedure. I allowed myself the indulgence of arriving after the proceedings had already commenced since there was always the typical delay of dealing with the cases of accused persons in custody. On my arrival, I went into the Court room and sat down on the back bench to wait for Murphy to show up. Murphy was more casual than anyone else and actually felt that it was sufficient that he showed up for his court appearances. If by coincidence he was on time, so much the better. He was fortunate that his attitude and his mannerisms had an endearing effect on judges and other lawyers. Because of that, they always made the endeavour to accommodate him and rarely commented on any delay that he caused.

After a significant amount of time had passed, I began to feel a little concerned that Murphy would not arrive before our case was called. Suddenly he appeared and immediately came over to speak to me. As he sat next to me, he whispered:

"Our case should be up soon. I've just spoken to Nash outside and everything should go smoothly. We'll just go up there and I'll explain everything to the Judge. After I get leave of the Court to withdraw, I'll leave the Court room. Then you can handle the final part of setting a new trial date. If you want to discuss anything, we can talk after this court appearance."

As Murphy finished, I nodded in agreement. He then stood up and walked to the front of the Court room to sit with the other lawyers. As I glanced around, I noticed Eileen Nash who was still attired in the same garments that I expected to see on her. Her physical appearance was worse than I remembered with a facial complexion of deathly pale grey. I assumed that she must have attended too many Christmas parties. Having heard so many stories of the private drinking parties that Crown Prosecutors and police hold, I was satisfied that these assumptions were probably accurate.

My thoughts were abruptly interrupted as my name was called by the Court Clerk. As Murphy and Nash rose to speak to the Judge, I walked toward the front of the Court room and then into the Prisoner's Box. The Court Orderly closed the door behind me as I turned to face the Judge. At this Arraignment Hearing, the judge was Tevie Miller, a senior judge who had steadily climbed through the ranks of the judiciary over the last fifteen years. Like many judges, he was pleasant but projected himself as aloof from the people of the Court. Thankfully, Miller was a pleasant change from the abrasive and demeaning attitude of Agrios who had presided over my earlier Arraignment Hearing.

While I stood facing Judge Miller, Nash and Murphy took turns explaining the situation to him and advising him that the trial date would have to be rescheduled. Everything proceeded as a formality and Miller immediately granted the application by Murphy to formally withdraw as my legal counsel. Murphy then thanked Judge Miller and walked out of the Court room, leaving me abandoned in the Prisoner's Box. As all the attention in the Court room fell on me, I fumbled around for the right words to make the request to reset the trial date. Nash then insisted that the next trial date had to be "pre-emptory". This meant that no further request for an adjournment by me or my lawyer would be considered. The new trial was scheduled for three weeks to commence on October 7, 1992. To conclude my appearance at Arraignment, Miller formally directed that the trial date would be changed and I confirmed that I would arrange a new lawyer to handle the trial on those dates.

During these proceedings, I was surprised to see Myra Bielby walk into the Court room from the Judges' entrance and sit down beside Judge Miller. This didn't cause any surprise to anyone else and I therefore assumed that she had recently become appointed as a Judge. Bielby became one of the new additions to the Court and was intended to bolster the presence of female judges in the judiciary to develop more equality among the sexes. This new criteria for appointing Judges was referred to in jest as "Anatomical Appointments" because a candidate had to have the correct body anatomy to be considered. So important was this criteria that gossip circulated of a transvestite lawyer who was considering a sex change operation to become more acceptable as a Judicial candidate. There was no doubt that allowing more women into the legal profession and elevating some of them to judges was a good way to improve the staid, old-boys club image of the legal profession and the Courts. Although it is a good objective to introduce new abilities and perspectives to the judiciary, the appointment of someone like Bielby as a Judge was probably too high a price to pay. The common joke among lawyers was that judges like Bielby would definitely be impartial, since they had never appeared in Court and therefore had no opinions about anything.

Bielby was quite young for a judicial appointment. According to many lawyers, she was too young and too inexperienced for the position. This seemed irrelevant however since the main consideration was political affiliation and not age or experience. Because she had attended Law School in a junior class to mine, her climb in the legal profession was easier to follow. Shortly after entering the profession (almost twenty years ago), she distinguished herself and made headline news at that time when she insisted on a marriage contract with her prospective first husband. Such marriage contracts were a unique and unromantic concept at that time but Bielby was a liberated feminist who knew what was important. When her marriage ended in divorce, no doubt she must have rejoiced in the idea that she had the foresight to plan for a divorce before entering into the marriage.

In theory, Bielby must have satisfied certain standards before she was selected to be a judge and therefore she had some qualifications. The reality was that all of these newly-appointed judges really only had to satisfy the qualification of being favoured politically by the then Minister of Justice, Kim Campbell. Although Campbell handled the Justice portfolio in a capable and responsible manner, there was nothing outstanding in her accomplishments. However, she caught the public attention by posing for a portrait hiding her suggestively nude body behind her lawyer's robes. With Campbell at the helm of the Justice Department, there was a sudden surge in the momentum to put women into visible positions in the Court. Unfortunately, most of these appointed Judges were selected because of political patronage rather than ability.

The appointment of Bielby was a classic example of this as she fit the criterion of being a woman but brought to the position very little, if any, court experience. Such experience in Court matters was significant as she would be presiding at trials, especially criminal trials. It was unfortunate for those whom she would judge that she had no knowledge or experience on how to conduct the trial or what law to apply. In such cases, the Judges typically make decisions which are arbitrary rather than based on the law. As a result, these appointments improved the Court cosmetically but lessened the integrity and the ability of the Court to deliver justice for society.

As I left the Court room, I looked for Murphy but he had already left. I decided that I would have to initiate some immediate efforts to arrange for a new lawyer on my case and then assist him in preparing my case for the Court of Appeal. I felt disappointed and alone now but I knew that I could waste no time in retaining a new lawyer since the new trial date was now set.

CHAPTER TWENTY

WINDOW SHOPPING

The task of hiring a new lawyer was not as simple as scanning the telephone directory and picking one. Traditionally, a criminal lawyer developed a reputation that became known in his community and received all his new clients by referral. When I first began to practice law, the acknowledged experts in criminal law were well known and instantly recognizable by the general public. In the sixteen years that followed, all of that changed and the old experts either retired or became judges. Now there were new experts who distinguished themselves by specializing in drug cases or impaired driving charges. The emphasis was on big money that was quickly and easily earned. This new crop of experts didn't even bother with legal aid cases because they could charge excessively large fees on the files that they did handle. Typically, these lawyers worked from their own independent law practices and were a stark contrast to the other lawyers who often struggled to survive as the economy dwindled.

The task of finding the criminal lawyer that was best suited for my particular case required a determined effort in "window shopping". Although the legal profession in Alberta and in other provinces was now allowed to advertise in a tasteful manner, most lawyers simply didn't bother. The advertisements that did exist provided very little information for the first time shopper to make a good selection. Inevitably, the inexperienced window shopper usually selected a lawyer who lacked the necessary ability to properly handle the case.

Promotion by word of mouth still seems to be the favoured medium for criminal lawyers to attract clients. The high profile cases naturally generate publicity through news coverage and that helps to attract new clients. Naturally, the ability to win criminal cases will distinguish a criminal defence lawyer and establish a favourable reputation. Ironically, it is the cases that a criminal lawyer loses that generate the most referrals or repeat business. Since over ninety per cent of the inmates in prisons will become repeat offenders, a criminal lawyer gets great advertisement from those clients that end up in prison. Most criminal clients that lose in Court remain loyal to their lawyer because they see the lawyer as the only person who fought for their innocence. As the client brags about his case to impress other inmates, he also exaggerates the abilities of his lawyer. Ultimately, it is this fantasy which consoles the client and also generates more business for the lawyer. In the converse situation, when a lawyer wins a case, the client will often discount the seriousness of the offence. This results in a limited amount of publicity.

When window shopping for any commodity or service, one must know the fine distinctions in the products or services to make a good decision. When relying on word of mouth advertising, it becomes more difficult to determine who might best be suited for one's needs. As one might guess, it is the repeat offenders who are the best authorities in evaluating the unique abilities of the various criminal lawyers. While in custody, they have the time to compare experiences with other inmates and to examine in vivid detail the expertise of all the notable criminal lawyers. They come to know which criminal lawyers are best qualified to handle specific types of cases ranging from impaired driving to drug trafficking and from robbery to murder. They also become proficient on how to "handle" their lawyers to present the best defence to the Court. Ironically, it seems that you have to be a convicted criminal to know who to select for the best representation in a criminal case.

Because of my inexperience in dealing with criminal lawyers, my window shopping for a new criminal defence lawyer quickly became a frustrating experience. After wasting a few weeks trying to speak to a few lawyers who I believed to have a notable reputation as criminal defence lawyers, I began to panic. I therefore decided to call upon a friend and classmate from my law school days, Jim Skitsko, for his recommendation. Skitsko had joined a small downtown law practice right after his articleship was concluded and had steadfastly remained with that firm. As the years passed, his senior partners retired, thereby allowing him to become a senior partner. With a positive outgoing attitude, he established a good clientele and enjoyed a comfortable living from his law practice. I always endeavoured to stay in touch with Skitsko by occasionally meeting him for lunch. Over the years, we consoled each other over the disappointments that each of us encountered and offered each other moral support and encouragement to face the challenges that lay ahead. I felt comfortable confiding in Skitsko and wanted some candid advice.

Skitsko and I met for lunch and it didn't take long before I raised the topic of my problem in arranging a new Criminal Defence lawyer. His immediate response was a recommendation that I contact Jim Brimacombe. What followed was a discussion of the other criminal lawyers in Edmonton and Skitsko assessed and rated them for me.

The first candidate to be discussed was Alex Pringle who was creating news headlines by representing Don Cormie on criminal charges relating to his failed financial empire. Skitsko rated him as too expensive and over-rated for his actual abilities in Court. The name of Robbie Davidson was raised but Skitsko also labelled him a bad choice. According to Skitsko, Davidson would not likely accept this case because of the complaint that I had filed against Christal. Since Davidson always represented police officers in criminal matters, he would naturally decline my case to avoid a possible conflict.

One final possibility was Rostyk Sadownik who served as my principal when I articled as a Student-at-Law. Skitsko pointed out that Sadownik was slowing down in his senior years and was not as vibrant or effective as he once was. Sadly, he had become a victim of alcohol abuse and over-indulgence and this gave him the physical appearance of a disgruntled Santa Claus. Although his mind was still sharp, his energy level was down and his enthusiasm was now lagging. Skitsko also pointed out that it was never a good idea for a former articling student to go back to his principal for help. Invariably, Sadownik would see me as a student who messed up rather than a client who was innocent and wrongly charged. I was again reminded of the Lesson in Life that time changes everything and you can never go back in time to relive those "Wonder Years".

Clearly, Skitsko felt that Brimacombe was my best choice out of the very limited selection of candidates that existed. Brimacombe had practised criminal law exclusively for over fifteen years. During that time, he developed a law firm that specialized in criminal law and handled criminal files exclusively. Furthermore, Skitsko assured me that he had referred clients to that firm and was satisfied with their work. When we finished our lunch, we walked to Skitsko's office. I then confirmed that I would take his advice on Brimacombe and Skitsko telephoned him and set up an appointment for me.

After my meeting with Skitsko, I now hoped that the distasteful task of window shopping for a new lawyer would soon be over. I continued to stay in touch with Skitsko and shared with him the developments in my case. A few years later, Skitsko secured an appointment as a Provincial Court Judge in Edmonton. I had no doubt that he would work hard at his new position and distinguish himself ultimately among his colleagues.

My appointment with Brimacombe was a week later and I worked to organize the material that I planned to discuss with him. When I arrived for my meeting, I brought a bag full of files containing documents for him to review. I wanted to impress him with the important elements of my case in the hope that he could give me an initial assessment. I was worried that he might draw negative conclusions about my case since I was switching lawyers. This was a hazard that I was hoping to overcome but I instinctively knew that the stigma always remains.

Brimacombe's office was located in a downtown office tower, which was a striking contrast to the offices of most criminal lawyers. Typically, criminal lawyers used to inhabit old, crowded and smelly office spaces in buildings that should have been demolished. A simple explanation for this is that criminal lawyers have nobody to impress. Their clients are attracted to them only because of their reputation in court and are unconcerned about the appearance of the office.

After waiting a few minutes in his reception area, I was heralded by Brimacombe personally as he directed me to an adjacent meeting room. Brimacombe was tall and thin in stature with a youthful face that was accented by dark rimmed glasses and a thinly manicured mustache. I was initially surprised to observe how young he looked and this reinforced the reality that I had grown old in the legal profession. In the seventeen years that passed since I had entered the legal profession, my class of lawyers had slowly become elevated to the status of seniority. The myth of finding a great legal mind was slowly shattered as I discovered that this top rated criminal lawyer and I shared a similar vintage in the profession but had simply selected different specialties in our legal careers.

I was flattered that Brimacombe remembered me from the days when we started to practice law. As we began to speak, I was surprised to learn that he had not heard anything about my situation either through the gossip brigade of the legal profession or through the news media. After giving Brimacombe a brief summary of what had transpired to date, I began to review the certiorari and stay of proceedings application with him. I then showed him the legal brief that I had prepared and the Notice of Appeal that I filed. As I completed my comments on the proposed Appeal, Brimacombe commented:

"Orest, there is certainly a lot to read here. If you want to leave it with me, I'll go through it with the assistance of another lawyer. We can then meet again and I will give you my legal opinion on the merits of the appeal. However, I can tell you this in a general way. It looks like you did a good job in your research. I have no doubt that there are good arguments on the certiorari and the stay of proceedings charter argument. The problem is that our Court of Appeal is not very receptive to looking at those types of arguments. In other provinces, you see cases where the Court of Appeal will throw out cases on a certiorari argument. Some of the other Appeal Courts have also thrown out charges based on the Charter of Rights and Freedoms. In the Alberta Court of Appeal, these arguments are ignored mainly because most of those Appeal Court judges don't understand them. Another factor is that all of them are very conservative and very reluctant to make such a major decision. Now having said that, I'm still willing to review your material. If the Charter argument looks good, then perhaps we could take that to the Court of Appeal."

What Brimacombe had just described was so incongruent with the way that I perceived the Court of Appeal. I immediately questioned him as tactfully as I could:

"Jim, I accept what you're saying but I find it hard to believe. If the case law is clear that the remedy of certiorari should be granted, why would any Court of Appeal refuse to grant it. Surely, we are talking about a simple matter of determining if the case fits within the stated law. If it does, then the remedy should be granted. How can the Court of Appeal ignore that and not grant the remedy?"

Brimacombe looked at me with a puzzled expression and then proceeded to explain the situation explicitly, showing patience and kindness:

"Orest, I'm sure that you know from your experiences before the Court that judges can do whatever they want. The Court of Appeal is the supreme judicial body in Alberta since few cases go beyond that to the Supreme Court of Canada. If they don't like certain arguments, then they simply brush them aside and there is nothing that you can do about that. Let me give you an example: Alex Pringle took a Charter argument to the Court of Appeal in the Don Cormie case. You've probably read about that case in the newspapers. I met with Pringle before the appeal was argued to review his legal brief and I was convinced that he had a winner. The Court of Appeal wouldn't go for it and I was as surprised as Pringle was. As I said, they don't like those types of arguments. However, if we've got a good charter argument here, it might be worth arguing it before them."

As I sat there feeling demoralized by what I heard, the name Don Cormie started bringing back memories of this well-publicized case. Cormie was once heralded as a financial wizard in Western Canada and captured everyone's attention with his economic philosophies and financial strategies. He created a large financial empire based on his ability to forecast and profit from economic cycles, thereby being able to invest and liquidate at the most opportune times. After becoming a lawyer, Cormie started his financial empire initially by selling mutual funds door to door. His investments in the real estate market ultimately led him to form a trust company, Principal Trust, and two large affiliated mortgage companies. His accumulated real estate holdings included many diverse properties, the most significant being a large commercial office tower named Principal Plaza. He also controlled a large tract of farming land outside of Edmonton which was ultimately purchased by Japanese investors with plans to develop a large golfing resort exclusively for Japanese tourists. The extent of his international holdings was largely unknown but it was revealed that he owned mansions and holding companies outside of Canada beyond the reach of the Canadian law.

Although Cormie's companies were able to weather the initial stages of the 1980 recession better than many smaller finance companies in Western Canada, his mortgage companies ultimately began to suffer. Defaults on mortgages led to defaults to their investors which soon thereafter resulted in a receiver-manager being appointed for the two mortgage companies. This loss of investor confidence caused a run on deposits at Principal Trust despite Cormie's desperate attempts to reassure investors that Principal Trust was not in trouble. Within days, a failure to meet deposit standards as required by the Treasury Department led to a receiver-manager being appointed for the trust company as well. Although depositors with Principal Trust got some relief from deposit insurance, there was no compensation available for investors and depositors of the mortgage companies.

The investors who lost money in Cormie's companies soon began to complain and then blame the Provincial Government for failing to protect them. In turn, the Provincial Government attempted to deflect the blame from itself by insisting that Cormie was the culprit who caused the losses of the investors. When it came to resolving the issue of whether Cormie had acted improperly, the Provincial Government could have simply followed the same process as it did in the Dial Mortgage demise. After all, the public complaints were about the operation of two mortgage companies which were monitored by the Alberta Securities Commission. If there was any wrongdoing by the directors of these mortgage companies, the Securities Commission could have laid criminal charges against the directors just as it did in the Dial Mortgage case.

In the Cormie situation, the Provincial Government avoided this direct approach of dealing with the situation. By this time, the leader of the Provincial Conservative government had changed from Peter Lougheed to Don Getty. The attitude of Getty was different from his predecessor in that Getty always remembered those that supported him and openly granted them government assistance. Since Cormie had donated heavily to the Getty leadership campaign, he had this

Premier's ear and merited special consideration. As a result the Getty Government ordered a special Royal Commission inquiry into the entire situation which cost the taxpayers millions of dollars. The effect of this protracted approach to examining the cause of the collapse of these financial institutions was to confuse and diffuse the situation for Cormie's benefit by giving him this expensive forum to argue that he had done nothing improper.

When the commission report was finally released, to nobody's surprise, it criticized Cormie's conduct. However, it also identified and criticized government officials for failing to take stronger measures when evidence of financial difficulties first came to their attention. Getty reacted immediately by firing Connie Osterman, the minister who had the misfortune of heading that department at the time. Getty then decided to pay partial compensation to the Alberta investors who lost money in an attempt to appease them. It was an interesting comparison that Getty did not hesitate to pay all the losses of North West Trust Company to bail out his friend, Larry Rollingher. However, Getty didn't have the same compassion for Don Cormie or the investors of his failed companies.

Because the investors were still upset over their losses, Getty and his ministers acted to further diffuse the situation. They first considered laying criminal charges against Cormie and his associates but it was obvious from the inquiry that they had committed no criminal act. As a final measure, the Government proceeded with charges of failing to make truthful disclosures in the Prospectus document that was filed with the Alberta Securities Commission.

The statements made in a Prospectus document were subjectively crafted and therefore could be criticized as not being totally accurate. This accusation became the only hope of casting any blame on Cormie and his associates. Cormie's lawyer attempted to have the charges struck out on the basis of a legal argument under the Canadian Charter of Rights and Freedoms. The case was competently argued but the Courts could not allow Cormie to escape prosecution even if his fundamental rights were arguably put in prejudice. Instead, Cormie would have to face a trial which would be watched by an audience of inflamed investors and satisfy their demand for frontier Justice. The news media ignited public sentiment to expect that Cormie and his associates would be ruthlessly punished for the hardships that had resulted.

Cormie's lawyer was able to avoid the consequence of "mob justice" by working out a plea bargain with the Crown Prosecutor. A plea bargain is an arrangement reached between the Crown Prosecutor and the Criminal Defence lawyer to resolve a case with a guilty plea to avoid a trial. A Crown Prosecutor is always open to such an arrangement because it allows a case to be resolved quickly and frees up Court time for other cases. The Criminal Defence Lawyer strives to get the best deal for his client by having as many charges dropped as possible and securing the lightest sentence possible for his client. The accused person is enticed into accepting the plea bargain by the fear that a harsher sentence may result if he is convicted after a trial. The only unsatisfied parties in this clandestine arrangement are the victims and the general public who are typically powerless and forgotten by the legal system.

The Judge who participated in this scheme was none other than Burkey Dea. As the trial date approached, the general public waited in anticipation of viewing a lengthy trial involving Cormie, his son and his associates on numerous criminal charges. To the surprise of a crowded Court room of spectators, this new arrangement was announced to the public on the first day of the trial. The Crown Prosecutor declared that all the charges would be dropped except for one against Don Cormie himself to which he would plead guilty. With the approval of Burkey Dea, the charge was then read to Cormie and a guilty plea was entered. Cormie's lawyer then spoke to sentence and Burkey Dea responded by handing down his decision of a $500,000.00 fine and no prison. Everything was handled with rhythmic precision and had the appearance of a well-planned performance with Burkey Dea quickly dispensing justice in his arbitrary style. Within two hours the fine was paid and Cormie vanished into obscurity. As he left the Court room, he left behind the enraged investors who now watched the mockery of a Justice system that failed to deliver for them any semblance of justice. From all assessments, the fine was a token monetary payment for Cormie. As the case was concluded, it was abundantly clear that justice was not achieved in the eyes of the general public who witnessed this melodrama.

The Cormie case will always be remembered as another example where justice was not achieved in the Courts through the application of the law but rather in spite of it. If the case had been decided strictly on the law, then the charges should have been dismissed to safeguard Cormie's rights to a fair trial under the Canadian Charter of Rights and Freedoms. If the case was really deemed important enough to proceed to trial in spite of the infringement of Cormie's rights, then nothing should have prevented the trial. Instead, the Court system allowed Cormie to circumvent the demand for Justice with a planned plea bargain. From Cormie's perspective, he had to achieve justice by making a deal with the Crown Prosecutor and paying a token fine, which had to be just as distasteful. The fault rests with judges who are not conscientious and sometimes not knowledgeable. Too many are improperly motivated by personal factors or events outside the law. Whatever the reason, it all perpetuates the mockery of injustice in the Court system.

All of this was discomforting as I struggled to find comfort and hope in Brimacombe's comments. I was grateful that he was being candid with me as there really was no time for polite gestures directed to appease me. However, he was leaving all the possibilities open so I had reason to be hopeful. As I concluded my meeting with Brimacombe, I agreed to secure a copy of the transcript of the decision of Burkey Dea in dismissing my Court application. Brimacombe agreed to look at my material and to call me once he had reached a decision on what needed to be done. I left my materials with him, feeling very unsettled about my future. I now realized the significant effect that the shortcomings of the criminal justice system were having on my case. It was also abundantly clear that the Court system was a forum that I didn't understand very well. I lacked a realistic and objective assessment of how it worked. A chilling thought struck me that I might become an innocent victim of a legal system that failed to deliver justice. Now, more than ever, this prospect frightened me.

I had already ordered the transcript of Burkey Dea's decision so only a few more days passed before it was ready. I personally picked it up and delivered it to Brimacombe's office. My next meeting with Brimacombe came almost two weeks later and I was anxious to hear his comments and opinions. Shortly after my arrival in his reception area, Brimacombe called me into his meeting room and began to give me his assessments:

"Orest, I reviewed all of your materials and I've also obtained an outside opinion. I'm convinced that you should not pursue your appeal of the dismissal of your application to the Court of Appeal. In my opinion, it would simply be a waste of your money because our Court of Appeal has shown such a reluctance on granting the certiorari arguments. Even when the arguments are good, they always make the accused go through a trial. Regarding the Charter argument, Burkey Dea simply said that it should be presented to the trial judge. In my opinion that is a good way to proceed. If the trial judge refuses it, that gives you one more ground of appeal to take to the Court of Appeal. For that reason, I feel that it's better to just make the application on the opening day of the trial and then see whether the judge will dismiss it. I feel that you have a good chance with that argument in front of a trial judge but that again depends on who you get for a Judge."

As I listened to Brimacombe's comments, I began to shudder at the sound of those same familiar words: "IT DEPENDS ON WHO YOU GET FOR A JUDGE." There were a few conscientious, competent and unbiased judges dedicated to their work. However, I understood the reality that many of the judges lacked Court room experience and competence and some were totally irrational. In a practical sense, one could only expect a just decision if one was lucky enough to appear before one of the "better" judges. Otherwise, justice only happened by accident.

The most important research that a Court room lawyer does is determining the abilities of specific judges and their reactions to specific legal cases. Some judges have strong biases against offenders of certain crimes. An appearance before such a judge inevitably results in convictions and a harsh sentence. A good lawyer knows which judges to avoid and how to delay a case until he can bring it before the "right" judge. Another important factor in many court cases is whether the judge likes the lawyer representing the accused person. A favourable decision often depends on the friendship between the lawyer and the judge rather than the legal argument presented. For this reason, it is better for an accused person to pick a lawyer who has a good social relationship with a number of Judges. In practical terms, that lawyer will succeed more often than a lawyer who is simply knowledgable in the law and experienced in the Court room.

As I considered Brimacombe's comments, I began to realize that I had no choice in the matter. I needed a lawyer, time was quickly passing and I now had his ultimatum. Reluctantly, I accepted Brimacombe's assessment and advised him that I would proceed on this file based on his recommendations. He then proceeded to advise me on how he wished to see this case proceed:

"For me to get started on this case, Orest, a Discontinuance of your Notice of Appeal to the Court of Appeal must be filed by you. You can simply fill out and sign a form at the Clerk's office to that effect. As soon as you confirm that the Discontinuance is filed, I will notify the Crown Prosecutors office by letter that I will be representing you at the trial. Then, I can expect to receive notice from them on any matters that arise concerning this case as the trial date approaches. By the way, I'm sure you've heard that Eileen Nash has recently been appointed as a Provincial Court Judge. The Crown Prosecutors office will have to appoint a new Prosecutor to this case. I'll probably find out who the new Prosecutor will be as we get closer to the trial date."

This news of the appointment of Eileen Nash as a Provincial Court Judge was yet another surprise in a case that was filled with unusual circumstances and ironical developments. For a moment, I was impressed to realize that despite her dowdy appearances and her cold, withdrawn mannerisms, Nash was also politically active. She had to be very strong in the Conservative Party to elevate her name in the political list of names for judicial appointments. Nash, of course, was capitalizing on the Anatomical Appointment Movement to appoint more women to the judiciary. It was rumoured that she was quite disappointed when her name was passed over for a Queen's Bench appointment in favour of someone with better political clout. However, she obviously retained some political clout because within two years, she was able to secure an elevation to the Queen's Bench Court.

As I contemplated the implications of Nash as a Provincial Court Judge, I wondered how she would perform in her new position of power and authority. Obviously, her experience as a Crown Prosecutor made her qualified in Court room procedure and her knowledge of the criminal law was excellent. However, she had always worked in an environment where an accused person was assumed to be guilty. Even when a Judge dismissed a case for technical reasons or for lack of evidence, a Crown Prosecutor still harboured the belief that the accused person was guilty. Now, as a Provincial Court Judge, she was expected to adjudicate on cases without any bias or favour. Each accused person had to be assessed on the basis that the accused person is to be presumed innocent until proven guilty. Although I knew that it was always possible for people to change their ideas and perspectives, I had serious doubts about Nash. For the moment, I felt happy and relieved that I would not find myself in front of Nash in this case. From what I had seen, Nash was like the Tin Man of Oz who didn't have a heart. It would take quite a miraculous transformation to change Nash into a Judge who could empathize with the accused people appearing before her.

As I confirmed that I would comply with his request, Brimacombe gestured that our meeting was completed. As he began to gather up some of the papers on the meeting table, he raised the topic of his retainer:

"The last thing that we should discuss is my legal fees. To do this trial for you, my legal fees will be $25,000.00. This fee only includes the trial and not any applications or any appeals to the Court of Appeal after the trial. I will need to receive this money long before this trial date, so you'd better start bringing it in as quickly as you can. Stuff some money into your briefcase the next time you come and start handing it in to my secretary."

As Brimacombe smiled to assure me that he had a sense of humour, I sat in my chair speechless at the thought of how I could possibly pay that amount of money for his services. For a moment, I struggled to gain a perspective on the situation by reflecting on my experiences with legal fees. The common practice was for a lawyer to bill for services on an hourly basis and a standard rate was one hundred and fifty dollars or more per hour. There was no maximum limit on a lawyer's hourly rate and the only requirement was that a lawyer document and prove the amount of time that was in his bill.

In contrast, most criminal lawyers handled legal aid clients and were paid pursuant to a schedule of sixty two dollars an hour for only specific services. The lower rate of pay has been the cause of complaints and threats of strike action by criminal lawyers. More recently, there have been desperate actions by some Criminal Defence lawyers to bill for services that were never performed. These dishonest actions were perpetrated to increase income and are indicative of a blatant reality that competition has diminished the income of lawyers.

The exception to this situation are the few Criminal Defence lawyers who have established themselves as experts. Their desperate clients will pay anything to guarantee success in fighting criminal charges. Such lawyers can demand a flat fee which is exorbitant and never have to justify what they charge. Because their clients are victims of the legal system, they will sell everything and borrow beyond their means to pay for experts that might save them from their ultimate demise. To the client, the hope of being vindicated is worth being impoverished and therefore no price is too high.

I was now one of those clients that was caught in the criminal justice system. I could not afford any mistakes and it was critical that this criminal charge be dismissed. If I was convicted, my legal career would end and I would be left in mid-life with the prospect of finding a new career. Even if I was handed a light sentence, the conviction would devastate my life and my family. There seemed to be no alternatives and I could feel the pressure on me to do whatever was necessary to get a good lawyer to represent me.

As I studied Brimacombe's expression for a moment, I realized that he was one of those established criminal lawyers who could "name his price". His expensive office was proof of that success. No doubt, he had many clients who could pay the amount of legal fees that he just quoted but it was simply beyond my means. I decided to appraise Brimacombe of my dilemma immediately:

"Jim, I'm sorry! There is no way that I could afford to pay you that type of fee. I've been suspended from the Law Society for over a year now. I only earn a small income by doing some occasional consulting work. From that income and my wife's income, we are lucky to cover our household expenses. I hope you have some suggestions as to how I can look after your legal fees. Is there perhaps another experienced criminal trial lawyer that you can refer me to?"

Brimacombe reacted to my comments in a defensive manner but was ultimately sympathetic to my situation:

"As you can appreciate, Orest, I charge high fees because I am the main draw in this firm. For that reason, I don't accept legal aid work and I don't make special arrangements with clients on fees. However, as you know, everyone in this firm specializes in only criminal cases. You may know Rick Stroppel who is one of my associates. He charges on a lower fee rate and even does legal aid work. He has handled jury trials and a number of fraud cases so he would have the experience that you need. He's even getting to be quite recognized by the judges because of a few cases that he's taken to the Supreme Court of Canada. If you wish, I would be happy to review your file with him. If he is prepared to handle it, then you can deal directly with him."

As I listened to Brimacombe's comments, I began to feel defensive about my personal circumstances. Impulsively, I made a gesture to relieve Brimacombe of any personal obligations to undertake a defence of my case against his firm policies:

"Jim, I totally understand if you or your associates decide that you can't handle my case. After all, you have financial commitments like everyone else and my financial problems are not your concern. If taking on my case is going to create any problems, feel free to say so and I'll simply speak to another lawyer about it. I wouldn't want Rick Stroppel or anyone else to handle this case if they really didn't want to do so."

As I finished my remarks, Brimacombe immediately responded to my concerns:

"Let me tell you this, Orest! Most of the clients that come into this office to hire our services are best described as pond scum. Typically, we find ourselves representing drug dealers, rapists, pimps and thugs. Usually they are repeat offenders and none of them are very nice people. Your case is such an exception! From what I've seen, you are a decent, moral person who didn't do anything illegal but unfortunately find yourself in a legal mess. I'm sure that Rick would be interested in taking on your case and I know that you'll be happy with his legal services. If Rick can't do it, maybe someone else in this firm can. Why don't you let me talk it over with them and I'll telephone you and let you know."

I appreciated Brimacombe's gestures and words of encouragement so I asked him to discuss this matter with Stroppel. It occurred to me that I didn't really know Brimacombe that well. Therefore, it didn't really matter if he or someone else represented me at the trial. What I needed was a lawyer with the appropriate experience in jury trials and specifically with fraud cases. This was now the most important consideration for properly presenting the defence in my case. I couldn't deny my uneasy feelings about this sudden change and my feelings of uncertainty about this new replacement candidate who would be asked to handle my case. I resolved that I would wait until I met with him before deciding if I would allow him to handle my case.

It is a sad epitaph that Jim Brimacombe died two years after this last meeting from a brain tumour. At the height of his career, he left the legal profession in the one way that is considered honourable among lawyers. Acclaimed as one of the profession's best, he would be honoured by his legal firm by having the office closed for the day of his funeral. There would be no elaborate processions or honour guards which typify the funerals of policemen, firemen or revered politicians. Instead, Brimacombe's files would be quickly dispersed among other firm members and his position in the profession would be quickly forgotten. In contrast, my departure from the profession by being suspended was the equivalent of a dishonourable discharge. However, I was getting out before the legal profession sucked all the life out of me. I knew that Brimacombe would have gladly accepted my fate in place of his if there was a choice. I felt sad for Brimacombe because he was truly one of the few decent, likable lawyers in the legal profession and a rarity in anything is always missed.

CHAPTER TWENTY ONE

FOUL PLAY

As the season of Winter gave way to Spring, I found myself embroiled in my legal problem more than ever before. At this point, I had already been suspended from the practice of law for more than a year. It was now obvious that no final decision would be made by the Law Society until there was a decision from the Courts on my criminal charge. All other avenues and all remaining hopes for resolving my legal ordeal had now been abandoned. The only alternative action left was to proceed as quickly as possible to trial. I felt a sudden regret that this matter had not proceeded to trial a few months earlier but that opportunity had passed. I would now have to wait another six months to resolve this legal calamity.

Brimacombe had called me to confirm that Stroppel would handle my case and a meeting was scheduled for me to meet with him. Having reflected on this new development, I felt partially relieved that I now had a new lawyer on my case. Consequently, I awaited this first meeting with renewed enthusiasm. Although I could not displace my feelings of apprehension, I was determined to enter this meeting with a positive outlook. I knew that it was important to receive Stroppel's comments in an objective frame of mind.

On arrival at their legal offices, I was asked to wait in the reception area. After a short wait, I was greeted by Stroppel as he introduced himself and then led me to his office. In physical stature, Stroppel was tall and thin with black hair and few distinguishing characteristics. His rounded small face seemed out of proportion for his tall, lanky body. His talk was always serious in spite of his attempts at humour, when he forced himself to display a smile. As I pondered my first impressions of Stroppel, I reflected on a wise observation that Court room lawyers are typically the oddest looking people. To belong to that group, you had to look and dress oddly. In time, I would come to respect and admire Stroppel's work which was thorough and precise and performed capably and efficiently.

Stroppel began by telling me about his background and experience as a lawyer. In addition to teaching a law course at the University of Alberta law school, he had sixteen years of legal experience in the field of criminal law. He was proud to mention that he had appeared before the Supreme Court of Canada and that he was awaiting a decision on a recently argued case. He confirmed that he had handled numerous Queen's Bench trials including a number of jury trials. He also had experience in fraud cases and in arguing cases before the Court of Appeal of Alberta. He concluded by saying that he felt quite comfortable with my case and was confident that he could achieve a dismissal of the criminal charge.

As I listened to Stroppel's description of his experience and abilities, it occurred to me that he had been in practice for approximately the same period that I had been. However, it was interesting to observe how different his course in life had been from mine. After law school, Stroppel's career seemed to continue in a normal manner. Nothing unusual had occurred to disrupt the routine that he had developed in his law practice. In direct contrast, I was now facing a shocking and devastating prospect that could end my legal career. At that moment, I longed to see my life return to normal and to have this ordeal resolved. I really wanted to return to the routine that I had enjoyed as a practising lawyer. Unfortunately, I had been away from the practice of law for so long that I was now wondering if my life would ever return to the state of calm that I once knew and enjoyed.

After Stroppel's brief dissertation on his qualifications, we began the task of identifying the various documents that I had delivered to his office. As we talked, Stroppel made notes of everything that might be relevant in the case. During this process, I identified documents that would be useful in our preparation for the trial. As we examined each of the documents, I provided him with a brief summary of how the documents were created and Stroppel made copious notes for his later reference.

I was enthused to see that Stroppel was careful and analytical in his approach. Unfortunately, not all lawyers take such care in studying details relevant to a case. This is especially true of some trial lawyers who pretend that they can remember what is important and then simply bluff their way through a case. As we completed the review of the various documents, I raised the prospect of receiving assistance from Patrick Murphy. Stroppel had a manner of pausing and then replying slowly in the characteristic manner of a University professor. In that fashion, he replied:

"I'm going to want to talk to Pat Murphy about his impressions of the Crown witnesses since he has seen them on the witness stand at the Preliminary Hearing. It's very difficult to judge the demeanour and the general quality of a witness from a written transcript. However, Murphy should have developed a definite assessment of the witnesses as he cross-examined each of them. Before I talk to him, I want to review the testimony of each witness and discuss the evidence with you to get your comments. Once I complete my review of the testimony of each witness, I'll discuss my impressions with Murphy and obtain his comments. Then, I can decide how the defence will be presented at the trial. Have we covered everything or do you have any further questions for me?"

Finally, an opportune moment had arrived for me to bring up the question that had been burning on my mind since I last met with Brimacombe. As Stroppel made some final notes, I slowly inquired:

"Rick, during my last meeting with Jim Brimacombe, we discussed the application that was made to get an Order for a Stay of Proceedings under the Canadian Charter of Rights and Freedoms. The facts and the case law are all set out in the material that you now have. The application was made and argued before Justice Burkey Dea. Has Jim reviewed this aspect of the case with you and have you considered it yet?"

Stroppel looked up at me from behind his work and offered a curt explanation to my inquiry:

"I had a brief conversation with Jim on that but I really didn't have a chance to look at any of that material yet. As we get closer to the trial date, we'll look at whether we should make any preliminary applications before the start of the trial."

As I listened to his response, I felt quite disappointed. I forced myself to maintain a positive outlook regarding Stroppel's comments. I acknowledged his suggestion with a respectful gesture and then he continued:

"That raises another matter which I feel we should discuss right now. Your case is unusual because you are not the typical kind of person who appears in criminal court. It makes the case easier for me because I will be able to present you in a credible way to the court. The difficulty that arises is that as a lawyer, you understand everything that is happening. There will be times when you may disagree with an approach that I'm taking or the decisions that I am making in your case. Naturally, I want to hear from you if you have any comments on what is happening. However, if you disagree with a decision that I am making, it has to be resolved or I cannot continue to represent you. What is your view on how such disagreements should be resolved?"

At that moment, I wanted to burst out in laughter but I was concerned that Stroppel did not have that much of a sense of humour. Here I was being asked a question by him when it was obvious that no answer was necessary. We both knew what the answer had to be. Stroppel's words were carefully chosen to insure that he did not offend me or trample my pride. Giving me the opportunity to answer was an interesting way of allowing me to make the ultimate decision. However, we both understood the implications of what he was saying. If I suggested that I would want to make the final decisions, it was obvious that he would refuse to act as my lawyer. It had become obvious that Stroppel believed that he knew what was best for me and did not want any interference in the way that he handled my case. If I felt that he should follow a certain procedure or employ a certain strategy, I had to be careful how I raised the topic. There was no doubt that Stroppel wanted to be totally in charge for making the final decisions.

I decided not to make a joke of his question or even jest with him as I would have done with Jim Brimacombe or Patrick Murphy. Instead, I simply responded in a serious tone of voice:

"Rick, you are experienced with criminal trials and you are more objective than I would be in this trial. Therefore, I will naturally expect you to make the decisions that are in my best interests. However, I want to discuss each of the matters in advance with you and I'd like to give you any feedback that I think may be helpful to you. This shouldn't interfere with your ability to make decisions. To answer your concerns, I will support any decisions that you make. After all, if I didn't have confidence in your abilities or your judgement, then I would get a different lawyer."

I was surprised when Stroppel showed an expression of relief. I concluded that he expected me to rebel at the thought that I would put such confidence in his judgement and not interfere with his decisions. In fact, I had hoped for a good working relationship in which I could evaluate each situation before a decision was made. However, it was his expertise in the trial that was crucial for presenting a good defence and rebutting the Crown Prosecutor's case. There was no benefit in limiting his ability to perform by placing any limitation on the decisions that he could make.

As we concluded our conversation, Stroppel agreed to telephone me when he had reviewed the material so that I could brief him and provide him with my impressions. We both agreed that this would be a lengthy process that would extend over the coming months leading up to the trial date. In fact, this preparation work would prove to be the best antidote for the tension and stress that I would have to endure over those months to come as I awaited my trial date.

When a lawyer speaks of a "brief", the reference is to a legal brief, a document describing the relevant facts of a case and the results of research on a specific legal issue. Lawyers typically prepare legal briefs on most of their files. If a unique point of law arises, a legal brief will be prepared to evaluate it. These legal briefs define the strategy to be employed by the lawyer in presenting a case before the Court. The task of preparing legal briefs on files is typically assigned to Students-at-Law or junior lawyers. However, it is becoming more frequent for judges to require lawyers to file legal briefs before and sometimes as a result of presenting legal argument. This simplifies the work of the judges at the expense of the lawyers and parties involved.

As a trial date draws near, the lawyer will begin the process of "briefing" or preparing. Often the client will be present to answer questions and to receive directions on the lawyer's strategy. In order to prepare a client for court, the trial lawyer will usually question him vigorously so that he is conditioned to the type of questions that he will be asked. These "dry rehearsals" are essential to ensure that the client will make a good impression in the Court room. However, a fine line exists between briefing and coaching. Unfortunately, too often that line is crossed when a lawyer wants the evidence of his client to suit the case that he is arguing.

Spring melted into summer and as the weather heated up, so did the activity on my case. As the trial date approached, I met with Stroppel more frequently in our bid to prepare for the trial. At each meeting we would discuss the evidence of a few of the witnesses from the Preliminary Hearing. During each meeting, I would give my impressions of the witness, the evidence and the contradictions. Our meetings would typically last one hour, after which time we would adjourn since this provided an easy time frame for concentration. This also allowed Stroppel a chance to respond to the needs of his other clients.

As we neared the end of the summer, the fall trial date loomed in my immediate future like the beacon light of a lighthouse beckoning us to approach with caution. My discussions with Stroppel were now more intense as we examined every detail of the evidence given by each of the witnesses. Even if it seemed inconsequential, we debated the implications of every statement made by each witness. The work was tedious, but necessary. We were both exhausted as we concluded the last of our briefing meetings.

With the arrival of September came the cooler weather which typically heralds the arrival of Autumn. It also brought me to the threshold of the event that would finally resolve my perpetual nightmare. The months of meetings and the frustration of waiting had taken a toll on me and my family and I was glad that this case would soon be resolved. The delays of the court system and the senseless procedural steps that I had to endure had drained my energy to valiantly fight for vindication. I needed to have this ordeal resolved so that I could have my life back again.

Late in September, Stroppel called to arrange a meeting to discuss some procedural aspects of the pending trial and the latest developments in the case at the Crown Prosecutor's office. As we sat down in his office, Stroppel immediately brought out a list of items that he wanted to discuss with me and we began our discussions on the various items. Stroppel was different in that way from other lawyers that I knew in that he was all business. He limited his personal and social comments to a few gestures during his greetings. Humour was more of a forced effort for him so we maintained a serious attitude during our meetings.

As I reflected on this noticeable characteristic, I concluded that this was a necessary practice for Stroppel just as it was for most criminal trial lawyers. Following this practical principle of conduct avoids the prospect of developing any sentiment or feelings for the plights of the clients. This is actually a prudent consideration if a Criminal trial lawyer wishes to avoid burn-out. It is a grim reality that a criminal trial lawyer will often witness the disappointment and distress of his clients if they lose in Court and the ultimate devastation of their lives by the justice system. For that reason, most lawyers try to distance themselves as much as possible from the plights of the clients. In addition, a criminal trial lawyer must witness the travesty of injustice that occurs when innocent clients are wrongly and improperly convicted and imprisoned. In contrast, the lawyer must accept that other clients who were clearly guilty of serious offenses will avoid any legal consequences because of technical defences. Legal scholars always defend the legal system for allowing technical defences to excuse criminal behaviour where the evidence is insufficient to prove the crime. However, there is no amount of rhetoric that can justify the ineptitude in the justice system that results when incompetent judges improperly convict an innocent person of a crime and then unnecessarily imprison him.

Stroppel began our meeting by advising me about his most recent discussions with the Crown Prosecutors office:

"I've just been notified that the new Crown Prosecutor who was assigned to handle this case has now been re-assigned to a different one. As a result, your case is now going to be prosecuted by Bill Pinckney. This is an unusual move at their office since Pinckney is the boss over there and a case like this one would generally be handled by one of the other Crown Prosecutors. I can't really understand why there was such a sudden change but it doesn't really matter who prosecutes it. I've been on cases before when Pinckney handled the Crown's prosecution. I've never had any problems with him and I don't expect to have any problems in this case either."

As I listened to Stroppel explain this recent shuffle in Crown Prosecutors, I could smell foul play. It was obvious that Pinckney had blatantly used his position as the Director of the Special Prosecutions branch to take over the file from the assigned Crown Prosecutor for a personal reason. As Murphy had explained to me, Pinckney and Christal were good friends and therefore Christal could influence Pinckney. This showed itself when Pinckney over-ruled the decision of Eileen Nash and authorized the criminal charge to be laid against me. Now that Nash was gone, Christal had to be sure that this case would be prosecuted vigorously and that a conviction was secured by any means possible. Christal and Pinckney had too much at stake with an investigation under way into the conduct of Christal in this case. Christal obviously had little confidence that the designated Crown Prosecutor would accomplish the necessary result. Therefore the only satisfactory course was for Pinckney to take over the prosecution himself.

I knew that this was more than paranoia because of the comments that Murphy made when he quit as my lawyer. He had warned me of a conspiracy to manipulate the legal system to guarantee that I would be convicted. To Stroppel, this last minute switch in Crown Prosecutors was unusual but he had no reason to suspect foul play. I knew that there was nothing that could be done about this sudden change since the Crown Prosecutor's office was at liberty to pick anyone they wished to prosecute this case. I decided not to explain this realization to Stroppel because I was concerned that Murphy might have wanted this information to be confidential. I knew that Stroppel would speak to Murphy on this matter and therefore Murphy could express these concerns directly to Stroppel if he chose to do so.

I therefore simply nodded my head to acknowledge what Stroppel had just described. He then looked down on his agenda before continuing:

"The next thing I want to deal with is the Judge. I spoke with the Trial Coordinator and he was finally able to confirm the name of the Judge who will be handling this trial. The Judge's name is Delmar Perras who is a recent appointment to Queen's Bench. Before his appointment he was a senior bureaucrat with the Attorney General's department. I was told by one of the Crown Prosecutors that Perras handled the negotiations for the Attorney General's department when the Crown Prosecutors were negotiating for better salaries. Perras showed how ruthless he could be when he stuck it to the Crown Prosecutors. As a reward from the department, he received his appointment as a Queen's Bench judge. His appointment came after you were suspended and therefore, I assume that you have never appeared before him or had any dealings with him. For that reason, we don't have any basis for asking for a different judge. Otherwise, I could have requested a different judge. In a case like yours where a lawyer is being prosecuted, it's typical that they will bring in a judge from Calgary to hear the case."

Although the name Perras was not familiar to me at the time, I was to receive shocking information later about Perras from another lawyer. I was informed that Perras was indirectly affected by a fraud that was committed on a Credit Union. The result was an obvious bias on the part of Judge Perras against anyone charged with fraud on a financial institution. The effect of this bias became noticeable as we progressed into the trial.

As Stroppel completed his comments, I anxiously interjected:

"Rick, you're right in your assumption that I have never had any dealings or appearances before Perras. Have you heard anything about him? What is he like in Court?"

Stroppel responded immediately as he continued his explanation:

"I was just going to get to that. I have never had a trial in front of Perras but I have spoken to a few lawyers that have. According to them, he is a terrible judge to get for a criminal trial. All those years at the Attorney General's depart-ment have definitely given him a bad attitude against accused people who appear in his Court room. One lawyer told me that he had Perras on a murder trial but the Crown Prosecutor proceeded on the basis of manslaughter which carries a lighter prison sentence. Perras not only convicted the guy on what was questionable evidence but also increased the charge to first degree murder. He then gave the poor guy the mandatory twenty five year sentence. Both the lawyer and the Crown Prosecutor were shocked when they left the Court room and they both agreed that Perras was totally irrational on the bench. Before a Judge was assigned, I was considering the possibility of doing the trial before a Judge only, without a jury. However, after hearing those stories about Perras, I've concluded that our only hope is to have a jury make the decision."

As I sat in shock and listened to Stroppel's latest revelation, I was mortified with disbelief as I contemplated what had transpired. I was aware that there were some bad judges that might have been assigned to hear this case, but Perras sounded like someone who was tailor-made in Hell. Although many judges pre-side over their Court rooms like the reincarnation of God, it sounded like I would be put on trial before Lucifer dressed in black robes. It was obvious why Stroppel was determined to proceed with a jury trial. Even though it is a longer and more difficult process, it was now the only hope that we had of obtaining a fair decision.

Now, I was convinced that Murphy's comments about a conspiracy were accurate. Christal and Pinckney had managed to arrange a judge who they knew would convict me. It was obvious that Pinckney knew Perras since they were both senior bureaucrats in the Attorney General's department. The odds were now being stacked very favourably for the Crown's case. The old adage of knowing the judge was now a big factor in my case.

At that moment, I also realized another set-back that Stroppel's decision to proceed with a jury trial would create: Prejudice. According to Brimacombe and other lawyers that I had consulted, a jury would likely be more prejudiced against me than a judge because of my occupation as a lawyer. The prevailing sentiment of the public is to generally dislike lawyers and especially those who are suspected of being dishonest. For that reason, it was more preferable that this trial proceed before a judge without a jury. However, this prospect now seemed to be closed because of the designation of Perras as the Judge. There didn't seem to be any options left and so we had to proceed to trial in spite of the "uneven playing field" in the Court room.

After a few moments of adjusting to this disturbing information from Stroppel, I began to slowly react by asking:

"Rick, it's obvious that we won't get a fair hearing before Perras. Why don't we apply for a new judge to be appointed. After all, if judges from Calgary have been brought up in the past to hear cases where a lawyer is put on trial, why not apply for one in my case?"

Stroppel looked up from his papers and responded in his thought-provoking manner:

"I've thought about that, Orest! I've decided against doing so. First of all, I'm not sure if they would do it in this case. Secondly, you could always get a worse judge from Calgary. There is an old saying with lawyers when it comes to changing judges: THE DEVIL YOU KNOW IS BETTER THAN THE DEVIL THAT YOU DON'T KNOW. That saying seems to say it all! At least with Perras, we can prepare our case better because we know what to expect from him. If we get a judge from Calgary who nobody I know has appeared before, it's more difficult for me to know how to present a case or an argument. When I prepare a case, I like to know how the judge will respond. For that reason, I'm prepared to stay with Perras."

While I sat and listened in anguish, I began to despair at the prospects of what was to occur. Stroppel had described it accurately when he quipped that I was about to be judged by the Devil. Sadly, the over-riding concern was that if we switched judges, we might get a worse Devil. Suddenly, we were not talking about justice but rather survival. Instead of preparing our case so that we could achieve a fair adjudication, we were now pre-occupied with damage control. The whole situation seemed bizarre and it was difficult to imagine that this nightmare would pass gently from my life without a painful battle to vanquish it.

With resignation, I acknowledged my compliance with Stroppel's conclusion. He then continued to comment on other procedural matters pertaining to the pending trial and concluded on the question of the Pre-trial application to the Court:

"I've also had a chance to review your material and research on the application for a stay of proceedings on your criminal charge. You have about five different arguments there and I'm sure that we could argue all of them. However, it's my assessment that with Perras, we have to use a different approach. In my opinion, the best tactic is to take the one argument that is the strongest and to argue it only. That way, there isn't much work for Perras to do and it won't be confusing for him. Otherwise, with too many arguments, he'll form the impression that we are grasping for excuses to avoid the trial. If Perras is prepared to consider an application, this is our best approach. I'm convinced that the best argument that we can put forward is the long delay between the time that the fraud happened and the time that the charge was laid. This pre-charge delay is a good objection to this prosecution since we can easily prove prejudice to you. It is clear that you suffered prejudice to properly prepare a defence. The biggest prejudice is that evidence has since been discarded and destroyed and we can't bring it before the Court in your defence. I feel we have a good chance with that argument and that Perras should consider it. Do you agree with this assessment of how we should proceed?"

As I listened to Stroppel, I understood the reality that the best legal argument in the world was not good enough if the Judge didn't want to hear it. It was difficult for me to believe that Perras would actually listen to the argument and I was sure that Stroppel felt the same way. However, Stroppel's job was to assess my case in the light of the bias and attitude of Judge Perras. As my lawyer, it was his obligation and responsibility to put forward any proper arguments supported by all available evidence. Stroppel pointed out that if Perras dismissed the application without considering it, at least the avenue was open to appeal that decision to the Court of Appeal.

By now, I was physically exhausted and so I simply nodded my head in acknowledgement. Stroppel then advised me that we would meet to discuss the testimony that I would present on the Pre-trial application just prior to the first day of the trial. He then continued with a final matter:

"As you are aware, the first step in the trial process is the Jury Selection which is set for Thursday October 3, 1991 at ten o'clock. You have to appear with me and I would like you to meet me at the Court room that is assigned for Jury Selection. That is the same one that is used for Arraignments. I will get the list of potential jurors earlier in the morning and review it to see if I recognize any names. If you meet me at the Court room about fifteen minutes before Court begins, I will get you to go through the list to see if you can recognize any names on it. The process itself doesn't take very long and we should be finished before noon."

As Stroppel completed his comments, I hardly was able to respond because I felt so devastated by the various revelations that had come to light. The dark and threatening aspects of the trial process were now being boldly imprinted on my case. I accepted the grim reality that it would no longer be an easy challenge to present our case and be quickly vindicated. Instead, I and my lawyer had to contend with the various shortcomings of the Criminal Justice system. We had to rise to the challenge of demonstrating the true facts which proved my innocence in the face of obstacles that would prevent our abilities to do so. The most devastating of these obstacles was the fact that I would be presumed guilty by Perras who was in a formidable position to influence the jurors by his subtle actions and words. I worried that this could prove impossible to overcome.

As our meeting ended, I agreed to meet Stroppel at the Court House for the jury selection and I left to go home to rest and reflect on this situation. As a consolation, I reminded myself that trials are highly unpredictable and that we were in an excellent position to present a proper defence. With an objective assessment of my case from two different Criminal lawyers, I had no doubt that the Crown Prosecutor lacked the evidence to secure a conviction. Ultimately, I would testify to remove all doubt about what happened and this would surely guarantee that the criminal charge would be dismissed. Furthermore, I knew that the jury had to apply the legal principle that I was to be presumed innocent and that I could only be found guilty on evidence which was beyond a reasonable doubt.

I resolved that I had to maintain a positive attitude and approach this trial as a challenge that would ultimately vindicate me. After all, we first had the Pre-trial application to challenge these proceedings because of the prejudice created by the long delay. If that was dismissed, the Crown Prosecutor still had a problem because there was no real evidence of fraud. Finally, I now had new evidence which had been covered up. If Stroppel used it properly, both Christal and Pinckney would be humiliated for even bringing this criminal charge before the Court.

I could see that Stroppel was now fully prepared and we were both ready to deal with any unforseen variables. I was now prepared to face my accusers and to demonstrate that I had been wrongfully charged with this criminal offence. This trial would be my opportunity to finally dispel all the negative effects that this prosecution had created in my life. The process of the trial was about to start with the selection of a jury.

CHAPTER TWENTY TWO

JURY SELECTION

With the arrival of October came unusually cool temperatures and the familiar predictions that this winter would be long and cold. There was nothing particularly scientific about these predictions but the topic always arose at this time of year. Supporting evidence for such a conclusion typically included: the predictions of an old Indian chief, the fact that geese and other migrating birds had begun their southward trek earlier, the fact that bears were fatter than normal and the fact that squirrels had gathered an extra large cache of nuts for this particular winter. The list was endless and featured as much common sense as the Ground Hog predictions in February about an early spring. Even so, everyone faithfully listened every Autumn with earnest desire to hear the bad news that we would surely endure another cold winter. I accepted this pre-occupation with the weather as a natural consequence of living in a climate where the changes in climate are so extreme.

The date for the jury selection arrived but I was determined not to stimulate any further anxiety in our household by discussing it. Instead, I endured the nervous trauma silently as I carried out my morning routine with my family. After my wife and children left the house, I prepared myself for Court and resolved in my mind that this would be "Just one more Court appearance" which had to be endured before my trial. At that moment, I was numb from the anxiety and stress that these court appearances had caused. Although I could physically function, all of my emotions had been drained from me. Initially, I resolved that I had to persevere and conclude this tortuous ordeal before it devastated me physically. However, the reality I now confronted was that it would be a long and gruelling journey before the trial was completed.

On my way downtown, I chose the scenic wonder of our river valley. This was best enjoyed down Keillor Road, as it meandered near the river through overgrown trees and shrubs. The leaves on the trees were now rich with the full spectrum of rainbow colours. The drive through this beautiful setting was a glorious experience, even on a dull and overcast day. Sadly, the road was slated for closure to eliminate the traffic flow through the river valley. Although this decision was a terrible blow for motorists who depended on this quick access to the downtown, we were assured by our environmentally-conscious Mayor and aldermen that this measure would actually benefit all of us. I had resolved long ago that common sense played no part in politics. No doubt, this passageway to downtown would have survived if the reasons for maintaining it had been ridiculous rather than practical.

After entering the Court House, I proceeded to the elevators and checked the Court schedules located on the elevator walls to confirm the Court room location. When I stepped out of the elevator, I was surprised to see the hallways and the entire reception area jammed with people. I assumed that these people had been summoned to be considered as jurors for the various trials that would be proceeding in the following weeks. It would have been ludicrous to wait for Stroppel in the hallway as it was difficult to recognize anyone who might be arriving or leaving the floor. I decided to wait for him inside the Court room so I proceeded inside. Instinctively, I sat down at the back of the Court room where I could see everyone coming in from the entrance on either side.

The Court room was alive with the same activity that I witnessed on my Arraignment appearances. Lawyers were decked out in their robes and chatting among each other or talking with their clients. Meanwhile, the clerks and the Crown Prosecutors made last minute preparations for the cases that would proceed. Court Orderlies milled around the Prisoner's Box and enjoyed the levity of the circus atmosphere. Everyone readied themselves for the main performance that would commence shortly.

During all this commotion, I reflected on how this event looked more like a carnival than a serious Court room hearing where Justice would be exercised. There were people dressed in funny looking outfits and acting like clowns. There were prisoners in cages who were brought out for the delight of the spectators. The orderlies and clerks were getting everything ready for the Ringmaster who would preside over this raucous event. The spectators were gathering outside with their numbered tickets as they waited in anxious anticipation of being picked to participate in the grand finale event. All that was really missing was the popcorn and the hotdogs to make this carnival event complete. However, by the look of some of the clowns dressed in black robes, one could deduce that they had already eaten more than their share.

While gazing around the Court room, I noticed Stroppel entering through a side door and waving for me to join him. I immediately stood up and followed him out and as we entered an adjacent meeting room, he exclaimed:

"Nice crowd, today! Looks like we have a wide assortment to chose from. I've got the list of jurors who may be called. I'd like you to examine the list and tell me if you recognize any names on it. I've already done that and I've noted a few names. If you recognize any, just let me know. I'll be back in a minute."

As he finished, Stroppel abruptly turned and left the meeting room, closing the door behind him. I began to read through the list of names quickly and in a few minutes, I had completed the task without recognizing any names. As I finished, Stroppel walked back into the room. While he closed the door, I advised him:

"I've gone through the entire list and I don't recognize any of the names on it. I notice that the list only gives you their names and occupations. Do you get any other information to help you decide if you want a specific person as a juror?"

Stroppel responded immediately to my inquiry:

"No, there is no other information on the jurors. I have to make a decision on a juror based on his name, his occupation, and his physical appearance. In the United States, a lawyer can question a prospective juror to determine if there is any hidden bias or prejudice. Unfortunately, in Canada, none of that is allowed. Therefore, I simply have to make a guess based on a person's appearance."

On hearing Stroppel's description of the jury selection process, I was immediately reminded of the exhaustive jury selection process that is used in the United States. In that jurisdiction, an exhaustive examination of a prospective juror is conducted in court to determine if there is any potential bias before that juror is allowed to sit on a jury. Although the system is not perfect, at least a defence lawyer has some prospect of identifying jurors who might have an intentional bias against the accused person on trial. Because the selection of jurors is so critical to the outcome of the trial, the American trial lawyers consult psychologists to assist and train them in determining which jurors would have an unfavourable bias or prejudice. In Canada, there was no way of determining if any or all of the jurors had a bias against the accused person. In that sense, having a jury was perhaps more dangerous that allowing the judge to determine the case. At least, in a trial with no jury, the Judge had to provide reasons for his decision which could be questioned on appeal. In contrast, a jury did not have to give reasons and there would never be any statement on the Court Record that might disclose their bias.

I quickly inquired of Stroppel regarding the selection process:

"Can you object to any person who you feel would not be a good juror?"

Stroppel remarked in his firm, unequivocal manner:

"I only have twelve objections that I can use during the process. The Crown has twelve objections and they can stand aside forty eight other jurors. If I use up my twelve objections, I have to accept any juror after that point that is acceptable to the Crown. The other problem is that I have to go first in advising the Judge of an objection, which gives the Crown Prosecutor a further advantage in the selection process. I have found in the past that I usually use up my twelve objections and the Crown Prosecutors tend to object even more frequently. For that reason, we'll probably go through quite a number of prospective jurors."

As I listened to Stroppel's explanation of the jury selection process, it became apparent that even this procedure was weighted heavily in favour of the Crown Prosecutors. It was hard to believe that judicial reformists had allowed a situation like this to exist. Where was the campaign to demand change to such an obvious affront to fairness in the justice system? Sadly, the people most affected by these situations were people accused of crimes. Unfortunately, their interests and objections were seldom measured with any degree of concern by the politicians who enacted the laws. More recently, the issue of the unequal number of objections to potential jurors has been declared by the Supreme Court of Canada to infringe the Charter rights of accused people. Although some change has been introduced, the system still remains prejudicial to an accused person and offers no method for determining bias of prospective jurors.

Once again, I felt dejected as I realized how the legal system functioned against the interests of an accused person. As a final lament, I responded to Stroppel:

"It's pretty obvious that the Crown Prosecutor has the advantage when it comes to selecting jurors that will favour their position."

As Stroppel rose to his feet and we readied ourselves to leave the meeting room, he remarked:

"You'll find that the Crown has all the advantages in the criminal trial process except one. The exception is that the accused person is presumed innocent and that any facts relating to his guilt must be proven beyond a reasonable doubt. However, because of legal presumptions that arise in almost every case, even that onus is easy for the Crown to meet. At best, the Court room should at least be a level playing field. In reality, you'll find that it is slanted in favour of the Crown. We'd better go into the Court room now. If you want to discuss anything else, we'll have to talk later."

I followed Stroppel back to the Court room and was directed to sit directly behind the Prisoner's Box. A few minutes later, the Court Orderlies opened the doors and all of the prospective jurors who were waiting outside were directed to come in. As they entered, they were asked to sit anywhere except on the front bench where I and the other accused persons were sitting. Over one hundred prospective jurors had responded to a summons to appear in court on this date. The confusion that persisted as they shuffled their way to a seat lasted for over ten minutes. Finally, everyone was seated, and the Court Orderlies closed the Court room doors. This was the signal for the Clerk to convene the Court.

The presiding Justice was Joanne Veit who was one of the first female additions to the Alberta Queen's Bench Court judiciary about ten years earlier. Veit was a likable, grandmother figure who had made her way to the Queen's Bench after serving as a Chairman of the Alberta Securities Commission. She was a typical candidate who had the right political affiliations and no court experience but satisfied the anatomical requirement. To her credit, she was approachable and sincere so because of that, her faults and weaknesses could be forgiven. Before the jury selection proceedings started, she gave a warm, political speech to all the potential jurors reminding them of how important their role was in the administration of justice. It was amusing to hear her advise these unwilling participants that they should not feel bad if they were rejected or not chosen for a jury. She then explained that she would consider excusing anyone who might suffer a financial or personal hardship as a result of serving as a juror.

The reality of the situation was quite different from the picture that Veit tried to paint for her reluctant audience. Few, if any, of these prospective jurors had come to court that day because of personal choice but rather because their failure to do so would result in prosecution. There was no meaningful remuneration for serving on a jury and the work was unpleasant, if not somewhat horrifying and disgusting in some cases. Typically, a jury trial would consume two to four weeks or perhaps more of a juror's time and was sure to create inconvenience and possibly hardship for the juror. For these reasons, most people are actually pleased when they are refused for jury duty.

Each prospective juror sat nervously in silent prayer hoping that his name would not be called to serve on a jury. A prospective juror who was called then waited to be rejected by one of the lawyers. Of those who were not rejected, some then made a plea to be excused. As Stroppel explained later, the trick was to find people who did not mind spending their time in Court for two weeks or longer. It was his assessment that anyone who was upset with being a juror might not listen to the evidence and might flippantly vote to convict an accused person just to get out of spending more time on a jury. For that reason, Stroppel favoured retired people and housewives since he felt that this provided them with a form of excitement that they otherwise would not experience. By his assessment, the work of a juror would become a live-action, soap opera in which the juror could play a starring role. The horrifying reality was that the amusement of the jurors in attending court was more relevant than the dire ramifications that an accused person might suffer.

The first accused person to be called was a man seated next to me who was charged with murdering his wife. He sat quietly on the bench next to me to give the prospective jurors the impression that he was not in custody. However, the Court Orderlies who hovered around him dispelled that notion for anyone who was watching their clumsy performance. As his name was announced in Court, the Court Orderlies moved the accused person into the Prisoner's Box. The Crown Prosecutor and the Defence lawyer then made their formal gestures to Judge Veit to identify themselves for the purpose of the Court record. As the accused person stood in the Prisoner's Box, the Clerk made a formal statement advising him that his jury was about to be selected. She then read out the criminal charge and stated that he had entered a plea of not guilty.

At this moment, I expected the jury selection to begin. Instead, Veit began to explain to the prospective jurors that the accused person was charged with murder. She then continued with some general details about the commission and the location of the crime as well as the witnesses that would be called to testify. I sat there in momentary amazement as I grappled with the effect of what had just happened. Veit should have already told these prospective jurors that this accused person was guilty of the crime but that they would have to hear the case to satisfy themselves that they agree with the Court's assessment. If there was ever a mockery of justice for an accused person, this procedure was the most blatant example that I had ever witnessed.

Although the prospective jurors may have found this procedure unusual, it certainly did not seem to affect any of the lawyers present. Many of them appeared disinterested and bored as they casually settled into their chairs for the monotonous task that awaited them. After Veit completed her short dissertation of the crime that the jurors would adjudicate upon, it was "Show Time". The moment that this large audience was waiting for had now arrived. On the direction of Judge Veit, the Clerk spun a prize barrel containing the names of all the potential jurors. She then began to draw out and call the names of the "lucky winners". These prospective jurors were asked to line up in the order that the names were called so that each might then be presented to the Court like an aspiring knight in medieval times.

After a set number of "lucky" names was drawn, the Clerk called out the name of each prospective juror again. This time, each one walked to a location in front of Judge Veit and faced the two lawyers. The lawyers, beginning with the Defence lawyer, then advised Veit if the prospective juror was "acceptable" or "not acceptable". If a prospective juror heard one of the lawyers say "not acceptable", there was often a noticeable sign of relief as the prospective juror returned to his seat. Those prospective jurors who were identified as "acceptable" by both lawyers were directed to have a seat in the special jury seats situated on the opposite side of the Court room from the Prisoner's Box.

The process continued until the full contingent of twelve jurors was selected at which point the process ceased. Veit then declared that they now constituted the jury which would hear the trial scheduled to proceed the following week. She instructed them not to talk to anyone about the case and to avoid reading or listening to anyone about the case outside the Court room. At the conclusion of her speech, the jurors were asked to follow the Court Orderly out of the room so that he could give them specific instructions regarding their attendance in Court for the trial. After they left the Court room, the accused person was removed from the Prisoner's Box by Court Orderlies and taken back to the cells through a door located behind the Prisoner's Box.

As I watched these "Carnival" proceedings come to an end, I sat on the bench frozen in a state of total horror. I now waited for my fateful turn when I would be presented as a criminal to a hostile group of prospective jurors. Nothing that I had ever heard or witnessed had prepared me for what I had just witnessed. Not even in my wildest imagination could I have visualized that the procedures would be so bizarre and devoid of any fairness or justice to the accused person. It was totally inconceivable that anyone watching this orchestrated event directed at purposely maligning the accused person would not be affected by what was said. Each juror was sub-consciously compelled to form a negative opinion from Judge Veit's comments which implicated the accused in the crime. This assessment would only be reinforced by the time delay between the jury selection and the trial. It was hard to believe that notable criminal lawyers who witnessed this atrocious procedure continually subscribed to and supported a system that featured such blatant injustice to the accused person. Yet, the system continued with no public outcry or legal challenge to this obvious miscarriage of justice.

While I pondered this paradoxical situation, I heard my name called by the Clerk. I knew that my time had come to face the Court and the prospective jurors who would decide my fate. Stroppel and Pinckney immediately stood up to identify themselves for the purpose of putting their names on the Court Record. Veit acknowledged them and each lawyer bowed his head to Veit as part of the pageantry of the occasion. As I rose to my feet, the Court Orderlies directed me into the Prisoner's Box. When I walked in, they closed the door behind me and stayed there to guard the door, presumably to insure that I wouldn't escape. Once inside the Prisoner's Box, I stood and faced Judge Veit while Stroppel remained seated at the lawyer's table beside Pinckney.

Before the proceedings started, Pinckney stated that he had prepared a revised list of Crown witnesses that included the names of more witnesses than those stated on the Court documents. He then provided a copy of his list to Veit. He also advised Veit that the trial would start on Monday October 7, 1992 but the jury would not be required until Wednesday October 9, 1992. The reason for this two day delay was to allow time for the presentation of our application for a stay of proceedings. At that point, the Clerk began with her formal statement on the Jury Selection process:

"Orest Rusnak, these good men and women that you shall now hear called and who do appear are the jury which are to pass between our Sovereign Lady the Queen and you on your trial. If, therefore, you shall challenge them or any of them, you must do so as they come to the book to be sworn, before they are sworn and you shall be heard.

Orest Rusnak, you stand charged that you, at Edmonton, in the Judicial District of Edmonton, Alberta, between the 1st day of July, A.D., 1984 and the 1st day of April, A.D., 1985, did, by deceit, falsehood or other fraudulent means defraud Heritage Savings & Trust of money of a value which exceeded $1,000.00, by causing a false mortgage application to be submitted to Heritage Savings & Trust, contrary to the Criminal Code."

Veit then interjected with a comment regarding my status on this charge:

"On this charge, the accused has pleaded Not Guilty and has chosen trial by judge and jury."

Stroppel acknowledged Veit's comments on my status and then signalled for me to sit down. I quickly complied and Veit then began her statement to the prospective jurors about my case:

"So, Again, to members of the jury panel, the charge in this case is essentially fraud on the Heritage Savings & Trust Company, and the fraud was committed by making a false mortgage application. The witnesses who are expected to be called in this trial are the following: Don Christal, Nadia Foster, Doug Hawryluk, John Gulayets, Peter Pilip, Kenneth Klushin, Prit Paul, Keith Gilmour, William Patrick, Marcel Notschaele, Doug Thompson, Walter Pevcevicius, Darrell Thompson, Juline Boucher, Mark Denman, Wiltrude Schwaiger, Stephen Robert Garmaz, Douglas Gahn, Gail Garmaz, John Chubb, William Osborne, Donald Foster, G.R. Brosseau, Doug Chorley, Heather MacDonald, Jim Sicoli, John Lynch, Morley Lee, Donald McLean, Paddy Hunter, Gordon Leversidge.

In this case, we're informed by counsel that the trial is expected to take three weeks, to start on Wednesday of next week and anticipated to go for three weeks. So, again, with respect to all the disqualifications and the potentials for exemptions that I mentioned at the beginning, these apply to this trial. Also, if anyone has knowledge of the facts of this trial or knowledge perhaps of any of these persons who are expected to testify, anything to do with this particular trial, again this is also something which, if you're called forward, I'd ask you to bring to our attention as you're called, before you're asked to face the counsel."

Veit then signalled for the Clerk to begin the "games". With that direction, the Clerk began to turn the prize barrel. She then drew the names of the first twenty "lucky winners" who were asked to line up in the order called so that they could be presented to the Court. During this process, Stroppel hastily made notes of the people selected in preparation of the selection process. Once the first twenty contestants were selected, the Clerk announced this to Veit who then nodded to allow the Jury Selection process to proceed. The Clerk then began the process of calling the names of the prospective jurors in the same order so that Stroppel and Pinckney could advise the Judge if each candidate was "acceptable" or "not acceptable" as a juror. For every five prospective jurors called, one was identified as "acceptable" to both Pinckney and Stroppel. The reason for this was that Pinckney immediately stood aside any candidate that did not look or dress conservatively. Stroppel labelled "unacceptable" anyone who was employed in any way by the Government or its agencies or by a financial institution.

At one point, a prospective juror was voted as "acceptable" by both Stroppel and Pinckney but the juror immediately applied to Judge Veit to be excluded. His reason was that he felt that his involvement in the jury would create a financial hardship in his business. Veit questioned him on this point and then ruled that he would not be exempted. She explained that the Court was now taking a firm attitude that people must serve on juries when summoned and that only in extreme cases may a person be exempted. Both Pinckney and Stroppel looked at each other and concluded that they did not want him as a juror. Pinckney acted graciously by using one of his surplus votes to stand aside that juror.

As the process continued, Stroppel's objections were slowly consumed. At one point, Veit interrupted to remind Stroppel that he had used up eleven of his objections and that he only had one left. Stroppel acknowledged that fact and with a strained expression, watched as the prospective jurors continued to be called. From the next few candidates, the last of the jurors was chosen and the process was now complete. I looked across at the jury, hoping that I was making a good impression. I tried to look relaxed as the twelve jurors stared at me. As we looked at each other from opposite ends of this oversized Court room, I could now appreciate how easy it was for them to form the impression that I was on the opposite end of the law from them. I was in the Prisoner's Box and being dealt with as a convicted felon. The jurors were the righteous people who were chosen to make moral judgements on behalf of society. They were selected to punish wrongdoers such as myself for one of the terrible crimes that they continually hear about through the news media. I knew that it was inevitable that the jury members would develop an immediate negative impression. After all, it was a logical progression because of the manner in which the "stage" was set at the commencement of the "games".

The twelve jurors selected to hear my case remained seated in their specifically designed jury seats. As they stared at me, I could feel them evaluating my guilt based on my appearance just as Stroppel had evaluated them as appropriate jurors based on their appearance. I was afraid to cough or even blink for fear of making a bad impression that might stay with them. I couldn't look confident, I couldn't look scared and I couldn't look indifferent. All I could do was sit there quietly to wait for this ordeal to end and hope that I didn't make any bad first impressions.

There seemed to be a reasonable mixture of ages on the jury with some seniors, some middle-aged, and one juror that must have just turned eighteen. There was nothing about the jurors that would lead a person to believe that they didn't have biases unfavourable to my case. I began to worry that this jury might be a worse situation than doing a trial before a hanging judge. At least then, the bias of the judge would be easier to detect and easier to deal with.

I decided not to make any assessments of these jurors since I didn't know any of them. All I would ever really know about them were their names, which were as follows

1. Vivian Hoeksema	7. Russell Yackimec
2. Ted Sakousky	8. Richard Harvey
3. Derek Newell	9. Romeo Pelletier
4. Ken Lee	10. Aki Romaniuk
5. Ron Grasdal	11. Barbara Juchli
6. Clifford Massel	12. Josephine McLaren

Veit then proceeded to tell the jurors that they were now the appointed jury for my case and that they should refrain from speaking to anyone about this case. The jury members were then directed to follow the Court Orderly out of the Court room to a meeting room where they would receive further instructions relating to their attendance at my trial. The jurors were reminded to return to Court on Wednesday October 9, 1991, which was the agreed date that the trial would start. The first two days were now reserved for the argument and adjudication of the application for a Stay of Proceedings. Once the jury had left the room, the Court Orderly opened the door to the Prisoner's Box to allow me to leave. I felt drained by this tainted procedure but I forced myself to my feet and stepped out of the Prisoner's Box. I then walked out of the Court room and waited for Stroppel outside.

The ordeal of this Court Appearance, although brief, had been worse than I expected it to be. Not only was it strikingly different from anything that I had read about but also grossly unfair in the manner that it was conducted. It was no wonder that juries are commonly used in the United States and yet only used in Canada in extreme situations. It was also more obvious to me why lawyers preferred to avoid jury trials if they felt confident that they could obtain a reasonable hearing in front of a judge. The Court procedures in selecting juries were simply too prejudicial to the accused person. I surmised that these Court procedures were probably developed to discourage lawyers from using the jury system. The reason for this was that jury trials were more costly, inconvenient and time consuming than a trial in front of a judge.

After waiting for a few minutes, Stroppel came out with Pinckney. Following a few parting words, Stroppel came over to talk to me:

"Well, I'm glad that this step is completed. I feel we have a few good jurors who should be willing to listen to our arguments but we'll have to watch how they react to the evidence as we get into the trial."

At that moment, I interjected:

"Rick, I don't see how you can be sure of any of them. I didn't get a good feeling about any of them. After Veit told them about my fraud charge, I'm sure they are all ready to hand in a guilty verdict. Didn't you feel that the Jury Selection process is slanted against the accused?"

Stroppel responded impatiently:

"Look, Orest! That's the process and there's nothing that we can do about it. You shouldn't worry about what was said today. The jurors will probably not remember anything that was said when they come back to Court next week. Regarding your impression of the jurors, it's best to wait until the case begins and you can then see how they react to the evidence. Now, if it's alright with you, I'd like to get back to my office to look after another matter. We have a meeting set for two o'clock so why don't we talk further then."

What Stroppel was ignoring was that first impressions seem to last longer than all the eloquence that follows later. For some people, first impressions are the decisive indicators that dictate how they feel about people they meet. Usually, all the information that a person receives about someone is judged on the basis of that all-important first impression. I knew that Stroppel was wrong to dismiss this first meeting of the jurors as inconsequential. However, I could see that this was not the time to debate this point and so I remained silent.

As I nodded my head in acknowledgement, Stroppel turned and walked towards the elevators and I followed him out. I was still shaken and disturbed by the jury selection procedure and I really couldn't talk about anything at that moment. I decided to hold my questions and comments until later as there would be plenty of time to discuss the implications of what was transpiring. What was important now was to prepare myself mentally for the afternoon meeting. The trial was now imminent and we had to be ready to proceed. These last meetings would be dedicated to planning our strategy in presenting our case for the defence. Also there was the application to Perras for a Stay of Proceedings which would be presented in four days time at the commencement of the trial.

CHAPTER TWENTY THREE

THE BIASED JUDGE

If there is one sacred principle which serves as the foundation for our Criminal Justice system, it is that every accused person can expect to receive a fair hearing. The law states that an accused person is presumed innocent and that the proof of his guilt must be demonstrated beyond a reasonable doubt. However, all of these legal principles are meaningless if an accused person does not receive a fair hearing. This is such an important principle that it was enshrined into the Canadian Charter of Rights and Freedoms and has always been a fundamental part of the Constitution in the United States of America.

One of the cornerstones to this sacred right of a fair hearing is that the judge must be free of bias. Unfortunately, few judges have the necessary expertise or motivation to guard against bias. As a result, it is common for judges to favour certain parties and to openly conduct themselves in a biased manner. In criminal matters, many judges tend to openly favour the police and the Crown Prosecutors in the cases that come before their court.

When a judge holds a bias, the law and the merits of the case become irrelevant since the decision is essentially pre-determined. This situation of bias can be compounded to the detriment of the accused person if the judge also harbours a personal dislike for him. Not only will the decision be a guilty verdict but the sentence will be unusually harsh. Unfortunately, bias is hard to prove to an Appeal Court because most judges know how to mask it and to justify their decisions. Furthermore, Appeal Court judges are reluctant to expose one of their brethren to criticism for personal bias.

In the end, the Criminal Justice system simply loses credibility because it fails to work as it was intended. Furthermore, when the rights of one person are ignored, the rights of all of the citizens of society are diminished. By allowing biased and incompetent judges to adjudicate, everyone in society suffers the erosion of their basic fundamental rights. Sadly, there are so few who are willing to speak up to protect those rights that are so sacred for the benefit of our society.

Now that the opening day of the trial had arrived, I felt unprepared for what lay ahead. Too much rested on the outcome of this trial. There was no time left for changes and any mistake could drastically alter my life. I wondered if I would have the strength to see this through without faltering.

Both I and my wife felt nervous anticipation as we readied ourselves for this eventful day. We had shielded our children from this ordeal by not discussing it in their presence and by suppressing any sign that we were upset by this ordeal. For our children, this was just another day at school and their breakfast chatter reflected this. Their lives were pre-occupied by the challenges of excelling on the school grounds and accommodating the demands of teachers in the class-rooms.

As adults, we view those childhood days as magical times when any prob-lems that arise can vanish instantly if a simple apology is provided. The serious problems, of course, require the intervention of parents but quick and expedient resolutions are the expected norm. Unfortunately, as we become adults, quick and expedient resolutions are the exception and the serious problems may pre-sent insurmountable challenges. It is no wonder that adults marvel and long for the happy and carefree times of their childhood.

Dressing for Court presented its own challenge as I had to now visualize what would make a good impression on the judge and ultimately on the jury. Although it was obvious that I should be well groomed and neat in appearance, it was preferable that I wore clothes that were modest but respectfully appropri-ate for the setting. Any expensive clothing might create a negative sentiment for the judge and would definitely alienate me from the jury as it would make it dif-ficult for them to relate to my situation. It was obvious that ultra-suede suits and silk shirts were out and that chords and blue jeans were inappropriate as well. In the end, I decided on clothes featuring a sports jacket, a conservative tie and coordinated dress slacks with subdued colours.

Since Stroppel had already briefed me on the procedure that he proposed to follow, it was not necessary for us to meet to discuss the application this morn-ing. Instead, we would meet for a few minutes before court to discuss any ques-tions that I might have. Otherwise, we would simply proceed with the applica-tion. Because I was unable to focus or concentrate on anything other than my pending court appearance, I decided to leave for court early and wait outside the Court room for Stroppel.

On my arrival at the Court House, I immediately went to the elevator and looked at the list posted on the wall inside the elevator for the Court room assignments. As I looked down the list, I found the description for my case: "R. vs. Orest Rusnak" and then the number of the Court room. My immediate thoughts were of the countless times that I had looked on these lists to find the names of clients to determine where I had to appear to represent them. I never could have imagined that one day my name would be on the same list relating to such a serious matter. Now, I was like my clients and was forced to defend myself from a consequence that would destroy my life.

On reaching the floor where the Court room was located, I immediately went to the large reception and waiting area where there were large, oversized leather chairs. These chairs were specifically designed to compliment the mod-ern theme of this institutional building. The seats were soft to sit on but not com-fortable to relax in. However, this was a welcome relief from the concrete ledges and the wooden benches that were otherwise provided for the public to sit on. These seats were aesthetically complimentary to the harsh concrete motif of the building and were not intended for anyone to use in comfort. The obvious purpose for this was to discourage people from loitering, which was viewed as inappropriate for such a sacred place as the Court House building.

As a further reminder to the public that this building was intended to be a temple, the Court Administrators placed a solemn plaque on the entrance to the building. It bears the inscription: "THE PLACE OF JUSTICE IS A HALLOWED PLACE." which is a quote by Sir Francis Bacon. Presumably, the atmosphere of the building was intended to generate a feeling of holiness which would embody the judges as they presided in Court. Unfortunately, most lawyers would agree that it takes more than building design and a plaque to stimulate some judges to act divinely in Court.

As the minutes dragged on slowly, I reviewed in my mind the evidence that Stroppel would be putting before the Judge in this application. To put in evidence that which would be the basis for the application, Stroppel decided to call me as a witness. I would be asked specific questions that would relate to the prejudice that I suffered because of the long delay in bringing this matter before the Courts. While I was conducting this mental exercise, Stroppel suddenly appeared from one of the elevators. On seeing me, he began to walk in my direction.

Once he drew near, Stroppel called out in a reserved and quiet voice:

"Orest, before we go in, do you have any questions about the proceedings this morning? Are you clear on the questions that I will be asking you on the witness stand?"

The sudden disruption by Stroppel's appearance caused my mind to go blank. After a few moments, I responded:

"No, that's fine, Rick! I'm ready to get started with the application. Let's find out exactly what kind of judge that Perras is."

I then stood up, followed Stroppel into the Court room and sat down in the back row. Stroppel walked to the lawyer's table and began to take his files out of his briefcase to set up for the proceedings that would soon commence. Pinckney was already at his table and was whispering comments to Christal. Meanwhile, the Clerk, the Court Reporter and the Court Orderlies all chatted among themselves to kill time while waiting for something to happen.

As I focused on Pinckney, I could see immediately from his expressive actions that he was quite friendly with Christal. Ironically, it didn't surprise me that he would conduct himself in the devious manner that was described to me. As a senior Crown Prosecutor, such antics were the "games" that relieved the boredom of a repetitive, stagnant career. The fact that he was playing with other peoples' lives was of no concern to him since he was now hardened to the pain of his victims.

Pinckney was tall in stature which accentuated his menacing features. He proudly displayed a protruding pot belly which he must have carefully crafted from years of over-eating and excessive drinking. Genetics had blessed him with a long nose that featured a bulbous point on which he supported glasses with half lenses to compensate for his failing eyesight. His thinning hair, facial complexion and slow responses would have caused me to guess his age in the late fifties. He fit the typical profile of the many senior civil servants that I knew who were simply waiting out the final years before retiring with a lucrative government pension.

As I watched Pinckney perform for those present, he reminded me of an exhibitionist who had to maintain everyone's attention on himself to appease an oversized ego. It was interesting to watch his flirtatious remarks with the Clerk and Court Reporter or to listen to his cute stories which only he thought were funny. In Pinckney's mind, he was a "ladies man" in the prime of his career. By his actions he must have imagined himself as a very desirable companion for any woman to have. No doubt, the women present saw a different image of a buffoon who looked at the world through rose-coloured glasses. Unfortunately, his behaviour did not make him an unusual specimen in the legal profession. In fact, lawyers with an inflated ego and matching self-images are perhaps more abundant than the conservative variety, especially in the Court room setting.

Stroppel and Pinckney exchanged a few final remarks about the procedure they would follow when the Judge entered. They then advised the Clerk that they were ready to proceed and she left through a back door to advise the Judge. At that moment, I was called up by Stroppel and asked to sit in the Prisoner's Box. As I stepped in, the door was locked behind me and the Court Orderly stayed by me, presumably to protect the Court from my criminal characteristics. This Prisoner's Box was different from the ones in Arraignment Court or Docket Court. This one featured a simplistic design and was made out of oak wood to match the panelling of the Court room. It featured a long, hard, straight wooden bench for the "comfort" of the prisoners and was built to accommodate as many as six people. This Prisoner's Box was joined to the side wall where a securely locked door offered access to the Prisoners holding area. A four foot partitioning wall enclosed me and prevented me from having any access to the lawyers table directly in front of me.

As I sat down on the hard wooden bench, it immediately occurred to me that the design of the Court room, the use of the Prisoner's Box and the callous treatment of accused people was so bluntly prejudicial. All of these features would work to negate the possibility of a just decision being rendered by the Court and by a jury. The Prisoner's Box put the accused person on display in such a manner as to label him a danger and menace to society. It was quite obvious that anyone would sub-consciously form that conclusion about an accused person brought before the Court in that manner. The American courts usually don't allow such an obvious charade of injustice. Even the older styled Court rooms in Canada simply allowed the accused person to sit next to the Defence lawyer. However, this design appealed to the Senior judges and the Court Administrators who felt that once charged, a person should be treated like a criminal until he is released by the legal system.

A few minutes later, the Clerk re-entered the Court room and called out: "ORDER IN COURT". Those words brought an immediate silence as everyone stood at attention. With pretentious pageantry, Perras swept by her and mounted the stairs to his elevated perch with his robes flapping behind him in the air movement that he created. From the top of his platform, he paused briefly to survey everything below him. Then, with the air of authority that he embodied, he ceremoniously sat down, greeted the lawyers and then permitted everyone to be seated in his presence. After taking a few moments to open his notebook to the appropriate page, he then called upon Pinckney to begin the proceedings. I suddenly got a sickening feeling that our application was in trouble with this Judge. He reminded me of the judges I had met who lacked compassion and were quick to pre-judge a case. Time would soon tell if this first impression was sound.

Perras appeared to be about the same age as Pinckney even though he maintained more hair. His face seemed to be skewered into a perpetual frown which complimented a scowling predisposition. He spoke slowly in a low, condescending tone of voice which gave the impression that he was trying to think of something to say while moving his lips. It was obvious that these characteristics were naturally developed during his tenure as a senior bureaucrat at the Attorney General's department. Like most judges, he now pompously flaunted his prestigious position and demonstrated his sub-conscious desire to gloat at his good fortune. His arrogant actions were purposely intended to generate as much envy as possible from the lawyers present who hoped and dreamed to one day aspire to the same station in life. With all this pompous pageantry, one might innocently imagine that we were reliving the majesty of the monarchy and paying homage to a new king rather than attempting to resolve a criminal charge in the legal system.

Pinckney began his opening remarks by describing the proceedings to Perras for the Court Record. It immediately became obvious from the smiles they exchanged and from Pinckney's overt behaviour that they were on unusually friendly terms. My earlier suspicions were now confirmed as I watched them openly flirt like two old hippies at a Love-in. It was easy to understand this deep friendship since both of them held senior positions in the same government department and must have worked on files and other department work together. It was now easy to perceive that these two government bureaucrats would have attended the same social functions and formed a friendly relationship over many years of close association. It angered me to know that Pinckney had so much influence with Perras and I wondered if Perras would even consider anything we had to say.

I began to reflect on the process that was followed to select a judge for my case. I was now convinced that it wasn't just a coincidence that Perras and Pinckney, both senior bureaucrats from the Attorney General's department, ended up on this case together. Just as Murphy predicted, it had to be arranged and such an event was very possible in our Court system. In order to insure fairness in the selection of judges to hear cases, many American Court jurisdictions follow the procedure of drawing the name of the judge from those available to hear it. To ensure absolute fairness and to eliminate questions of impropriety, this selection is made in the presence of the two lawyers and the accused person. In our Canadian Court system, the assignment of judges falls under the control of the Chief Judge or Associate Chief Judge of the Court. It is therefore possible for judges to ask to be assigned to certain cases and for favoured lawyers to request specific judges for certain cases. Naturally, these procedures are handled discreetly and are dependent on a good relationship with the Chief Judge or Associate Chief Judge who has the power to assign judges to cases. Above all, these arrangements are kept secret as it would be embarrassing if it became known that the assignment of judges was not as impartial or arbitrary as everyone believed that it was.

One further factor that was irregular about this situation was that Perras, as a newly appointed judge, was handling a criminal jury trial. Normally, these assignments went to judges with considerable experience in criminal trials. This was a critical factor since the handling of a jury by a judge required a greater degree of knowledge and expertise than conducting a trial without a jury. When I began the practice of law, all criminal jury trials were essentially handled by the Chief Judge himself. At that time, he was the only one on the judiciary who had the experience to properly handle and instruct a jury. More recently, with the increase in the number of jury trials, other judges have developed the expertise to handle these specialized trials. However, it was typical to expect a judge to have a significant amount of experience with criminal trials before being assigned to such an important responsibility.

Although one might first assume that a criminal trial with or without a jury is the same for a judge who hears the case, the difference becomes manifest once a person observes a jury trial from beginning to end. In a jury trial, it is an obvious fact that the jury, not the judge, makes the decision of whether the accused person is "guilty" or "not guilty" of the criminal charge before the court. However, the jury is told at the beginning and throughout the trial that they must accept and follow any instructions and directions that the judge gives them. At the end of the trial, the jurors are told that they must consider the facts and the law as the judge describes it to them. Therefore, everything that the judge says and does is a significant item to the jury. Furthermore, the sentiments and remarks of the judge as it relates to witnesses and the accused person make a significant impression on the jury. Ultimately, even the actions and comments as well as the statements of the judge during the trial have the greatest effect on the decision of the jury.

I wanted to ignore the warning that Murphy had given me about a conspiracy to convict me. However, I knew that it was improbable that it was only a coincidence that Pinckney and Perras were both involved in my trial. Stroppel had already confirmed the fact that Pinckney intentionally took over the prosecution of this case from another lawyer who was assigned and was working on it. The role of Perras as a judge at this jury trial was inconsistent with the usual candidates chosen to handle such specialized trials. All of this was compounded by the obvious friendship between Perras and Pinckney that was now being openly displayed at the opening of my Court case. I began to wonder if Stroppel had reached the same conclusions and was simply making a valiant effort against odds that were formidably stacked against us. I knew that Stroppel was very cautious about making comments relating to these types of matters as it was viewed as unprofessional to criticize judges or other lawyers. For this reason, he probably would not express these types of concerns to me even if they were blatantly obvious and would have a dramatic effect on the decision of the jury in this case. The only thing that I could do was to monitor the conduct and comments of both Pinckney and Perras and to raise these concerns with Stroppel at an opportune time during one of our meetings.

Pinckney finished his remarks by advising Perras that before the trial proceeded, Stroppel would be making an application to the Court. With that statement, Stroppel stood up to present the application to Perras and Pinckney sat down. Stroppel began the application by explaining the basis for it and then advised Perras that he would be leading evidence in support of the application. He then advised that Pinckney intended to call evidence in rebuttal and that the application would be concluded with legal arguments from both himself and Pinckney. At that juncture, Pinckney stood up to confirm that he was in agreement with Stroppel's description of the proposed procedure. Perras then directed Stroppel to proceed with his evidence.

Stroppel abruptly announced that he would be calling me to give evidence in support of the application and then directed me to proceed to the witness stand. As I rose to my feet, I felt faint as if all the energy in my body had drained out. For a moment, I thought that I might collapse. I took a deep breath and slowly felt some of my strength return. I then began to move toward the door of Prisoner's Box which was now being opened by the Court Orderly. As I slowly moved across the front of the Court room, I began to feel better. My mind began to focus on what was to happen in the witness stand located adjacent to the elevated podium that Perras occupied. I climbed up the steps into the witness stand and stood there facing Stroppel and Pinckney, with Perras staring at me from my right side.

One of the strange traditions followed in Canadian courts is that witnesses are expected to stand while giving their evidence in court. No doubt, this is how the name "witness stand" originated although other theories regarding the origin of the phrase exist. This practice was one that Canadian courts inherited from English custom and have clung to it for the sake of tradition. Canadian courts have progressed slightly by dispensing with some silly and outdated traditions like the need for lawyers and judges to wear white wigs in Court. However, too many of the other antiquated English court customs continue to exist although some practices only receive lip service from the Courts. One blatant example of this is the special treatment that is supposed to be afforded to lawyers with Queens Council designations. Originally, the English courts gave special treatment in all procedures to lawyers with this privileged designation. Fortunately, such customs have virtually vanished in Canadian Court rooms, although the politically astute lawyers who secure such designations love to flaunt them whenever possible.

This court practice of requiring witnesses to stand while they give their evidence creates a difficult and exhaustive stress on witnesses. Often, a witness may be required to give evidence for an hour or longer and the need to stand often creates a problem for the witness. Ironically, it appears to be more of a problem of design than necessity. Aside from tradition, witnesses are told that they must stand so that their voices will be more easily heard and they will be more easily seen by the judge, the jury and the lawyers. Of course, all of this could be alleviated by better Court room design and perhaps a better microphone system. Such a system could easily be adapted to the sound system currently used to record the words of the witness for the benefit of the Court Reporter.

In American court cases, the witness is typically seated while giving evidence from the witness stand. This practice is one that is traditional in their courts and is far more comfortable for the witnesses than the situation in Canadian courts. Although this witness stand had a wooden bench built into the back of it, this is clearly to be used only when the witness is unable to stand because of physical inability. In exceptional circumstances, a judge might offer the witness the option of sitting if the witness appears frail or medically unstable. More typically, judges are the first to direct witnesses to stand if the witness mistakenly sits down in the witness stand. This happens often since most people develop that impression of Court room procedures from American television dramas.

As I stood in the witness stand, the Clerk approached me and asked me to state my name and address for the Court record. When I had done that, she asked me to take the Bible in my right hand and then asked me to swear the standard oath to tell the truth. I acknowledged that I would and she then returned to her seat while Stroppel began to question me. Because we had reviewed all of his questions in advance, I was prepared to answer them. As he continued, I found myself relaxing somewhat from the high degree of tension that I had felt to that point. Because of my nervous anxiety, the Court Reporter, who sat directly below me, had to ask me to repeat some of my answers. I had to make a conscious effort to slow down so that she could properly record my answers. It seemed ironic that after the number of times that I had appeared in court and given slow, effective presentations for my clients, that I would have such difficulty doing the same during my trial. The problem was that my anxiety had developed to an acute condition with the stress that I had endured to this time. I was now unable to relax and calmly testify in these proceedings because the outcome was so critical to my future and I had such doubts about receiving a fair hearing from Perras.

The purpose of my evidence was simply to confirm when the mortgage transaction was completed, namely December of 1984, and that the seven year delay to the time of the trial resulted in files being discarded or destroyed. My evidence also confirmed that because the files of so many witnesses were now missing, there was a real prejudice to me in being able to properly present evidence to the Court. I then proceeded to identify six different witnesses in addition to myself who had discarded or misplaced their files on this transaction. Because the evidence in this case relied so heavily on documents, these missing files created a significant prejudice in developing and presenting a defence to the Court.

According to Stroppel's research, this evidence was sufficient to prove prejudice and to justify an Order from the Court for a Stay of Proceedings on the criminal charge. There was no need to prove that anyone was at fault in creating the prejudice so long as there was prejudice in presenting a defence. There was certainly no doubt that we had a good argument on prejudice in this case but the question was whether Perras would follow the law.

The cross-examination by Pinckney was brief as he intended to support his arguments on the rebuttal evidence to be presented by Christal of the reasons for his delay. Once Pinckney concluded his questions, Perras then looked over the notes which he had made of my testimony and proceeded to question me about the date that I had been suspended from the practice of law. Although the question was irrelevant to this case, I responded to the question. From his expressions, I could see an unfavourable attitude brewing within. Perras then advised that he had no other questions and Pinckney and Stroppel also confirmed that they had nothing further to ask. At that moment, Perras directed me to stand down and I immediately turned to step down from the witness stand.

As I reached the Prisoner's Box, Stroppel advised Perras that he would be calling one further witness: John Chubb. Chubb was then called into the Court room and directed to the witness stand. After his oath was administered, Stroppel began to question him on the dates of each steps that he took while handling this file to demonstrate the unusual and lengthy delay. Chubb confirmed that Heritage Trust completed this mortgage transaction in December of 1984 and the foreclosure of the property in 1985. After that date, all actions and delays on the file were due to the efforts of Heritage Trust to collect the shortfall on the loan from CMHC. In April of 1987, Chubb finally contacted the Edmonton City Police.

Chubb's testimony also explained why there was such a delay of four years from the time that the loss was realized to the time that the criminal charge was laid. The main delay was attributable to the failure on the part of Christal to investigate the charge more expediently. There was a lengthy delay between the time that he received the initial complaint and the time that he finally brought the case to the Crown Prosecutor's office for their first assessment. The other delay was attributable to Heritage Savings & Trust in simply allowing the file to be dormant for a significant period of time. About two years expired where the only activity was the infrequent attempts of various employees to collect the outstanding funds.

After Stroppel concluded his questions, Pinckney and Perras directed questions to clarify certain dates and then Chubb was excused. Although Stroppel could have presented more evidence to support a number of alternative arguments, he chose to rely on only one argument based on the delay of Christal and Heritage Trust. This delay took place before the criminal charge was laid and was excessive in Stroppel's assessment. The argument of Pre-charge delay would be the only grounds used in this application for an Order for a Stay of Proceedings. Presumably, even Judge Burkey Dea felt that it was an appropriate argument for consideration by the trial judge. Although Stroppel felt that we would succeed on this argument, the unknown variable was Perras.

Stroppel then advised Perras that he would be calling no further evidence. Pinckney stood up to advise Perras that he would be calling one witness in rebuttal: Detective Don Christal. He then motioned to Christal, who was seated directly behind him in the public seating area, to take the witness stand. Christal walked arrogantly to the witness stand. He appeared to be prepared for this moment and carried a file with him. As he acknowledged the oath that was administered by the Clerk, he looked towards me with a smug expression. Pinckney then advised Perras that Christal wished to refer to his notes which he had specifically prepared for this occasion and Perras agreed to permit this. Pinckney then began his questioning of Christal.

The evidence of Christal was primarily a dissertation of the times and dates that he worked on the file with occasional details of what he did each time. In his testimony he would specifically mention that he stopped work on the file to attend to another investigation that received priority. It became obvious that this would be their main argument for justifying the delays in completing the investigation more expediently. On the completion of his testimony, Stroppel began his cross-examination, and focused on the time delay issue. He asked Christal how much sooner this case would have been completed had he not taken time out for other investigations. Christal admitted that it would have been completed one year earlier. This final admission was all the evidence that Stroppel needed for his argument.

When Stroppel finished his cross-examination, Perras again reviewed his notes and asked a question to clarify his understanding. It was now obvious that Perras was intent on having the last word with each witness rather than being just an impartial adjudicator. When everyone acknowledged that there were no further questions, Perras directed Christal to stand down. Stroppel then rose to present his legal argument and cited various legal cases that supported his position. He argued that the pre-charge delay as shown by the evidence could have been avoided and caused an unnecessary prejudice to the Defence case. For that reason, an Order for a Stay of Proceedings was requested to end these criminal proceedings.

Pinckney then rose to present legal argument in rebuttal. He contended that the delay had caused the same prejudice to both the Prosecution and Defence. For that reason, he suggested that the case should be allowed to proceed in spite of the prejudice to my rights under the Canadian Charter of Rights and Freedoms. Pinckney's argument sounded ridiculous but Perras was accepting it with the same authority as a Gospel reading. Had Perras listened to Stroppel's legal arguments and case authorities, he would have realized that this was not an exercise in determining if equal prejudice was suffered. On the contrary, the only issue in this application was whether I had suffered any prejudice because of the long delay.

When Pinckney concluded his legal argument, Perras looked at both lawyers and advised them that he would adjourn to consider the evidence and the legal arguments. Because the jury would not be available until Wednesday morning at ten o'clock, he directed that his decision would be given at nine o'clock on that date. If he dismissed the application, then the trial would begin at ten o'clock. Ordinarily, such a tightly scheduled time frame would create a concern for the Crown Prosecutor. After all, he would not know if he should prepare witnesses for giving evidence at the trial or whether there would be a need to be ready to proceed.

Curiously, Pinckney must have had good reason to believe that the application would be dismissed even though nothing to that effect had been expressed by Perras. His actions seemed so unusual that I had to suspect that he knew something that we didn't about Perras and the decision that he would make. Pinckney immediately rose to apply for an Order from Perras that would allow him to set up the exhibit documents on tables to be situated immediately behind the lawyers. He also asked for an Order that the Court room be locked with special access for him and Christal to enter so they could arrange and review the exhibit documents. All of this flowed so naturally between Pinckney and Perras that it seemed like it had been pre-arranged. The certainty of the plans that were being made left no room for any contingency, other than the conclusion that there would obviously be a trial.

After granting Pinckney's requests, Perras declared that Court was adjourned and everyone rose to their feet on the Clerk's command of "ORDER IN COURT". Perras quickly gathered up his notebook and pompously strode out of the Court room. Stroppel and Pinckney then gathered up their files while the Court Orderly opened the door that allowed my free access out of the Prisoner's Box. As I stepped out, Stroppel moved away from his counsel table and we walked out of the Court room to the adjacent meeting room for a short discussion.

As soon as we walked inside and I closed the door, Stroppel started to speak:

"Well, it looks like we have this afternoon and tomorrow all day to prepare for the trial. Pinckney has given me a list of the witnesses that he will be calling and the schedule that he will be following. What I'm going to do is start arranging my notes in a binder so that I can easily follow the witnesses. I would like to meet with you to discuss the evidence of each of the first witnesses. To prepare for Wednesday, we should plan to meet tomorrow afternoon. Why don't you call me this afternoon at the office and I'll be able to confirm the time for our meeting."

While I listened to Stroppel speaking, it became strikingly evident that he believed that the trial would proceed on Wednesday. There was no hesitation in his voice and he expressed no doubt on what needed to be done. His impressions of the proceedings in court must have been the same as mine and his assessment of Perras' attitude was obvious from his immediate reaction. We had presented a good application but Perras was showing an obvious bias against me. Although his decision was obvious, Perras simply needed time to prepare reasons that would justify his decision. It now seemed that this application was destined to become one more instance where justice would not be obtained in Court. As in too many cases, the judge had already made his decision based on personal bias rather that the law and the evidence before him.

For a moment, I wasn't sure how to respond to Stroppel. I then decided that instead of venting my frustrations on him, I would simply solicit his comments:

"I'll see you tomorrow afternoon and I'll call to confirm the time. Tell me, Rick! How do you think the application will be decided?"

I detected a reluctance in Stroppel to discuss the matter but I was sure that he was marginally upset about the shenanigans of Perras and Pinckney in the Court room. After a few moments, Stroppel began to respond in his typical, diplomatic style:

"Well, Orest, it's hard to predict! I'd rather not speculate on the outcome of the application. It's best for us to prepare for Wednesday on the basis that we are proceeding to trial. If Perras decides to grant a Stay of Proceedings, then we won't be in jeopardy for failing to be ready. My philosophy in these situations is to hope for the best but prepare for the worst."

Stroppel's response was a reasonable reaction to the situation but it was obvious from the tone of his voice that he knew what the decision would be. His expressions revealed that he believed we should succeed on this application. However his doubts were evident in his response. I knew that I would not be able to penetrate the cold, impersonal barrier that Stroppel maintained with his clients. I therefore decided not to pursue my questioning any further. We then agreed that we would speak later on the telephone and we both left the meeting room and headed for the elevators.

One cannot measure the frustration that I felt at that time for the ineptitude of the criminal justice system. Had we failed to present a good case or if our legal argument was weak, I'm sure that Stroppel and I would both have accepted the situation better. However, to have a good case and a good legal argument and to still be denied a legal recourse is insulting and discouraging for any lawyer. Frustrating cases like this one create the greatest disillusionment for lawyers and their clients. This ultimately contributes to the increasing rate of alcohol and drug dependency in the legal profession. The problem is that this is the only solace that some lawyers can find to deal with such a perpetually hopeless situation.

Naturally, the harshness of the consequences is actually endured by the clients only. For Stroppel, this would simply be another unfortunate set-back on one of his many cases. However, for me, this was yet another instance when I had to endure the frustration as a victim of the legal system. I was glad that I could go home to rest because I needed time to recover from this mockery of justice.

On the afternoon of the following day, I met with Stroppel for over two hours. We reviewed the evidence and the conflicts in the anticipated testimony of the witnesses that Pinckney proposed to call on the first day of the trial. Stroppel had already reviewed the testimony of each witness from the Preliminary Hearing and we now examined in detail the various contradictions and inconsistencies. Stroppel had made notes regarding the important issues in his review of the evidence and now he needed my feed-back. As we spoke, Stroppel finalized his notes that would ultimately serve as his guide and check list for the evidence to be presented at trial. On the conclusion of our meeting, we agreed to meet the following morning at the Court room to hear the decision of Perras on our application. If he dismissed the application, we would have some time to discuss any further questions and to address any final comments before starting the trial.

On my return home, the most important task was to comfort my wife as we contemplated this pending horror. We were now stressed to unbelievable limits as we tried to cope with the uncertainty of proceeding to trial. I decided that I would not worsen my wife's fears by describing to her the obvious bias that was evident from the attitude and actions of Perras. Instead, I simply endured that anguish in silence. During those difficult moments, it was impossible to concentrate on anything else. Even reading or watching television was insufficient as a distraction from the reality of the nightmare that we now had to endure and survive.

After a restless night, I awoke the following morning mentally exhausted as I laboured to understand the unfair proceedings that now embroiled my life. I struggled to complete my morning routine without showing any signs of distress. I was determined to shield my family from the agony of the trauma that I endured. Luckily, a normal morning with four children is pandemonium at its best so my distracted movements were easily camouflaged. Immediately after breakfast, the children left for school and my wife left for work. I decided to leave for the Court House early to ensure that I would be there on time.

Because of the driving and parking problems, I arrived at the Court room only ten minutes before it was scheduled to convene. When I entered, I saw everyone busily preparing and chatting as the appointed time approached. After greeting Stroppel, I walked into the Prisoners Box. The Court Orderly secured the door and then prepared himself for another long and boring day in Court.

It never failed to amaze me just how much wasted manpower was expended in our Court system. Court Orderlies were typically hired from applicants who were retired from the police force or army service. These applicants could accept a lower salary as they already drew a comfortable income from their pensions. Their job was filled with ceremony, waiting and errands but featured little paperwork or responsibility. For them, it was a way of passing the time and earning an extra income for easy work. Most of them were pleasant and talkative. Although Court Orderlies must occasionally deal with accused people who are in custody and considered dangerous, their work does not require them to apprehend or subdue anyone. In actuality, their position in Court is ceremonial and for the convenience of the judges but is otherwise largely unnecessary. With careful planning and coordination, these tasks could easily be covered by the police service.

Similarly, the role of the Court Reporter is unnecessary as everything that she records in written shorthand is also tape recorded. In Provincial court, the Court Reporters are now being replaced in the similar situations by tape recorded transcripts that are typed when requested. This would be a satisfactory solution in the Queen's Bench Court but tradition has continued to preserve that role. It could also be said that the role of the Clerk who administrates oaths and organizes documents could be reduced and perhaps eliminated. A judge can easily perform these extra functions and these are often done by Provincial Judges on circuit. When one considers the total manpower that is utilized for one trial and the attendant costs, it is no wonder that the taxpayer is paying so much for court services. Yet ironically, the legal system is unable to account for the increased waiting time for getting a case to trial. As with most government services, it is simply a case of misplaced manpower and superfluous positions to complete unnecessary tasks. Because efficiency is not a necessity in government services, it is not even a consideration in the Court system.

As I sat in the Prisoner's Box, Pinckney walked over to Stroppel to apprise him of the changes that he was making in the order of witnesses. They also discussed the arrangement of the documents on the tables directly behind them. On the tables were the original documents that had been marked as Exhibits in the Preliminary Hearing and Pinckney provided a binder with photocopies of the documents to Stroppel. I stared at the documents on the table and contemplated the work that had been done to orchestrate this elaborate scene for the jury. It was evident that Pinckney and Christal were making all the right moves with calculated precision to impress the jury with my guilt so that they wouldn't have to prove it.

Finally, Pinckney and Stroppel acknowledged to the Clerk that they were ready to proceed and the Clerk disappeared through the back door to advise Perras. As we waited in silence, the suspense began to build within me and the nervous apprehension made me feel sick. Suddenly, the Clerk reappeared and made her announcement. Perras then flashed by her and quickly mounted his pedestal. After everyone was seated, Perras began to read out his speech and the Court Reporter hastily recorded the decision and his reasons. He began his dissertation by reciting the facts from the evidence as we had presented it. On completing the facts, he then touched on the legal arguments and the law as he proposed to apply it.

As I feared, Perras decided to dismiss this application. He had to acknowledge that we had proven that there was prejudice in presenting a defence to the Criminal charge. However, he justified his view on the basis that the Crown might suffer prejudice as well and therefore this factor in some way diminished the prejudice that I would suffer. What Perras said didn't really make sense but it did follow the arguments that Pinckney had made. From the perspective of the general public, he was simply agreeing with one lawyer and refuting the legal arguments of the other. In reality, he was ignoring the law and justifying a decision based on a pre-existing bias. In a few minutes, his speech was finished and he then adjourned Court to ten o'clock for the trial. Hastily, he whisked out of the Court room so that he could enjoy another coffee before Court was to resume.

Once Perras had left, Stroppel asked me to join him in the meeting room. As I walked in and closed the door, he began to speak:

"Orest, I know you must be disappointed but this is not the last word on the topic. If we have to go to the Court of Appeal, that will be one of the first grounds that I intend to argue. I would even be prepared to argue this one at the Supreme Court of Canada and I'm sure that this legal argument would succeed. However, let's hope that none of that is necessary. We've done a thorough job preparing for trial and I'm certain that Pinckney knows that he has a real flimsy case. I'm satisfied that we will win this case. Therefore, I want you to keep your spirits up. Just don't worry about what happened here today."

I appreciated Stroppel's remarks and as I listened, the shock of what had happened now began to settle onto my thoughts. I was now embarking on the uncertainty of a trial before a jury. I began to panic as thoughts of further disasters flashed through my mind. In those few moments, I stood before Stroppel in silence and then I began to respond:

"I appreciate what you are saying, Rick! It's just that nothing is happening the way it should. This is all a frightening experience for me. But, I'll be fine! I just need to take some time and go for a walk outside. The fresh air should help to clear my mind. If you don't need me, I'll meet you back here just before ten o'clock."

Stroppel stared at me in silence and simply nodded his head. I then turned and walked out the door to the elevators. At that moment, I felt totally betrayed by the law. During my legal career, I had proudly represented the law and expounded its virtues. I had defended the legal system from criticism and lauded it for its impartial and fair adjudications. Now, I was witnessing the darker side of the law, where legal principles were manipulated and ignored. The law was no longer used to bring justice to the public but rather to justify the course of action that a judge with unquestioned authority wished to follow. My life was now being slowly consumed and devastated by Christal and Pinckney, two experienced practitioners who knew all the right means to achieve the ends that they desired. My only hope was that Stroppel was capable of effectively presenting my defence in a Court room where all the odds were stacked against us.

Instead of lamenting over our latest set-back, I decided to focus on what lay ahead and any advantages that we had in our battle to prove that I was innocent of wrongdoing. At this point, the only logical salvation appeared to be the jury. It occurred to me that if at least one person on the jury could understand this case and Stroppel's arguments, then I could expect to succeed with my defence. It was logical and comforting to think that at least one juror would prove to be a reasonable and independently-minded individual. After all, it was Stroppel's assessment that all twelve jurors would likely reject Pinckney's arguments and throw this case out. All I could hope for was that at least one juror would not be duped by Pinckney's unscrupulous tactics to secure a conviction.

I resolved in my mind that I would proceed bravely into these uncharted waters and be guided by faith and my trust in Stroppel's judgement. From my experience as a lawyer, I understood that criminal trials looked more overwhelming to a client because the client is not objective. To the objective eye of the lawyer, everything is viewed in a better and more positive light. This is probably the main reason for the saying: A LAWYER WHO REPRESENTS HIM-SELF HAS A FOOL FOR A CLIENT. I knew that it was imperative that I calmly sit through these proceedings and not react adversely to the testimony of any of the witnesses. The task of presenting my defence was now in the hands of Stroppel and my role was essentially that of a concerned spectator.

As the appointed time approached, I ended my walk and returned to court to meet my jury. The time had come to be judged and I was about to embark on one of the most important journey's of my life.

CHAPTER TWENTY FOUR

THE JURY TRIAL

A s Court reconvened for the commencement of the trial, the harsh reality struck me that I had never participated in a jury trial before nor even witnessed one. Unlike American trial courts, a jury trial in a Canadian Court room is very much a rarity. The main reason is that few lawyers and judges know how to conduct a jury trial and therefore most of them avoid juries. Presumably, a trial before a judge without a jury is easier since a judge can overlook the errors and inappropriate comments of a lawyer in the presentation of his case. However, an error or an improper comment before a jury could result in a mistrial. A further detraction of jury trials is that they are more time consuming and tedious for everyone. The reason why jury trials are more protracted is that a jury must be excluded from the Court room during any applications relating to the admission of evidence. Also, there are more adjournments to accommodate discussions between the judge and the lawyers relating to procedure that the jury is not supposed to hear. In a trial featuring a judge without any jury, the judge simply pretends that he didn't hear those remarks which he should not have heard.

Ironically, the reason for having a jury trial is the same as the reason for avoiding one. This anomaly is the unpredictability of jury decisions. In criminal cases, the main reason for choosing a jury trial typically arises in cases where the physical evidence is persuasive that the accused person committed the crime and the only arguable issue is that of intent. A Defence lawyer often chooses a jury because judges are usually more callous on these questions. Most judges will conclude that the accused person had the required intent by drawing inferences from the physical evidence that the accused person intended to commit the crime. A jury, on the other hand, may sympathize with the plight of the accused person. Because the jury members have no legal background, they often ignore legal presumptions in favour of personal sentiment. In such cases, the Defence lawyer employs the tactic of making an emotional appeal to sway the opinions of the jury members to reduce the charge or to acquit. Indirectly, the jury is asked to ignore the factual evidence and the case law that would influence a judge to otherwise enter a guilty verdict on the criminal charge.

When the evidence of the Crown Prosecutor is conclusive, there really is no gamble in proceeding with a jury trial since a trial before a Judge would guarantee a conviction. However, if the Crown has a weak case based on circumstantial evidence, then the most sensible course is to present the case to a judge without a jury. Under such circumstances, an impartial and unbiased judge will consider the evidence and exercise his discretion to dismiss such a case. It is therefore quite unusual to be forced to proceed with a jury trial because of the assignment of a biased judge but that was my dilemma.

It is because of the fact that the jury members have no legal background that the unpredictability of jury trials presents a problem for both the Crown Prosecutor and the Defence lawyer. In presenting a case to the jury, both lawyers must attempt to impress them with theatrical performances. Suddenly, it is an important factor for the jury to like the lawyer and therefore agree with the arguments that the lawyer is presenting. The Defence lawyer cannot rely on legal presumptions since the jury members don't understand them. Furthermore, the Defence lawyer cannot hope to present arguments on the law since only the judge is allowed to instruct the jury on the law.

The lawyers must also make the case interesting to the jury to insure that they don't simply assume that the accused is guilty. After all, the jurors don't really want to be in court, are compensated minimally for expenses and receive no compensation for time away from their work or business. Furthermore, most jurors expect to be entertained by this experience of serving on a jury. Some jurors expect this experience to resemble a live human drama from a soap opera that they would ordinarily have watched on television. It becomes a challenge for the Defence lawyer to simply get the jurors to appreciate the serious implications of the decision that they will be making.

The actual adjudication of a case can be compared to a scientific process of "weighing the evidence" to determine if there is sufficient evidence to justify a guilty verdict. Symbolically, this process is referred to as the "Scales of Justice" and is represented by the image of a balance weigh scale. Since most crimes are based on what a person said or did, they are proven by sworn evidence from witnesses. In the process of weighing the evidence of a witness, the juror must assess the reliability of the witness. Unfortunately, the factors which discredit a witness are not easily understood by jurors or even by many people with Court room familiarity.

What the witness saw and heard has to be evaluated by the jurors to determine if it proves anything. A juror must recognize the distinction between comments that raise suspicion of possible involvement by the accused person and specific observations and statements that prove that the accused person committed a wrongful act. Because jury members have no experience in assessing evidence, they are prone to accepting comments from witnesses that raise suspicion as evidence of wrongful conduct by the accused person.

The most ironic feature of a jury trial is that the jurors usually know nothing about the law that applies to the assessment of the evidence in the case before them. They are expected to hear all the evidence first, to make notes of the "relevant evidence" and then are given a brief, selective description of the applicable law by the judge at the end of the trial. By that point in time, most jurors have formed their opinions based on their own evaluations and any directions that they receive at the end of the trial are simply considered in the context of supporting their viewpoints. In contrast, judges and lawyers understand legal principles such as the "standard of proof" and the "onus of proof" that must be satisfied by the Crown Prosecutor to achieve a conviction. The specific facts that must be proven are well known to lawyers and judges from prior cases and research of case law. However, all of this is foreign and unknown to jury members.

A notable example of how jury members often fail to appreciate the effect of the evidence given by witnesses became a top news story on the appeal of an accused person against his conviction. In an unusual move, the judge in the case, Justice W. Girgulis, wrote a letter to the Court of Appeal in support of the appeal. He declared that if he had heard the case without a jury, he would NOT have found the accused person guilty of the crime or entered a conviction. In his letter, Girgulis clearly stated that there was insufficient evidence for a finding of guilty. However, he was unable to interfere with the verdict, making it necessary for a conviction to be entered and for an appeal to be taken. What was unusual about the situation was that this judge chose to speak out against an unfair conviction at the risk of being criticized for doing so. Most judges would have followed the usual practice of remaining silent and treating the case as simply one more example of a wrongful conviction by a jury that he would have to forget.

These wrongly made convictions by juries arise because juries have the sole responsibility for deciding what statements from witnesses to believe and what statements to ignore. Unfortunately, jury members are ill equipped to assess the value of statements made by witnesses or what such statements prove. Also, jury members may be wrongly impressed by the number of witnesses called by the Crown Prosecutor to give evidence. In many cases, only a few of the witnesses contribute any factual evidence to the case. Often, a witness may confirm nothing more than an acquaintance with the accused person. However, a juror may assume that the presence of a large number of witnesses is indicative of a strong case against the accused person.

One further variable that causes concern for lawyers undertaking jury trials is the limited opportunity for presenting arguments to the jury. The use of opening remarks and closing remarks by either lawyer is strictly monitored. Only the judge is allowed to describe to the jury what law is applicable and how it is to be applied in the particular case. A lawyer's argument on the law may be totally ignored in the judge's instruction to a jury. Furthermore, the jury is instructed from the start to take all their directions from the judge. It is therefore typical for jury members to be impressed and subtly influenced by incidental remarks emanating from the judge. Such remarks are not confined to the closing statement when the judge instructs the jury but also includes all those remarks during the trial. When the judge asks questions of the witnesses or admonishes anyone, the jurors form impressions that ultimately affect the decision they will make. Unfortunately, it is difficult to prove to an Appeal Court what effect any remarks may have had on the ultimate decision of the jury.

Although it is assumed that a judge plays an insignificant role in the jury's determination of a verdict, the reality is shockingly otherwise. The judge is in an unquestionably authoritative position to discreetly influence the jury during the trial. Additionally, he is also in a critical position to direct the jury on how to reach the verdict on the conclusion of the trial. After the trial, both lawyers are allowed to address the jury with their final remarks. However, after that is concluded and before the jury retires to consider its verdict, the judge addresses the jury. In his statement to the jury, he advises them in general terms about the principles of law that they should consider. He may also advise the jurors what evidence was given to prove the facts required for a conviction. The judge's remarks are based on his assessment of the evidence which may conflict with that of the lawyers. The judge's instructions to the jury typically contemplate that the jury will accept his statement of the evidence and decide the verdict based on his assessments. In many cases, the verdict of the jury is a magnification of the judge's specific directions and reflect his personal assessment and preference for the disposition of the case.

This was the actual situation that awaited me as I embarked on the most important trial of my life. Twelve strangers had been picked to be my jurors but they would already bring a negative impression of me into the Jury Box from the jury selection process. They would listen to the judge who already demonstrated a bias against me. My only hope was that Stroppel was equipped to repel these negative influences and demonstrate my innocence to them. I now had to put my full faith in the justice system that often didn't work and I had good reason to be concerned for my ultimate fate.

As I entered the Court room, both Pinckney and Stroppel were at their tables reviewing their notes prior to the beginning of the trial. Christal was talking to Pinckney and getting ready to leave the Court room before Court resumed. It was a relief to know that Christal would not be sitting through the trial in the public gallery. Otherwise, he would try to influence the evidence of witnesses through his gestures as he began to do at the commencement of the Preliminary Hearing. Normally, a judge will direct that witnesses who have not testified be excluded from the Court room while other witnesses gave their testimony. This avoided the possibility that the evidence of one witness might be influenced by the other. Since Christal was a possible witness, he too was excluded under this procedure. However, he could still influence witnesses as they arrived at the Court House but at least his role in affecting the testimony of witnesses would be reduced.

As I approached Stroppel, he turned and stared at me. With concern in his voice, he asked:

"I was beginning to wonder where you were. Are you feeling okay?"

I slowly responded by nodding affirmatively. The Court Orderly then directed me into the Prisoner's Box and closed the door behind me. As I settled into my uncomfortable seat, I looked up at Pinckney who was passing the remaining minutes by chatting flirtatiously with the Court Clerk. Under other circumstances, I might have found his actions which flattered his egotistical self-image to be amusing. However, my thoughts were now riveted to the reality of the pending ordeal that continued to consume all of my waking energy. As I watched the final minutes pass by, my body was gripped in the anxiety and stress that immobilized me. I could no longer think positively about the outcome of the trial and instead had to focus on surviving this ordeal and to mark my progress with each passing witness.

As I looked around, I noticed that the Clerk had disappeared to find Perras. Suddenly she reappeared, the Court was called to Order and Perras mounted his lofty perch. Perras had now adopted a stern and foreboding expression that signalled his desire to complete this case in an expeditious manner. Once settled into his nest, he asked both lawyers if they were ready for the jury to be brought in. Stroppel immediately rose to his feet to inquire about a problem that had arisen earlier:

"My Lord, there was some mention on Monday about a juror asking to be excused. I understand that we'll be addressing that issue at this time."

A concern had arisen prior to court being convened two days earlier with one of the jurors who now did not want to serve on the jury. The apparent problem was that he would be missing too much work and he wanted to be excused. Naturally, if he had made this known at the time of jury selection, one of the lawyers would have voted to exclude him even if the judge did not grant his request to be excused. However, at this late date, this would have left the jury one member short and this was an undesirable situation. When the issue arose on Monday, Stroppel had requested that the concern be settled in Court so that he could make representations on this critical question. Perras agreed that the situation would be settled just prior to the start of the trial. However, Perras decided to direct the Sheriff's officer to meet with the juror to deal with this problem.

In response to Stroppel's inquiry, Perras responded in a defensive manner:

"Well, what I have been advised is that he wasn't asking to be excused so much as he was apparently what they call a hardship case. He has spoken to the sheriffs department and I understand that they are handling it so that he has no problems with serving and is quite content."

Stroppel acknowledged this comment and sat down. However, it was obvious to everyone that the tenor of the conversation with the dissatisfied juror would have been stronger than acknowledged by Perras. A juror would typically be told that he had to serve on the jury. His failure to do so would be enough for the judge to declare him to be in contempt of court and to be sent to jail. On this kind of direction, it was obvious that any juror would attend when required. However, such a juror would likely adopt an attitude of being unresponsive to the work that had to be done. Naturally, such a juror might look for the quickest resolution to the trial so that he could return to his work. Such a juror was a detriment to the whole system of adjudication by juries and would obviously jeopardize the prospect of a fair and just verdict in this case. What Perras sanctioned was a blatant interference with a juror to the detriment of the Defence case but nothing could be done about it.

Perras then looked at the Court Orderly and directed him to bring in the jury. The jury walked into the Court room through a door on the back wall located on the opposite side to the one used by Perras. The jurors walked in an organized single file and sat in the specific order that they were chosen. It was obvious that they were coached on this procedure and I wondered what else they might have been coached or influenced to do. It was also obvious that they would use the same corridor as the Judge to enter and leave the Court room and therefore some interaction between them was inevitable. As soon as the jurors were seated, the Clerk proceeded to call out the name of each juror for the Court

Record and each one stood and responded in acknowledgement. During this time I tried to assess how each juror might respond to my case. I wondered which ones would understand my situation and believe that I was innocent of wrongdoing. While I carefully studied each one, I tried not to stare at any one juror to avoid making a bad impression. Somehow, it seemed to me that the jurors lacked any interest in their role as jurors. I had to ultimately accept the fact that I could not form any proper conclusion about any of them.

The Clerk then proceeded to administer the oath to the jury in which the jurors committed themselves to fulfilling their obligations to deliver a fair verdict in this case. The jurors were then seated and Perras proceeded with his opening remarks to the jury. His remarks included the standard warnings not to speak to anyone about the case while it was in progress and to disregard anything that they might have heard or read about this case. They were then told that if anyone approached them to talk about this case, they should decline to say anything and to report this incident to the Court Orderlies. Perras then advised them that all their directions on how to adjudicate the case would come from him. They would decide the case from the evidence they heard in the context of his directions on how the case should be decided. All of his remarks sounded like they were quoted from a textbook but there was no doubt from his remarks that he remained the key person in the Court room. Although the jury would provide the verdict, Perras would be in charge of how that verdict was reached and would direct its determination. When I heard these directions from Perras, it became clear that this jury was effectively nothing more than the puppet that was controlled by the Master Puppeteer. If the jury made the decision that Perras desired, nobody could blame the jury and Perras could shield himself from criticism. The shocking reality was that I was still on trial before Perras and the role of the jury was actually secondary in importance.

Perras then advised the jury that the trial would start with opening remarks by the Crown Prosecutor who would describe what he proposed to prove in this case with the evidence of the Crown witnesses. Perras then remarked that the jurors should not treat these remarks as evidence or proven facts but merely as an indication of what the evidence of the Crown Prosecutor would prove. As I watched the jurors listening to these comments, it was evident that some were listening intently while others were noticeably bored as they waited for the case to proceed. Each of the jurors held a notepad and pen which was provided to them for the purpose of making notes. To this point, none of them made any gestures to record anything or even to create some doodle-artwork. I tried to remain hopeful that this would not be a sign of their efforts and energy in the trial.

As soon as Perras completed his remarks, he called on Pinckney to begin. Pinckney rose to his feet, adjusted a speaking stand that he positioned on his table to face the jurors and then adjusted some notes on the stand. With comic-like exaggerated gestures, he peered at his notes though half-lens glasses that dangled at the end of his nose. Slowly, he began to speak solemnly about the grave and sinister crime that they would soon hear about in evidence. As he

326 The Lawyer in the Prisoner's Box

began to warm up, he gave his description of the real estate transaction to the jury. I assumed that his script for this speech much have been developed by an experienced fiction writer as it bore only an incidental resemblance to the evidence that was presented at the Preliminary Hearing. A gracious assessment of Pinckney's remarks was that it was the Crown's theory but it was a gross misrepresentation of reality.

I suddenly became aware, as I listened to Pinckney's remarks in his opening address to the jury, that his derogatory remarks bore a strong resemblance to those of Nash at the Preliminary Hearing. Both Pinckney and Nash had used the same tactics of exaggerating the evidence in its darkest pretext to improperly influence the Court. However, Pinckney decided to make his speech even more colourful by stressing how deceitful, dishonest and fraudulent I was in my actions. It really didn't seem to matter that prior to or since this transaction, I had never been accused or charged with doing anything dishonest. Instead, Pinckney simply contended that on this one real estate transaction, I decided to deceive everyone and to mastermind a devious plot to create a fraudulent deal that was nothing more than a "sham". According to Pinckney, everyone in the transaction was merely my pawn and everyone acted honestly except me. He declared that the only reason that Heritage Trust lost money was that I circumvented the honest intentions of everyone. He concluded that I did this to deviously mislead Heritage Trust and to effect a profit on a real estate deal. Pinckney left the impression that such a person was obviously guilty of fraud and should be convicted and punished before society is exposed to an even more dangerous and sinister plot.

As I listened to Pinckney's description, I began to wonder if he practised any moral ethics in the way he conducted the prosecution of his cases. Not only were his statements to the jury a total misrepresentation of the evidence that emerged at the Preliminary Hearing but also a vengeful character assassination. His accusations about devious and dishonest actions were nothing more than malicious slander for a gullible jury. Naturally, the jurors were ready to accept these fictitious rumours because of a general public desire to believe that any lawyer on trial is a crook. The fact that I had been a lawyer for seventeen years and had never improperly mishandled anyone's money was now ignored in Pinckney's sleazy tabloid narrative.

Pinckney's unfounded accusations completely ignored the realities in my personal life. As a lawyer with a real estate practice, it was common to have large deposits in my trust account. Often my banking trust balance was in the millions of dollars. Had I truly wanted to steal money from others, all I had to do was write the cheque. With the type of cunning and planning that Pinckney attributed to me, I could have moved to a Caribbean Island and retired as a millionaire at an early age. After all, there had been several lawyers in Alberta who had done just that, leaving the Law Society to settle the claims of their clients. One lawyer was even clever enough to leave before he was detected so that he could enjoy a retirement that the rest of us only dream of. However, there was no concern about my past honesty since Pinckney was now drawing on the general resentment of the general public against lawyers to win the hearts of these jurors.

The truth was not really relevant to Pinckney as his single goal was to secure a conviction against me that would ultimately justify his decision to allow Christal to lay the fraud charge in the first place. From Pinckney's perspective, if there was no dishonesty, all he had to do was convince the jury that there had to be dishonesty involved to cause a loss to the mortgage company. The jury would easily conclude that the reason that I was in the Prisoner's Box was that I was the guilty party. Pinckney's main strategy was actually simple: all he had to do was plant enough suspicion in the mind of the jury. The decision of the jurors to convict would be natural since this would justify their presence in this long and boring procedure. Since Pinckney had no evidence of dishonest conduct, he would simply parade a number of witnesses before the jury who would confirm their contact with me during the time of the transaction. Ultimately, the suspicion would continue to be aroused until the jury, weary and tired of all the evidence, would conclude that there was a connection between me and the loss of the money. At that point, the jurors would be willing to accept Pinckney's theory since they really didn't understand what was going on. I suddenly recalled a description by Murphy about this tactic which seemed to eloquently but crudely describe it: IF YOU THROW ENOUGH SHIT AGAINST SOMEBODY, SOME OF IT IS GOING TO STICK. There was no doubt that Pinckney was going to do just that and I was the sitting target in the Prisoner's Box. The jury would watch this contest and as my character became blemished, they would naturally become revolted at the sight of me.

At the conclusion of his dissertation, I expected Stroppel to stand up and rebut all of these comments while presenting the Defence position on the case. Not only did this seem to be the fairest procedure to follow but it was also my impression that this was a standard procedure. After all, the legal system is supposed to be a forum where fairness is practised to allow the two opposing sides to have an equal opportunity. In Canada and the United States, the criminal justice system is supposed to protect the rights of the accused person by giving him every opportunity to rebut the case of the Crown Prosecutor. The jurors had now heard a series of negative accusations and it was only proper that they should hear the position of the Defence case.

The problem that was created by Pinckney's opening remarks to the jury was that it provided them with only one perspective. A failure to answer it would leave the jury with that one perspective as they assessed the evidence that they would then hear. Without hearing the opening remarks and rebutting remarks of Stroppel, the jury would naturally assume that there was no rebuttal or defence. They would therefore only listen to the evidence in the context of watching "the fulfillment of a prophecy" as described by Pinckney. It was essential for them to hear the position of the Defence lawyer so that they could assess the evidence as they heard it to determine if it supported the Crown Prosecutor's theory or the explanation of the Defence lawyer. In short, without a rebuttal from Stroppel, this would become a one-sided trial where the obvious verdict was the one being proposed by Pinckney.

The final remarks of Pinckney were an explanation of the documents arranged on the tables directly behind the lawyers. He explained that photocopies of the documents had been made and inserted into binders with tabs to identify the number of the Exhibit as marked in the Preliminary. He proposed to enter each of the documents as Exhibits at the trial. The procedure contemplated that as each document was identified by a Crown witness, the original document would be marked by the Clerk. The binders were created to provide the jury, judge and lawyers with a reference to follow during the trial. However, the jurors were reminded that at the conclusion of the trial, they would be given the original documents in the deliberation rooms. The binders would be left in the Court room so that the jury's decision would be based on an assessment of the original documents actually entered as Exhibits. Because photocopies tend to distort details on documents and sometimes fail to reproduce a document accurately, they are viewed as inferior evidence in Court. Pinckney's premise was that the jurors would view the photocopies throughout the trial but make no assessment until they viewed the originals at the end of the trial. The reality was that the jurors would formulate their assessments on the photocopies and assume that the originals were the same. In spite of this obvious problem, Perras approved the procedure and Pinckney began to hand out binders to the jurors. Perras and Stroppel also received a binder. Strangely, no binder was provided for me to view even though I was the one who ultimately had to respond to all of this evidence.

Once this was completed, Pinckney announced to the Court that as his first Crown witness, he was calling Nadia Foster. As the Court became quiet, I stopped breathing as I stared at Stroppel and waited for him to react. Stroppel continued making notes and there was no reaction in Court that something had been missed. I tried to get Stroppel's attention but he was looking away from me and I was seated out of his range of vision. As the Clerk called Nadia Foster into the Court room, she walked in with nervous hesitation and was directed to the witness stand where the witness oath was administrated. Pinckney then began his examination and I slumped back in my chair, realizing that there was nothing that could now be done. This blatant procedural injustice was just one more blow that would make it difficult to convince the jury of my innocence. Sadly, I was forced to endure it without even a complaint regarding this obvious unfairness. What was so shocking was that nobody, not even Stroppel, reacted to this situation!

The evidence of Nadia Foster was similar to the evidence she gave at the Preliminary Hearing. Her role in the transaction was that of the vendor of the acreage property that she and her husband sold to my company. She had no direct contact with me and provided very little tangible evidence so her testimony was short. The next witness was her husband, Donald Foster and his testimony was even shorter since he had no direct dealings with anyone. Donald Foster was not called at the Preliminary Hearing and the only logical reason for his appearance at the trial was to provide the jury with a repetition of evidence. I suspected that their testimony showing lack of knowledge was only used to create suspicion for the jury.

At the conclusion of these two witnesses, Perras called for the mid-morning adjournment and the jury filed out in their proper order through their back door. Meanwhile, Perras disappeared through the other back door, only to meet the jurors in the corridor behind. The jurors were directed into a holding room in the back where they were treated to coffee and other beverages, gourmet doughnuts and gourmet muffins. Although the government pays only a token daily allowance for the expenses of jurors, they treat the jurors to first class refreshments and nobody has ever questioned the irony of this.

The bizarre effect of this festive atmosphere is to encourage jurors to socialize and to form friendships which continue after the case is concluded. Stories abound of entire juries that meet socially on a continual basis to foster friendships that form from these social introductions. Some social courtships that began in the jury room even resulted in marriages. The unfortunate consequence of these social alliances is that they diminish the desire and concern of those initially serious jurors to consider the verdict and vote according to their own conscience. Instead the jurors tend to vote according to the sentiments of their newly-found friends. The result is that Court system does not maintain twelve independent and impartial jurors during the continuation of a case but rather creates twelve jurors who influence each other through social pressure. The timid introverted jurors become more susceptible to accepting and maintaining the biases of the more dominant members of the group rather than making independent assessments.

As soon as Perras disappeared, the Court Orderly opened the door to the Prisoner's Box. As I stepped out, I told Stroppel that I wanted to speak with him. We both then slipped out to the meeting room and I immediately began by protesting to him.

"Rick, I was absolutely flabbergasted by what Pinckney told the jury in his opening remarks. All of it was pure science fiction. How could he make up stuff like that and then present it to the jury to mislead them on what actually happened? It's an outright lie! Yet, the jury seems to be swallowing everything he said and is now salivating for more. Is there anything we can do to set the record straight?"

Stroppel looked up at me and his forlorn expression told the whole story. This trial had taken a bad turn when Perras dismissed our application. Now, Pinckney was using disreputable tactics to improperly influence the jury. It was easy to feel disillusioned with these types of developments. However, Stroppel was an experienced trial lawyer and he showed confidence in dealing with these unfortunate set-backs.

After pausing for a few moments to collect his thoughts, Stroppel responded in a philosophical tone:

"Well, regarding a statement to the jury, I am not allowed to say anything until the Crown's case is finished. Before leading Defence evidence, I can make a statement to the jury about our case. One tactic that I'm considering using is to order a written transcript of Pinckney's remarks. When I make my opening remarks, I'll go through them and point out that none of them have been proven by the evidence. His remarks are so far out that I think he'd be in trouble with the jury if we did that."

It was easy for Stroppel to be philosophical and objective. After all, he was not the one enduring these abusive accusations and character slurs. I couldn't simply accept Stroppel's comments without questioning him further:

"I'm really concerned, Rick! I was watching the jury while Pinckney delivered his remarks. Despite what you say, I think Pinckney's remarks really had an effect on the jury. If we can't respond to the evidence right now, what we do later may not help our case. By the time Pinckney finishes his case, the jury will already have their minds made up. By the time we get to present our defence, it will be too late to get them to change their minds. Now, I have to admit that I don't have any experience with juries. However, I saw how they reacted and I'm sure that I'm right on this."

Stroppel hesitated for a few moments and then calmly responded to my excited reactions:

"Well, first of all, I don't think that you should conclude that the jury will decide anything before they hear our evidence. As the days pass, they will tend to forget Pinckney's remarks as they follow the evidence that he is leading. Because there is no real evidence of wrongdoing on your part, the jury is going to be curious and more accepting of my remarks when I make them at the end of Pinckney's case. Don't forget that I will be cross-examining each witness and pointing out the weaknesses in the Crown case. As far as my initial assessment of the jury, I find them difficult to get a reading on. None of them have taken any notes so far. I find that really strange. I'm wondering if they are really following what is happening or even know what the case is all about. I'm going to continue to watch their reactions carefully but I'm concerned that I may have to keep everything as simple as possible. Otherwise, they won't understand what the issues are and what our defence is. We'll discuss this more as the case progresses."

Stroppel was about to stand up and leave to get a coffee when I confronted him with a final remark

"I'm just starting to realize just how many advantages the Crown Prosecutor has over the Defence lawyer in a trial situation. I always thought that the situation was supposed to be fair to both sides with the benefit of any doubt in favour of the accused. Now I don't see it that way. Am I missing something?"

As Stroppel reached the door, he looked back and provided me with this insight:

"Orest, I've found that the Crown has every advantage in the Court system except one: that the accused is presumed innocent and that the Crown must prove its case beyond a reasonable doubt. All we have to do is make sure that the jury understands that and we'll be just fine in your case. So just relax! Let's just wait and see what develops."

I sat slumped in my padded chair in the conference room, which was a delightful improvement over the wooden bench that was straining my back. When Stroppel disappeared, I began to reflect on his comments and tried to develop a positive outlook on the continuation of the trial. I realized that Stroppel was right in saying that one could not prejudge the jurors or the progress of the trial at this early stage. It was only natural for me to react with such distress as I watched everything evolve so unfavourably. I was clearly skeptical of the way the trial was proceeding but I resolved to watch the proceedings with an open mind. It was my job to assist Stroppel by offering helpful suggestions rather than complaints. It was going to be a long and painful trial but I was determined to see this trial through with courage. I was now in for the fight of my life and I had to vindicate myself at last.

CHAPTER TWENTY FIVE

THE DEFENCE CASE

Many misconceptions about the legal system originate from the growing influence of television. The amount of time that the average person spends in front of a television set is increasing as each successive generation becomes more dependent on it. Soon, it will become our main source of learning with educators projecting themselves to larger audiences more efficiently.

From its earliest programming, television offered dramatic programs featuring Court room trials for the entertainment and enlightenment of its audiences. Of course, since these programs were produced in the United States, the procedures in the Court room were loosely modeled after the American procedures. Although these may vary significantly from those in our courts, Canadian viewers readily accepted what they saw as their legal system in operation. Fictional Court room dramas drew large audiences who happily watched as good prevailed over evil and the innocent were vindicated while the evil were punished.

The problem with television programs is that accuracy in depicting realism in the Court system is secondary to the main goal of presenting an entertaining program. Furthermore, television programs must condense a court case that might have continued in the legal system for two years or longer into approximately forty minutes. A television trial is depicted as a forum in which both parties stand before a jury to explain their stories. Before the program is concluded, the jury delivers a verdict providing an obvious and fair resolution to the case. Television Judges are typically portrayed as impartial and fair-minded people with integrity that is beyond reproach. The Defence lawyers are the heros of the under-dogs as they fight with unwavering dedication to defend the innocent client from harm. These television Defence lawyers usually possess an inexhaustible array of tactics and explanations to satisfy any juror that the accused person may appear to be guilty but is actually innocent. A viewer of these programs is forced to accept the inevitable conclusion that the justice system never fails. On television, only guilty people are convicted and punished for serious crimes.

Because of this multitude of misconceptions, people often find it very disillusioning to appear in court on a case and experience how the legal system actually works. In addition to court delays and tedious procedures, the actual results are seldom consistent with what the general public typically expects. In too many cases, the Court proceedings lack any semblance of justice in the eyes of those involved. Most Judges flaunt an attitude of noticeable pomposity and openly display their short tempered and biased dispositions. Often, Criminal Defence lawyers handle cases unsympathetically and arrogantly and openly distance themselves from the plights of their clients. The actual court procedures are far more technical than anyone imagines and often inappropriately favour the Crown's position, creating a hardship on the accused person. Sadly, the idealism portrayed on television is just as absent from our legal system as are the legal philosophies of text-book scholars.

One misconception that was particularly significant in my case was the strategy that was employed to defend criminal charges where there was no real evidence of wrongdoing. Stroppel's main strategy was not focused on presenting evidence to rebut the Crown Prosecutor's case but rather to argue simply that there was no evidence of wrongdoing on my part. His tactic was therefore to carefully cross-examine witnesses who made statements that could arouse suspicion of wrongdoing. The questions were specifically directed to clarify their testimony and to insure that no adverse inference could be drawn from it. Because the Crown Prosecutor had already defined the wrongful act as "causing a false mortgage application to be made to Heritage Savings & Trust", it was only the testimony of a few key witnesses that was actually relevant. Stroppel ultimately fashioned my Defence on the basis of what these witnesses conceded on cross-examination.

The art of cross-examination by a Defence lawyer is a scientific talent in that the lawyer must determine if anything that was said is proof of any wrongful conduct. The real skill of a Defence lawyer is to avoid cross-examination on points which are not relevant and may confuse the jury or become counter-productive. Stroppel's primary task was to keep the jurors on task by focusing them on the main question. This also meant that Stroppel had to prevent Pinckney from confusing them with his tactics of raising irrelevant issues, more commonly referred to as "red herrings". Unfortunately, Pinckney was calling a large number of witnesses with the intention of leading evidence on irrelevant or fringe developments in the case. In doing so, it was inevitable that he would place a number of "red herrings" before the jurors to feast on. The challenge for Stroppel was to make sure that the jury understood that such testimony was irrelevant.

As the trial proceeded, the same witnesses that appeared at the Preliminary Hearing were called to again testify at the trial. These witnesses were now well rehearsed on what needed to be said. For their added assistance, Pinckney and Christal arranged for each of them to receive a transcript of the questions and their corresponding answers from the Preliminary Hearing. With this written transcript and the coaching of Pinckney and Christal, it was assured that the evidence of the witnesses would be more precise, definitive and improved than the evidence heard at the Preliminary Hearing. Since the witnesses could now confidently predict the questions and were well rehearsed on the answers that the Crown Prosecutor expected, the task of cross-examining these witnesses became more difficult. Unfortunately, the jury was unaware of these earlier proceedings or the procedure used to prepare these Crown witnesses. Therefore, they would naturally assume that these Crown witnesses possessed remarkable skills to recall the many incidental details of this typical transaction after the passage of seven years!

Of the twenty-one witnesses that were called by the Crown Prosecutor at the Preliminary Hearing, two were not called as Crown witnesses at the trial because they gave testimony favourable to the Defence case. Of the nineteen Crown witnesses that were recalled for the trial, only four of them gave testimony that was relevant to the wrongdoing specifically described in the criminal charge. Yet the remaining Crown witnesses were called by Pinckney on the pretext that they could provide incidental information on how the transaction in question proceeded. Typically, a Crown Prosecutor will significantly reduce the number of witnesses being called at the trial to avoid calling anyone who can't provide material evidence on the issue before the court. Pinckney, on the other hand, chose to call all these extraneous Crown witnesses. In addition, he called ten new Crown witnesses who offered no evidence that related to the issue before the court. His tactic of trying to create suspicion worked not because of what the Crown witnesses said but rather because there were so many of them. All of the Crown witnesses could identify me now and this was enough to add to the suspicion of the jury.

As each Crown witness was called, Stroppel first made notes of their testimony with a view to noting any contradictions from prior testimony. During his cross-examination, he was entitled to bring up any irregularity with previous testimony and in fact to demonstrate this by quoting from the prior testimony. I soon became aware that Stroppel appeared very timid and cautious with his questions to the Crown witnesses. During a break in the proceedings, I raised this question and he advised:

"There are actually a few reasons for the approach that I am following in the cross-examination of Crown witnesses. My main concern is to avoid alienating the jury. A juror could turn against you for attacking a witness if he feels that you are wrong for doing so. If it's a point that isn't that important, you loose more by alienating the juror. Another reason is that I don't want to create a backlash with Perras on anything if it is avoidable. Certainly on something inconsequential, it's easier to simply let it slide. Finally, it's not a good tactic to confuse the jury by making an issue out of a minor point because it draws their attention away from the main question. Pinckney is already confusing the jury enough with all these unnecessary witnesses. It would only hurt our case to create more confusion with irrelevant issues. I have therefore decided to limit my questions to the main issue and I'm sure that we'll win this case by doing so."

Although I wasn't satisfied with his approach, I knew that this was an area where I had to let Stroppel decide how to handle the case. I would have preferred a more aggressive cross-examination of each witness to challenge credibility and to demonstrate our position. After all, this is what we see on television and it always works in those Court cases. However, I had to accept that this was the real world and there were other factors that had to be considered.

One of the unwritten rules of Court procedure that made our legal system more subdued than the American Courts is that of protocol. Some of the antics and tactics that Criminal Defence lawyers try in American Courts would immediately result in a harsh reprimand in a Canadian Court room. In our legal system, judges freely intervene to limit questions and to even regulate the tone of voice used by the lawyer. Unfortunately, witty and polite cross-examination is only effective before a judge who readily understands the purpose of the questions. To most jurors, such a performance is boring and meaningless and leaves them unimpressed.

As Pinckney got entrenched in presenting the Crown case to the jury, it became evident that Perras was not prepared to play a neutral role in the proceedings. As the Crown witnesses presented their evidence, Perras put on a display of making copious notes of the testimony. After EACH witness was cross-examined, Perras would question the witness on an item which would reaffirm the position of the Crown. It was obvious that as a result of Perras's conduct, the jury would hear and remember only those points that the judge raised. All of this had the effect of planting an obvious message in the minds of the jurors of the "important" statements made by each Crown witness. This deliberate tactic began early in the trial and noticeably irritated Stroppel. After all, this form of blatant interference in the conduct of a trial was totally inappropriate and would have a persuasive effect on the jury.

As I watched Stroppel wrestle with his emotions while he endured these continual interjections by Perras, I understood the dilemma that he faced. The conduct of Perras was obvious and it was Stroppel's responsibility to deal with the situation by raising an objection. However he was already concerned about alienating and upsetting Perras, especially in the midst of an important trial. There was no recommended approach for telling a Judge whose arrogance was symptomatic of an oversized ego, that he could not do as he wished in HIS Court room. Any remarks by Stroppel would be received by Perras as an affront on his unquestionable rights. Such a move would almost certainly guarantee that Perras would thereafter use every opportunity to hamper Stroppel in his defence of my case. However, to do nothing would also guarantee that the Crown's case would be the only one considered by the jury, since Perras made his bias so obvious.

On the third day of evidence from Crown witnesses, Stroppel had endured as much as he could of the inappropriate conduct of Perras. At the conclusion of the morning session, Stroppel abruptly called me into the Meeting Room outside the Court room. As we entered, he immediately blurted out:

"Orest, I'm sure that you must have noticed that Perras is continually interfering in this case. I'm satisfied that his actions are influencing the jury. Since the trial started, he has consistently questioned each Crown witness after my cross-examination was concluded and he always raised the same points that Pinckney did. In my experience, a jury is usually swayed by anything a judge says or does during the trial. His comments and tactics are helping to build the case for the Crown and that's not fair. A trial is supposed to be a one-on-one contest. I don't mind matching skills with Pinckney but Perras is making this contest TWO AGAINST ONE. The jury will accept anything that Perras says because he is the judge. I've been reluctant to do anything to this point but I feel that I must put an objection on the Court record. If we lose this trial, we can then at least present an argument to the Court of Appeal about his interference. Unfortunately, Perras isn't going to like what I'm going to say but I feel that we have no choice. I'd therefore like to know what your feelings on this matter are?"

We had now reached a critical moment in this trial. This decision would probably affect the total outcome of the trial. There was no scientific means for assessing the damage that was done or would be done by Perras in the course of this trial. The only certainty was that any objection directed at Perras would not be accepted graciously by him. On a positive note, the objection might cause him to be more careful but he could always find other ways to influence the decision of the jury. The prospect of doing nothing would not solve the problem and would lead to further interference from Perras. Furthermore, a failure to object would be tantamount to acceptance of his conduct and would diminish the likelihood of the success of our position before the Court of Appeal.

I wrestled with the dilemma for a few moments and then proceeded to respond to Stroppel's inquiry:

"Rick, I couldn't help but notice how Perras is interfering in the trial. I'm watching the jury closely and they seem to nod and agree each time Perras opens his mouth. I agree with you totally that the way that he is questioning the witnesses is directed at developing the Crown's case. It probably negates some of the effect of your cross-examination in clarifying the testimony of the Crown witnesses. I'm really concerned about the final impression that the jurors are getting. It's likely that any answers to Perras' question are the only ones that the jury will consider or even remember. I'm also convinced that Perras is definitely influencing the jury. I don't think there is any real choice here. If you don't do something to stop Perras from openly influencing the jury, then the obvious verdict is going to be a conviction. Therefore, I agree that you should make an objection on the Court record. Hopefully, this will cause Perras to change his approach in handling this trial."

Stroppel seemed to appreciate my support of his decision to raise this sensitive question in court. He was ready to leave the meeting room when I raised another question:

"I'm wondering if you have formed any impression of how the jury is reacting to the evidence that they are hearing on the Crown's case. Do you feel that they understand what the issues are, or do you feel that they are struggling with this case?"

As I finished speaking, Stroppel quickly interjected:

"Actually, Orest, I'm having a hard time reading the jury. We have already gone through a number of Crown witnesses and NOT ONE juror has even lifted a pencil to make notes of the testimony they heard. This is really strange because they are instructed to make notes to remember important points. Anyone would expect that at least a few of them would be seriously making notes to refer to later when they will be deliberating. Perhaps it's too early to tell or perhaps they are simply not impressed with any of Crown's case to this point. We'll have to wait and see how this develops during the trial."

As he finished, Stroppel walked out of the meeting room and I followed him. We both needed time to rest before resuming the tiresome ordeal of continuing a trial where so many witnesses had essentially nothing to say. As I thought about Stroppel's remarks about the jury, it occurred to me that there was another possibility as to why the jurors were not bothering to make any notes: PERHAPS THEY HAD ALREADY DECIDED ON THE VERDICT. The thought was too devastating to contemplate. I refused to accept the conclusion that this jury could be so easily influenced or that all of them would neglect their duties to consider all of the evidence. Surely, one of them would be able to see that there was no evidence of fraud and vote to prevent the jury from simply entering a conviction to expediently dispose of this case.

As my thoughts frantically contemplated this shocking scenario, I immediately reminded myself that these jurors looked like reasonable men and women. The defence that Stroppel would argue was a reasonable conclusion to form from the evidence presented by witnesses. When the trial was over, it would be obvious that there was no evidence of wrongdoing. It would therefore be difficult for all twelve jurors to simply enter a conviction without realizing that they must have a reasonable doubt about the Crown's case. Furthermore, any testimony that they heard would have to be considered in light of my personal testimony. This would surely satisfy anyone that the Crown Prosecutor had failed to prove wrongdoing on my part beyond a reasonable doubt.

I then resolved to maintain a positive perspective on the proceedings and the adjudication by the jury. I always had faith in the justice system and I had never feared to be judged by anyone for my conduct. I had nothing to hide and I was not afraid to be judged by the Devil himself. I felt confident that even the Devil, sitting in judgement with Perras, would have enough conscience to enter an acquittal in this case even if Perras did not. If the jurors were properly doing their job, they would have to consider the defence that was being presented. No matter what was said, there would have to be at least a few jurors who doubted that I was involved in any wrongdoing as proposed by Pinckney. I had to believe that the legal system worked and that I would see a just result in my case.

During the noon Court recess, I decided to go for a walk to distract my mind from generating more anxiety over the "showdown" that was about to take place between Stroppel and Perras. I tried to comfort myself by assuming that Perras would react in an objective manner and accept Stroppel's comments as an expression of legitimate concerns. He wouldn't have to acknowledge that his inexperience as a judge may have caused him to improperly interfere with the conduct of the trial. However, I understood clearly from experience that most judges typically accept any comments as personal criticisms. Instead of being objective, they become bitter and vindictive to lawyers who dare to question their conduct. The waiting caused my body to be totally stricken with nervous apprehension as I completed my walk and returned to Court. As I settled into my seat in the Prisoner's Box, I prayed that Stroppel's actions would not escalate into a major confrontation.

After three days of testimony at this trial, the week-end had arrived. Perras instructed the jurors not to discuss any part of the trial with anyone and to report any attempt by anyone to discuss the trial with them. Each of the jurors seemed to nod or acknowledge Perras' direction but it was evident that the jurors were now relaxed in these proceedings. I wondered if any of them would seriously comply with such a request. Instead of the solemn mood that these trials create for lawyers, the jurors were jubilant. They chatted and laughed with each other and it was obvious that friendships and alliances were forming that would ultimately affect the way that each juror would deliberate and vote.

It was Friday and Court would soon be adjourned for three days because of the Thanksgiving holiday. Stroppel chose to wait until the jury was dismissed for the week-end before stating his objection. As the jury left, Perras was about to adjourn Court when Stroppel rose to his feet and began to address Perras in his most respectful tone of voice:

"My Lord, I wonder if we could raise a point before we break for the week-end. I'll try to do so briefly. My Lord, it is apparent in the course of this trial that Your Lordship is from time to time questioning witnesses at the conclusion of the Examination-in-chief by my learned friend and cross-examination by myself. And, My Lord, I have decided to put a comment on the record because the manner of the questions put to the witnesses by the Court gives us some concern. My Lord, in our respectful submission, most, if not all, of the questions put by the Court to the various witnesses seem to be for the purpose of advancing the theory of the Crown. And I am aware that it is customary in this jurisdiction that a Judge may put questions to witnesses at the conclusion of examination and cross-examination for the purpose of clarifying certain points and we would certainly have no particular objection to that. But in my respectful submission, the questions being put by Your Lordship have tended to go beyond that. And I think it will be clear to Your Lordship where our concern lies. When the trial began, Your Lordship told the jury that the carriage of the case was in the hands of counsel and clearly that is where it should stay. I just wanted to put that objection on the record because it is a matter that is causing us concern as the trial proceeds."

While Stroppel was speaking, the Court room was deathly quiet. Everyone held their breath and waited to hear the reaction of Perras. As I watched his facial expressions, it was becoming obvious that he was not happy that Stroppel DARED to question his imperial authority to speak and to do as he wished in his Court room domain. When Stroppel finished speaking, Perras was silent for a few moments as he visibly struggled to calmly respond to this insolent remark that was questioning HIS conduct of HIS trial.

I truly expected Perras to react harshly by firing back at Stroppel to condemn his comment as a contempt of HIS court. However, Perras was now treading lightly because he must have realized that his conduct was obvious to everyone and Stroppel was right in making this objection. Perras ultimately responded in a defensive tone that his questions were only directed to clarify testimony. With indignation, he insisted that he was not asking questions to intentionally develop the case for the Crown. Then, he abruptly asked Pinckney for his position on this matter.

With an affectionate gaze in his eyes, Pinckney rose to his feet to offer support to his beleaguered comrade. Pinckney stated in a righteous tone of voice that he believed that the questions asked by Perras were appropriate. Pinckney then declared his support for these actions by declaring that in his opinion, it was a judge's right and even his duty to ask questions if he wished.

After Pinckney finished his complimentary tribute, Perras appeared bolstered by this valiant and loving demonstration of support. He then adjourned Court with a grand show of pomposity and left his perch. The confrontation was now over but the issue was certainly not resolved.

When Stroppel finally emerged from the Court room, he walked over to me and proffered one of his business smiles. He waited silently to allow me to ask him any questions that were on my mind. I reacted by asking about his assessment of the Crown's case and he immediately advised:

"All the evidence is coming just as we expected. There were really no surprises and Pinckney has already called most of his key witnesses. The evidence is very weak and I am satisfied that Pinckney has a serious problem in proving that you did anything fraudulent. All that the evidence shows is that you did a real estate deal and made a profit but that is a long way from being fraudulent. On the specific issue of the false mortgage application, it is obvious that the real culprit is either Stephen Garmaz or that broker with Premier mortgage. So from the point of view of the Defence case, everything is going well and I feel very confident about it."

I was relieved to hear his encouraging words, and I felt good that Stroppel had assessed the Crown's evidence in the same manner that I had. In the end, the jury would have to consider the evidence and determine what the verdict would be. Where the evidence is quite incriminating, a jury will often deliberate for a lengthy period of time to arrive at a verdict. In a case like this, it was obvious that I was innocent of any wrongdoing and especially fraud. Therefore I knew that the verdict was obvious and would take very little time to decide. I only hoped that the jurors were following the testimony carefully and not being blindly influenced by Pinckney and Perras.

Before I could respond to Stroppel, he continued:

"I've also had further thoughts about how this case should be presented to the jury. None of them seem to be responding to the evidence in the way that I expected. I don't see any of them taking notes and that bothers me. My assessment is therefore that we should play it safe and keep our defence as simple as possible. That's why I've decided to present our defence in a real simple way. Instead of arguing the technical questions of whether or not there is any real proof of fraud, I think that we should simply admit that there was a fraud. The issue then is simply who did it. The evidence is clear that it could have been either the mortgage broker or Garmaz. The way things stand with the Crown's case, there has to be a reasonable doubt right there. Don't worry about this now! We can discuss this tactic further after all the Crown evidence is before the Court and I have to proceed with my submissions."

What Stroppel now suggested really shock me up. It was now clear that Stroppel was prepared to assist the Crown's case by admitting part of their case: that a fraud had taken place. However, there was no real proof of any fraud and in fact it was obvious that Heritage Trust did not lose any money and that the mortgage loan was flawed by negligence and not fraud. Yet Stroppel was prepared to concede this point. Our only defence now was to argue that Garmaz and the mortgage broker were responsible for any resulting loss and not me.

As I took a moment to reflect, I found this proposal to be totally unacceptable. I had done the research for the certiorari application and I knew that there was no evidence on any of the elements of fraud. How could anyone, especially my lawyer, take the position that we would defend this case on the basis that a fraud had occurred? In that situation, my only hope would be that the jury would find me Not Guilty even though I was the only one in the Prisoner's Box. Every witness was called by the Crown Prosecutor to identify me as a participant in the transaction. The bias of Perras made it obvious to the jurors that he felt that I was guilty of the crime. It just didn't make sense that we were safe in assuming that the jury would find me Not Guilty after we made such an admission about the evidence.

While these thoughts flashed through my mind, I realized that I would have to consider this carefully and discuss it with Stroppel later. He was gesturing that he wanted to leave and I wasn't really prepared to discuss this question until I thought about it more. I knew we still had time to develop our ultimate strategy and I was glad that the evidence in Court was so favourable.

Stroppel then advised me that we would have to meet on Sunday to prepare for my testimony in Court which would be heard later in the week. I was feeling partially relieved that this case was finally being resolved. In spite of the grave concerns that we had about the conduct of Pinckney and Perras, I was anxious to see this nightmare dispersed from my life. As we parted from the elevators, I began to relax and savour the relief of the short rest that I would have over the week-end. The new week had to be more promising than the set-backs that we had witnessed during this first week of the trial.

During our Sunday meeting, Stroppel reviewed the questions that he proposed to ask but followed a strict policy of avoiding any comments on how to answer the questions. In Stroppel's world, it was improper to coach a witness by suggesting answers and so he simply wouldn't do it. Our meeting was routine and simply gave us both an opportunity to review our notes on the Crown witnesses. It was important to identify statements that raised suspicion of wrongdoing so that I could respond to these allegations.

Before I concluded our meeting, I expressed my concerns about conceding that the evidence showed that a fraud had taken place. Stroppel then explained his reasons for this unusual strategy:

"In a jury trial, I always prefer to put forward the strongest defence for their consideration. I try to avoid arguing about the side issues because that takes away the jury's attention from the main defence. From my experience, I can tell you that this is the best way to proceed. In your case, the main defence is that you were not involved in the mortgage deal at all. There is no evidence that you had anything to do with the mortgage except the questionable statements of Garmaz and the mortgage broker from Premier Mortgage. I've already shown in cross-examination that it is doubtful that you had any involvement there. Your evidence will further confirm that position. It therefore doesn't make sense to argue that there was no fraud since that becomes a side issue. Whether there was a fraud or not really doesn't matter to us since it is clear that you had nothing to do with it in any case."

I reluctantly agreed with Stroppel and simply hoped that he was right in his assessment. Because I had no experience in jury trials, I couldn't really debate this strategy with him. It was also obvious that his mind was made up so this was one of those times when I had to allow him to follow his judgement. I felt apprehensive about this strategy but I comforted myself with the thought that Stroppel had considerable experience and knew what was best.

Thanksgiving is a holiday that holds no special significance to a child and is usually viewed simply as a day off from school. For adults, however, this holiday becomes more meaningful with each year as we take time to truly give thanks and express our gratitude for all the blessings that we enjoy. On this day, more than any other holiday, we can reflect on the joys that fill our lives and cherish our family and friends for making this world such a beautiful place.

I especially enjoyed this Thanksgiving holiday because I could see a brighter future ahead. I knew that the painful ordeal that I endured with my family would soon vanish. For a change, I felt truly relaxed as I enjoyed the warmth of my family as we exchanged greetings with relatives and friends. I could visualize everything soon being like it used to be before this ordeal started.

The new week in court began with Pinckney calling the last of the Crown witnesses who had testified at the Preliminary Hearing and the testimony was predictable. Stroppel effectively demonstrated inconsistencies in the evidence of the various Crown witnesses during his cross-examination. Perras continued with his tactics of asking pointed questions of witnesses but he was now more careful and discreet in favouring the Crown's position. It was interesting to note occasional facial reactions from some jurors. However, throughout all the evidence, NOT ONE juror made any noticeable effort to take notes of any testimony. Yet, there were obvious items in the testimony presented that they would want to consider when deliberating on the evidence. Nevertheless, I was happy to see some reaction from the occasional juror which at least indicated that they were listening. However, I could not avoid the uncomfortable realization that they still continued to show very little interest in the actual issues in the trial.

The trial continued in the same manner as it had before but Perras was now noticeably more careful in his tactic of questioning each witness. As Pinckney continued to parade witnesses before the jury, I watched the jurors and tried to gauge their reactions. However I wanted to avoid staring at any one member of the jury for fear of making a juror uncomfortable with my presence in Court. With each witness, I became steadily more concerned that not one juror was making any notes, anywhere. This was in sharp contrast to both lawyers, the judge, myself, the Clerk and Court Reporter. As we carefully followed what was being said by each Crown witness, each of us made careful notes for our later reference. The jurors, on the other hand, had apparently come to this trial with the same attitude that most lawyers take to a legal convention. They obviously had no intention of learning, noting, or remembering anything from the speakers. This was certainly unusual and I wondered if any of the jurors really cared about what these witnesses were really saying. I now worried about the effect that this attitude would have in deciding the question of whether I was innocent or guilty.

On completing these witnesses, Pinckney began calling witnesses who had not been called at the Preliminary Hearing. These witnesses could offer no evidence relating to the actual mortgage application in issue. Instead, each of the witnesses commented on their incidental knowledge of one of the many documents which had no relevance to the real issue. Each of these Crown witnesses could easily have been excluded without affecting the Crown's case. The only real effect that these witnesses seemed to have is that their testimony seemed to raise unanswered questions about some documents marked as Exhibits. However these documents had no relevance to the issue that the jury would have to decide. It was obvious that Pinckney was trying to create as many "red herrings" as he could to confuse the jury. Presumably, this tactic would make it easier for Pinckney and Perras to influence the jury to decide the case as suggested.

Pinckney finally concluded his case on Wednesday October 16, 1991, and Perras adjourned the trial so that the Defence would begin its case on Thursday morning. I met with Stroppel in the Meeting room outside the Court room to discuss what would happen when Court resumed. Before he could speak, I asked Stroppel for his assessment of the Crown's completed case. Stroppel paused for a moment and then proceeded with his explanation:

"Well, Orest, you've asked several times for my opinions of this trial as it progressed. I didn't want to say too much until I could hear all of the Crown's case. Now that I have, I am happy to say that I am satisfied that Pinckney has a real weak case. All that he put forward is his theory and a lot of suspicion. In terms of real evidence in this case, there is really nothing. There is no real proof that you had anything to do with any false representation that might have been made to Heritage Trust."

As I listened to Stroppel's words, I felt excited about his assessment and relieved that everything was turning out as we had hoped. As I listened carefully to Stroppel's explanation, he continued with a further observation:

"I've also tried to assess whether it is really necessary for you to give evidence in this trial. Having considered the Crown's evidence, I am satisfied that there is insufficient evidence for a conviction. Therefore, I am ready to conclude this case and argue for an acquittal without you giving evidence. However, if you want to give evidence, you may do so. That is the one decision in a trial that I feel is the exclusive right of a client to decide and I will abide by your decision."

At that moment, I felt surprised and somewhat unprepared for this question. I had always assumed that I would be giving evidence at my trial. However, I understood Stroppel's inquiry since an accused person may choose to refrain from testifying. Typically, this happens when an accused person is afraid of incriminating himself or is found to be lying under oath. However, the law provides that an accused person is not required to testify and no inference can be drawn from the fact that an accused person does not testify. Therefore, in a case where there is insufficient evidence for an acquittal, an accused person may decide not to testify. This avoids the fear of saying things that might provide the additional proof of other criminal activity.

After pausing for a few moments to consider what Stroppel had suggested, I responded by asking:

"Rick, I had always assumed that I would be testifying and I am prepared to do so. However, I would like to know if you feel there is any reason why I should not testify. Will my testimony be helpful in arguing my defence to the jury?"

Stroppel responded in an anxious tone to my inquiry:

"As I said, Orest, I am ready to proceed either way. If you want to testify, I think it would be positive for our position. Your testimony would repeat many of the points that I made while cross-examining Crown witnesses. I believe that you would be a good, credible and believable witness. Your testimony should also dispel the suspicions that Pinckney is trying to develop in the minds of the jurors. Therefore, I would be happy if you were to testify in your defence."

With this endorsement, I agreed to testify. We then proceeded to discuss the other possible witnesses that might be called to give evidence for the defence. Stroppel suggested that he would wait until the following day to decide if he would call any other Defence witnesses.

I then asked Stroppel about all the information that I had collected relating to the re-organization of Heritage Trust. Stroppel stated that the information was another side issue that he preferred to avoid. When I stated my disapproval, he agreed to allow me to present that information through my testimony in response to his questions. I could then simply explain what I had discovered.

I now felt pleased that this information would be put to the jury so that they could see what a farce this whole situation was. I knew that if the jurors were aware that there was no loss and no need for a criminal charge to be laid, then they would have little sympathy for Pinckney's arguments. I had hoped that further Defence witnesses would be called on this point but I was satisfied to explain this to the jury personally.

We concluded our meeting and I left the Meeting room knowing that my day in court was finally about to arrive. I would finally have a chance to tell this jury my side of the story. I now could set the record straight about all the accusations that had been subtly made about my conduct in the Crown case through the testimony of some of the Crown witnesses. I was ready to be judged and I was enthusiastic about having the chance to testify in Court.

When Court resumed the following day, I was sitting anxiously in the Prisoner's Box as I waited for the minutes to pass. Soon I would begin my testimony and then I would finally emerge from this negative image that was created by Pinckney. Finally, I would answer all the suspicions that had been created and present myself as a real person to the jurors. When Court resumed and the jurors were in place, Stroppel rose to his feet and began to make his opening remarks to the jury. Stroppel was at a distinct disadvantage to Pinckney because he had to speak from his table, which was farther from the jury than Pinckney was. Thankfully, Stroppel did not drone during his dissertation as Pinckney did. Instead, he spoke clearly and forcefully. I expected Stroppel to repeat Pinckney's opening remarks containing the exaggerated and imaginative Crown theories. Stroppel had agreed to do this to demonstrate how fictitious these remarks were. To my surprise, Stroppel did not do this as he said he would. Instead, he simply pointed out to the jury that the criminal charge required them to determine if a false representation had been made to Heritage Trust and if so by whom. Stroppel's explanation to the jury sounded so simple. I wondered if the sheer simplicity of Stroppel's explanation might cause the jurors to wonder why Pinckney and Perras were so pre-occupied with all the meaningless details throughout the Crown's case. My concern now was that Stroppel had made the whole case sound too simple and that could raise skepticism with the jury of our Defence case.

Once Stroppel concluded his opening statement to the jury, he then announced that he was calling me as the first Defence witness. As adrenaline raced through my body, I rose to my feet. I then slowly walked out of the Prisoner's Box and across the Court room to the Witness stand located between Perras' perch and the jury. Because I was so nervous, I had to focus carefully to make sure that I did not trip over any of the steps that lay in my path. As I stood in the Witness stand and took the oath from the Clerk, I tried to relax so I would make a good impression on the jury.

As Stroppel began to question me, my nerves began to betray me as I responded quickly to the questions. On a few occasions the Court Reporter asked me to repeat an answer so that she could properly record it. I then apologized and agreed to speak slower. As I gave my testimony, I looked directly at the jurors and tried to make eye contact so that they could appreciate the person who they were about to cast judgement on. As I continued, I began to feel more relaxed and confident about my defence. I wanted the jurors to understand my sincerity as I answered each question.

My evidence was flowing smoothly and my answers were having a good impact on the jurors when Pinckney decided to interrupt the testimony with a technical objection. With pretentious ceremony, he arrogantly announced that my answer had offended the hearsay rule of evidence. His obvious ploy was to discredit me in the eyes of the jurors. Perras immediately responded by agreeing with this objection and then began to lecture and scold me before the jury. His tone of voice and his expressions conveyed the unmistakable message that he disapproved of what I was saying. I knew that this action by Perras would leave a permanent negative impression in the minds of the jurors. All I could do was softly agree to do as he ordered.

By this point, any confidence that I had developed in the jury was gone. Perras and Pinckney had now successfully cautioned the jury to be suspicious of anything that I said. I decided to continue my testimony without any indication of being upset with them. I knew that the jury was still watching me closely and any adverse reaction could damage my Defence case. As Stroppel continued his questions, I proceeded to elaborate on vital points to our case. As soon as Stroppel completed his examination of me, Perras ordered an adjournment so that everyone could have their mid-morning coffee break.

This was the seventh full day of trial for the jurors. By this point, they had all noticeably evolved into social friends and this made these adjournments the most meaningful times of the day for them. The obvious highlight was the exquisite selection of refreshments complimented by gourmet doughnuts and muffins. It was now apparent that the adjournment times were getting longer and the pace of the trial slowed considerably. Naturally, there would inevitably be the comments about the evidence that was being presented even though the deliberation was to begin only after the final arguments were presented and the judge instructed them on the law. Since jurors fail to appreciate this procedure, it is natural for them to discuss and debate these points before the appointed time for doing so. As a result, attitudes and actual decisions are formed long before the trial is concluded and the jurors are instructed on what the issues are that they must decide. For that reason, an accused person may be judged by the jurors' attitudes and not based on the actual issues to be decided. My only hope was that I had impressed them sufficiently to keep the discussions about me in a positive light.

Since my cross-examination was still to be conducted by Pinckney, Stroppel advised me that he could not talk to me until I was excused as a witness. He then disappeared for a coffee so I waited in the Meeting room until the adjournment was over. I spent the time relaxing in the comfortable padded chairs and subdued my anxiety with prayer. When I returned to the witness stand, Pinckney began his cross-examination by trying to focus on incidental facts that did not relate to the main issue. His tactic, of course, was to try and trick me on something to make me look like I was either holding back or not openly telling the whole truth. On each occasion, I responded with a short, clear answer and avoided any argument with him although he did his best to provoke me. After an hour of cross-examination, Pinckney requested an adjournment so Perras ordered a two hour adjournment to two o'clock.

When court resumed, Pinckney again attacked me with further questions that continued for approximately one more hour. Only a few of his questions ever came close to the basis for the charge: a false representation in the mortgage application to Heritage Trust. Pinckney obviously didn't like my answers since he avoided any further cross-examination on this point. Finally, after cross-examination on tedious, irrelevant points, Pinckney gave up and Perras ordered a mid-afternoon adjournment.

At this juncture, I was able to speak to Stroppel once more and I was anxious for his assessment of my evidence and the response of the jury. As we entered the Meeting room, I immediately asked Stroppel for his comments to which he responded:

"Everything went great with your testimony, Orest! You really covered all the main points in your first examination. Then, in the cross-examination, you responded real well to all of Pinckney's questions. I'm sure that the jury must have been impressed with your evidence. From my perspective, it couldn't have gone better."

I was pleased to hear that Stroppel felt confident about my testimony. I was ready to see this case concluded and to get a decision from the jury. I had never felt this much confidence during this entire ordeal and I was sure that my night-mare would soon be over. As I began to relax from the euphoria of the moment, I asked Stroppel about one area of evidence that we hadn't covered:

"I noticed that you didn't ask me any questions about the re-organization of Heritage Trust and the fact that Heritage Trust in fact lost no money on this deal. Are you planning to call the evidence through another witness?"

The evidence that I was concerned about was the discovery I made that Heritage Trust had suffered no loss on this mortgage. During the re-organization of the two trust companies, Heritage Trust and North West Trust, the Government of Alberta paid out this mortgage claim to Heritage Trust. The Government then took over this mortgage and the foreclosed property into a private holding company. Therefore, the mortgage and the foreclosed property were never owned or adminis-trated by North West Trust Company. Chubb, as an employee of North West Trust Company, had no right to even cause this investigation to proceed. This fact had been covered up by Christal for obvious reasons. I was sure that it would have a sig-nificant effect on the assessments by the jurors. Naturally, it was my assessment that this evidence should be placed before the Court. When I met with Stroppel to pre-pare for testifying in Court, he agreed to ask questions that would allow me to explain these facts. Since Stroppel hadn't asked these questions during my testimo-ny, I started to assume that he planned to introduce this evidence in some other man-ner.

Stroppel responded immediately with confidence and reassurance:

"Actually, Orest, I've decided that I'm not going to call any evidence on that point. I know that it is a valid consideration but we don't need it. It doesn't relate to the mortgage application and I don't want to take a chance that it might confuse the jury."

At that moment, I was a little disappointed but I decided that I had to main-tain my faith and confidence in Stroppel's judgement. I therefore simply allowed this concern to pass. I then asked Stroppel about the other witnesses to testify for the Defence:

"Orest, I've decided that your testimony is really all we need. There is no point in introducing more evidence. After all, there is always a danger that something might be said to confuse the jury or diminish what was said. I feel that we should just wrap it up now and put it to the jury. It's obvious that there is no evidence to support the Crown's case and your evidence should reassure them that you did nothing wrong. In my experience, that's as good a case as you can get."

What Stroppel said made sense and I silently prayed that he was making the right judgement call. I was happy to know that we were so close to concluding this case. I then asked Stroppel for his opinion on when the case would now be concluded and he advised:

"As you are aware, the final summations to the jury should be given tomorrow. The problem is that tomorrow happens to be Friday. If we give our summations tomorrow, the jury would have to start deliberations late in the day, and continue into the week-end until a verdict is reached. Pinckney doesn't like this prospect and frankly, neither do I. The better course is to adjourn the trial until Monday. That will give the lawyers more time to prepare. It would also eliminate any pressure on the jury to make a fast decision to avoid missing out on being with their families on the week-end. Unfortunately, the jury may forget some of the points that were so positive in your testimony. In any event, we have a good defence and I don't think it will make much of a difference."

As I listened to Stroppel, I felt a little disappointed but I could understand his comments about not requiring a jury to deliberate through a long week-end. One could almost visualize the haste at which a jury would act to reach a decision and then hurry home to avoid being away from family and friends. Certainly, this type of behaviour would not be a proper exercise of their duties as jurors. However, I could easily understand why they might hastily conclude a deliberation on this case which had no special significance to any of them and undoubtedly presented a financial and personal inconvenience to each of them.

When Court resumed, Stroppel advised Perras that there would be no further evidence from the Defence. Before the jury was brought in, the question was raised as to whether the jury would be asked to deliberate on the week-end. It was mutually agreed that this would be unsatisfactory. Instead, we would all take a three day break and Court would resume on Monday. At that time, both Stroppel and Pinckney would give their final summation arguments. Perras would then instruct the jury with his comments on the facts and the applicable law. At that time, the jury would begin the deliberation to reach a verdict.

I was relieved that everything had gone so well. Now, our case had progressed to the stage of an airplane coming in for its final approach on landing. Everything looked good, the conditions were clear and all the instruments were working perfectly. We were about to successfully conclude this rather difficult mission. The likelihood of a crash was inconceivable. Soon the ordeal would only be a memory. The thought of a sudden disaster like the military plane crashes at Alert, N.W.T. or Wainwright, Alberta was not even a realistic possibility. With these optimistic thoughts, I was happy to return home to my family for a reprieve from these exhaustive proceedings.

CHAPTER TWENTY SIX

THE VERDICT

On this third week-end in October, we enjoyed beautiful and perhaps unseasonably warm weather. However, the days were now noticeably shorter and the nights were cooler than a month earlier. Reluctantly, we had to accept the reality that we would soon be confronting another winter. Thankfully, the weather was still radiantly warm and the prospect of winter seemed so far away. What none of us could visualize was the sudden drastic change in weather that would soon befall us on Monday morning and the effect it would have on my trial.

In our typical morning routine, my wife and I woke up to our radio alarm clock and listened to the morning news and weather reports. We usually tried to concentrate on the weather forecast to assess how we should dress for the day and what to expect when we leave the house. The forecast for the day was foreboding with news that a winter storm was moving in rapidly from the north. This weather pattern was bringing freezing rain followed by large snowfalls and frigid temperatures. Naturally, we hoped that this was simply a mistake and that the storm would by-pass our city. Nonetheless, we proceeded to prepare for this situation.

The first winter storm always creates chaos since it typically forces everyone to respond to emergency winter conditions. Although we are conditioned to expect this dramatic change in climatic conditions, inevitably everyone is caught unprepared. Slippery road conditions always generate a record number of traffic accidents and road crews struggle to clear roads of snow and sprinkle sand on the main intersections. Heavier clothes need to be rustled out of storage closets and organized. Everything outdoors must now be secured or stored for the long cold winter that will soon reclaim its seasonal outdoor domain. The prevailing mood is panic and confusion as everyone braces for the onslaught of a frigid and raging snow storm. Without delay, everyone must develop new routines to cope with these sudden storms which soon become normal occurrences as winter tightens its grip on the frozen landscape.

After a relaxed week-end of warmer Autumn weather, it was difficult to organize our household for the dreaded winter storm that was predicted to begin as early as twelve o'clock noon. Normally, in this type of situation, I would re-arrange my work schedule and plan to be home early to handle any emergencies. However, I wasn't sure how long the proceedings on this day would continue and when the proceedings would be adjourned. I could only hope for an early adjournment so that I could be home before this raging winter storm made the road conditions treacherous for driving.

After sending the children off to school with winter clothing, my wife and I both decided to leave early as well to avoid traffic problems in the event that any form of precipitation had started. I had also agreed to meet Stroppel before Court started to discuss his final summation to the jury and any final concerns before the trial was concluded. I knew I had to remain calm so I tried not to anticipate what would happen in Court today. Instead, I consoled myself by recalling that everything had proceeded well and that my destiny was safe in the capable hands of my lawyer.

During my trip downtown, I tried to relax by listening to the car radio but this was a useless distraction. Frequent news reports focused on the approaching winter blizzard which had already paralysed some northern Alberta towns with slippery roads and large deposits of snow. Temperatures outdoors were falling quickly and the ominous prediction was that our city would soon be traumatized with this terrifying storm. It was also predicted that this weather pattern would continue to rage for the balance of the week and would cause continual physical hardship for everyone to endure.

Fortunately, I arrived downtown well in advance of my meeting time with Stroppel so I decided to park my vehicle in the underground parkade that was connected by a pedestrian tunnel to the Court House. As I walked to the Court room, the general mood of the pedestrians that I encountered was noticeably gloomy. It was evident that everyone was mentally pre-occupied by the pending storm that would undoubtedly create traumatic personal problems and discomfort. As I neared the Court House, it suddenly occurred to me that this pending storm would also be on the minds of the jurors. The inconvenience of this trial would certainly now become a pressing concern for them because of this new emergency.

I surmised that this new development might create a desire on the part of some jurors to quickly finish this trial so that they would be allowed to return to their personal lives. Naturally, this type of attitude was a contradiction to their role as sworn jurors. They were expected to conduct a thorough, detailed review to assess all the evidence that was heard during the trial. Then, a time-consuming debate would be held to consider how the law should be applied to the fact situation to arrive at a properly reasoned verdict. Whether any jury ever lived up to this idealistic expectation was difficult to know but I wanted to believe that my jury would.

On my arrival at the reception area outside the Court room, I peered out the window. As a prelude to the blizzard, the wind was already increasing noticeably in velocity which meant that the snow storm was soon engulf the city. Pedestrians on the street hurried to their destinations and everyone became gripped by a quiet panic as we contemplated the effects of this oncoming disaster. I began to feel stress and anxiety forming in my body as I wrestled with thoughts of how I and my family would cope with this unexpected storm. I suddenly realized that each of the jurors would experience similar anxiety. This circumstance would probably create a mental attitude in the minds of the jurors to arrive at a hasty, flippant verdict so that they could end their involvement in this undesirable obligation. As my heart began to pound wildly at the thought of this possibility, I realized that this was not a good time to panic. I was desperate to believe that the jurors would be reasonable in their actions and that they would fulfil their obligations properly. I consoled myself by recalling the comments of Stroppel that it was an obvious case for the jury to decide because there was no evidence to support a conviction. In spite of my determined efforts, my anxiety continued to grow within me as I waited for Stroppel to appear.

As people began to arrive for their various court matters, I observed the arrival of some of the jurors in my case. Without exception, each one tried to avoid looking at me and walked directly to the jury room behind the Court room. I understood these deliberate actions as this was an awkward situation for them and for me. After all, any contact between a juror and myself would be deemed improper and might result in a mistrial. It suddenly struck me that a better building design would eliminate the likelihood of jurors coming into contact with the other parties in the trial. Unfortunately, this inappropriate building design and utilization of the Court House facility stemmed from the misplaced priorities of providing comfort to the judges rather than convenience to those involved in the court system.

When Stroppel finally arrived, we proceeded to the Meeting room for our final preparatory meeting. Once inside, Stroppel sat down at the table and removed a file from his briefcase. As he opened it to glance at his notes, he began to explain what would transpire in Court:

"Well, this is the day you've been waiting for, Orest! I've spent a few hours yesterday reviewing my trial notes and preparing my final summation to the jury. As I've said before, I see the issue in this case as being really very simple. That is the way I intend to present my remarks to the jury. The Crown has specifically identified the false representations on the mortgage application to Heritage Trust as the fraudulent act. It is obvious that there is no evidence that you committed such an act. The balance of the evidence that Pinckney has put before the jury is simply a smoke screen. He is trying to hide the fact that he has not put any real evidence before the jury of the fraud that is alleged. I'm convinced that if we keep it simple and direct, this jury will have no difficulty in acquitting you on this charge."

Because Stroppel's comments were a reiteration of his assessment that he shared with me earlier, I was not surprised by any of it. I was more concerned about Pinckney's summation and asked Stroppel for his assessment, to which he replied:

"Regarding the Crown's position, Pinckney has followed the same strategy throughout this trial. You have probably heard the expression: "GUILT BY ASSOCIATION". Basically, he has called so many witnesses who had nothing relevant to say about the main issue. Instead each one has testified to your involvement in some aspect of the real estate deal. If you recall his opening remarks, he painted you as being a grand schemer who masterminded an incredibly complex real estate scam. I'm sure that the jurors realize that there was nothing that complex about the real estate deal. The only thing that he has shown as sinister about the deal is that you made a profit. Because he has no real evidence that you did anything wrong, he's hoping that he can create enough suspicion so that a naive jury would convict you. I suspect that Pinckney is getting desperate because his case is faltering. In his notes to Perras on the law to be included in the instructions to the jury, Pinckney introduced the possibility of an alternate theory. What this means is that Pinckney is going to argue that the jury can convict you even though there is no evidence that you committed a fraud. Basically, Pinckney is going to take the position that the jury should convict you if they believe that Garmaz or the mortgage broker committed the fraud and you were aware of it. Obviously, this is a pretty weak argument and a bit far fetched considering the facts in this case. It really shows how weak Pinckney feels the Crown case is."

I was aware of the legal summaries that both Pinckney and Stroppel had provided to Perras. Typically, judges will use this ploy to avoid doing the legal research themselves. Since these summaries would serve as a guide for Perras to prepare his final instructions to the jury, it made it easier for him to know and favour the Crown's case. I was now concerned about the remarks that Perras might make to the Jury because he was acting like a loose cannon. I knew that Stroppel shared this concern also. As I raised the topic of what Stroppel expected in the instructions to the jury, he confided to me:

"It's hard to guess what Perras will say to the jury. It's obvious that he favours the Crown's position from what I've seen of his conduct throughout the trial. We can also expect that his remarks will have a significant influence on the jury. As you may know, he's not confined in what he can say. He can go as far as to tell the jury that he thinks you are guilty of the crime. Naturally, he shouldn't do such a thing but nothing can stop him from doing it. Although Pinckney and I have both given him our summary of the law that should be put to the jury, he can give them whatever legal directions that he wishes. All we can do is appeal the decision if he makes an error in law during his instructions to the jury."

Stroppel's comments once again re-enforced the fact that a judge can dramatically influence the decision of a jury if he chooses to favour one side over the other. Indeed, a judge can make a mockery of a jury trial by coaxing the jurors into "puppet duty". By influencing a jury to make the decision that he desires, the judge can avoid criticism for a conviction if it is successfully overturned by the Court of Appeal. In theory, the judge is supposed to be neutral and unbiased to insure that the decision of the jury is fair and just. However, Perras had already made it obvious that he was very biased. I was now concerned that he would not withdraw from the action and let justice work as it was intended.

It was the jury that could make all the difference in this case. Although I had asked Stroppel this question so many times, I now needed to know his final impressions of the jury. This was a difficult question and Stroppel took a moment to collect his thoughts before responding:

"I've really had a problem trying to assess this jury and I'm still not sure how to read this jury. Throughout this whole trial, NOT EVEN ONE of the jurors made any notes of what was said. This is really strange because nobody could remember the details of this trial without making notes. Yet, none of them even opened their note books to write down anything. I wasn't able to see much reaction from the jury either except for a couple of times when the Crown witnesses really contradicted evidence given by other witnesses. It was obvious that some of the Crown witnesses were lying and a few of the jurors did pick up on that. But basically, they all just sat there and listened to the Crown witnesses and did nothing else. It's possible that for some of them, this whole trial is so complicated that everything is just going over their heads. However, you would think that a few of them would be taking it seriously and making notes or something. Either they don't care or they've made up their minds already. It's possible that they don't understand the real issue and are waiting to hear the final arguments. Perhaps they feel that the whole case is nonsense and they've decided from the start to throw the criminal charge out. Whatever the case is, we'll probably have a better impression of the jury when the final summations are finished and they leave to deliberate."

The time was drawing near for us to go into the Court room but I wanted to get Stroppel's opinion on how long this stage of the proceedings would take. Stroppel was more confident on this question as he remarked:

"My summation to the jury will take about an hour and Pinckney will probably spend that long on his. That means that the morning will be spent on these summations to the jury. Perras will probably take a little less time and he will probably start his instructions to the jury in the afternoon. By mid-afternoon, the jury should begin their deliberations. Because of the amount of documents and evidence, I suspect that it will go right into the evening. If no decision is made by a certain time, they will be sequestrated and lodged in hotel rooms until tomorrow when they will continue. My guess is that they will reach a decision by this evening and certainly by tomorrow. In the meantime, we all have to stand by and wait. Therefore, I'd like you to stay downtown and keep in touch with my office. As soon as the verdict is in, the Court Orderlies will reach me on a beeper that they will provide to me. My secretary will then notify you to meet me in Court. At that point, we will have to be back in Court, even if it's late in the evening, so that the verdict can be delivered and Perras can dismiss the jury."

As Stroppel spoke, the anxiety of what was about to transpire was now building within me and I began to tremble. I decided to walk out into the reception area to calm myself down. When I entered the Court room, Stroppel and Pinckney had already set up their files on their tables. As I moved forward, I noticed the Court Orderly waiting to lock me into the Prisoner's Box for this eventful moment in my life. Looking around the Court room, I realized that this setting had now become second nature to me. The uncomfortable seat in the Prisoner's Box was nothing more than another inconvenience. I had now become conditioned to these surroundings in spite of the horror that they created in my life. I began to appreciate that everything was now secondary in importance to the verdict that would soon determine my future: either I would be vindicated or I would be devastated.

In a few minutes, Court was reconvened. Perras again assumed his lofty perch with the ceremonial bowing after which the jury was brought in. After the requisite cordial greetings from Perras, the proceedings began with Perras asking Stroppel to present his final submissions. Stroppel again spoke from his table which was farther from the jury than Pinckney's table. Unfortunately, this made it more difficult for Stroppel to be as forceful as he might otherwise have been. Furthermore, Court rules require that both lawyers stand stationary at their tables and not move about as the lawyers portrayed in the American television dramas are allowed to do. For this reason, the speeches of the lawyers are far less dramatic and far more reserved, which is in keeping with the English tradition that still dominates the Canadian courts.

Stroppel's remarks were presented as he described to me. He emphasized to the jury that they should read the charge carefully before starting their deliberation. Stroppel suggested that they should take the opportunity to study the written charge and the actual exhibit documents in the jury room during their deliberations. The jurors were asked to examine them carefully as they recalled the evidence of the various witnesses. He then identified a few of the documents and reviewed the evidence of the few key witnesses that related to the documents. As he concluded his remarks, he emphasized that I was not on trial for getting involved in a real estate deal and making a profit. He again directed their attention to the wording of the criminal charge which described that I was accused of making a false representation to a mortgage company. Stroppel asked the jury to conclude that there was no evidence that I was involved in any way in making any representations to Heritage Trust. Therefore, such a verdict was appropriate because the Crown Prosecutor had failed to prove its case beyond a reasonable doubt as required by law. For that reason, the only proper verdict was an acquittal.

I watched the jury carefully while Stroppel presented his summation. I began to feel uncomfortable as they displayed stone-faced expressions while gazing up across at Stroppel. Occasionally, a juror would look at his binder to find a document that Stroppel was referring to. Otherwise, the jurors just basically sat there and showed no reaction to anything that was said. I often assumed that a jury was like an audience listening to a speaker or watching a drama. I was hoping that the facial expressions of the jurors would reflect what was going on in their minds. I concluded that if this assumption was correct in this case, then there was really nothing going on in the minds of these jurors. If that was actually the case, then they were probably day-dreaming of more pleasant pastimes than the one they were now experiencing.

When Stroppel concluded his comments, Perras ordered an adjournment for a mid-morning break. At that moment, the jurors became animated like cartoon characters and eagerly filed out to enjoy their gourmet treats and refreshments. After commenting with approval to Stroppel on his summation, I walked out of the Court room and stood by the window staring out at the changing weather outside. Although the weather was getting colder, there was no precipitation of either rain or snow. Yet, I only hoped that it would not be as severe as we were told that it would be. In any event, I now knew that I wouldn't be home early and it was quite possible that I would be staying at the Court House late into the night. I realized that this last part of the ordeal would be the hardest to endure. However, the trial was now concluding and there was nothing that could be done except to watch everything unfold before me.

After the mid-morning break, the Court resumed. Perras and the jury resumed their positions and Pinckney was called upon to present his final summation. The jurors appeared to have livened up somewhat and I guessed that they would need this extra energy to endure the boring dissertation that Pinckney was about to inflict on all of us. His remarks were basically a repeat of his opening address and his tactic again was to ignore the criminal charge and to dwell on my involvement in the total transaction. From Pinckney's prospective, anyone who gets involved in buying and selling real estate that results in a loss to a mortgage company must be guilty of fraud. It didn't matter that the default occurred in the mortgage loan at a later date or what actually caused the loss to the mortgage company. Pinckney wanted the jurors to conclude that the blame for any wrongdoing must fall on the person who put the real estate deal together. He suggested that everyone in the transaction was innocent and naive and that the only person who knew anything about the real estate deal was me. This was therefore a good reason to convict me of the criminal charge of fraud.

As I listened to his comments, I felt infuriated that Pinckney would try to colour and misrepresent the facts in such a open display of dishonesty to the jury. It was obvious that he rated the jurors as being naive and dependent upon him. He acted confidently that these jurors would accept his exaggerated and re-constructed description of the evidence as being a fair representation of what they heard. One had to appreciate the reality that Pinckney was working desperately to achieve a conviction in a flimsy case. However, he had a duty to the Court to act ethically and this professional mandate required him not to act in such a disreputable manner. Had I held any respect for Pinckney, I surely would have lost it while watching his arrogant display of manipulation before the jury.

The jury appeared to treat Pinckney with the same expressions that they provided to Stroppel. This gave me hope that it was still an open contest and that my hopes for a fair verdict could still be realized. After Pinckney finished his remarks, Perras then ordered that the Court be adjourned to two o'clock. At that time, he would give them his instructions and then direct them to deliberate until they reached a unanimous verdict. Perras and the jurors then left the Court room. Stroppel also left but advised me that he would speak to me before Court resumed. As everyone disappeared, I decided to go for a long walk using the underground walkway system to avoid being outside in the mounting storm. This change in activity would provide me with an opportunity to walk briskly and to calm down before returning to Court for the final moments of the trial.

I returned to the Court room early to wait for Stroppel in the reception area near the elevators. As I sat, I noticed a few of the jurors returning and congregating at a window to stare at the escalating blizzard outside. Snow was now falling and the wind had noticeably increased in velocity. The feeling of panic instinctively settled upon all of us as we silently visualized the treacherous road conditions that this blizzard would quickly create. A natural impulse was to return home as soon as possible before the road conditions became impassable. Unfortunately, nobody would be allowed to leave the Court House until the trial was completed and the verdict was decided and delivered in Court.

I realized at once that this unpredictable event could cause the jurors to make a quick decision so that they could be excused and allowed to return to their homes. With a biased judge and a theatrical Crown Prosecutor, all I could really hope for was a common sense decision based on a proper examination of the evidence. However, this was not a likely prospect if the jurors simply panicked and made a flippant decision. Such impulse decisions usually favour the position of the Crown Prosecutor and typically result in a conviction. The reason is that usually, those jurors that may be inclined to acquit will relent and agree with the other jurors just to end their participation in a protracted trial. I knew from my various conversations with Stroppel that my only hope for a fair verdict was a thorough deliberation by the jury. With all the documents and evidence, such a deliberation would last well into the evening and perhaps continue to the following day or longer.

As I sat in silence, contemplating how this unusual blizzard might dramatically alter the decision of the jury, Stroppel appeared. On seeing him, I followed him to the Meeting room for a quick discussion before Court resumed. As I closed the door, I asked him about his impression of the jury's reaction to Pinckney's final summation. Stroppel replied cautiously:

"I didn't really see any form of reaction by any of them. I really believe that they are going to have trouble with this case. I expect that there is going to be a long deliberation and it could go on for days. Ultimately, there has to be a lot of doubt in their minds about the Crown witnesses so they'll have to acquit you. I think that everything will work out fine."

It was nice to hear Stroppel's positive comments but I still felt uneasy as I retorted:

"Rick, I have a bad feeling about the blizzard that has moved into the city. Do you think that this storm might cause the jurors to make a hasty decision so that they can be excused and allowed to return home immediately?"

This was an impossible question to answer but Stroppel responded sympathetically:

"I don't think that should be a factor in any jury decision. Most jurors will take their roles very seriously. However, it's impossible to know what motivates a decision by a jury. I think that once they get into the jury room to deliberate, they'll start going over the evidence and the documents. As they get involved in discussing this case, they'll forget about what's going on outside. That's why the jury deliberations generally take so long. I wouldn't worry about them making a quick decision on this case for any extraneous reason. Instead, you'd better prepare yourself for a long wait."

As Stroppel finished speaking, he rose to his feet and we both walked out and into the Court room. Everyone was almost ready to start again. In a few moments, I was settled into my familiar seat in the Prisoner's Box waiting for this ordeal to finally end.

When Court resumed, Perras proceeded to deliver his instructions to the jury. Many of this remarks appeared to be taken from a textbook and then incorporated into a standard form of instructions. Perras sputtered them out from his written notes like a pre-rehearsed speech without any expression in his monotonous tone of voice. Because I had never been involved in a case where a judge instructed a jury, the comments by Perras on the procedural matters were a new experience for me. However, the jurors seemed lost or oblivious to what Perras said as he droned from his lofty perch. His talk would have made an excellent bed-time story simply because it was so uninteresting that it was guaranteed to put anyone to sleep.

My worst fears began to be realized as Perras began to instruct the jurors on the facts that they should consider from the evidence that they had heard. The approach that Perras took was similar to that of Pinckney. Instead of reminding the jury that they were to adjudicate on the criminal charge as stated on the indictment, he began to recite the evidence as it related to the entire transaction. He advised the jury that they should draw inferences from certain testimony and that their decisions could be based on these inferences. The only thing that Perras left out was what the verdict should be but he made his feelings quite obvious from his instructions.

It was disturbing to see how captivated the jurors now were by what Perras said. As they stared up at Perras on his pedestal, they looked like loving servants who would do anything that their master desired. I reminded myself that I had to remain objective and not to make judgements of people before seeing their actions. I immediately blocked out all images of my darkest suspicions of the jury and resolved to wait for the verdict. On completing his instructions to the jury, Perras advised the jurors that they would now be sequestrated in the jury room until a unanimous verdict was reached. They were also reminded that they could only take their notes into the Jury room but not their binders of documents. Perras further advised them that when the Court was adjourned, the Court Clerk would deliver the original copies of all the marked Exhibits into the Jury room. In addition, a copy of the Indictment and a copy of the relevant sections of the Criminal Code of Canada would be provided to them. At that time, they would be able to review those documents and then begin their deliberation of the evidence and ultimately decide upon a verdict.

Once the jury filed out, Perras confirmed with Pinckney and Stroppel that each of them had a beeper on which the Court Orderly could summon them when the verdict was reached. Perras was about to adjourn the Court when Stroppel rose to his feet to make an objection about the instructions to the jury. Stroppel then stated that the definition that Perras gave to the jury of fraud was not a proper definition. He further objected to Perras that his statement of what one of the witnesses said at the trial was also incorrect. Stroppel asked Perras to recall the jury so that these two items could be clarified. Perras slowly reviewed his notes and then responded to Stroppel that he considered the definition of fraud that he gave to the jury to be correct. He then looked to Pinckney for a reassuring nod before declaring that his statement of the evidence of the particular witness was also satisfactory. On both items, he ruled that the jury would not be recalled for any further clarification.

During this brief exchange that lasted only a few minutes, the Court Orderly who had taken the jury to the jury room had returned. On entering the Court room he blurted out a comment about the verdict. When he realized that Perras was still talking about his decision regarding a recall of the jury, he stood impatiently at the door in silence. When Perras was finished, the Court Orderly then commented again in a clear voice that a verdict had been reached by the jury. Everyone looked at each other in surprise! As we looked at Perras, it was obvious that even he was surprised. For a moment Perras was not sure how to react to what had happened. It was obvious to everyone that there had been NO deliberation by the jury. They did not even read the indictment or the legal definition of fraud on which they were pronouncing a verdict. Furthermore, the jury had never seen the original documents marked as Exhibits on which they were supposed to rely to make their findings of fact before deciding a verdict. This whole situation was blatantly improper and it was obvious that the jurors did not appreciate the task that they were to perform.

Perras then looked at the Court Orderly and asked again if he actually meant that a verdict was agreed upon by the jury. The Court Orderly again acknowledged that they had and Perras then instructed him to recall the jury to the Court room. For the brief moments that passed, I became convinced that the jury had decided on a "Not Guilty" verdict. Otherwise, they would have taken the time to consider and discuss all of the factors that Perras had listed in his textbook speech. I assumed that the jury had concluded that there really was no evidence of wrongdoing on my part. They obviously avoided delving into all of the technical aspects of the case that Perras and Pinckney had stressed in their speeches. Instead, they were obviously content to simply look at the singular issue as described by Stroppel and reached the obvious conclusion that he stressed. As I sat there in silence, I said a silent prayer while I waited for the jury to return to the Court room.

In a moment, the door to the Court room opened and the jurors filed in again with eager expressions on their faces. In my silent prayers, I pleaded that this would be good news. Nervous energy raced through my body as I waited anxiously for the jurors to take their places. Once seated, the Clerk addressed the jury:

"Members of the jury, have you arrived at a verdict? If so, say so by your foreman."

A man in the middle of the back row responded:

"Yes, we have."

The Clerk then inquired of the foreman of the jury:

"What is your verdict?"

The foreman of the jury again responded:

"Guilty as charged."

Both Stroppel and I sat motionless and in shock. Perras displayed a faint smile and Pinckney gloated with satisfaction on achieving the verdict that he desired. The jurors were also smiling and were undoubtedly pleased that this lengthy trial was over. The mood of the jury became jovial as they basked in the warmth of the smiles of Perras and Pinckney who had guided them in arriving at this "difficult" verdict. Perras then instructed the Clerk to "poll" the jury. Immediately, the Clerk began to call the name of each of the jurors to ask them if they agreed with the verdict. As each juror acknowledged affirmatively, I sat in disbelief and wondered if this was really happening. I could only hope that I would wake up in a cold sweat and realize that it was all an unbelievable nightmare.

At that moment, I could not rationalize why the jury had reached such a perverse verdict. They could not have logically decided this by evaluating the evidence and considering the wording of the criminal charge. Much later, I reviewed this verdict and obtained the opinions of Stroppel and other lawyers. The consensus was that the jury did not actually deliberate on the criminal charge but chose instead to arbitrarily choose a side as one might do in a spirited debate. They obviously did not fulfil the role of jurors who were making a decision that had grave implications on the operation of justice in a significant trial. Instead, these jurors were content to adopt a whimsical attitude and to agree with Perras and Pinckney just to end their involvement in this protracted trial and to return home before the blizzard got worse. It was clear throughout the trial that Perras favoured a conviction. Pinckney had called so many witnesses just to support his contention of the suspicions that he believed actually existed. Sadly, the jurors lacked the ability and the desire to seriously examine the merits of the case. Instead, they made the decision that would obviously please the Crown Prosecutor and the Judge and would excuse them from further involvement. Now that the trial was over, the jurors could once again return to their lives, feeling satisfied that they had fulfilled their duty to their country and knowing that they would never have to endure this inconvenience again.

As I sat in the Prisoner's Box, I now realized how deeply influenced the jury was by the campaign of suspicion engineered by Christal and Pinckney. The cooperation and assistance of Perras throughout the trial was the persuasive influence that enabled Pinckney to effectively carry out his program during the trial. Because he couldn't win this case by producing real evidence of fraud, Pinckney succeeded by simply casting suspicion and discrediting me in the eyes of the jurors. The process was made easier by the growing sentiment of the general public to dislike lawyers. Pinckney's "dishonest lawyer" campaign made it easier for the jurors to show no sympathy for my plight. As one juror would later remark:

"He was just another crooked lawyer but we fixed him. We made sure that he got what he deserved."

When the polling of the jury was concluded, Perras then thanked the jurors for their work in sitting through this trial and discharged them. Once the jury left, Perras looked at Pinckney and Stroppel and announced that he would be adjourning the court to the following morning for sentencing. Pinckney then asked that I be remanded in custody and Perras immediately agreed and made the order without considering the request or even asking Stroppel for his comments. I was still in shock so I couldn't even react to this new horror. Perras then declared that the court was adjourned and everyone stood up to watch him triumphantly leave the Court room. Pinckney bore a noticeable smile as he gloated over his victory and began to assemble his files. I glanced over at Stroppel who appeared to be in shock as he struggled with the reality of what had to be done next.

As the Court Orderly prepared to take me into custody by escorting me into the cell area behind the Prisoner's Box, I asked if I could speak to Stroppel first. The Court Orderly agreed and allowed me to meet with Stroppel for a few minutes in the Meeting room. This was unusual since there was no security that would prevent an escape in this situation. However, the Court Orderly must have realized that there was no likelihood that I would consider anything like that.

Once inside the Meeting room, I struggled with my speech as I asked Stroppel about what just happened:

"I don't understand this, Rick! How could the jury find me guilty? They didn't even take a minute to consider the case. They just handed in a guilty verdict. How could this happen?"

I was so much in shock that I could hardly speak. Stroppel was slow in answering my question. For a moment, he couldn't even look directly at me. Finally, Stroppel made a laboured response:

"Orest, I'm just as shocked as you are! I can't believe that any jury could find you guilty on the evidence in this case. But, don't worry, Orest! We have good grounds for an Appeal. In addition to the grounds that Perras interfered in the trial, we also have the argument that he misdirected the jury on those two matters that I raised in the objection. Because I put my objections on record, the Court of Appeal should have no difficulty in setting aside this verdict for those reasons. Once I review this case, I may find other grounds to argue as well. This case isn't over yet!"

As I listened to Stroppel, I was already losing hope that my case would ever be resolved properly or that I would ever see any justice. It was difficult for me to visualize that the Court of Appeal would be objective, fair and unbiased. In my devastated state of mind, I could no longer hope that my life would return to normal. Instead, I was convinced that this situation would now take a greater toll on my family and marriage and that nothing would ever be the same again. The torment and trauma would now quickly increase as I became branded a "criminal of society". The publicity by the news media would soon follow to make the devastation of my life complete.

With my whole self-image shattered, I struggled to maintain my composure as I asked Stroppel:

"What is going to happen now?"

Stroppel now looked at me with sympathy. Like most Criminal lawyers, he endured too many occasions when he had to console shattered clients after a verdict destroyed their lives. After a few moments he seemed to instinctively respond:

"Well, as you heard, the sentencing is tomorrow morning. I'm going to go back to my office to prepare my submissions for sentencing. It's obvious that you will be sentenced to some time in jail. I'll call your wife to get some information that will be useful in speaking to sentence. In the meantime, you'll be taken to the Remand Centre where you will spend the night. I know it won't be pleasant for you but I hope you'll be alright. I'll see you tomorrow morning before the sentencing."

As Stroppel spoke, I had difficulty comprehending what he said. My mind was now frozen by the horror of what had just happened and what now lay ahead. My expressions must have explicitly told the story which caused Stroppel to comment:

"Look, Orest, I'm really sorry about this! I was sure that we would win this case. But don't give up hope! We have an excellent chance at the Court of Appeal. Try and keep your chin up and don't let this get you down. I'm sure that you're strong enough to make it through this. I'll have to leave now but I'll see you in the morning."

I didn't realize how shaken Stroppel was by my conviction. In his later conversations with my wife, Stroppel confessed how stressful this case had now become because of his failure to present a stronger defence. Behind his objective and callous exterior, he was able to disguise his feelings of guilt for failing to appreciate the effect of Pinckney's tactics on the jury. Because of his failure to properly appreciate the effect of the presentation of the Crown case, Stroppel also failed to appreciate that a simplistic defence would not be sufficient. Sadly, Stroppel had the opportunity to present evidence that would have demonstrated all the various weaknesses of the Crown's case. Unfortunately, he chose not to do so because he felt so confident that he could succeed on a simplistic legal argument. He now felt responsible for my disastrous situation but I was the person who was really going to suffer for it. Despite all of this, I continued to support his efforts to rectify my situation and accept his shortcomings which he demonstrated during the trial.

I acknowledged what Stroppel said and then we got up and left the Meeting room. The Court Orderly waited inside the Court room for me to return. Stroppel then disappeared to go back to his office. I was now alone and about to enter a darker, sinister world. My life was about to change forever. I could visualize the trauma that this ordeal would cause for my wife and children because of the sensational news stories that would be broadcast and published the following day. Unfortunately, there was nothing I could do but try to survive the fallout of this ongoing ordeal.

CHAPTER TWENTY SEVEN

THE SENTENCING HEARING

As with any disaster, natural or man-made, the damage and destruction as well as the pain and suffering are usually greater in the aftermath of the event. Since the disaster itself is presumed to be the real devastation, the fallout is usually ignored and receives little sympathy. So it was to be in my case where the verdict was only an initial disaster that set in motion a much larger series of consequences. In many ways, the fallout would be more devastating for me and my family than the actual verdict. Like an area affected by an earthquake, my world continued to feel devastating and destructive tremors that continued for weeks after the initial tragedy.

At the same time as the verdict was delivered by the jurors that afternoon, a ferocious snow storm intensified in the City with extreme blizzard conditions. The City quickly became engulfed in this unseasonal catastrophe which would set the tone for a long and difficult winter season. I would now be protected from all of this as the loss of my freedom also meant that I would not be allowed to go outdoors.

The Court Orderly led me into the cell area in the back of the Court room where he completed a form to document information on me. After taking my belt, my rings and my personal possessions, he led me to an elevator that took us to the basement of the Court House. I was then directed into a large cell holding area monitored by video cameras. When I asked if I could telephone my wife, I was told that there were no telephones in this area. Before I would have access to a telephone, I would have to wait until I was admitted into the Remand Centre. The waiting began as I was slowly shuffled from one cell to another and grouped with other prisoners. About an hour passed before I was called out, handcuffed to other prisoners and then led down a long tunnel that led to the Remand Centre, about one block away.

Throughout this time, my mind remained in a state of shock. As the Court Orderlies and Prison Guards made demands of me, I responded without emotion or comment. As I moved to their directions, I was trying to comprehend how this could happen. The horror began to settle in as I wondered if I would survive in this bizarre environment. As the time slowly passed, I continually thought about my wife and family and how they were going to survive this devastating situation. I knew that I had to get to a telephone as soon as possible to telephone my wife and tell her what happened. However the waiting just continued with no telephone in sight and soon I lost track of what time it was. My only salvation was that I was still in severe shock so I remained in natural sedation as I endured the horrifying situation that I now found myself in.

The Remand Centre was actually the facility that processed and held people in custody while they awaited trial or placement in a prison facility. The admission process in the Remand Centre was an exercise in patience. Prisoner's waited in crowded holding cells while the guards slowly processed the paperwork. The waiting became longer with the growing number of people who were being taken into custody. The inefficiency in processing people was mainly attributable to the lack of desire on the part of the guards to do the work. Any processing that seemed to occur was only as a result of necessity. Eventually, I was fingerprinted and then questioned by a doctor about medical concerns. I was then directed to the area where I had to surrender all my clothes, take a shower with strong hair shampoo that is supposed to kill off lice, and then dress in standard prison clothes.

The clothing issued to me consisted of shorts, tee-shirt, blue jeans, socks and running shoes. All of these were faded and well-worn. I was actually happy to change into these clothes as this was the outfit worn by the other inmates. To this point, my suit and leather overcoat made me stand out very noticeably. I had often heard stories about lawyers who were sentenced to prison and then beaten by prisoners. I feared that this could easily happen to me in this crowded environment. After being shuffled through the system, I was finally escorted with other inmates to a cell equipped with bunks where I would spend the night. It was after eight o'clock in the evening when I reached this final holding tank. I had been waiting in the admitting process for over five hours from the time I first entered custody. I was to learn later that this was actually good timing and that many inmates experience much longer waiting times.

When I finally reached the holding tank, all the inmates were directed to immediately make up their beds with blankets and sheets that were provided. Although we got pillow cases, there were no pillows. From the obnoxious attitudes of the guards, it was obvious that we would all have to sleep without pillows. Fortunately this holding tank was equipped with one wall mounted telephone. Everyone immediately rushed to make a telephone call and I once again found myself waiting for an opportunity to telephone my wife. Finally, about nine o'clock in the evening, I was able to reach the telephone and I anxiously dialed my home number.

In my dazed condition, I hadn't thought of how I would explain this situation to her. I could hardly speak when I heard my wife answer the telephone. When she heard my voice, she immediately asked:

"Orest, are you okay? We were all worried about you! We've been phoning the police and the hospitals to see if you were in an accident. Where are you?"

For a few seconds, I could not speak. How could I tell her that I was now in jail? There seemed to be no easy way to explain such a horrible situation to her. I realized that the best way would be to tell her directly what had happened. I proceeded to blurt out what I knew would be the most devastating news that she would ever hear:

"Pat, I'm in jail! The verdict came in this afternoon. The jury found me guilty."

I could hear my wife gasp as I blurted out these words. I knew that this was even more difficult for her to understand than it was for me to accept. I could tell that she was shaken and I knew that this new ordeal would be more stressful and more difficult for her to endure that it would be for me. While my wife remained speechless on the telephone, I continued:

"Rick Stroppel will be speaking to my Sentencing Hearing tomorrow. He told me that he will call you to talk to you about it. I hope you don't mind talking to him. Please don't come to Court tomorrow! I know that you may want to but I don't want you to go through that ordeal. Don't worry! I'll be fine! I'll call you tomorrow after I'm sentenced and tell you what happened."

I then burst into tears as I told her how sorry I was that this case had turned out like this. I told her that I was sorry that she and the children had to go through this difficult situation. My wife responded strongly by reassuring me that everything would be fine with them. She insisted that she could handle the home situation and told me not to worry about them.

Because of the line-up to use the telephone, I had to hang up quickly. After I composed myself again, I went to my bunk bed and laid down to rest. The surroundings were loud and noisy but none of this bothered me now. The lights remained on all night, making any form of rest impossible. We were awakened early in the morning to be led back to the cell area under the Court House. When I asked for my street clothes back so that I could wear them to my Sentencing Hearing, the guards refused to provided them. They even refused to allow me to shave or brush my teeth. At that moment, I looked like a haggard and pathetic soul who could pass for a street dweller. I now fit the appearance of the stereotype prisoner who was being presented in Court for sentencing.

The process of waiting in cells and being shuffled from one cell to another started again. About three hours later, I was finally taken to the cell behind the Court room where I would meet with Stroppel. As I entered the secured room, Stroppel simply stared at me. His reaction to my appearance prompted me to explain that the guards had refused to return my personal clothes or allow me to shave. Stroppel assured me that my appearance would not affect my Sentencing Hearing. I knew that this meant that there was no point in trying to impress Perras with my appearance as he already had made up his mind. Usually, it is preferable for an accused person to be dressed reasonably for these types of Court appearances. Unfortunately, I would not be appearing in front of a reasonable judge so this was now an inconsequential detail.

Stroppel then reviewed his notes with me and advised me what representations he would be making to Perras. When Stroppel finished his comments, I asked him to proceed immediately with the Appeal against conviction and sentence. Although Stroppel tried to be optimistic about the Sentencing Hearing, we both knew that the sentence would be as outrageous as the conviction. Stroppel assured me that we would meet later in the day to discuss the Appeal process. He then notified the Court Orderly that he was ready to return to Court. As Stroppel left, I prepared myself for this final torment that I would have to endure. Anxiously, I tried to mentally prepare myself for the anguish that waited for me in the Court room.

A few minutes later, I was led into the Prisoner's Box inside the Court room. I was surprised to see so many spectators waiting for this circus event to begin. Naturally, there were a number of news reporters who were anxious to report this sensational event. I was surprised to recognize a few lawyers who wanted to get the "fresh dirt" on what was said in my sentencing. There were also a few people who had come to show me their moral support for the ordeal that I was enduring and I nodded in acknowledgement to them for their concern. In the middle of the public seating area sat Christal with a few of his colleagues. As he stared at me, he proudly displayed his pleasure and gloated over the victory that he had secured in "nailing a lawyer for fraud." No doubt, this would now become one more stepping stone in his frantic climb to the top of the police hierarchy. Very soon, the accolades would begin for the recognition of this worthy achievement.

The quiet commotion in the Court room caused by people whispering was suddenly shattered as "ORDER IN COURT" was called. From a back door, Perras made his grand and triumphant entrance. After settling on his perch, he glared at me with a look of disdain. It was now obvious that I had become one of the wretched, unwanted criminals that he would soon rid from society. Perras began the proceedings by calling on Pinckney to make his representations on sentencing.

Pinckney rose to his feet and tried to present as much flair as he could show for the spectators who now made his speech so meaningful. Although Pinckney was speaking to Perras, his remarks were actually designed for the benefit of the news reporters who were busy making notes. Now that a conviction was in place, his exaggerated accusations became proven facts in his mind. Nothing would prevent him now from portraying me as the worst menace that was ever unleashed on society. According to Pinckney, nothing more than the most severe sentence would possibly protect society from me and from others who might be tempted to trade in real estate for profit. Pinckney then cited a series of cases that showed that sentences of between one year and two years had been given by the courts in first time fraud conviction cases. However, he acknowledged that such cases involved breach of trust which was not present as a factor in this case. Therefore, according to Pinckney, my case should receive a shorter jail sentence than the cases he cited. Perras appeared receptive as he listened to Pinckney and I wondered how much of this performance was really pre-rehearsed.

When Pinckney finished his comments, Perras asked Stroppel for the Defence submissions. Stroppel first gave the usual description that is necessary in these Hearings. He described my background, my family life, my good character and the fact that this was an isolated event that had happened over seven years ago. He then advised Perras that this conviction would unquestionably result in my disbarment by the Law Society of Alberta. This meant that my career which I had trained for and practised all my life would be taken away from me. He emphasized that the stigma of this Criminal conviction would be one that would affect me for the rest of my life. As I watched Perras, I became convinced that he wasn't concerned about any of this. It was distressing to see that my life had been shattered and that Perras had no compassion for my devastation. The reality became more evident as I realized how callous and heartless Perras really was.

Stroppel then pointed out that this Criminal conviction and the loss of my career would cause a financial and social hardship for my wife and family. Perras made a note in his notebook but showed no emotion on this. Nothing seemed to impress Perras and I became more convinced that he had already decided how he was going to sentence me.

After these submissions, Stroppel then provided Perras with photocopies of a few legal cases setting out the decisions and the reasons for sentencing in a few specific fraud cases. Stroppel then stated that he would be using these cases to demonstrate what an appropriate sentence would be in my case. The first case was an Ontario case involving a lawyer who had been found guilty of fraud in a real estate transaction that did not involve his law practice. The judge in that case ordered probation. I was amazed for a moment that Stroppel found a case with a fact situation that was so close to my case. There was no doubt that this case should have received the most careful consideration of any judge hearing my case. Perras reacted immediately when Stroppel finished his description of the case. He declared that he would not consider probation for me and it was now obvious that a prison term would be ordered.

Stroppel then reviewed a few other Court cases that demonstrated that the sentence in my case should not be more than six months, and certainly no more than one year. Stroppel had accepted the reality that Perras was undoubtedly going to order a prison sentence. There was therefore no point in presenting legal argument for any alternative sentence.

At the conclusion of Stroppel's remarks, Perras directed that Court would be adjourned to two o'clock so that he could consider all of these submissions. Since he knew that he would be addressing the news media as well, Perras now wanted to make sure that his speech in Court was dramatic to generate news coverage that would feed his ego. Everything was now in his hands and there was nothing that I could do except wait and pray. After Perras left his perch, I was escorted back to the cell area in the basement of the Court House where I waited patiently for the next three hours.

As I waited in the holding cell, my thoughts focused on the Sentencing Hearing that would soon take place. Perras had a wide discretion regarding the sentence he could impose. The Criminal Code of Canada defined a maximum sentence of ten years in prison. However, the usual sentence was a fine or probation on a first offence unless there were extreme factors such as breach of trust or the loss of an extremely large sum of money. My case did not have any of these factors so a prison sentence was not appropriate. Both Stroppel and Pinckney had cited legal cases that were intended to give Perras guidance on the appropriate sentence to impose. It was now a question of how much compassion that Perras felt for my situation. From my earlier assessment, I feared that Perras could not relate to my circumstances and therefore a harsher sentence was most probable.

I recalled from my law school classes the various legal principles that were applied in justifying the sentence to be imposed by a judge. Of the three most common factors to be considered, retribution was perhaps the one that seemed to concern judges the most. By this standard, the judge had to decide on a punishment that would be sufficient to satisfy the public regarding the offence committed. Since my offence was an isolated one that happened over seven years ago with no actual complainant or resulting loss of money, an appropriate punishment would have been probation. Two obstacles prevented this type of consideration. The main obstacle was that Stroppel in his haste to complete this "simple trial" neglected to lead evidence in the Defence Case that would have proven that there was no complainant and no resulting loss of money. Therefore Pinckney's contention, based on the skeptical evidence of John Chubb, would now be accepted as the only facts before the Court. The other obstacle was the unfortunate attitude of Perras to sentence me harshly and therefore a more lenient sentence was really unlikely in my case.

Another legal principle to be considered in determining an appropriate sentence is that of deterrence. By this principle, a sentence must be one that will deter the convicted person and also others like him who might be tempted to commit the same type of crime. In my case, I was already suffering a most serious consequence with a pending disbarment by the Law Society. It was therefore unlikely that I or any other lawyer would ever consider committing a fraud in a real estate transaction and risk their entire livelihood. However, this was certainly not the way that Perras saw my situation and I worried that he might impose a harsh sentence in spite of all these mitigating factors.

Another legal principle that is touted in Sentencing Hearings is that of rehabilitation. A judge has an obligation to select the type of punishment that would serve to re-integrate a convicted person back into society as a productive citizen in the shortest time. Obviously, a prison sentence was counter-productive in my case and probation with community service was indeed the most logical sentence for my circumstances. However, I now knew that Perras would likely ignore all of these considerations even though other judges and most prison administrators consider this factor to be the most important of all.

Ironically, a prison sentence was the least appropriate sentence in my case. According to legislation relating to prisons, the primary purpose of a prison is to confine people who are a threat to the protection of the public. It is widely recognized now that prisons do not deter people from re-offending or committing crimes. It is also recognized that prisons cannot rehabilitate criminals and in fact, prisons often have the exact opposite effect.

Because my case did not involve any violence or danger to the public, there was really no need to consider a prison sentence. Certainly, the other consequences of my Criminal conviction would be a greater deterrence than a prison term. Finally, there was no conceivable way that a prison sentence could be justified on the basis of rehabilitation in my case. However, I knew that judges can use any type of logic to justify personal ideas and opinions. Common sense is not one of the traits that a prospective judge needed to possess. I also knew that rational thought was not a strong characteristic trait with Perras. My hopes for a reasonable sentence were gone and I considered myself fortunate that Perras could not order the Death penalty.

As the Court Orderly led me back into the Court room for sentencing, I noticed the same faces in the audience. I was surprised that the audience was still just as large, if not somewhat larger. I concluded that either the outside gossip was promoting my case as really sensational or perhaps there wasn't much happening in the other Court rooms. Shortly after I was brought in, Court resumed and Perras again made his grand entrance. After settling into his nest on his perch, he began his speech on my Sentencing Hearing.

It should not have been a surprise for me or for Stroppel that Perras began to reiterate all of the statements that Pinckney had outlined in his speech. Perras, however, added some of his own social commentary and emphasized how the Courts must make an example of ruthless and despicable people such as me. It was obvious that Perras had a particular disdain for people who profit from real estate deals which later cause losses to financial institutions. To Perras there were no redeeming factors in anything that he had heard. He also declared that I was not remorseful because I didn't plead guilty to the criminal charge but instead proceeded with a trial and professed my innocence. Perras concluded that he was obligated to impose a severe penalty to discourage others from considering the same opportunities of profiting from real estate transactions.

As Perras concluded his remarks he then announced that he was sentencing me to three years in prison. With that, he closed his note book and majestically rose to walk out of court. As I listened to the sentencing, I didn't react in any way because I was still in shock over my circumstances. It would not be until much later that I would truly appreciate how ridiculous the sentence was. As Stroppel prepared my Appeal, we realized how unreasonable Perras had been during his sentencing and also throughout the trial. Unfortunately, none of that could spare me and my family from the statements that he made about me. All of his comments were highlighted in the news stories which became lead stories on television and radio that day and in the newspapers on the following day.

With the sentencing concluded, the Court Orderly led me back to the cell holding area and my prison ordeal now began. I knew that I would encounter many difficult and emotional situations while in prison and that I had to develop a strong mental attitude to survive this ordeal. It would take a triumph of the spirit to function in this bizarre environment and to emerge again without physical or mental injury or devastation. However, there was no doubt that my life had now changed and nothing would ever be the same again.

EPILOGUE

My story of abuse and corruption in the legal system is actually one of many stories that are currently prevalent. Some cases are far more extreme and resulted in innocent people serving significant portions of a life sentence before being released from prison. My prison sentence, although extreme for the offence, resulted in a short incarceration. However, whether the prison term is long or short, the imprisonment of an innocent person diminishes the freedoms that every citizen relies upon in a free society like ours. The need to identify the cause of these flaws in our legal system are critical if there is ever to be any solution to the corruption and abuse that now exists.

One significant realization is that it is too simplistic to assign blame to specific individuals and to believe that under the guidance of more just people, the system is flawless. In fact, it is the flawed system that allows manipulation and abuse to be practised without detection or punitive measures for those that utilize them. The obtaining of justice in a legal case should not be a game of chance. Our system of justice is premised on the doctrine that everyone should be treated equally and fairly before the law. Therefore, the legal system should be reformed to eliminate the opportunity for abuse and corruption and to allow for easier detection and removal of those that inappropriately resort to such measure.

In my case, the actions of the police officer, the Crown Prosecutor and the Judge were carefully examined to show how the legal system allows for manipulation and corruption. These abuses can be eliminated by changing the legal system to make these public servants more accountable for their actions. Those individuals who perform the functions of their positions in a proper manner will have little concern about these reforms. However, a significant lobby will exist to block these types of reforms since these individuals are currently not required to be accountable and their indiscretions are conveniently covered up. It is for the sake of our future generations that we must act now to end the abuse that is becoming so rampant.

On a personal basis, I was forced to confront the ugly realities of our legal system. This is an exercise that I would have readily avoided at the time but the experience is one that has left me changed and enlightened. Having been forced to leave the idyllic shell of ignorance that protected me from the harsh realities that others endured, I have now learned to appreciate our legal system in a more objective manner.

Furthermore, when this ordeal ultimately devastated my reputation and my professional career, I began to appreciate more clearly how important family and friends are. In spite of everything that had happened, I still believe that I am blessed to be able to enjoy my relationship with those people who define my very purpose in life. Through prayer and with the help of family and friends, I was able to survive this ordeal and to develop an optimistic outlook on the future.

From devastation and depression, I began to re-examine the legal system that I always defended and then proceeded to rebuild my hopes for a brighter future. One course of action was to forget this experience and just start a new life. Unfortunately, I just couldn't do that because of a number of practical factors. It would also have been a conflict with my character to hide or deny what had happened to me. For better or worse, this event had now shaped my life. I had now become another victim of our justice system because it didn't vindicate me. I also acquired a different insight into our legal system where manipulation and corruption make a mockery of the ideals of our just society.

My curiosity prompted me to study the issues of abuse in the justice system and the blatant malfunctioning of our entire legal system. I conducted countless interviews with people who had experienced injustice and suffered from the corruption of the system. The clear message that emerged from this awakening was that the general public as a whole had little appreciation for the extent of the deterioration that existed in the justice system. There was an obvious need to develop a reform and advocacy organization that would help people in general to identify the areas of corruption and manipulation and to lobby for change.

After considerable soul searching, I accepted the challenge of working as a legal reform advocate. It was my conclusion that effective change could only be accomplished if people and politicians became better informed of the flaws in the Justice system. Ironically, the very people who have the best perspective of these problems are never consulted. These forgotten experts are those people who have experienced the injustice of the entire legal system and have suffered the effects of its malfunctions and flaws. Having become one of those victims, I know that my experiences are a valuable tool in identifying those features in the legal system that must be reformed. With the help of others, the task of exposing the causes of the deterioration to our legal system will be easier than it is for those who have no actual experience with the system

To effectively organize the efforts of the many volunteers who enthusiastically support these goals, a non-profit organization was formed called The Justice & Prison Reform Foundation. As its President, I have dedicated myself to organizing programs and services which are lacking in the legal community. The primary function of our organization is to research and advocate changes to make our Justice system more effective and responsive to the needs of the general public. To do this, our organization must lobby to eliminate the corrupt practices and the flawed operations of our legal system. Another important goal is to offer counselling, support and assistance to the many people who have been disappointed or disillusioned by our legal system and the legal community. Whenever resolutions can be reached outside of the legal system, our organization is instrumental in effecting these desirable results.

To take our message to the general public, I have also undertaken a career in public speaking. Topics deal with various aspects of the legal system and are intended to identify concerns and stimulate discussions on the solutions. It is undeniable that dramatic reform will be achieved when the general public begins to make their voices heard regarding the need for change.

The need for reform in the legal system can only be approached by identifying the flaws and demanding changes to cure them. Left untreated, our justice system will deteriorate to a nightmare of rampant injustice. If we are to leave a desirable legacy for future generations, then this important foundation of our society must be re-examined and revamped to ensure that it protects the rights of all its citizens, now and in the future. There are few goals that are nobler or more deserving of sacrifice than to develop a legal system that guarantees justice for all. I hope that my story will serve as an example of the abuse and corruption that exists and the need to act now to achieve these changes.

There is also a desperate need to reform the Prison system in our Country, and indeed in all of North America. Our prison system is not only flawed in archaic objectives but also has become the most wasteful and objectionable institution in our country. Its only reason for continuing to exist is a lack of desire on the part of politicians to find new solutions to rehabilitate offenders in society. Because of my experiences, I have now undertaken a second literary project and am dedicating it to my life in prison. It is my hope that this book will serve as a basis for identifying and exposing the flaws of our prison system and inspire discussion for solutions to this antiquated institution.

INDEX